think of no better legacy to leave than the one she did: that we are spiritual beings in a physical body sustained by nature; to eat right, be nutrition minded, and know that you are the only one that can produce health or illness in your body, and because of this to always be responsible to the health of your mind and body. She was also very adamant about maintaining vigilance against the products of irresponsible food companies that denature and poison our food. My grandmother grew up on a farm in Fresno, CA. so I think the farm girl in her started getting a little disgusted at what companies were doing with the earth's foods that she grew up with such a respect for.

Living by these simple guidelines, just think of the many illnesses and diseases, as well as the pain and suffering associated with them, you can save your family by instilling and practicing the importance of nutrition – for those family members in the present and those who will come down the line that you may never know.

So first, this book is dedicated to Gladys Petralli. Without her influence and the real life experiences she provided me proving her case, this book would never have been written. So remember, when you start reaping the rewards of this program to give a shout out to Gladys.

This book is dedicated to my daughter, Justine, whose birth taught me that God has something grander in store for me than I could ever imagine for myself. I spent nearly every moment from the time I found out I was pregnant envisioning what a perfect daughter would be like, and she made my wildest dreams dull in comparison. This made me realize how limited the best I could conjure up for myself was. So I have learned to be more receptive, listen to God, put my best out there and let the universe take care of the rest; essentially, to not restrict the magical universe and God's abundance in my life with my own agenda. We truly have everything we need in abundance; the only lack in our lives comes from the limitations we put on ourselves. Thank you, Justine, for lifting my limitations and for the best lesson of my life- it's a gift that keeps on giving.

To my brother, Michael Chukov: your support and humor carried me through the entire process of writing this book. I was blessed to have your comforting voice of encouragement

4

and the excitement of your pride in what I was doing and the ethics my work rests upon. Our talks, which would sometimes last for hours, provided the refuge I needed, while at the same time keeping me on track. You helped me to see the world more clearly, we resonate so deeply on all subjects that matter it is no wonder that we arrived on this planet as not only brother and sister of the flesh but of the soul. Your belief in me helped me to understand better why I should believe in myself. Your devotion to helping others, combined with the expansive life force I receive by simply being in your presence, is proof that we resonate together on this earth, as in heaven, and are a team in God's plan. You are a being of brilliant light. I have always and will always look up to you- I do every time I raise my head to the heavens. And thanks to his beloved wife, Arlynn, for giving him 15 wonderful years on this planet. You are truly the best thing that ever happened to Michael; thank you for all the many ways in which you enriched his life through your love for him.

To my father who has always believed in me and supported each and every endeavor I have approached with love, guidance, sustenance, and encouragement... and for saving me from myself long enough for my daughter to come and take over.

To my very best friend, Esther Adler, whose friendship, support, and belief in what I do has helped carry me to this point and will always be of the foundation to my success as well as the success of The 101 Program. Her friendship, encouragement, and guidance are angelic, while her example of worldly strength and conviction has helped fuel my own, always when I needed it most! She is truly the best friend anyone could have and I am blessed to call her mine.

To my dearest friend, Christiana Wyly, who has an enchanting way of entertaining me with her wisdom, heart, playful insights, and treasure of a friendship. Her journey for the truth took her on the path of most brilliant, caring people who seek the truth at the cost of all comfort- she, like many of us, was fragmented by the pain of the honest stark view of humanity her clear eyes were willing to see, but she, like not so many of us, found her foundation within, held on, and rebuilt her house from the inside out. Now she heals the world that once tried to destroy her. She is a testimony to the

capabilities of an innocent soul fueled by pure intention. Watching you reinvent yourself has given me some of the most heart-felt joy I have ever experienced; you are hope's hope. Thank you for not only providing a testimony for the natural healing process, but also the way for so many others. Thank you for enchanting my life and helping to keep the earth alive. I worship your beauty in all respects and will always love you.

I thank Heather Noel Culin, the most recent jewel in my life. Thank you for proofing this book, thank you for putting all else aside to accommodate my crazy schedule developing Green Body and Mind, and thank you for looking after my health and comfort. Your contributions to every action item on the long list of helping victims of our present mental health care system get off of psychotropic medications as well as the business development which is giving life to Green Body and Mind are not only appreciated but I thank you for adding to this vision with your own brilliant mind and caring heart. Green Body and Mind would not be what it is today without your insightfulness and dedication- you are one of the progenitors of this organization and the movement that will save millions of lives- and while this has manifested in your life at such a young age, your contributions are those of a sage. You are a rare breed; a true nurturer, and your friendship is quickly becoming one of the pillars of my life. You are my muse. You, unwilling to exchange integrity for comfort and adopt the way of mass consciousness to escape your own pain and struggles have built "of your imaginings a bower in the wilderness" which has kept your truly angelic qualities channeled through a vision for a better world alive. You live in truth and have endured it alone for most of your life; I hope our friendship marks the end of that era and the beginning of a beautiful integration between you, your new-found purpose and the world so that you may shed the isolation, free your soul and breath freely with the universe again. I hope you have found your dharma here because I want to work with you for a lifetime. You have helped to heal others while healing yourself- your strength and character responds eloquently to the reality that for any one of us to ever be completely whole and healed, we must do our part to heal the world we live in. The ability to do so only comes from

those pure in spirit; it is a joy to be in the company of such vibrancy. You channel God's work with flair and grace! While you and those like you are here, we can all count on a much brighter future!

I would also like to thank Dr. Abram Hoffer M.D., Ph.D. for writing the foreword to this book. To receive such consideration from a man who's heart alone ranks him among the finest of souls this world has ever known is an honor of such caliber that it leaves me speechless (and if you have ever attended one of my seminars, you know how hard that is to do!). However, beyond the purity of heart this man possesses, to receive such professional reinforcement from a person that has focused his heart and brilliance into the *humane* application of medicine that has resulted in the historic and unprecedented accomplishments and contributions to orthomolecular medicine counted by the thousands of lives he has saved, and the quality of lives his treatments have provided for those suffering from schizophrenia, cancer, and alcoholism is the crowning achievement of my career second only to the lives and quality of lives the 101 Program has saved.

To all my friends that entertain me, laugh, and cry with me, pray with me, cook and eat with me, play with me... each and every one of you have helped in one way or another teach me how to love wholly, unconditionally, and without limitation, thanks for sharing your sandboxes with me... every moment has been treasured.

To planet Earth for making life such an enchanting journey; for nurturing me in mind, body, and soul; healing me, providing peace of mind, for lifting my spirits when they needed lifting, for the recreation and fun, for the delectable pleasure of her natural cuisine which is as beautiful to the eye as is tasty to the tongue; for the daily hikes that keep me resonating with her energy, for the inspiration, for teaching me the importance of harmony, for bursting with mind-boggling beauty and enchantment with every turn of my head, for her beautiful museum of land and sky art, her crafts, and for being there for me in every capacity imaginable whenever I needed her. She has truly been my medicine.

Dedication

Thank you for sustaining everything that matters to me with such beauty and grace! You are truly the channel to our abundance.

-Genita Petralli

Table of Contents

Alcoholism: The Cause & The Cure

The Proven Orthomolecular Treatment

&

The 101 Program

Bringing the Most Advanced Holistic Alcohol Detox and Health Recovery Center to You

Table of Contents

Table of Contents

Table of Contents

Table of Contents

14

Table of Contents

Table of Contents

Foreword by Dr. Abram Hoffer

Alcoholism is not a disease, though it has been so considered for many years. A chronic drinker is not well, and seeks relief and comfort from the consumption of alcohol in the same way that people seek help from aspirin, or eating too much sugar, or are given medication for their discomfort.

The person genetically predisposed to becoming dependent on alcohol often experiences a personal combination of chronic daily anxiety, excitability, uneasiness, depression, mood-swings, nervousness, self-disapproval, and mental and physical fatigue. Often plagued by the feeling that something is missing – a feeling that is caused by imbalanced brain chemistry – and seeking to relieve these symptoms, they will self-medicate with anything available that seems at first to help. This person will show a tendency to over-indulge in simple or refined carbohydrates, coffee, and alcohol.

Essentially, people who have become dependent on alcohol have found a way to self-medicate that creates unhealthy (and potentially deadly) brain chemistry … one that further destroys their ability to maintain healthy states of mind and choice. Alcohol consumption, for those prone to dependency, provides more comfort than any other drug available for the symptoms of their dis-ease. And alcohol is readily available and acceptable within certain boundaries by our society.

So why do we call it alcoholism? Do we call a diabetic who has to take insulin, an insulinic? A schizophrenic who has to take zyprexa, a zyprexic? Or a person who has to take steroids for Addisons disease, a steroidic? Should we call an arthritic that takes aspirin to control pain an aspirinic? The term "alcoholic" was helpful in the past to specify a reference to a person who drank too much, but the term is totally illogical and indefensible today, in light of the scientifically valid information we now have about the real factors that lead to excessive drinking, and indeed, to all addictions.

The real problem is that the alcohol-dependent person to be (typically regarded as an alcoholic) is not well. None of the common medical tests will show where the problem is because it is a case of severe malnutrition – not of calories, but of the

nutrients essential to properly metabolizing food ... the proteins, fats and carbohydrates.

Since I first started working closely with Bill Wilson, co-founder of AA, I have believed that a person who is actually well will not become addicted to alcohol. It doesn't mean s/he will not drink. It means that, like most of our population, s/he will use alcohol on occasion – and not to the detriment of themselves, their families, and society. This idea of nutritional malfunction preceding addiction first began to take shape during our research on the therapeutic effect vitamin B-3 had on schizophrenic patients. We found that patients with the double diagnosis of alcohol addiction and schizophrenia could not recover until they were treated with optimum (meaning large) doses of niacin or niacinamide.

In 1960, a woman complained that she was very troubled by voices, which were incessant and loud, and that the only way she could control them was to drink enough alcohol to be drunk. She became addicted to alcohol and joined AA, but whenever she stopped drinking for any length of time, the voices came back, causing her to go back to the treatment that helped her send them away. She was desperate to be free of both the voices and the alcohol. She was started on 3 grams of niacin daily, and within a few months she was a good member of AA and was free of the voices. She became a member of the first schizophrenic anonymous group I organized in Saskatoon, and was in fact a leader in this group. She had been drinking not because she liked the alcohol, but because it was the only way, until she started taking niacin, to be rid of her voices. This observation showed me that there was a sub group of alcohol dependent people who needed niacin in order to control their underlying biochemical pathology.

Bill W. and I explored this niacin connection very thoroughly. Bill understood it first hand, for even though he had been abstinent for many years, he was still unwell. He suffered from immense anxiety, tension, and fatigue, but was able to function in spite of what might have been disabling. After taking 3 grams of niacin daily for two weeks, his symptoms vanished and he remained free of addiction. This was a peak experience that he never forgot. He became determined to give as many AA members as possible the benefit of the same healing vitamin.

Without telling me that he was doing so, Bill conducted a trial of niacin on 30 friends and colleagues in New York. Most of them were very productive and sober members of AA, but they all suffered from the common mind and mood afflictions that people formerly addicted to alcohol experience, even when they are not drinking. After three months he showed me his data. After one month, ten of the subjects were well. After the second month another ten had recovered, and the remaining one-third had shown no improvement after the third month. By this time I had also treated a number of people addicted to alcohol and had seen similar recoveries. Ms. Petralli describes what happened thereafter in this book, where she sheds light on the fact that the physicians of AA not only refused to respond to the promising results of our research, but also dismissed Bill Wilson's efforts to introduce nutritional treatment methods into the AA experience.

Interest in the role of vitamins, and the possibility of addressing nutritional deficiencies as a treatment for alcoholism, inevitably drew my attention to the problem of hypoglycemia. This became the "H word" for the medical establishment, but is a real condition that is now given a different name and is often diagnosed as diabetes type 2. I tested over 300 chronic drinkers with the five-hour glucose tolerance test and found not even one patient who had a normal sugar tolerance test result. The treatment then became that of avoiding sugar, which is especially difficult for alcohol-addicted individuals, since sugar becomes their secondary medicine if alcohol itself is not available. Alcohol is a liquid sugar, and harms the body in ways identical to those of actual sugar. Alcohol and sugar are also identical in that they both provide relief to those suffering from the symptoms caused by deficiencies of neurochemicals. Those symptoms are caused by nutritional deficiencies in a person's diet. This easily explains the well-researched fact that the addiction to sugar in early childhood carries with it a strong likelihood that the problem will progress to an addiction to alcohol. The conclusion: addiction to sugar and addiction to alcohol are interchangeable.

At a doctors' meeting in AA, one well-known member came in with a huge cardboard box on his shoulders. I was told that each year he would bring a box full of chocolate to give to doctors at the meeting in order to help them deal with the

severe anxiety commonly experienced by the dry drunk. And when I looked at some of the empty coffee cups, I found that they had been drinking not coffee, but saturated solutions of sugar. So we now had a second group who needed to eliminate sugar before they could recover.

The basic dis-ease of alcoholism is caused by one or more metabolic defects in the body, which creates the anxiety, tension, and fatigue that can actually be treated quite effectively by alcohol for some time. Overall, and in the short-term, alcohol is probably more effective and safer than modern anti psychotics are. But over time, the side effects of alcohol become terrible to the drinker, to the family, and to society.

I am utterly convinced that the propensity to become addicted to alcohol stems from a metabolic disorder caused by the initial symptoms in the person – the symptoms that encourage them to turn to alcohol in the attempt to self-treat their condition. Alcoholism is a syndrome for which we do not know all the generating biochemical abnormalities, although we are getting much closer.

An experiment done many years ago with rats gave me an idea of what might be wrong. These laboratory animals were placed in running cages, where the number of rotations of the cage would be counted as a measure of activity. Normal, well-fed rats ran about 3 to 4 miles daily. When the rats were starved, they doubled that mileage. This makes sense, for hunger drives animals to seek food. If a lion never got hungry, he would never hunt, but would instead spend the whole day sleeping or making love. Hunger activates. An herbivore that did not graze would die of starvation. And even for humans, there is nothing as effective as hunger to motivate activity such as work, and even anti-social behavior such as stealing.

There is an evolutionary drive that forces hungry mammals to become active in their search of food. So that experiment was not very exciting. But the investigator (who later received the Nobel Prize for his work with vitamin A) now fed the same rats a diet adequate in calories but deficient in B vitamins. The rats were not advised to sign consent that they would not be getting their B vitamins. And they ran as much each day as they had done during the starvation diet.

The deficiency of the B vitamins created the same need in the rats as the starvation diets had. They were still starving.

These vitamin-B-starved rats suffered from "affluent malnutrition". This is our modern diet: too rich in calories and too depleted of the essential nutrients. I see hyperactive children suffering from the same problem. Their genes are desperately looking for the missing nutrients and are driven to hyperactivity. I see obese people in the same way. They are hungry for the essential nutrients, and the only way they can get them is by eating a lot more. The price is obesity.

The problem of dis-ease is in the complex biochemistry of the cells, and, in the view of orthomolecular medicine as described by double Nobel Prize winner Linus Pauling, is due to a deficiency of required natural substances such as vitamins, minerals, amino acids, EFAs, and enzymes. Therefore, to heal dis-ease or alleviate the symptoms of a disorder, what the cell is deficient in must be identified and restored so that the cells function as they were designed to do. Cells, functioning as they should, will restore health. Two early pioneers, Sir Archibald Garrod, and later Dr. Roger Williams, made the scientific observation and theoretical conclusion that no two individuals are alike, and that we each have differing biochemistry and nutritional needs specific to our unique biogenetic structures. In 1902, Sir Archibald Garrod described chemical individuality, and later, the great chemist and nutritional pioneer, Dr. Roger Williams, attempted to popularize this conclusion. We are all individuals and different in the same way: we do not have the same finger prints, look the same, or have the same biochemistry or nutrient needs. Now, 100 hundred years after Garrod, modern studies of genomics have confirmed these findings. But human genetic variation is more complex and subtler than even modern geneticists have realized, and throws into question many of the conclusions currently accepted as true.

To illustrate this, Dr. Roger Williams used a symphony analogy. Visualize that you are at a concert with a superb orchestra, enjoying a world-renowned conductor and superb music. The symphony is great because every player, and every instrument, is perfectly performing the important role it is meant to perform. But during the concert the lead violinist suddenly loses her memory. What can the conductor

do to ensure that the show goes on? He must find a replacement for the violinist. If there are no other violinists available for her position, and he invites instead his lead drummer to move up with his drums, you can guess that the result will be a cacophony, no longer a symphony.

Williams is pointing out that each essential nutrient must play its role in the same way that each member of that orchestra must, if the thousands of simultaneous reactions in the body are to continue. Pauling made it clear that molecules cannot replace each other in the body's complex biochemical systems, so adding the right nutrients to the body is like putting the right musician back in the right place in the orchestra. Putting in any other drug to replace the lost nutrient is like asking the drummer to replace the lost first violinist; or even worse, is similar to calling someone up from the audience, who cannot play an instrument at all. The result is chaos, and for the living cell this means death.

Modern drugs convert the symphony of life into a cacophony. Only by the miracle of the body's ability to maintain some kind of stability is it able to more or less function with these faux substitutes, and at an enormous cost to the person and to our society. Quality of life diminishes with the degree that the structural integrity of the cell and cell communities is compromised. We do not need any more xenobiotics. Let's assume that niacin represents the violinist in our symphonic analogy. No other chemical can have the same properties in the cell as niacin does, due to the remarkable sensitivity of the relationship between the molecule and its receptor. A replacement drug may be partially acceptable to the cell, but it will also be only partially successful. The only cure for a deficiency is providing the substance that is deficient. This may be the actual substance itself or something that will release/rebuild it in the body. If, for example, niacin is deficient, it may (to a lesser degree) be replaced with tryptophan, because some of the tryptophan provided will be converted into niacin. Another possible cure is inositol niacinate, which is split in the body and releases niacin.

If the missing member of the orchestra is folic acid, the result is depression. Giving that orchestra Prozac will not re-form the orchestra. Neither will it cure the depression. Let's call the pianist thiamin. If the pianist is not up to par and

there is not enough thiamin, the whole orchestra will suffer. We can diagnose this malaise of the orchestra as a deficiency of piano players, or as a deficiency of thiamin. The integrity of the musical composition can only be re-established by replacing the intended instrument defined by the composer. The integrity of the human body during dis-ease can only be re-established by replacing the intended nutrients required for each biochemical process, as defined by the creator, not a pharmaceutical company.

In this book, Ms. Petralli describes in careful detail how these essential nutrients play a role in the cause and the treatment of alcohol addiction. Further, <u>Alcoholism: The Cause & The Cure</u> enlightens the reader by clearly demonstrating that alcohol addiction is truly, at its core, a Nutrient Deficiency Disorder, and provides a fascinating account of how to properly treat it. It provides the course of action that must be taken to cure an orchestra of the malaise created by one or more defective musicians. The results are immensely superior to those that depend upon psychosocial methods alone, though these are important. Every practitioner of orthomolecular medicine specializing in treating addictions sees the same very good results – very high recovery rates. And if preventive measures are started early, the results will be even better. To carry the orchestra analogy even further, every excellent conductor knows that rehearsals must be done to ensure the peak performance of every individual in his orchestra. Why should we expect less from every cell in our body?

Once it has been diagnosed, a search will be made to find out which nutrients are lacking in a person's body. During this search, there is sometimes a trial and error phase to pinpoint the exact deficiencies in the person's biochemical structure; however, there is no loss in this method since providing nutrients, even if they are not needed, is not dangerous, as is the case with pharmaceutical drugs. Ms. Petralli demonstrates how, once the biochemical malfunction has been identified, the treatment becomes rational and relatively simple, while illustrating the details of the proper procedures for treating alcohol addiction.

The education you will find in <u>Alcoholism: The Cause & The Cure</u> is that there are underlying nutritional deficiencies that create the symptoms that you use alcohol to relieve,

which leads to alcohol dependency. <u>Alcoholism: The Cause &</u>
<u>The Cure</u> exposes these deficiencies while providing a proven
dietary and nutritional supplement program that reduces or
eliminates these symptoms. This method of approaching
NDD, or alcohol dependency, diminishes the likelihood of
relapse with the degree of health and balanced brain
chemistry that is achieved with your treatment. When the
symptoms are gone, so is the craving or need for alcohol.

Dr. Abram Hoffer
Canada, November 28, 2006

The Biochemical Solution for the
Biochemical Epidemic

Dr. John P. Cleary, noted for his research regarding B3
deficiencies in problem and chronic drinkers as well as those
predisposed to addictive biochemistry, "...observed that some
alcoholics spontaneously stopped drinking in association with
taking niacin supplements. Cleary's preliminary research
findings suggested that niacin supplementation helped wean
some alcoholics away from alcohol. Activated vitamin B3 used
intravenously has also helped alcoholics quit drinking." Bill
Wilson (AA Co-founder) reported that about 70% of alcoholics
who took niacin (vitamin B3) found that they felt much
better: "Evidence has mounted that many of this group
reporting recoveries from depression, anxiety, tension, etc.,
are actually hypoglycemic, people in whom B3 is, to a
considerable degree, preventing the abnormal drop of blood
sugar which is characteristic of that malady."[1]

These were early findings that certainly inspired
numerous doctors of both traditional and alternative practices
to research the holistic methods of balancing the body and
curing addiction in greater detail. However since alcohol
addiction is now known to travel multiple biochemical
pathways, and adversely influence at least six known vital
biochemical processes which parent addictive biochemistry, I
endorse the "full spectrum approach". This means that The
101 Program is designed to address and heal each of the
addictive biopathways and the damage that alcohol does to
the body and mind comprehensively. I do not endorse the
idea that simply taking mega doses of B3 will meet with any
sustained success, nor will it produce the results of enhanced
health that The 101 Program advocates and provides detailed
guidance to achieve. No single supplement can reach the
depths and travel the biochemical labyrinth that alcohol
destroys. Because of this, each chemically destructive
pathway is studied, and thoroughly addressed in The

---

[1] Joan Mathews-Larson, PhD. <u>Seven Weeks To Sobriety</u>.
New York, New York: Fawcett/Columbine, 1997; 133.

Program with a dietary and therapeutic nutriceutical protocol. The 101 Program reaches far beyond simple sobriety because limiting your goal to just that, without addressing your health and the special needs of your biochemistry, is the premiere cause of relapse and will imprison you in a purgatory of compromised mental and physical health. Remember, it's not just about being sober; it's about being healthy and happy, and living an inspired life with the energy and presence of mind to do so. That is what keeps you hooked on sobriety!

Through this program, you will achieve enhanced physical and mental health because all the known biopathways of alcohol addiction are addressed and healed, and the road for vibrant, healthy living is paved for those who once demonstrated addictive biochemistry. Both recovering drinkers and those with inherited imbalances are freed to truly enjoy life. When you successfully complete The 101 Program you will be delivered to an enhanced state of health and a sense of well being; you will no longer seek alcohol, because that which drinking once offered will now be achieved naturally.

Important! Please Read!

The bio-medical information in this book is based on the training, experience, and research of the author. Because each person and situation is unique, you should consult with a qualified health professional (preferably one disciplined in naturopathy or orthomolecular medicine) before following this program. The author and publisher specifically disclaim any liability, loss, or risk, personal or otherwise, which is incurred as a consequence, directly or indirectly, of the use and application of the contents of this book. In the event you use any of the information in this book for yourself, which is your

constitutional right, the author and the publisher assume no responsibility for your actions.

Regarding The 101 Program Formulas:

Taking any of the supplements suggested in this book or on any of our websites including http://the101program.com should be a decision based on personal research and assistance obtained from consulting with one of our accredited consultants or any other competent accredited nutritional biochemist, naturopath, or homeopath that specializes or has proven competence in addictive biochemistry. A professional with a solid background in addictive biochemistry will always be able to suggest the accurate nutritional support you require in the best combinations for ultimate efficacy. A trained professional in holistic health can also ensure the safety of your nutritional supplemental protocol since interactions between prescription drugs, vitamins, herbs, and health conditions need to be considered for each individual.

The information provided within this book and our websites is for informational purposes only and is not intended as a substitute for advice from an accredited holistic health care professional or allopathic physician that is formally educated in holistic health (these are professionally referred to as "integrative" physicians), and should not be used for diagnosis or treatment of any health problem or for prescription of any medication or other treatment. A holistic health care professional should be consulted before starting any diet, exercise or supplementation program, before taking any medication, or if you have or suspect you might have a health problem. Do not discontinue any other medical treatments without first consulting your doctor.

Introduction

I truly believe that many of those addicted to alcohol today, who master themselves through embracing the healing process required to cure addiction, will be the progenitors of true healthcare for the future. They will serve as models for the type of healthcare that we, as a species, will have to embrace if we want to survive the irresponsible food processing and distribution methods developed for profit as opposed to health, and the toxic assaults that are increasing in our environment and food every day. Without the blunt, unforgiving, and symptomatic life-threatening forces which ultimately brings one with a serious drinking problem to make the changes necessary to heal, many people with many milder health problems live half-lived lives; they are able to get by because their moderately compromised health does not jeopardize their life or lifestyle, at least not in the blaring manner required for recognition for change. Chronic alcohol consumption brings on such severe mental and physical suffering that it transforms into a life crisis that becomes the catalyst for the personal transformation that leads one with a serious drinking problem to in mind, body, and soul whole-heartedly accept not only the need for change, but the requirements for that change. A fierce conviction is born from within that personal transformation, which surfaces as the strength and perseverance required to endure the initial stages of the changes necessary for the transformation to be complete.

People that are not blessed with the experience of the naked truth staring them in the face every day they continue to drink, slowly adapt to failing mental and physical health due to practicing diets not meant for humans (or any other creature) and many other assaults on our physical, psychological, emotional and spiritual health. They will ingest, for a lifetime, things that companies misrepresent as food (food is meant to nourish the body, not poison it), pharmaceutical and OTC drugs to mask their mounting ails and ills, environmental pollution, etc. In so doing, they cut themselves short of the true joys of living; the awareness of how precious life is, the enchantment of every day, and the full potential of their life accomplished by being present for

the always expanding broad spectrum of their human capacities that all culminates into an awareness every day of what a blessing it is to be alive and living that life with the passion and appreciation it deserves. Instead they live in a "getting by" fashion, hypnotized by daily routines without ever being aware of the treasures missing in their lives. A trance dictated by various addictions to foods, stimulants, and drugs supported by a society that many of them serve through maintaining the responsibilities they are barely able to serve. The fact that they are unaware of the thrill of life they are missing and how wonderful they could be feeling is the saddest part; if they only knew how they were capable of experiencing life, they might do something about it. We were designed in mind, body, and soul not only to receive abundance through resonating harmoniously with the vibrations and processes of creation, but also to recognize it and celebrate with it every day.

The problem and chronic drinker doesn't have the choice to "just get by". Their lives and health progressively deteriorate until they are forced to do something about it. To truly heal alcohol addiction, one must hit the biological reset button and not only detox and remove the biochemical pathways of addiction, but learn how to take exquisite care of themselves, their environment, and their body chemistry's particular needs. This will require a holistic transformation and will touch on all aspects of human experience; physical, psychological, spiritual, and emotional which will influence every aspect of their lives and environment. When they do this, they will learn how to achieve the type of health that will enable a full, joyous, inspired, purposeful, addiction-free, and grace-filled life. There are no in-betweens for those with addictive biochemistry. After the addiction has been achieved, a road has been paved in the biochemistry that creates cravings for products that will provide relief from their symptoms. Until the addictive biochemistry is completely healed, use of products such as sugar and caffeine can open the gates to these roads again and in doing so, derail them from the practices of true health for their specific needs, and that derailing will nearly always land them in trouble again and again. On the other side of that, though, staying on track and attending to their health will deliver them to a bliss that many without their type of body chemistry experience

naturally. The pendulum swings with the same intensity both ways. These people have the most to gain from choosing a healthy lifestyle; joy becomes bliss when it is enhanced by a truly grateful and appreciative heart that feeds even more joy into every day! After having lived through the hell of alcohol addiction and then achieving the mental and physical health The 101 Program provides; their joy, enthusiasm, and inspiration is truly ten-fold compared to the average person who has never experienced the anguish, isolation, and desperation of alcohol addiction. When health and a vibrant spirit fill the dark holes and mental vacuums a recovering drinker's consciousness has endured through the years, an awe-inspiring zest for life enters their being-ness.

In order to achieve true health and freedom from addiction, they must do what everybody should be doing – but aren't. They must completely avoid the commonplace food items distributed by irresponsible "food" distributors that actually encourage addictive biochemistry; they must avoid what is slowly killing people and in the process, landing them in doctors' offices for arthritis (and all other degenerative diseases), depression, eating disorders, cancer, bi-polar disorder, obesity, anxiety, ADD, ADHD etc.. They must make their health the top priority; in doing so, they pierce through the lies told about the health benefits of dead, denatured and poisoned foods and refuse to fall victim to the convenience irresponsible food processing and distribution companies provide with their products to make their profits, and learn the true mechanics of mental and physical health while accepting and enjoying the time it takes to prepare the right food and dine properly. Nothing else will "work" for them. Their sensitive bodies can't lie; they will tell the truth through the horrific mental and physical symptoms they develop.

Mental and physical diseases are becoming epidemic due to the "dead food" (sugars, additives, toxic lab-produced drugs put in foods, processing, junk food; empty, poisonous calories) and pharmaceutical and OTC drugs people are consuming in alarming quantities in today's society; things that render them not only malnourished, but literally poisoned and mutating. People are falling apart from the inside out and too fog brained to realize it when the progression begins at such an early age; they truly don't notice it, or they think that their

semi existence is what living and life is supposed to be like.
They slowly adapt to the aches and pains, ills and ails, mental
and emotional imbalances, and compromised mental function
(again unaware that it is compromised) for a lifetime, which
eventually takes them from their health purgatory to an early
grave.

I have been blessed with a very unique opportunity; to be
there to accommodate an individual's health care needs with
the tools and practices that will truly heal them, and to
witness the transformation and the bliss that comes with it
when they find, in such a short period of time peace, joy,
serenity, and excitement about life for the first time in many
cases since their youth. When those addicted to alcohol come
to me, they are ready – they have already begun the
transformation (when the student is ready, the teacher
appears)… they simply can't go on the way they have been
feeling and living anymore. That type of desperation feeds
purposefulness, conviction and perseverance that is fierce and
grounded. When people in this state are given the solution
they need – one that works, one that they have searched for
in quiet desperation for years -- their lives become recharged,
and in heart and soul they become like kids again. It is truly
like watching someone fall in love; only they are falling in
love with life.

Once someone learns how they feel when completely
unobstructed by toxicity, they become very protective of it.
Having learned what led them to addiction, they recognize
the dangers to their newfound health in the foods, sugars,
drugs, and drinks that plague our existence, and they create
healthy habits and lifestyles that avoid them. They are truly
tomorrow's health experts – the progenitors of purist (true)
healthcare who practice the methods we are meant to in food
consumption and taking care of our bodies. These practices
will one day evolve from being a luxury practiced by those
who seek enhanced health today over addiction and illness, to
the survivalist's healthcare all people will one day be required
to practice to survive as a species. Those who embrace this
truth now will learn and travel the right path; the path that
everyone needs to take to avoid addiction and illness today as
well as protect their offspring's health.

A challenge is simply the universes way of telling you it
has something better in store for you. You have been blessed

with the challenge of alcohol addiction. If you respond properly, your physician within will awaken and your newfound health will lead you to the abundance you are meant to experience and the life you are meant to live.

- Genita Petralli

Chapter One

Services and Support Network

For many, the road to freedom and complete wellness is simply about removing alcohol from their lives and healing their body and mind; however, for some, the road to complete wellness requires more than just detoxification and neurochemical / neuroendocrine rehabilitation. If you are on psychiatric medications; need help in developing or evolving in your spiritual, emotional, interpersonal, psychological or functional bodies or simply would like to network with others taking the holistic approach toward full recovery, I strongly suggest the three services below. They are filled with passionate, talented, professional and caring people that are here to help *you* and are very good at it!

Green Body and Mind

Green Body and Mind is reforming mental health care from a lifelong dependency on toxic psychiatric medications that gradually destroy every healing process of the body and initiates many other diseases, to a "green" mental health care model. Green Body and Mind will help you get off psychiatric medications with the same approach promoted in this book. With minimal transitional discomfort during withdrawal (tapering), in a very short period of time you will find your way to natural mental health utilizing targeted nutritional therapy (TNT), detoxification, diet, and specific laboratory testing to unearth the root cause of your mental distress and address it holistically.

If you need help getting off of psychiatric drugs please visit www.greenbodyandmind.com.

Integral Recovery

Addiction to any substance, be it illicit drugs, alcohol or psychiatric medications (which are also toxic drugs) affects every aspect of our lives. You can not harm one aspect of your life without it affecting all others and you can not heal one aspect without it affecting all others. That is why

detoxification, focus on healing the body and mind from the ravages of alcohol abuse, and neuroendocrine health and brain chemistry balance cause people to feel "on top of their game" and they begin naturally healing all other aspects of their lives.

However, depending on the degree of damage to any aspect of a person's life during their addiction crisis which affected all others, or because that person may be wounded by an event or series of events, or possibly may be in the midst of a life crisis besides their addiction- caused by it or not, the person seeking peace within, freedom from addiction, and a full life would certainly benefit from guidance and being provided the tools and support systems to carry them through their healing event and evolve as a person toward their highest vision of themselves.

I have never been a fan of conventional psychology and addiction counseling in the past because it simply did not touch on the core issues that I saw my patients struggling with such as trying to function in a world while their bodies and mind were fighting them every inch of the way. Conventional psychology, talk therapy and *of course* psychiatry do not recognize that a person struggling with addiction can not create lasting change or healing by just meditating or thinking differently through counseling or talking about their problems. So long as they are fighting the cravings from the addiction, the symptoms that brought them to it, and then of course whatever damage the addiction caused they will be struggling with the very core of their survival system: to find a way to reduce their emotional, psychological, or physical pain and most of the time in conventional therapy that results in relapse.

That is where **The 101 Program** comes in and cancels the symptoms by healing the mind and body, freeing the person to seek a full life. However, because in all cases a portion of their lives were spent with a space between them and their environment and circumstances there is an adaptation and growth stage that needs to be nurtured.

There, in that space, in-between the mind and body and environment there is an adaptation phase that is initiated on every level and in every aspect of that person's life when healing from addiction. Here good, functional medicine in the way of support and guidance in how to take command of those

spaces in-between and look at all the aspects of one's life and address them on their terms so that they may grow toward the person they see in their mind's eye is certainly going to be a prescription for success on all levels. And since every person is different the combination of tools to accomplish this is going to be different for each individual.

John Dupuy of **Integral Recovery** understands the space in-between and has brought together a combination of the most powerful tools available to not only fix but operate that space in-between.

The 101 Program will give you the "presence"; the healthy body and mind full of inspiration, calm, focus, enthusiasm, energy, peace within, and most importantly the ability to successfully follow through with any mind/body energy medicine or therapy program you choose. **The 101 Program** "makes the soil rich" for new growth and awareness. **Integral recovery** will help you choose and then plant the seeds for new growth in every area of your life that will bring you closer to your highest vision of yourself and will assist you in the process of nurturing all growth in all aspects of your life. There is nothing more exhilarating after becoming healthy in mind and body than to quickly sweep away the residual issues and begin planning and nurturing your new life. Experienced, professional assistance with an organization focused on the needs and challenges of one recovering from addiction would not only ensure success but accelerate its manifestation.

Integral Recovery is a bold and totally new approach to the treatment of *alcoholism* and *addiction.* I say "totally new" not because it breaks with other approaches past or present, but because it unites—or *integrates*—them, preserving what is best of existing modalities, while negating their weaknesses.

At the core of Integral Recovery is **Integral Life Practice™**, a sophisticated system of personal development that engages body, mind, heart, and spirit to produce *extraordinary health* and *awakening* on all levels of our being. Also central to Integral Recovery is the **AQAL Map,** a conceptual framework that helps illuminate the dis-ease of addiction—and the journey of recovery—in comprehensive and compassionate terms.

John Dupuy combines two decades of on-the-ground addiction counseling experience with the cutting-edge tools offered by Integral Life Practice and the AQAL map, to offer a fresh and extremely promising approach to treatment for chemically-dependent individuals and their families.

For more information on **Integral Recovery** please visit www.integralrecovery.com.

*Zaadz

The 101 Program Online Community

When it comes to recovery, engaging with others who can share and understand your challenges and successes is one of the most profoundly healing things you can do for yourself – it's good orthomolecular medicine! Visit The 101 Program link at www.zaadz.com at: http://pods.zaadz.com/the_101_program to *Join The 101 Program Online Community!* Hang out and have fun with other wonderful people like yourself while you learn, grow, integrate and empower yourself in the art and science of holistically healing addictive biochemistry! And remember: all that is necessary is the exchange of experience, compassion, vision, good vibes, knowledge, and healing ambition; not your name. You can join and remain entirely anonymous!

A Holistic Detox Operations Manual

Welcome to the most advanced holistic alcohol withdrawal, detox, bio-repair, and health recovery program in the field of orthomolecular medicine as applied to healing addictive biochemistry. This recovery program, designed to successfully heal the body and mind of both the biochemical conditions that attracted you to alcohol and the damage inflicted by excessive alcohol abuse which embeds the addiction deeply into the brain chemistry, is The 101 Program. The success of The 101 Program is in working to literally change the biochemistry of those with the known genetic/environmental influences that cause 'addictive' biochemistry, as well as those who have earned 'addicted' biochemistry through irresponsible food and drink

consumption and/or alcohol abuse. Successful completion of
The 101 Program will transform addictive biochemistry and
all the symptoms known to it such as anxiety, panic attacks,
cravings, depression, mental and physical fatigue, and
nervousness to a healthy independent biochemistry that
naturally produces what you once looked to alcohol for such as
relaxation, peacefulness, joy, good times, and contentment.
The healthy states of mental and physical well being you seek
can be reestablished, and in this book you will learn how it is
done.

What is The 101 Program?

The 101 Program integrates nutritional bio-repair, and
mind/body energy healing to correct addictive biochemistry at
the cellular level and deliver you to your natural, healthy
non-addicted state, free from not only addiction but the
symptoms that brought you to it.

There are five primary influences that encourage either
the health or dis-ease of our cells. They are nutrition,
emotion (heart), thought (mind), toxicity (internal and
environmental - you can not separate them) and EMF -
Electro-Magnetic Frequencies. The 101 Program addresses
all of these with a scientifically researched and successfully
practiced holistic protocol.

The 101 Program is founded on the view that
the microcosm mirrors the macrocosm and vice-versa; when
your molecular biochemistry is in chaos, so is your life, and
one way that chaos can manifest is in creating an addiction.
Using the principles and practices of orthomolecular
medicine, this Program educates you in the biology of your
challenge, arming you with all the instruction and
information you need to free yourself from addiction once and
for all. *Through balance and harmony with the earth's
farmacy you will find the path back to your original self and
in a state of enhanced health.*

The 101 Program is an in-home holistic treatment that
uses the most advanced diet and therapeutic nutritional
therapy (TNT) methods based on the most recent research in
holistic alcohol treatment. The foundation for this program is
the non-addictive biochemistry diet; throughout the book this
diet will be referred to as a 'condictive biochemistry diet': a
diet opposed to addiction. This treatment has a very high

rate of success in combating addiction and alleviating the symptoms that caused you to drink in the first place. By following the condictive diet and employing the therapeutic nutritional support in the ensuing Krispy Klean Detox Program, most participants lose the craving to drink within a week; no participants have been known to crave alcohol by the end of the eighth week of the program. Shortly into the program you will begin to experience the peace of mind, joy, inspiration, purpose, and energy that you may not have known in years. That is just the beginning of the freedom from addiction. After the detox you will enter into The Ark module of the program. This period lasts from 10 to 18 months, depending on the extent of the biochemical damage sustained by your body before entering the program. Picking up where the detox period left off, The Ark aims to heal the damage done to your body and mind, and to change your metabolism from one predisposed to addiction to a healthy one. The most important point to keep in mind while becoming acquainted with The 101 Program is that it is not just about being sober and no longer drinking. It is about being healthy, happy and living an enriched, productive, full, and inspired life; it is about feeling good inside your own skin. The goal is to become physically AND mentally healthy; to restore completeness in body and mind, and to be comfortable there. In order to accomplish this, you must hit the biological 'reset' button, and bring your body and mind back to where it was before becoming addicted, protect your body from future addictive biochemistry invasions and then learn and practice the aspects of integral healing so that you may evolve in other areas of your life to make the transformation complete which is explained in the final chapter. Here is where you will have the opportunity to address the lifestyle and environmental influences that developed when you removed yourself from the driver's seat and succumbed to addiction. In doing so, you will erase the remnants of the addiction in all areas of your life and live in the driver's seat manifesting peacefulness, joy, strength, and health in mind, body and spirit in all your endeavors.

The Purpose and What Will Be Accomplished

This book serves many purposes in the multi-layered journey of recovery from alcohol addiction. It will help you

accomplish this journey with a simple explanation of the metabolism disorder called alcoholism; a disorder often referred to as a disease. Understanding how you became addicted and why your biochemistry is prone to addiction is the foundation of understanding how to heal it. This book will also demonstrate the biochemical root causes of the symptoms expressed by a body damaged by alcohol toxicity, and show you how to heal them. Once moderate or recreational alcohol use turns into addiction as a result of the damage inflicted by alcohol, the resulting symptoms such as depression, anxiety, fear, and fatigue encourage you to further self-medicate with alcohol. This is the beginning of a vicious biochemical addiction cycle, since continued use of alcohol will further the damage that is creating the symptoms. As alcohol abuse continues, the symptoms intensify and so does the need to self-medicate.

This book will not delve into the psychology of alcoholism. Personal clients, who have completed the program, have demonstrated that much of the negative feeling and 'head speak' disappears when you heal brain chemistry. Correcting brain chemistry means working to clear out the poisoned addictive biochemistry that encouraged you to harm yourself with alcohol and feed depressed, negative, and fearful ideas and emotions into your head. Those thoughts and emotions are products of the damage done by chemical poisoning to your brain and a lifetime of ingesting poisons "food" companies call food, not a product of their true consciousness. So instead of using a 'talk therapy' approach to treat something that shouldn't be there in the first place, you will remove it by correcting your brain chemistry, leaving nothing to treat.

To cure addictive biochemistry, you must heal your body and mind. In doing so, you will no longer be biochemically predisposed to respond to stimuli compulsively as a fractured network of frayed, unfocused, mechanically driven neurons with every circumstance and situation owning you. You will be able to once again focus and consciously create the life you were born capable of living. How to accomplish this, cure addictive biochemistry, and personally witness all the rewards of enhanced health is presented in the ten chapters of this book.

This chapter will start with definitions of many key words that are used in recovery jargon. It is important that when a term such as addiction or addictive biochemistry is used, you understand exactly what is meant. This way you can fully respond to the information being shared and understand how to implement it in your personal recovery. I will also explore some of the politics behind alcoholism, the methods and results of various treatment options, what to expect during recovery with this program, and what's behind the attacks on the supremely effective holistic and orthomolecular methods for curing dis-eases such as alcoholism.

It is a well-known fact that people can either be born with addictive biochemistry (although it is not genetic!) or acquire addicted biochemistry through irresponsible lifestyles. In any case, the biochemical markers are identical, well researched, and established. Chapter Two, "What Makes Addictive Biochemistry Different", describes the biochemical markers of alcoholism in brain chemistry, blood sugar metabolism, and damaged neuroendocrine function. The question: "Why can't someone with addictive biochemistry have just one drink?" is thoroughly explained.

Chapter Three, "The 101 Program", is an overview of the entire program. Chapter Four, "Detoxifying and Healing the Liver", reveals the mechanics of a thorough detox program aimed at removing waste and awakening the body's natural healing processes, known as the physician within, which will be the bedrock of an individual's recovery.

Chapter Five, "Lab Tests", explains the blood, urine, and saliva tests that are given at strategically timed intervals of the comprehensive program to reveal the extent of the damage done to your body by alcohol toxicity, propensity toward addictive biochemistry, and any inherited or environmental / lifestyle health risks. Results from these tests are used to prepare highly effective and sophisticated nutritional supplement protocols referred to as Targeted Nutritional Therapies (TNT) that will assist and accelerate healing.

Chapter Six, "Krispy Klean Detox Instructions", contains the step-by-step details of the 8-week detoxification process.

Chapter Seven, "The 101 Program Condictive Diet", instructs you on how to modify your food choices and culinary practices to adopt a condictive diet. This diet, along with the

therapeutic nutritional supplements you will be taking, is the foundation of The 101 Program. It will use nutrients as 'medicine' to provide what alcohol toxicity has made absent in the body, and to initiate and direct the body's resources toward healing the addiction. This chapter includes the Krispy Klean Detox Meal Companion, which highlights healthy dietary basics and will guide those unfamiliar with healthy foods and their preparation through the question marks they may experience when walking into a health food store for the first time. The food restrictions required for a successful detox and healing process can be a leap into another dimension for some people, delivering them into an area that they are entirely unfamiliar with. The Meal Companion section is included to help those doing the program through the detox by teaching them some staple items that specifically serve healing and detoxification for alcohol toxicity. Also listed are resources on the Internet that showcase an abundance of foods within the restrictions of the Krispy Klean Detox module, and recipes that will help you prepare healthy foods to your liking. These links will serve as helpful sources of information regarding natural foods, to help you get more familiar with their medicinal qualities while scientifically reinforcing the importance of migrating away from industrial foods, especially for those that have demonstrated addictive biochemistry.

Chapters Eight and Nine, "The Cause" and "The Cure", are devoted to the science behind this groundbreaking program. These are biochemically detailed chapters that will answer questions many people have had for years. The information shared in these chapters scientifically validates the dietary practices, lifestyle changes, and therapeutic nutritional protocols developed and included in The 101 Program.

Chapter Eight, "The Cause", reviews the true cause of alcohol dependency, and explains how one becomes dependent on alcohol to 'feel right'. "The Cause" thoroughly explores the effect of alcohol on each organ and how long-term alcohol toxicity contributes to a 'broken' metabolism, and thus dependency. It reveals how that damage causes the addiction to be seated in your biochemistry, and how this becomes the platform for health conditions that most people do not realize are alcohol-toxicity related. Long-term alcohol abuse destroys the brain's natural state of balance, or 'inner wisdom' which

knows how to and is capable of providing the neurochemicals you require for healthy states of mind; that one-time healthy brain chemistry is altered by alcohol and its toxic metabolites to produce compulsiveness. This is the primary biochemical pathway that gives life to the dependency.

Chapter Nine, "The Cure", responds to the damage and nutritional deficiencies demonstrated in "The Cause" with nutritional therapies known to correct them. You will receive an easy explanation of how these nutriceuticals accelerate and assist in the healing of addicted biochemistry, returning the distorted brain chemistry to a healthy one. The biochemical value of each nutriceutical used in The 101 Program is explained to shed light on the scientific reasons for its effectiveness toward curing alcohol dependency. This chapter will address the underlying cause and proven methods of healing symptoms such as depression, anxiety, paranoia, fatigue, low self-esteem, mood swings, compulsivity, emotional instability, irritability, alcohol cravings, cravings for simple carbohydrates, and even suicidal tendencies associated with alcohol dependency.

The education provided in this book will help you understand why you must heal your body and mind to ultimately cure the addiction to alcohol. The body is a majestic orchestra of light and atoms, and our health requires that the various musical instruments (organs) that comprise that orchestra are able to "play" their part and follow the conductor. They must perfectly express their individual purposes, working together to create the rhythms of healthy bioenergetics that harmonically resonate with the natural laws of health. "The Cure" will teach you exactly what must be done to 'tune up' each instrument in your body so that you may fully enjoy your life with the vibrant health that comes from nutritionally supported, harmonious bioenergetics.

Learning to take care of your body to achieve harmonious bioenergetics also means that you will know how to protect yourself from future chemical and environmental assaults.

This journey will be an education that can serve not only as the bedrock for a long life, but also as the foundation for the quality of that life. The world is constantly bombarding us with unhealthy stimuli, stress, and chemical toxicity that is ingested, inhaled, and absorbed from every orifice of our being. Also, far more grave to consider is the genetically

modified foods that are making their way into our food systems, and causing mutations in human, animal and plant life. These known mutations predict many very alarming consequences, that even the smartest of scientists (including the ones that created them) can not begin to project what the final picture of dis-ease and destruction to the human race will look like. People are literally mutating today as a result of the toxic, unnatural conditions they live in and "foods" they eat. Knowing how to take care of yourself is the most important factor in maintaining your health, and avoiding the "mutate and die" future that denatured and toxic industrialized products are sentencing many to. In addition to healing addictive biochemistry, this book will serve as your survival manual in preventing mutations in your gene expression (pool), and the painful, slow progression of dis-ease that leads to premature death.

The Natural Laws of Health

The laws that dictate health are not negotiable. Any and all digression results in health issues, and if you don't respond to the initial warnings they will lead to illness and disease. Hence the true meaning of the word DIS-EASE – earned by detaching (dis) from (ease); our biochemical grace or health. In life, when you do the right thing, events and circumstances tend to flow with harmony and ease toward 'good'. A person who responds to his or her environment – the needs of the home, family, career, and personal enrichment– does not experience the same chaos as someone who neglects these pillars of life. The same principles apply to health. If you ignore your body's needs, your inner wisdom will turn instead to turmoil and chaos. This chaos causes physiological damage that will affect you both physically *and* psychologically. It renders you incapable of seeking, nurturing, and maintaining healthy personal and professional relationships. Just as you cannot grow roses in a toxic waste dump, you cannot expect to derive personal enrichment and growth from life's experiences if you are poisoned. Alcohol toxicity literally disables your ability to respond in a healthy way to your environment, cutting you off from the natural flow toward good known as 'grace'. This is where your mental, physical, and situational suffering begins: opportunities for a healthy and productive life are lost

because your vision is blinded by the inner chaos caused by alcohol toxicity.

What can, when given the opportunity, exacerbate the harmful effects of alcohol toxicity is the fact that much has been done to destroy our environment. The environment is our natural foundation for health; the once perfect, unpolluted, and unadulterated ecosystem that our bodies' cells have adapted to for over three million years is being contaminated at such a rate that our bodies can't adapt or detoxify the chemicals and pollutants. The result is showing in the rise in cancer, diabetes, addiction, cardiovascular disease, degenerative diseases, and a plethora of other health issues. While we won't get the purity of the earth back in our lifetime, we can certainly refine our personal dietary choices to the cleanest, most nutritious foods available and reap the benefits still left to us while helping to heal our suffering planet. This clean nutrition is most important in combating the toxicity and damage of addiction.

Definition: Addictive Biochemistry

Those with the genetic biological influences known to encourage addiction to substances that the majority of the population enjoys in moderation are known to possess addictive biochemistry. This biological tendency is caused by an inborn deficient neuroendocrine system, which produces an imbalanced brain chemistry, which then provides a 'short cut' to dependence on any drug that relieves the psychological, emotional, and physical symptoms caused by being naturally under medicated due to a deficiency in key neurotransmitters required for healthy states of mind and physical comfort.

There are many known contributors to an inherent potential for biochemical imbalance. However, these biochemical abnormalities are easily fixed given the right environment. Because there are inherent conditions that you can be born with such as a compromised or malfunctioning neuroendocrine system that can produce addictive biochemistry, this does not mean that a gene is responsible for them. Genes are nothing but a blue print that the cellular environment uses to make more parts (proteins) as needed to maintain homeostasis, replicate, and survive in its environment. Genes can only express what the environment

asks of them. It is a molecular chain of events whereas a signal from the environment will trigger a receptor protein on the cell, which then passes this information to an effector protein, which then encodes the regulating proteins with information they use to decide what genes to unsleeve and read from. Based on the information provided to the regulating proteins from the environment via the receptor-G-protein-effector communication pathway, only that which the cell determines from the information provided by the environment will be read from genes to produce what the environment through the cell has determined necessary to facilitate the biochemical functions required for that cell to survive in that particular environment.

In <u>The Biology of Belief</u> by Molecular Biologist, Bruce Lipton, Ph.D., he writes:

"Defects in the gene programs, mutations, may profoundly impair the quality of life in those possessing them. It is important to note that the lives of less than 5% of the population are impacted by defective genes. These individuals express genetically-propagated birth defects, whether they are manifest at birth or appear later in life.

The significance of this data is that more than 95% of the population came into this world with an intact genome, one that would code for a healthy and fit existence. While science has focused its efforts at assessing the role of genes by studying the %5 of the population with defective genes, it has not made much progress as to why the majority of the population, which possesses a fit genome, acquires dysfunction and disease. We simply can not "blame" their reality on the genes (nature)."[2]

Alcoholism is not a result of defective genes and the proteins they build- that is why there will never be such a thing as an alcoholic gene. Alcoholism is a result of the cellular environment being drastically changed by the chronic invasion of a chemical that it must either learn how to accommodate for (adapt to) or die. While trying to adapt and at the same time responsible for repair and replication, the cells' resources are drained which makes it impossible for

---

[2] The Biology of Belief, Bruce Lipton, Ph.D. Mountain of Love / Elite Books 2005

them to function and healthfully co-exist with their natural environment which will translate into many ill-health conditions including addiction- or maladaptation. The key to curing addiction is providing an optimum cellular environment which provides genes and proteins the signals they need to produce healthy bioenergetics, not addiction. Health is entirely dependent on providing cells the environment they have learned to thrive in over 3 million years; the nutrient rich, natural environment where the energy forces of health can penetrate and dictate cellular bioenergetics. Human cells have adapted to the characteristics of what nature provides in its environment in order to survive, you can not denature your environment and expect to be healthy; you can not separate humans from nature, we need nature to survive.

Health is really all about providing the cells of the body the most agreeable environment for them to adapt to which just so happens to be the most nutritive environment containing only those things it requires to produce energy, repair itself, and build new cells.

The absolute king of engaging the potential for addiction is the consumption of industrialized, denatured, and processed foods that constitutes more than 95% of what is at the supermarket. These "foods" are barely recognized by the body and are adulterated with sugars, toxins, hydrogenated fats, sympathetic nervous system stimulants (neurotoxins/excitotoxins), and foods so processed that there really isn't any nutrition in the product anymore. These so-called foods cause malnutrition and damage the delicate workings of the HPA axis in similar ways as alcohol toxicity.

Excessive dietary sugars, OTC, prescription, and street drugs, malnutrition, disease, and environmental toxins (especially acetaldehyde) can create a deficiency of neurotransmitters and imbalance or even damage the neuroendocrine system. This imbalance creates an immediate requirement for restoration and rebalancing of neurotransmitter levels before illness and disease have a chance to develop. Alcoholism is extremely responsive to neurotransmitter repletion since their deficiencies and imbalances give life to the symptoms and addiction. Address this and you are addressing the very root of alcohol addiction.

Everyone needs a healthy supply of key neurotransmitters and hormones to protect them from physical, mental, and emotional pain or discomfort. However, not all of us are born with a system capable of adequately produce them, and when alcohol or other substances are introduced they can, for a short period of time, medicate and relieve the symptoms that neurotransmitter deficiencies cause. This often leads to dependence and then health problems, because drugs and alcohol are toxic and will take their toll on the mind and body as they further disrupt a biochemistry that was already naturally compromised.

The genetic potential for addictive biochemistry has early signs and, if properly addressed, can be successfully managed, healed, and avoided. Just because you have addictive biochemistry does not mean that you have to live with a disease for the rest of your life or that you can't change it – you can.

Addictive biochemistry (not addiction) can be inherited, but it can also be achieved by a prolonged unhealthy lifestyle involving bad diets, drugs, stress, and over exposure to exogenous (environmental pollutants) and endogenous (internally produced) toxins. Any of these conditions will cause your neuroendocrine system to become deficient and unable to sufficiently medicate the mind and body, which will produce identical symptoms to those suffered by people with inherited addictive biochemistry. The terms 'earned' or 'acquired' addictive biochemistry refer to these imbalanced metabolisms caused by prolonged use of toxic substances such as alcohol, drugs, (OTC, prescription, and street), food additives, and excess refined simple sugars that have damaged the body and mind to such a degree that a once-healthy biochemistry is no longer able to naturally "medicate" the body.

Definition: Addiction

The only difference between addiction and addictive biochemistry is that addiction implies that a person's relationship with a substance has progressed to the point where it has caused an imbalance in the person's life, loss of quality of life, and health problems.

Simply put, alcohol addiction is a person's dependency on alcohol to feel 'right' in body and mind. This includes the use

of alcohol to achieve states of being such as relaxation or cessation of worry, as opposed to being able to achieve these states in a healthy way without the use of a chemical. Once the symptoms of alcohol addiction and excessive use appear, they cause you to become compulsive and driven to self-medicate with alcohol and the symptoms become progressively more difficult or impossible to control.

To further explain, addictive biochemistry is engaged at this point due to the nutritional deficiencies that alcohol, sugar, and excessive refined and simple carbohydrates induce. This establishes dependency because the resulting altered brain chemistry causes symptoms to which the compulsive disorder of alcohol addiction will force you to respond. These symptoms will vary depending on genetics, lifestyle, and diet. The most common symptoms related to alcoholism and the so-called 'dry drunk' are depression, anxiety, mental and physical fatigue, emotional instability or outbursts, mood swings, decreased attention span, short- and long-term memory loss, inability to concentrate, constant aggravation and frustration, and lack of inspiration. These symptoms 'parent' the addictive symptom of engagement: compulsiveness, which in turn gives life to the addiction.

These nutritional deficiencies become more and more serious until the body and mind eventually become unable to carry out vital biochemical processes for themselves. In the neuroendocrine system, the damage involves the inability to manufacture healthy levels of specific neurotransmitters and hormones, which are required to facilitate physical and psychological health; emotional feelings like joy, peacefulness, inspiration, and self-esteem, and cerebral functions such as learning, focus and memory.

Nutritional deficiencies make it impossible for the brain to produce the right amount of its own healthy neurotransmitters, and give toxic alcohol metabolites the opportunity to step in and bind to the receptors meant for healthy, naturally produced neurotransmitters. The toxic displaces the natural, and you become progressively more dependent on the external chemical to help your body function and feel normal.

Withdrawal symptoms occur between when the chemical (alcohol) is discontinued, leaving receptor sites essentially emptied, and when the brain re-establishes its own healthy

chemical flora of neurotransmitters and balances its chemistry. During withdrawal, the symptoms of alcohol addiction can reach painful extremes, until the brain has registered the need for, and begins producing and utilizing, its own neurotransmitters again. The duration and extent of discomfort endured during withdrawal depends entirely on how quickly one is able to replenish the nutritional deficiencies and detoxify the body and mind so that the brain can function properly again.

Those that continue to include coffee, cokes, refined and excessive simple carbs (sugar) in their diets and do not restore a favorable, nutrition rich environment to aid withdrawal and support the much needed healing that must be achieved, will be sentenced to a lifetime of daily withdrawal symptoms and progressive dis-ease- which is the number one cause of relapse!

Definition of Disease:
Separating Addiction from Disease

The word disease is used loosely and inaccurately in recovery circles. The general definition of disease is "any departure from health in which a patient suffers. It can be defined as a disorder of bodily function or destructive processes in organs, organs' systems or in an organism with recognizable signs and symptoms, and in many cases a known cause." There are many classifications for disease, each having its own set of implications as to the impact on one's health, lifestyle, and options available for effective treatment. Though alcoholism easily fits the description, it is more accurately classified specifically as a *metabolic disorder* resulting from *nutritional deficiencies.* Alcoholism is no more a disease than menopause, pregnancy, or aging; although the FDA tried to have them classified as such.

There is a large difference between the properties of a physical disease and those of a physiological metabolic disorder. A physiological metabolic disorder creates an imbalance in the neuroendocrine system (CNS and hormonal system) and other critical organ functions. This imbalance shows itself through psychological, emotional, and physical

symptoms, which, if the body can't re-balance internally, will give life to a compulsive disorder, and drive you to seek balance externally. The nature of the human body, when speaking in biochemical terms, is automatic- it takes care of itself without input or thinking on our part; this is called homeostasis. If your body is unable to take care of itself, it will assuredly seek help externally in the same way, which will lead to the compulsiveness that is the parent of addiction. Once the super natural intelligence of a body (the physician within) has begun seeking to keep the body balanced through external sources, the situation becomes very difficult for one to manage because they are fighting with what the body thinks is its quest for survival- which is the genesis of compulsiveness.

Internal biochemical systems that help us adapt to our environment is at the core of our survival as a species; it is our adaptation mechanism, and is also the master system responsible for relief from psychological, emotional, and physical pain. When our internal environment is healthy, the body naturally provides healthy neurotransmitter and hormone levels as needed to meet the demands of everyday life and changes in our physical, social and personal environments. It will also provide the neurotransmitters and hormones required to mediate any stressful or difficult circumstances by drawing from its own healthy nutritional resources. When those resources aren't available rendering the brain incapable of producing the "feel-good" neurotransmitters required to mediate the stress in our environment, our natural instinct will work through our neuroendocrine system to literally instruct us to find them externally, and we will automatically do so because it is natural to seek relief from pain; this is the inherent autopilot of the physician within. Unfortunately, we are not as intelligent as our internal physician, which communicates directly with the supreme intelligence of our bodies; in not knowing exactly what their bodies need, those who fall into addiction are the ones that dismiss or don't know how to draw from healthy sources such as nutritional replenishment, relaxation, and environmental hygiene (stress reduction as well as toxic assault) and typically draw from unhealthy resources instead. The unhealthy is always more accessible and we have been cultivated to prefer that over the healthier

choices. So alcohol addiction can be summed up as a very misguided and uneducated attempt at providing what our body requires to establish internal chemical balance.

When a person doesn't think about his or her actions and does not have the internal fortitude to avoid substances and activities that they know are bad for them, it is called compulsiveness: one example is addiction. However, it is also a compulsive act of a parent to run in front of a car to save their child from getting hit, or run into a burning building to do the same, yet that is called instinct. In the case of alcohol addiction, during daily withdrawal the brain thinks something is wrong and sends out alarms that our survival instinct interprets as impending danger. This drives the person to seek their medication (food, sugar, alcohol, cigs, OTC and street drugs) to turn those alarms off. The original intention in both the addicted person and the parent saving their child is the same; to survive, however, toxicity in the case of withdrawal or symptomatic psychological dis-ease causes the original intention to be lost somewhere between the original message to survive and the person's resulting actions. Excessive, prolonged exposure to exogenous substances disrupts the inner wisdom of the body to cause life-threatening compulsiveness: addiction.

Addiction is the compulsive act of a person repeatedly self-medicating the symptoms they suffer with something they know to be harmful; it is compounded by their inability to deny the substance, due to the overwhelming and agonizing symptoms they seek to escape. Chemically driven compulsiveness is the hallmark of addiction, and an alarming number of people today suffer from addiction caused by a number of reasons, mainly industrial diet related. This book will show you how to turn ill-informed and compulsive nature into a well-educated, conscious lifestyle that will provide a healthy internal environment for your neuroendocrine system to produce the enhanced mental and physical health you seek. Your internal physician will never be required to seek external assistance again, once you begin providing it with the tools it needs to create an efficient adaptation response and enhanced mental and physical health.

With that understanding, you will now be taken on an enlightening journey as you learn how, through healing key biosystems that serve to awaken the physician within, to heal

and balance your neuroendocrine system. This healing will also serve to protect your body from profound neurochemical fluctuations that it might experience in response to typical internal and external environmental changes such as stress, foods, stimuli, or stimulants, so that you will be freed from alcohol addiction and chemically driven compulsiveness.

Contrary to what is believed today, alcoholism can be cured. First, you must take the toxic substance out of the body; this is the act of becoming sober. Then, and this is the step that most people don't consider, you target the damage done by alcohol toxicity and correct the metabolic disorders that created the symptoms you were self-medicating. If there was genetic influence that predisposed you to an addictive biochemistry, you address that as well. Curing the addiction to alcohol rests in healing the symptoms that encourage you to drink, and maintaining the correct diet and lifestyle so that those symptoms never resurface.

In summary, alcoholism is a metabolic disorder because there is a dependency on alcohol to feel right. It is coupled with the compulsion to medicate the symptoms (addiction) that the distorted metabolism produces in reaction to the absence of the alcohol, or withdrawal.

Definition of Addiction

Until alcohol toxicity manifests into a disease, such as cirrhosis, you are treating a metabolic disorder with roots in extreme nutritional deficiencies and the damage it causes. I know it's hard to think that while you eat plenty of food that you would be suffering from a nutritional disorder, but that is exactly what is occurring and this subject will be thoroughly presented throughout this book.

Let's compare a metabolic disorder to a disease such as lung cancer. Lung cancer is a disease that is usually brought on by smoking cigarettes and yes, a person's genetic make up and lifestyle factors determine if and when they develop it, just as genes and lifestyle factors determine if and when they develop cirrhosis from drinking. However, society does not consider a smoker to have a disease until they are actually diagnosed with lung cancer. Smoking does cause metabolic abnormalities and disorders, which cause lung cancer and addiction to nicotine, but we don't classify any of them as diseases. Up until the point of a cancer diagnosis, all a

smoker is afflicted with is an addiction. This addiction plays a very similar tune as alcohol does in brain chemistry: the overwhelming compulsion to medicate the withdrawal and compromised health symptoms with continued smoking. Should one quit smoking and be lucky enough to cure the cancer, loved ones celebrate the fact that they are cured and it is over; everyone moves on. He or she is not sentenced by the medical community, society, support group dogma, urban legend, or family and friends to a disease label to carry for the rest of their lives like long-term alcohol abusers are.

The difference between disease and addiction is that while the toxic substance leading to the metabolic disorder of addiction can cause disease, the metabolic disorder is not a disease in itself. With a metabolic disorder all you need to do to stop its progression is to discontinue use of the toxic substances that created it and suffer through a withdrawal phase. Withdrawal is actually the process of correcting the brain chemistry and metabolic disorders: it is a symptom of healing. In the case of alcoholism, it is not just alcohol that needs to be discontinued; the modern diet of sugar, junk food, and refined carbs needs to be removed as well, because they produce the same metabolic disorders as excessive alcohol consumption, and continue addictive biochemistry and the propensity for compulsive disorders. This is the premise of the well-known AA claim that alcoholism is progressive even in the absence of alcohol. It is, unless you discontinue the dietary practices that produce the same damage as alcohol does, at the same time as you quit drinking. Failing to address the unique dietary requirements of someone with addictive biochemistry is the number one reason for relapse because the psychological, emotional, and physical symptoms continue and become worse with time as the biochemical damage progresses.

Alcohol addiction can lead to serious health issues, disease, and death. However, alcohol addiction itself is a metabolic disorder. Since metabolic disorders create all the symptoms that define a disease it is too easy to mistake one for the other. For the interest of this book, the word "dis-ease" needs to be qualified as referring to two things. First, it refers to the metaphysical address of dis-ease: being detached from 'biochemical grace'; the body is in physiological discord because it has been detached from the natural systems that

dictate healthy bioenergetics, which produce well being. And secondly, the word refers to the metabolic disorder that creates the symptoms that make you aware that you are diseased, and encourages uncontrollable unhealthy appetites for toxic substances. This book does not refer to or endorse the idea that it is a disease in the traditional terminology, especially when it comes to the incorrect claim that alcoholism is a disease with which you will be living with for the rest of your life.

This text will clearly demonstrate how this claim is inaccurate and how alcohol addiction is not a to-death sentence; that drinkers are not doomed. In so doing, you will learn how a metabolic disorder and the genetic and environmental influences that inspire it can be corrected, thus curing the "dis-ease".

Because you are really suffering from a metabolic disorder that has caused an addiction, The 101 Program does away with the unhealthy and inaccurate self-image label of "alcoholic". For one, metabolisms can be changed. You once changed your metabolism from un-addicted to addicted, and you are entirely capable of changing it back.

Secondly, you are one of the most majestic creatures created and I, spiritually and scientifically, dispose of any notion that a human being can be reduced to a label representing a product of fermented sugars. There is simply no such thing as an alcoholic.

Definition: Cure

Alcohol addiction is associated with specific genetic, environmental and biochemical abnormalities, which are contributing factors to the dis-ease. These abnormalities are known to be rooted in nutritional deficiencies that ultimately alter brain chemistry and parent addiction by making it impossible for the brain to naturally self-medicate you and provide adequate "feel-good" neurotransmitters and hormones that produce mental and physical states of well being as well as the neurochemicals required to help you respond to stress in a healthy way. In orthomolecular practice, vitamins, amino acids, minerals, and essential fatty acids are used therapeutically in preventing, treating, and ultimately healing the dis-ease. Provision of these supplements helps to correct the nutritional deficiencies that the body has been

experiencing, and provides a foundation for re-balancing internal chemistries. This is the premise of proven orthomolecular methods that detoxify the body, correct the brain chemistry, and heal all afflicted organs, thus curing the addiction. When the body and mind heal and the genetic and environmental markers of addictive biochemistry are addressed, the addiction is cured.

Curing alcohol addiction is not just about being sober; it's also about being healthy, happy, inspired, enthusiastic and infused with a generous capacity to live life fully. Those who don't address their health when trying to quit drinking set themselves up for relapse because they short themselves of these very important states of well being. The success of The 101 Program rests in the fact that it actually heals the root cause of the symptoms that problem drinkers suffer, to correct imbalanced brain chemistry. Relapse happens primarily because of the continued symptoms caused by the damage alcohol once inflicted on the mind and body, and by the typical diet the dry drunk adopts after getting sober, of sweets, coffee, junk foods, and excessive amounts of simple carbohydrates. These "foods" feed and continue the root cause of the dis-ease: imbalanced brain chemistry caused by the damage they inflict on the neuroendocrine system. Depression, anxiety, mental and physical fatigue, frustration, low self-esteem, low self-confidence, irritability, reactive outbursts, and emotional instability are symptoms that follow former heavy drinkers into sobriety and will eventually lead them back to drinking in an attempt to self-medicate those symptoms. Permanently healing the body and mind of the damage alcohol has inflicted is the most sensible way of healing the symptoms and avoiding relapse. Using the orthomolecular model for restoring health, the bonds of addiction are not only lifted but the addictive biochemistry that attracted the individual to alcohol in the first place is identified, rooted out, and replaced with a healthy biochemistry. This is the true foundation of a new life free of compulsive desire and behavior.

The definition of a cure, when referring to alcoholism, is the state where the body and mind have healed from long-term alcohol toxicity and the genetic and environmental deficiencies pertaining to addictive biochemistry have been successfully addressed. In other words, a healed body is

entirely capable of sufficiently self-medicating in a natural way. The addiction is cured because the former problem drinker no longer has any appetite for alcohol, is no longer compulsively driven to drink, and no longer suffers the standard symptoms most dry drunks exhibit: those symptoms that are the cornerstone of relapse. What better cure is there for an addiction than losing the desire for the addictive substance and being healthy enough to once again live a fulfilling life on one's own terms?

The Premise of The 101 Program
What is Orthomolecular Medicine?

The foundation of The 101 Program is orthomolecular medicine, used to correct known imbalances in the brain chemistry of people addicted to alcohol, as well as those who possess the genetic, nutritional, and other environmental influences that predispose them to addictive biochemistry. The 101 Program integrates nutritional bio-repair and mind/body energy healing to correct afflicted biochemistry at the cellular level caused by genetic and environmental (epigenetic) influences that promote alcohol addiction, as well as the damage from alcohol toxicity which embeds the addiction. Your corrected metabolism provides you the sound body and mind health necessary to carry through in other disciplines that will evolve various areas of your life that may need nurturing to develop a truly "whole-istic" healing transformation. This promotes an integral approach that truly meets the needs of the transformation necessary to truly cure alcohol addiction. In the end, addictive biochemistry is cured at the cellular level as well as in those dimensions that out picture your relationship with your environment such as personal relationships, work, healthy interests, personal development, and community and you are delivered to your natural, healthy non-addicted state, free from not only addiction but the conditions and symptoms that brought you to it.

"Orthomolecular Medicine", as conceptualized by double Nobel laureate, Linus Pauling, "aims to restore the optimum ecological environment for the body's cells by correcting imbalances or deficiencies on the molecular level, based on individual biochemistry, using natural substances such as vitamins, minerals, amino acids, enzymes, hormones and

essential fatty acids."[3] Orthomolecular medicine is being employed today to cure mental and physical illnesses from cancer and schizophrenia to arthritis. It is also the lead therapy for successfully treating alcoholism. The 101 Program offers the most effective treatment known to the medical community; one that comprehensively addresses all damaged biochemical pathways attributed to alcohol addiction. It traverses and rebuilds the biochemical labyrinth that alcohol destroys, in order to heal the body and mind.

Bill Wilson – The First Fan of Orthomolecular Treatment

The first major advance in addressing alcoholism was the formation of Alcoholics Anonymous by Bill Wilson, based on the premise that alcoholism is a dis-ease with major physical or biochemical factors and symptoms. Bill also made the second major advance, when he recognized and later promoted the view that orthomolecular treatment was essential for the treatment of those addicted to alcohol. Dr. Abram Hoffer, M.D., Ph.D. discovered that Niacin (vitamin B3) was therapeutic for patients with schizophrenia, including the 10% of the schizophrenic population that was also addicted to alcohol. Learning this, Bill became very enthusiastic about Dr. Hoffer's work and set out to study the effects of vitamin B3 on members of Alcoholics Anonymous in New York, who were not drinking, and were not schizophrenic, yet remained very tense, restless, depressed, and tired. He found that out of a series of 30 patients, 20 were relieved of all these symptoms in about two months with the supplementation of vitamin B3.

Bill Wilson distributed this information to AA in a series of three Communications to the Physicians of Alcoholics Anonymous urging them to consider these therapies and introduce it into the AA experience. These publications generated a lot of controversy from the International Board, which Wilson had created, down to local AA groups. The main opposition came from the medical members of that group, who believed that no layperson such as Wilson had the right to

---

[3] http://www.orthomed.org

lecture them about the medical aspects of alcoholism and possible treatments (i.e. the use of vitamin B3). This comment, coming from conventional medical doctors, is truly astonishing. These doctors demonstrated a shocking lack of understanding about how the body works and heals. Even today, mainstream allopathic medical doctors remain predominately clueless as to the function and use of natural substances in the human body. Allopathic doctors are not provided an education in nutrition in medical school, have no respect for the role natural substances play in sustaining life and healing, and have absolutely no training in this area, so their response was not an educated one and should not be given the credibility that AA gave it. And their position should never have been used to dismiss what was proven to be helping people! Bill was eventually forced to do his work outside the International Board because of this close-minded attitude and ignorance-based ostracism from a group of physicians with no credentials in the field. Dr. David Hawkins and Dr. Russell Smith did corroborate Bill's findings, in publications of the Journal of Orthomolecular Medicine. However, AA and the physicians of AA steadfastly refused to acknowledge these promising developments and favorable clinical experiments.

Today, the 'medical experts' that have the attention of those in AA and related 12-step programs, as well as the facilitators of these programs and conventional treatment facilities, are freely drugging people with Naltrexone, which can cause serious health risks in addition to the side effects that take the glory of sobriety away. Anti-depressants are also a favorite drug for those treating alcoholism to push on their patients. In addition to the serious side effects and health risks these drugs impose, anti-depressants basically turn the patient into a cross-linking zombie, just alive enough to experience the drug's side effects, including in some cases, a risk for cancer more profound than that of a person who smokes a pack a day. It is criminal and very sad that these people who are seeking AA and 12-step programs to be healthy and happy again are misled down another road of dependence, sub-optimal lifestyle, and health risks.

Little has changed since Wilson was ostracized by the very group of physicians he had assembled and who preferred to ignore – as they do today – the success of orthomolecular

medicine regardless of its profound success. The real-life success statistics of orthomolecular treatment clearly prove that it leads the fight against alcoholism over all other treatments.

Alcohol Abuse and Body Chemistry

Up to this point, addicted biochemistry has been defined as a metabolism that has lost its 'inner wisdom'. Cellular poisoning and exhausting the body's nutritional resources in metabolizing alcohol and its toxic byproducts which creates dangerous deficiencies in vitamins, minerals, amino acids, enzymes, and essential fatty acids cause the overwhelming, debilitating symptoms that lead to the compulsive desire to self-medicate in order to feel right again.

Evidence has mounted over the last 20 years to the point that the effect of alcohol on the brain and body is no longer debatable. It has been proven time and again that the psychological symptoms of problem drinking such as emotional outbursts, anxiety, fear, irritation, mental fatigue, depression, and the cravings to continue drinking are due to physiological damage. The evidence also proves that addressing this damage by eating the way we were meant to eat and through the use of supplemental nutrients and herbs to target the deficiencies of a broken metabolism, you can reverse the problem and cure the addiction. For too long, healthcare professionals have tried (unsuccessfully) to diagnose and treat the symptoms of alcoholism rather than the damage that creates the symptoms – the root cause of the alcohol addiction. Joan Mathews-Larson's words at the Holistic Addiction Treatment Symposium in 2007 ring very clear here, "If you don't treat the cause, you're going to be treating the effects forever." The science and practice of orthomolecular treatment has proven over the last 25 years that through healing the body and mind, we can break free from the biochemical addiction and the psychological baggage that follows. Breaking free of the addiction empowers you to successfully engage an integral approach toward healing and practice various systems of repair and renewal required for a healthy lifestyle that will free you from the depression, anxiety, mental and physical fatigue, emotional instabilities, and hopelessness that normally follow the problem drinker into sobriety. These symptoms and conditions will prevent

you from being able to experience the presence of mind necessary, and exercise the follow-through it takes to benefit from these very valuable mind/body energy healing modalities. Being freed will enable you to approach life with a positive joyful disposition, allowing you to heal relationships and other areas of your life that suffered from drinking, thus enhancing the experience of recovery. This is the beauty of the orthomolecular method of treatment: when employed in all aspects of one's life, all influences that affect the health of the cell are addressed and a full spectrum of holistic health systems can be explored to correct what is deficient by employing what attracts the individual.

Adopting a Healthy Perspective

In order to accept and execute the work and sense of responsibility necessary on the path of liberation from addiction, you need to adopt a healthy, take-charge attitude. Unless one is tagged for a miracle, praying on its own is not going to provide the cure. There is a certain amount of personal responsibility involved in engaging the healing spirit. If the perfect, God-given body is riddled with alcohol and healthy biochemistry is damaged, you have to do your part to restore it, in order to restore your God-given abilities. We are disconnected from God's grace when our bodies and minds are poisoned, and these unnatural and unhealthy conditions that we have created are ones that we need to remove. Our bodies were made the way they were to be perfect vessels or temples of God's light; poisoning it is like putting layers of cloth over that light, and it won't shine like it was intended to until we remove those layers and that is entirely up to us. You must re-purpose your energy to heal your body instead of harming it. Prayer is good for empowerment, staying focused and connecting with God, but in the end it is up to the individual to actually do the work of getting out of the rut of addiction and into a healthy lifestyle. This takes an education and motivation, since the industrialized world environment works against health rather than for it.

Our bodies are remarkable healing machines when we get out of our own way and open ourselves to the powers that created us by removing the roadblocks that poisons such as alcohol create between the supreme intelligence that should

be running things and our physical mind and body. It is your natural state to be healthy, and when you get out of your own way and awaken the physician within you will return to your natural God-given health. It is truly amazing how quickly the body and mind can heal from 20 plus years of heavy alcohol abuse – absolutely fascinating.

It may be helpful for you to understand that God has not taken anything away from you, nor is God punishing you like many chemically depressed individuals think. Rather, through drinking heavily, you punish yourself and compromise your own health, which then shows itself in a host of difficult circumstances and illnesses. There is absolutely no judgment from the heavens, only that which is levied against the physical body from the toxicity it suffers which out pictures itself in deteriorating mental and physical health. The spirit has not changed: it is just as whole, perfect, and present as the day you were born; it simply cannot express itself through the veil of a poisoned body and mind. It is your responsibility to restore your mind and body to the condition in which it was given to you, as best as possible. In this way you connect with the divinity within, and enjoy the well of enchantment, intuition, joy, strength, power, peacefulness, and grace that comes with the awareness of God within.

Remember, the purpose and perfection of the spirit itself is never lost; you simply lose your awareness of it, and the ability to use your divine inheritance to take command of situations in your life when there is a sheath of poison between you and your divine inheritance. However, once you clear the path, your divinity is allowed to flow through you again, resulting in joy and peace of mind as well as freedom from alcohol addiction – you return to your natural perfection.

Treatment vs. Support Groups

It's extremely important to emphasize the difference between a support group and a treatment, and their different roles in recovery. It is also important to research and understand the processes and health risks involved with various treatment options. While support groups may or may not work on an individual basis, the worst that can happen is relapse, which is extremely common when one opts for a support group as a stand-alone solution for their illness. The

wrong treatment, though, can set you on a path that deteriorates your health and frame of mind, adding anguish, hopelessness, and even more desperation to the addiction itself. Many times the wrong treatment will actually aggravate the addiction and bring about a very dangerous level of multiple chemical dependencies.

Treatment Options

There are four conventional methods promoted today for approaching recovery from alcohol addiction. The 101 Program makes a fifth, unconventional, choice. Only through serious soul searching, research, and then consideration of all five approaches does one find the most logical solution toward truly ending alcohol addiction.

Aside from orthomolecular treatment, the four standard options are:

- Support Groups (this includes AA and other 12-step model programs)
- Drug-centric treatment, which is usually prescribed by a psychiatrist and is popular in rehab centers
- Talk therapy
- Rehabilitation centers, which essentially use their own branded combination of the other three techniques

Support Groups

If it works, it's good medicine; that's my creed, but what exactly does "works" mean? To me, it means happiness, enthusiasm, inspiration, and health as well as being able to meet with life's challenges in a healthy way while entirely free of the bonds of addictive biochemistry. Not just being sober. And while AA as a support group does help many people stay sober for a while, it does not 'work' for their physiological, mental, and emotional health. That is, in most cases, debilitating to the former problem drinker due to the physiological and physiological-turned psychological/emotional damage caused by long-term alcohol toxicity. AA helped many people in the 70 years since it was started; it is free, accessible, and somewhere for people to go

when they are feeling overwhelmed by the desire to drink. For someone who isn't addressing their health and the symptoms that create the need for that drink and for support, a support group can be a very good thing- even a life saving one. However, the better path, the one that serves quality of sobriety and ultimately no need for a support group is orthomolecular treatment.

The fact is that AA has dismal success statistics: the statistics from numerous unbiased medical and psychiatric reports is a rate of 95% to 97% failure. These same statistics also reveal repeated relapse, suicide, and the common practice of taking other prescription drugs to medicate the symptoms that follow those trying to get sober in the AA experience. This does not fault AA as an organization, since they clearly and officially state that it is a support group, not a treatment. Yet people continue to go to meetings as a stand-alone solution, expecting a full recovery, and never considering treatment. AA as an organization needs to acknowledge the crucial importance of treating the illness in a way that will permanently heal the symptoms that cause their members' relapse, alcohol-associated illnesses, and suicides if they are to ever hope to be a support group for and help the other 97% and change these very discouraging statistics. There is a reason for those numbers and science has come a long way in being able to explain them!

However, since conventional and corporate medicine and its investors, the pharmaceutical companies, either directly or through advertising dollars own the airwaves and the ink and paper of mainstream magazines and newspapers, they control the information released to not only AA but also to the general public. This selective information in turn drives the choices and belief systems of the mainstream public. While multi-national pharmaceutical companies are in the background lobbying to have supplements taken off shelves worldwide, mainstream conventional medical doctors and practitioners subdue and even publicly shame holistic practices. This is done not because they aren't accurate and effective treatments, but because they are more effective than conventional medical treatments and pose a serious threat to some of the largest profits made by business in the world. This is why large pharmaceutical companies spend millions of dollars trying to block the public's constitutional right to

information and nutritional supplements. (How interested can they be in the public's health if they are trying to take what is healing millions of people of thousands of illnesses away from them?) So AA, like the general public, has been forced to follow the propaganda of conventional medicine and treatment.

This cultivation of the American public's opinions has given full license to conventional doctors, who don't understand the biochemical deficiencies that cause addiction, and continue to practice their methods, which are repeatedly proven not to work, and dispense drugs that further aggravate addicted biochemistry. These doctors, fueled by the interests of the for-profit pharma-cartel, are the ones that have permeated the AA culture and have full access to those with a specific problem who are seeking a healthier lifestyle. What better market could they find? They use this access to propagandize their ultimately dangerous methods, and because people have been forced into the darkness by the hold they and pharmaceutical companies have on mainstream advertising and propaganda, leaving no access to the type of information you are currently reading, the general public is entirely unaware of the healthy choices available to actually cure the addiction to alcohol. Blinded by doctors who are promoting drugs and not health, which are able to mask but not cure, people who are vulnerable, desperate, and in a state of chaos believe that they have no other options. They are consistently led to try these perpetually failed methods, continually finding themselves in deeper trouble; in many cases they develop multiple dependencies and more severely altered brain chemistry from the prescription medication.

The saddest part of this cycle is that these people are further harmed, and then blamed for the failure of the treatment. They are led further down a path that does not really achieve their original goal: to be happy, healthy, and free of the bonds of alcohol addiction... to return to the body they knew before becoming addicted.

So while corporate for-profit "health" systems and practitioners have the attention of AA and a stronghold on its members' values and acceptance / endorsement of treatment modalities, that beautiful day when AA encourages their members to seek proven holistic methods of healing their addiction will not show on our calendar.

Unfortunately Bill Wilson died before he could better develop his orthomolecular research with the physicians he was working with outside of AA, and use his influence to implement it into the AA program. Many chronic drinkers were reporting relief and release from symptoms known to be the catalysts for relapse during the nutritional supplement-based trials Bill and his team of like-minded physicians were conducting. Yet the AA physicians continued to ostracize Bill and ignore the successful results of his research, even after physicians in the top of their fields validated Bill's findings with their own. Isn't the purpose of medicine to heal, not profit? Why did they dismiss something that was helping people quit alcohol? What right did they have to do that? They were outside of their professional jurisdiction. Why did AA indoctrinate this attitude and allow them to do this? If Bill Wilson were alive today, many of the orthomolecular-oriented pioneering practitioners, such as Dr. Abram Hoffer, Joan Mathews-Larson Ph.D., and myself, would be working *with* him. Because of the way mainstream medicine and advertising have cultivated people, there is still great resistance from AA members, and often outright attacks on orthomolecular and holistic therapies and their practitioners from members of the organization.

Another problem is that people have become cultured to approach their recovery backwards by seeking a support group like AA exclusively and not a treatment. In the case of every other illness, people first seek a treatment and then, if they feel they need it, a support group. The opposite is true of alcohol addiction due to the fact that there were no viable treatment options 70 years ago when AA was started, because not much was known about the premise of alcohol addiction and what caused it. But times have changed! At this point, research is well documented in the field of addictive biochemistry, and science demonstrates that orthomolecular medicine is now not only a valid method of fixing what is known to be broken but has been proven to be supremely effective over all other treatments in both length of sobriety and the quality of that sobriety. Since support groups were the only option in the past, people have been cultivated to seek support groups first and ignore promising treatment options. This method of approaching recovery has become so engrained in our society that even today, when there is

effective and successful treatment, people join a support group without even considering anything else. The proper approach to any dis-ease is to first seek treatment and then, if needed, find a support group that satisfies your needs in that area. Support groups are wonderful for addressing and airing some of the emotional trauma associated with an illness and its challenges, but they cannot provide the full spectrum healing required unless they are paired with an effective, bio-repairing treatment protocol. AA is part of the answer for some and rarely the entire answer. Even if the person does remain sober for any length of time, the quality of that sobriety would be enhanced to levels unimaginable to many if they were to adopt a healing, corrective, holistic treatment. The emotional and psychological symptoms that make the support group necessary aren't going to go away unless there is a treatment adopted for healing the root cause of their symptoms they built a life around self-medicating.

While the mind/body healing energy derived from a hug, a group of friends whom are compassionate about your struggles, a place to air your dreams, concerns, and struggles does promote good feelings and thoughts experienced to the cellular level helping to heal, AA as a stand-alone approach to breaking alcohol addiction is limited because attending meetings and 12 stepping does not address the root cause of the addiction which is deeply embedded in the biochemistry and can override the subtle in comparison effects of meetings. This is why those using AA as a stand alone treatment are engulfed in a daily battle; the battle between good intention and the benefits of the support group and the deeply damaged addictive biochemistry. The benefits of a support group are enhanced ten-fold when the appropriate treatment is being sought. Each and every body of science and medicine of any credibility will support the evidence that the best success rates are from those representing people who combined the mind/body energy healing methods (support groups included but not necessarily AA), with nutritional bio-repair. Support can also be found in traditional settings like church, temple, spirituality, family, clubs, hobbies, and internal/external exercise like Yoga, Tai Chi, and Qi Qong. Meditation has been a phenomenally successful method for former problem drinkers in learning how to calm the mind and manage stress. Meditation done properly actually increases endorphin and

enkephalin levels in the brain, as does Yoga, Tai chi, and Qi Qong, naturally reducing the desire to drink, which can benefit people who are at a biochemical disadvantage when it comes to being "naturally sufficiently medicated": those who do not produce sufficient amounts of endorphins, GABA, serotonin, and enkephalins to meet with life's bumps in the road in a healthy, non-reactive or health threatening way. However, nutritional bio-repair is required to enable one whom has suffered the damage of alcohol toxicity to sit still and focus for any length of time! Many clubs and activities that accommodate healthy common interests can provide the much-needed release of stress and provide a healthy sense of connectedness that is also the fundamental purpose of support groups and systems. There are numerous mind/body energy healing techniques available today that help to balance brain chemistry, create healthy states of mind and awareness, boost the immune system and produce general good health such as HeartMath, PSYCHE-K, EFT, and belief clearing just to name a few. All of these methods have a tremendous offering for those suffering from the psychological baggage and limited belief systems created by addictive biochemistry and many of their practitioners are specifically trained in treating addictive biochemistry very well. Since everyone is different, part of the healing journey is finding the one that resonates best with you which will be the one that provides the best results.

For those who have tried AA or any number of conventional treatments and are back to problem drinking, do not carry the weight of failure on your shoulders; the outcome of your passionate resolve and desperate attempt to recover was absolutely in most cases the fault of the treatment and so-called support you received. In many cases, the support you received was to continue drinking! There is an abysmal gap between what science knows the alcohol addicted person needs and what conventional treatment provides. For instance, in the case of AA meetings, they do not *treat the biochemical cause of the addiction or address how to cure the symptoms* that drive an estimated 95% of their members back to drinking. *AA is a support group at best, not a treatment.* And because of this and other facts I will point out, an overwhelming majority of problem drinkers seeking recovery by going to meetings as a stand-alone method of treating their

addiction will relapse back into self-medicating, often times with added intensity. There are many reasons for this, however, if AA is the primary influence addressing recovery much of the problem rests in the fact that AA *prescribes relapse*. AA prescribes what science knows to be the number one cause of relapse; high refined carb and sugar diets, and stimulants such as coffee and tea. Also, in the framework of mind/body energy healing aspects required for recovery, your perspective is your master pharmacist, and your belief system is what will create your experiences in life and what you get out of them. What you believe in is the primary vehicle that will create the future you manifest. If you view the world as an alcoholic with a life-long disease of which has rendered you powerless, that is exactly what you will get; you will be an alcoholic with a lifelong disease bearing witness to a future full of struggle, the depression that comes with that view, victimization, helplessness, and despair. Combine that with the sugar bowl and coffee cup you're living in and the symptoms this diet produces and you have got a full clad recipe for failure brought on by the torment of attempting to endure such a life! In our culture, the common experience has been all the things that I've just mentioned because that is the road to "recovery" these people have chosen- albeit because mainstream television is owned by the sugar and pharmaceutical industry bent on not only keeping people ignorant to successful holistic options but ridiculing them. However, now that you have in your hands the information and guidance that will deliver you to freedom from addictive biochemistry and a vibrant life, *it does not have to be your experience!*

Not one conventional treatment or practice in AA actually aims to and supports the premise of healing the damage and curing the addiction. This is exactly why these methods produce the perpetual pathetically unsuccessful statistics they do. And please never forget: *"statistics" means people's lives and the quality of those lives.* It is petrifying to think of what those failure rates have produced in terms of disease, suicide, violence, murder, broken families, beaten and abused children, homelessness, pain... loss, loss, loss experienced by themselves, families, and communities- the world. Dr. Abram Hoffer M.D., Ph.D. whom is credited for developing orthomolecular treatments that have healed and saved the

lives of thousands of schizophrenic and cancer patients, and who has also successfully treated those suffering from alcohol addiction wrote in his biography, *"I give my critics full credit for having delayed the full introduction of orthomolecular medicine into the medical world and for having denied life, health, and happiness for innumerable patients. Supporters of old paradigms never realize how much damage they do by their remarkable rigidity and adherence to old theories."* I can not find better words to express my exact sentiments for those that have dismissed the success of orthomolecular treatment and purposely prevented integrating orthomolecular medicine into mainstream society, including AA, for the treatment of addictive biochemistry!

Another thing that is very important to consider if you're looking into conventional treatment: AA gets to catch the blame in their statistics for the utterly unsuccessful methods conventional medicine is using to treat addiction because those being treated by conventional medicine and rehabs are typically in AA. So this fact truly provides a dismal picture of the efficacy of talk therapy, rehabs, and drugs as a treatment for addictive biochemistry.

Do not let these statistics fill you with despair. You now have the information you need to avoid the path to relapse and actually heal and enjoy your life again- living a life quite opposite of what mainstream treatment has in store for you.

The art of healing any dis-ease requires the involvement and evolvement of all aspects of the human experience – physical, mental, spiritual and emotional. A treatment program like The 101 Program, which cures the physical and mental addiction to alcohol and the plethora of symptoms from long-term alcohol toxicity, will deliver you, the seeker of health and wellness, to the success you desire and the happiness and peaceful centeredness you seek. It will enable you to find a complimenting lifestyle and empower you with the ability to make and sustain healthy lifestyle choices and support systems. Your rewards are then experienced thoroughly in all aspects of your life.

The process of healing and the personal needs of every person on the path of recovery are different. AA is not for everyone, and is not the quintessential divine passage to recovery – there is no such thing. By nature, support groups involve things like a person's spirituality, sense of reason,

beliefs, education, cultural influences, lifestyle, personal views, sexuality, etc.; all of which makes the type of support system chosen extremely personal. However, every person addicted to alcohol shares the same established biochemical damage; damage that needs to be addressed to break the addiction. Treatment is as essential as spirituality and other support systems: they all work together. It is impossible, save a miracle, to effectively employ the benefits and principles of any support system or spirituality with a poisoned, suffering mind and body.

The process of recovery is a multi-layered one, and if you find value in meetings then it is good medicine. However, your quality of life and odds for success are proven to be exponentially better served with a bio-repair treatment that actually heals and delivers you to a state of mental, emotional and physical health. Anyone attracted to AA should learn how to use it for the real value it is capable of providing such as a sense of support, social contact, and spirituality and avoid the aspects of the group that prescribe relapse.

One thing is absolutely certain: when you are healed such as in the way that the 101 Program and orthomolecular medicine provide, meetings are no longer necessary.

Talk Therapy

The American Medical Association's (AMA) position on alcoholism is that it is a biochemical addiction and only through treating it biochemically can you break the addiction: no amount of 'talk therapy' will address the true nature of the addiction. Talk therapy can be helpful to people in difficult situations, who do not have the ability to address their circumstances in a healthy manner. But it is not for chemical dependencies and their symptoms.

The techniques of professionals who use talk therapy to treat addictive biochemistry can be harmful for your recovery, and will sometimes even sabotage it by setting out to unearth bad memories or traumatic experiences as causes for harmful drinking in an already chemically depressed person and this has a tendency to keep them focused on these negative experiences and other less than ideal circumstances in their life. They also tend to push the wrong belief that the person has a disease for which there is no cure and substantiate their claims by demonstrating how it manifests in your

shortcomings. They go on to convince their patients that they can teach them how to learn to live with this disease. All of this talk is about a psychological disease that doesn't exist; further, this type of treatment has a tendency to inflame an already-low self-esteem created by the chemical depression. A low self-esteem that the person, in their true, un-poisoned self, does not own in the first place; it is one of many mental and emotional symptoms caused by the biochemical damage to the brain. Remember, when you correct the biochemistry through healing the damage, these symptoms disappear and are replaced with a good self-image as well as peacefulness, joy, centeredness, and inspiration. This is the natural state of being.

For recovering drinkers, paying a therapist $125 an hour to look for and find that dog that bit them when they were seven is not going to go a long way in helping them stop craving alcohol or relieve them of chemical depression. Instead, conventional psychological treatment and therapy models designed for addiction treatment can make life more unbearable for the alcohol-depressed frame of mind. It sets one on a path that focuses on negative feelings and issues, while at the same time wrestling with the painful physical and emotional symptoms of unhealthy brain chemistry. This is an overly expensive and self-destructive approach for a person seeking to recover.

Those in the field of nutrition and holistic healing are not the only ones aware of the fact that talk therapy is useless for problem drinkers attempting to find relief from alcohol abuse. Noted for his extensive research in alcoholism, endocrinologist Dr. John Tintera, who was a charter member of the New York State Commission on Alcoholism, considers psychoanalytic treatment "utterly unsuccessful (in rehabilitating alcoholics) since the deep-rooted emotional factor is, in reality, physiologically based."

Joan Mathews-Larson, Ph.D., author of the book <u>Seven Weeks to Sobriety</u>, and Founder and Director of the Health Recovery Center (HRC), is an outspoken advocate of the orthomolecular approach toward successful abstinence. In her book she states, "The notion that nutritional deprivation can have devastating effects on behavior is not new." She continues by noting that "research verifies the link between depression and biochemistry and no amount of psychotherapy

or counseling can help people who suffer from biochemically induced depression." She also asks the question: "Couldn't much of the hopelessness and depression, the violent mood swings and other psychological symptoms be the effects of heavy alcohol use rather than its cause?" Orthomolecular treatment answers that question with a resounding YES.

Going right to the source and correcting the real damage that has been done means that a person won't care what the name of that dog was that bit them when they were seven. They will find everything to once again be in proper perspective, and deal with life's real challenges with a positive frame of mind. To get there, it is necessary to focus on health and accept the rules that dictate it, rather than thinking that addiction is simply a mental issue, or a destiny decided by genetic influences; genes do not define your destiny.

Talk Therapy Does Not Correct an Addicted Metabolism

One of the difficulties of recovery, regarding the very real thoughts and emotions produced by alcohol toxicity, is that negative 'mind speak' slowly develops with the progression of brain chemistry distortion. People dependent on alcohol develop a psyche of thoughts and emotions over the years that believes the negative perspectives and feelings that they experience. The view of circumstances in life and self is warped by chemical toxicity, which disrupts the ability to produce healthy thoughts and emotions, especially in response to any difficulty. The other side of this problem is that the study of mind and body medicine has proven time and again that this sort of 'negative feedback' also biochemically influences the body toward disease and various psychological symptoms: it is a vicious circle. It is of paramount importance that you invalidate and dismiss these thoughts and emotions by remembering that most of them, if not all, are not actually yours- you, in your true self, do not own them. Your response to difficulty is weak and depleted because your mind and body have been weakened and depleted. Your view of life is damaged because your mind and body are damaged. Your attitude is toxic because your mind and body are suffering from toxicity. Your environment is in disarray and in disharmony because your mind and body are

in disarray and in disharmony. The macrocosm mirrors the microcosm – vis-à-vis.

The truth is that most professionals who use the old analytical models are just chasing the symptoms of alcoholism around. They are not pinpointing or addressing the root of the addiction, which is why their methods are so utterly unsuccessful. When the root of the addiction is pulled out of the system, those symptoms that they "treat" go away, as well as the behavior and compromised mental conditions associated with a damaged biochemistry. No amount of talk therapy will ever heal the symptoms of alcohol toxicity or cure the addiction. The best they can provide is that therapy may help the patient to find a better way to live with the symptoms; but wouldn't it be better to heal the symptoms altogether and stop the suffering?

Talk-therapy cannot effectively address chemical addiction nor cure it, but if you feel that you need psychological therapy even after the body is healed from the mind-altering damage of alcohol addiction, you should seek it because there are circumstances that can truly be helped by this model of therapy. I simply suggest that you find out which thoughts and emotions you actually own by first cleansing and healing your mind from the chemicals that are causing your thoughts and emotions to be distorted.

During The 101 Program, clients have made it obvious that issues that were paramount in their hearts and minds, as well as a host of problems they thought they had and the perceived intensity of those problems, simply disappeared during the healing process. It is remarkable how many health issues, both of mind and body, simply disappear when you detoxify and heal the damaged biochemistry inflicted by alcohol. So first find out which feelings are real and which ones are brought about by a distorted brain suffering from alcohol toxicity. Within a month or two a large amount, if not all of this 'mind junk' will disappear, and the radiant health that was hidden beneath the surface of this layer of addiction will begin to show itself. Approaching recovery this way will also help any therapist involved to get to the bottom of any real issues without having to dig through the fog of addiction. This will save lots of money and make any therapy that much more effective.

Drug-centric Treatment

The idea of using a drug to treat a chemical dependency is ludicrous and criminal, defeating all common sense. Using medication to mask symptoms that exist because the body and mind are crying out to be healed only aggravates imbalanced body and brain biochemistry. This leads to more damage to the body and mind, undesirable symptoms, further prescription drugs for support, and more opportunity for a metabolism to go astray and lead to illness.

Drugs prescribed for illness typically mask or treat only the symptoms, and drugs prescribed for addiction will do the same, while metabolic disorders continue to take their toll on a body's health and ultimately lead to disease. An addiction is a metabolic disorder and needs to be addressed on biochemical terms that return the body to its natural state, rather than lead it down another path of discord. The methods used to accomplish this need to encourage balance of the essential bioenergetics for health in the mind and body, not poison them further creating more cellular deficiencies which eventually cause more symptoms.

And regarding the liver, anyone who has been drinking heavily for a long time has done enough damage to their liver; additional drugs will only serve to harm it further.

One of the most popular drugs used for alcohol addiction, Naltrexone, is claimed to be the safest option in drug-centric treatment. However, the relapse statistics for people using this drug are only slightly lower than for those who do not (and remember, these stats are dismal to begin with), and there are some very serious risks and side effects that accompany this attempt at a shortcut to recovery.

One of the side effects noted is yellowing of the eyes, which is a very serious condition. It is a sign of the damage being done to the liver. The yellow in a person's eyes is caused from a build up of bilirubin, a metabolism byproduct that is normally dismissed by the liver. Bilirubin is a byproduct of hemoglobin metabolism, the molecule that carries oxygen in the red blood cells. When the liver is sick or sluggish, it loses the ability to process and remove bilirubin, which then backs up and causes the yellowing of the eyes. Bilirubin is just a flag that indicates trouble; if bilirubin is not being processed, you can be assured that toxins and other metabolic waste are also backing up in the body and leading to many health

issues. Those presently and formerly addicted to alcohol suffer from hundreds of health issues stemming from a damaged liver, and they don't need yet another toxin like a prescription drug increasing their vulnerability to these diseases.

The liver is responsible for over 500 processes on which the body depends for healthy bioenergetics. If the liver is not detoxing properly then other processes like protein synthesis for proper brain neurotransmitter availability are being compromised as well.

Some other side effects of Naltrexone are:

- Severe stomach pains
- Dark-colored urine
- Diarrhea or constipation
- Headache
- Joint or muscle pain
- Mild stomach pain
- Nausea or vomiting
- Nervousness
- Anxiety
- Insomnia
- Kidney damage

*Naltrexone has been shown to cause birth defects in animal newborns.

We all know that discomfort is the body's way of telling us something is wrong; something is wrong when these types of side effects occur. One of the edicts of a healthy lifestyle is listening to and responding to the body, not trying to manipulate it, shut it up, or fool it; it can't be fooled. If you take a drug to cure a drug addiction, you are the only one being fooled, but your body is going to continue to deteriorate until you begin responding to its needs in a healthy way.

There are warnings in nearly every Naltrexone journal that suggest that it, as a treatment for alcoholism, may cause liver damage when taken in excess or by people with liver disease due to other causes. Anyone who has been drinking excessively for the length of time that it takes to become dependent on alcohol, and who comes to the place in their life where they need to seek treatment to quit, has compromised liver function. It is strongly advised that you think long and

hard before considering use of a drug that can further damage you. One of the steps in the biochemical chain of events that leads to addiction is the failing of the liver to efficiently remove acetaldehyde and other toxins from the body and synthesize the proteins necessary for the brain to function properly. The obvious answer is to give the liver a break and an environment in which it can heal, not to further tax and damage it.

There are many other ways in which using a drug to treat addiction adversely impacts the quest for health.

- Using a drug such as Naltrexone, which blocks opiate receptors, disables a person from responding to life in a fully present human capacity. Since it blocks the opiate receptors in order to reduce the enjoyable effects of alcohol, endorphins and enkephalins (the natural feel-good molecules) are also prevented from lodging onto these receptors. This keeps the person from feeling the same heights of joy that they should, in the moments that warrant it. The brain will not respond to sadness or benefit as it should from natural endorphins, which should be released and received in their corresponding receptor sites in times of emotional distress to buffer pain. Sadness and pain are excellent catalysts for change – if the situation warrants it, we should feel sad. The goal is for you to get back in your body and learn to treat yourself right so that you can be 'present' for life. Life is about ups and downs, joy and sadness; the losses make the wins sweeter. A drug that blocks opiate receptors essentially cuts that person off from experiencing life as it should be experienced, with a full range of feeling and emotion. In today's overworked and undernourished economy, we should be very protective of what time we do have with what and who truly matters to us and stay attached to the majesty of life, so who wants to be a zombie during these precious moments? Naltrexone also detaches a person from the capability of experiencing a natural sense of peacefulness, because a balanced flora of endorphins and their complimenting receptors are required for that state. This drug can literally shut a creative person down by blocking their sensitivities. When emotional range is restricted the response to the environment is restricted as well, and inspiration and insight, which are

products of being absolutely integrated with your environment and feed creativity, will suffer as a result.

- People experience natural states of euphoria when they are healthy and the time / event warrants it. Naltrexone robs its victims of this.

- Taking a drug that shuts you down also retards your progress in developing skills with which to handle all that life has to offer, while at the same time experiencing your full range of emotions. These emotions are the unique aspects that make you who you are. They represent your past, beliefs, experiences with family and friends, wins, losses, and all that is important to you in life. Shutting that down, even moderately, affects personality, and detaches you from who you really are.

- As with any drug you will build a tolerance to it and, in time, be afflicted with a brain chemistry that is further altered. You will have to start back at square one in worse biochemical shape than that in which you began.

- Since anti-depressants mask the symptoms, you will not be inclined to correct the dietary and lifestyle problems that caused the trouble in the first place, forgiving (on the surface) your irresponsible lifestyle. This is dangerous because the mortality rate of problem drinkers and former problem drinkers continues to be high even after getting sober, directly because they adopt unhealthy diets as a result of their imbalanced brain chemistry and insatiable sugar cravings in the absence of alcohol. In this way, the addictive biochemistry and path of damage continue; no real healing is taking place, only continued biochemical injury and progressive illness and disease development.

- Using a drug to treat addiction continues the psychological association of taking an outside substance in order to feel right, instead of submitting to the laws that dictate health and adopting a truly health-oriented lifestyle. Doing what must be done and actually curing the dis-ease would feed confidence and self-esteem, creating a new self-image that the person can take into all new challenges in life. It will also increase the odds of success in many other aspects of life. Continuing the cycle of substance dependence does just the opposite, reinforcing addictive behavior in all aspects of the individual's life.

- The dry-drunk symptoms will continue to plague the recovering drinker, compounded by the side effects from the new drug itself. They will respond to this by going to the doctor for more pills to combat the various mounting psychological and physical discomforts.
- Added to the fact that after all of this, the relapse rates for those on Naltrexone are only slightly lower than those who do not take the drug, pharmaceutical cures are not cast in a particularly positive light. It is even more disturbing to realize that this is the drug that the medical establishment claims to be the safest.

Rehabilitation Centers

In a nutshell, conventional rehabilitation centers employ their own branded combination of support groups and conventional treatments. They are also proponents of prescription drugs and talk therapy, due to the financial gains they find in these areas. It certainly can't be due to the success rates because those are again, dismal. It's a system of using two methods that are known not to produce favorable results for those trying to heal addictive biochemistry. They are simply not the right tools for what needs to be fixed!

Disturbingly, conventional rehab policies and procedures for treating addiction are based on analytical models that were developed decades ago, when little was known about alcohol addiction other than the outward symptoms of continued drunken behavior and dysfunction. These analytical methods do not hold water when faced with our current understanding of the premise of addiction, as provided by today's more sophisticated research tools and scientists in the fields of biochemistry and orthomolecular medicine. Possibly the more educated facilitators and employees of these establishments privately recognize orthomolecular medicine's validity. However, switching these programs over to a holistic process would be financially impossible. This is because, as of today, insurance does not pay for nontraditional treatments; any treatment dispensed by doctors must be sanctioned by the AMA. The AMA, in turn, will only approve what the FDA, which is controlled by big pharmaceutical money, approves. This means that insurance companies will only insure what the FDA approves. If the AMA were to digress from this plan, doctors across the

nation would lose research grants, medical school scholarships, funding, and a long list of other incentives that are provided by the pharmaceutical companies, including the luxury of being insured. M.D.s' have literally had their medical license taken away for practicing orthomolecular medicine. This provides a peek into the corrupt world the pharmaceutical companies through the FDA have established to protect their interests. So your corner rehab will continue their proven unsuccessful methods simply to stay in business until people wise up and stop going to them.

Ideally, you need to learn how to maintain healthy lifestyle habits and take care of yourself if you have demonstrated addictive biochemistry. It's easy to stop something if someone else is controlling your environment and actions. Traditional rehab centers have a way of 'taking charge' of their patients instead of teaching them how to take charge of themselves; a situation very similar to addiction, where the addiction is in charge. This calls into question what exactly the benefits are in rehab centers, and what growth can realistically occur there. No conventional rehab to my knowledge educates people on the most fundamental requirements for healing addictive biochemistry – detoxification, therapeutic nutrition, what foods and substances to absolutely avoid, and how to follow a diet that not only discourages addictive biochemistry,

but heals it. Nor do they teach extremely successful mind/body medicine such as HearthMath, Psych-K, EFT, Biofeedback, Jin Shin Jyutsu, Thought Field Therapy, Energetic Rebalancing, or forms of relaxation, balancing, and focused concentration such as meditation, Tai Chi, and Yoga. These are all activities and disciplines that actually help the brain produce and properly utilize neurochemicals those with addictive biochemistry are known to be deficient in. Ultimately, learning the true nature of your biochemistry and how it became imbalanced in the first place is the best education toward avoiding trouble in the future.

The goal is for you to learn to take charge of yourself rather than being cared for by a team of doctors, nurses, and counselors because in the end only you can make yourself sick or well. The 101 Program requirements can be quite a leap into another dimension for some people simply because they have never learned or lived the basic edicts of a healthy lifestyle, which is in many cases what got them into trouble in

the first place. Because it is such a big change, a very high percentage of 101 Program clients have asked me to provide a retreat that employs the practices of The 101 Program; to teach them through study and in a hands-on environment about their specific biochemistry, and how to migrate away from damaging industrial products and eat the right foods that will help them heal. You need to learn how to prepare the right foods, find and connect with your inner person, and create a routine that provides for your own enrichment and physical and mental health. Many of you need to be afforded the time and environment to reconnect with your interests so that you have a sense of who you truly are once again, and a venue for self-gratification. The maintenance of daily life can be distracting and demanding when one is trying to learn an entirely new lifestyle that employs the practices of condictive nutrition and therapy, and true mind/body /spiritual health and transformation because there is so little of it out there! You really have to know what you're doing and cut a new path to health stores, restaurants, spirituality, healthy socializing and recreation; and many times even what doctor you see. Managing both daily life and implementing your new life can be challenging in the beginning.

It is important that you learn to take care of yourself and the quicker the better because once you have learned how to embrace and implement the practices of The 101 Program, the education will last you a lifetime, and the bonds of addiction will be dismissed as naturally as the grass grows. So that is where a retreat is helpful. In an orthomolecular treatment setting you would also be afforded the opportunity to benefit from mind/body energy healing such as Yoga, Tai Chi, Qi Qong, acupuncture, exercise, Heartmath, Psych-K, EFT (as well as other forms of psychological/emotional clearing and healing). These disciplines will help you learn techniques that are proven to reduce stress, boost the immune system, and induce healthy brain chemistry further paving the way to healthy states of mind, which are just a few of the benefits they provide. Some of these techniques can actually be used to help you create the future you desire through learning how to manifest your dreams and bring life to your desires. When you learn the mechanics of orthomolecular medicine and the results it provides, you will learn how your thoughts and emotions influence not only the health or dis-

ease of your cells but how your brain cells, when provided the right environment, are capable of tuning into higher states of consciousness that produces thoughts and emotions that guide you toward manifesting your dreams and desires naturally with ease, and in perfect alignment with what is in your mind's eye for yourself. Remember, the microcosm mirrors the macrocosm- "As above, so below." Vis-à-vis.

After looking into The 101 Program, many people find that they do want a retreat to do the program and take the time necessary to retrain their habits and focus; a time to rebuild their lives from the ground up; learn and embed the practices of a condictive lifestyle and diet, refocus their minds from their true-self out, and reconnect from the heart out. A time where they can stop answering to all the responsibilities that consume the much needed focus they need to educate and retrain themselves. A time to remove themselves from old triggers that distract them so that they can reconnect with and get to know themselves again and provide the person they find with the type of peace of mind that will no longer even recognize the triggers; a time where they can build from within the empowerment necessary to continue on in the industrial jungle (actually, I've had some people leave the concrete jungle and head for open land and small town living!). Essentially a retreat focused on providing them all the tools and education to start their new life that will not only initiate that change but will sustain it when they leave. For that reason, we have begun hosting one week and two month retreats to provide an environment that facilitates this type of growth and healing through a thorough education which teaches how to take care of their specific biochemical and environmental/lifestyle needs. They receive all the instruction, experience and education required to do The 101 Program and integrate the therapeutic nutritional bio-repair, and mind/body energy healing to correct addictive biochemistry at the cellular level and deliver them to their natural, healthy non-addicted self, free from not only addiction but the symptoms and conditions that brought them to it. More information about the location, dates/times, curriculum, and services offered at the retreats can be found through the "Retreat" link at http://www.the101program.com/retreat.html

Summary on Treatment Options

The medical institution needs to take a new look at the entire health care approach to problem drinking, and change it from a treatment-based model to a curing-based model. There is not a lot of push out there to focus on the curing models because there are only big profits in treating. If a treatment facility of any kind does not have a reasonable success rate, insurance companies should stop paying their invoices. This would not only force people to find something else that does work, it would also help reduce our health care premiums (yeah, right in a perfect world- well, at least people would be getting the help they really need and that is what matters). And those in authority should not be sending individuals in need of help to these ineffective facilities. If you hired a gardener to care for your dying garden and the garden continued to wilt away, wouldn't you fire the gardener? That is exactly what we must do with health care systems that don't work; this would repurpose the millions of dollars being absorbed by these unproductive treatment methods into the ones that do work. Orthomolecular practitioners are proving their case daily through their successes, and doing it at a fraction of the cost of rehabs, drug-based treatments, psychiatry, and psychosocial programs.

For an inside look at how important it is and what some "treatment professionals" will do to fill rehab and hospital beds for insurance money, read <u>Coyote Medicine</u> by Lewis Mehl-Madrona, M.D., a Stanford Medical School graduate and Shaman Healer. It may change your life forever, and it will certainly give you an insider's education about the corruption that flows through hospitals, health care systems, and especially psychiatric wards, which is where many problem drinkers and substance abusers end up. It's in these wards that many people, due to being diagnosed (or purposely misdiagnosed) as mentally incapable of making their own decisions, or harmful to themselves and others, are imprisoned against their will. They are forced to take extremely toxic drugs, poisoned with substances with uncharted negative side effects, severely victimized, mentally abused, made guinea pigs, and stripped of self-dignity as they fade into the fog and twilight of the drugs they are forced to take. In the process they lose touch with themselves,

becoming empty vessels aware only of the anguish of their condition. As the drugs, distress, fear, and anguish take their toll on their mental health they truly do become mentally ill. They are nowhere near where they need to be to heal because they are actually suffering from the conditions and treatment they are receiving. Many very sane people who are in the wrong place at the wrong time find themselves essentially imprisoned in these wards for no reason but to fill a bed so that hospitals and practitioners can collect insurance money. It happens every day and it is not only morally corrupt and disgusting, but criminal.

Rehabs, psychiatrists, and the physicians who dispense pills to cure addiction, and the pharmaceutical companies that provide them, are making millions of dollars while alcoholism is on the rise and people are dying from alcohol addiction and its related health issues at record numbers. More people are currently dying from the treatment than from the dis-ease. This fact is being made public by a new brand of doctors who are tired of the pharma-centric push to approach every illness with pharmaceuticals, which they now realize do not heal but rather mask the problem. Hidden under the surface the illness continues to progress, resulting in a downward spiral into chronic symptoms and more complicated health issues, invariably ending in death. One example is in the prescription of antidepressants, which accelerate damage to the liver, further distort an already unhealthy neuroendocrine system, and prove ultimately harmful to the brain of a recovering drinker who needs to be cleaned up, not further polluted. A further cause for concern is that it doesn't take much research to find the incredibly high rate of cancer suffered by those on today's popular SSRIs (antidepressants). Western Medicine; ergo, allopathic treatment is the number one cause of death in the U.S., and alcohol treatment is no different than the plethora of other treatments people are dying from.

While many doctors are awakening to the truth and taking action such as getting naturopathy degrees to become integrative physicians which allows them to provide the best of the east and west including orthomolecular medicine, on the other side of the fence many doctors these days are becoming nothing more than white-collar drug pushers. This is the result of the pharmaceutical company monopoly over

education, money, sponsorships, media, and information in the medical and healthcare industries. This influence promotes the use of extremely toxic so-called medications, which are criminally pushed through the FDA by pharmaceutical money and muscle. As a result of the pharma-cartel owning their education through grants, research money, sponsorships, full-page color ads in physician targeted medical books and magazines (essentially all advertising streams, even to the consumer); traditional medical doctors are being forced to fall in line with what the big companies want. Unfortunately, due to this method of educating and cultivating our medical students, the medical profession is filled with doctors who will prescribe nearly anything that doesn't kill you before leaving their office. Having to drag your lifeless body out of the way for the next patient would slow down that 15 minute per patient policy for maximum profit many doctors aim for. Worse, the majority of doctors will prescribe these medications without warning their patients about the health risks and side effects. For them, the adverse reactions to these drugs mean that these patients will be back for more, creating for them a flourishing practice and thicker wallets; people will be back for more pills to mask the symptoms and associated health problems caused by the first one that they were given. For their patients, this could mean more illness and early death.

These biases in the medical field are not entirely the fault of the doctors. Patients tend to want a magic pill, or a doctor that can wave a magic wand; they want an easy way out with minimal work or change of lifestyle on their part. If one doctor can't provide them with the easy answer they're looking for, they'll continue to look until they find one who will give them what they want; a pill capable of masking the negative symptoms of their unhealthy lifestyle so that they may continue indulging themselves in this toxic world until they keel over.

This attitude is what got them in trouble in the first place and this is where the change and healing process must begin. Pills do not heal people, changing the environment that caused the disease heals people. Although many doctors do act as if they are gods, it is irresponsible for patients to expect doctors to be able to reverse years of an unhealthy lifestyle. It is entirely up to the individual to practice what makes the

body whole and avoid what depletes it. The laws of health are not negotiable and the decision to abide by them or not is an individual one.

The results of holistic and orthomolecular methods, which help make the body whole again and assist the foundation of the healing process, are proven to be superior to drug-centric, psychiatric, and rehab approaches on many levels. Beyond successful sobriety statistics, holistic methods include quality of life via mental and physical health not experienced with conventional treatment, and education so that the individual can employ and maintain the practices that will deliver them to the potential of health they provide.

Most importantly, as an endnote to this review of treatment options, it is important to comment on the most popular and most debilitating belief promoted by all conventional treatment models: that you are powerless over alcohol. Nothing could be farther from the truth. Never choose to adopt a perspective or belief that does not empower you! The alcohol addicted person that believes that they are powerless has been keeping these ineffective practitioners and organizations in business too long! You will always manifest what you believe in!

Legal, Illegal, and OTC Drugs

The fact is that a drug is a drug. The body does not care if it came from the street or a doctor. Everyone should avoid physiatrists who are quick to dispense drugs. Always seek holistic or complimentary/integrative practitioners in all medical disciplines unless there is an emergency. The origin of allopathic medicine is war injuries and this is where it is at its best. Physical trauma is this medical profession's expertise; if you get hit by a bus, you don't want to rub herbs on your broken ribs and mangled organs; you want the life-saving expertise of the emergency room personnel. However, in all other cases other than life-threatening injury, choose the non-toxic, non-invasive solution that employs the body's natural healing mechanisms. Drugs are not the answer- so "JUST SAY NO" TO DRUGS!

As for treating alcoholism with a drug, there is always a price to pay, and the patient will pay it while living in a drug-induced fog. The goal should be to naturally heal the body and mind and return to where you were before the addiction

took root and caused its damage, not load it down with more chemicals. God provided an army of natural pain buffers and feel-goods: endorphins, enkephalins, dopamine, serotonin, norepinephrine and GABA are all capable of meeting life's challenges. Learn how to produce and engage them naturally so you can be in your body and present for this enchanting journey and all life has to offer.

You must take charge of your own health if what you are seeking is a fulfilling, exciting, and happy life, free of addiction. In order to embrace that life you must be fully present, and nothing that the established medical community or talk therapy has to offer is going to achieve that when it comes to addiction. There is no middleman that can save you! The body must be detoxed and healed from the damage long-term alcohol toxicity has inflicted, and then the known genetic and environmental influences should be nutritionally addressed if there is a predisposition to addictive biochemistry. Trading one drug for another, or chasing the symptoms with talk, is not the answers. In order to heal, you must make a commitment to get yourself back into the condition in which you were put on this earth, so that you can live the life you were born capable of, and want to live.

The Best Intervention – How to Avoid Addiction

Up to this point there has been nothing introduced in the U.S. as far as education between the first drink and AA to help people understand how not to become addicted. If people knew how, they could prevent inherited addictive biochemistry from manifesting, recognize it early on, discourage it from progressing and taking its toll, avoid the damage alcohol does to the body and brain chemistry which enables the addiction to alcohol, or privately heal it once it begins to take its course. They would be provided with a sensible, realistic, tangible and pragmatic course of action. Private action is far more acceptable in the beginning stages of realization than going to meetings and being exposed, a step which most people avoid at all cost. Having the option to privately heal themselves would guide people into the idea of doing something about their problem before they progressed into the chronic stages of alcohol addiction. AA is simply not anonymous enough for most. Without the option of privately engaging a method that actually heals the addiction (which

makes far more sense to the rational person whom has not bottomed out and in a desperate state, than talking themselves out of their addiction), most people are forced by their fears of the stigma associated with AA and alcoholism to wait to seek help until their lives and health have reached such a level of chaos that they collapse.

Education: The Best Intervention

In a world as environmentally, physically, and mentally destructive to the human condition as this one is becoming, personal management, true health care and environmental responsibility should be our highest priorities. These issues should be given the attention they deserve in our educational system. Most people will take care of themselves if they know what it is that they need to do, and understand the real price they will pay if they don't. They should be taught at an early age how to take care of themselves, starting with their diet, since the propensity for addiction starts at birth and depends largely on the diet and whether or not there are genetic combined with epigenetic influences that promote addictive biochemistry. And remember, genes do not cause alcoholism: alcohol abuse causes alcoholism, and symptoms of a metabolic disorder create the appeal for alcohol which can lead to alcohol abuse.

Approximately 90% of what is sold in our supermarkets as food is the type of lifeless, refined carbs that underwrite addiction by setting the stage for it in our biochemistry at an early age. Children become primed to become mainlining adults when they grow up consuming industrial sugars, refined carbs, and the multitude of junk foods and drinks pushed upon them everywhere they turn by irresponsible junk food distributors. Irresponsible food distributors have made children the primary target for these products and it's a very profitable business. The art is to get children addicted early so that they will continue to buy the product and self-medicate with them for their entire miserable, short lifetimes. If we educate our children and raise them on the earth's foods as opposed to industrial foods, we give them the best chance possible at never developing addictive biochemistry.

True nutrition is not the type promoted by old school doctors, dieticians, the USDA food pyramid, or today's mainstream food distributors, who misrepresent their foods

as healthy. If it doesn't nurture the body *and* mind it is not food and it is not healthy. The characteristics of a truly healthy lifestyle, not "sugar coated" by irresponsible food distribution systems, the pharmaceutical cartel, or sugar industry, needs to be taught to our children. The best way to do this is in a purist's manner on a biochemical level, so that they will truly understand it and recognize the scientific facts. In this way, we can help to prevent them from being misled by commercialism and propaganda. They need to be taught the truth and reminded that what they see and hear on TV, billboards, magazines, etc. are lies; sugar- and caffeine-drenched "sports" drinks are only good for you if you are racing to your grave.

Truthfully, we live in a dollar-ocracy, not a democracy, and the sugar and pharmaceutical industries are powerful multibillion-dollar industries with major investments all over the world. This money and power influences laws, medical research, public education, and social acceptance through their advertising dollars, educational grants, various well-advertised sports sponsorships, and richly compensated representatives in legal and political offices. The sugar industry even has a manipulating influence on the World Health Organization! Last year, the WHO published a report that suggested, "people wanting to avoid chronic diseases should limit daily consumption of free sugars to less than 10% of total energy intake," (we believe they were trying to be diplomatic here, because 10% is far too generous for one going for excellent health or with addictive biochemistry).

The sugar industry was outraged; if people were to begin questioning the impact of sugar on their health, that would cost companies not only in future sales but in the billions of dollars they have spent in advertising and payoffs to create an image that sugar is fun and harmless. Just as cigarettes were promoted as chic and harmless in the past while they were in reality causing cancer and many other chronic illnesses, this kind of press coverage might open the doors to courtrooms all over the world for those seeking financial restitution for having been misled by the industry's false claims. Consumption of sugar has been proven to be harmful, resulting in diabetes, cancer, arthritis, depression, ADD, Chronic Fatigue Syndrome, etc...

The sugar industry's response to the WHO's report was summarized as:

> "The UN recommendations have outraged US sugar producers, who have indicated they may lobby the Bush administration and Congress to link US funding for the WHO to changes in research methods at the UN agency. The US supplies 22 per cent of the WHO's budget."

The response from the UN and WHO was:

"The United Nations food and health authorities drew back from a full-scale confrontation with the world's sugar industry on Wednesday by saying their latest recommendations on sugar consumption were guidelines rather than standards requiring regulation."

They went on to retract their statements implying that sugar was linked to obesity and a multitude of other diseases including cancer.

This sort of playing with the truth and facts goes on everyday in the press, which is controlled by the billions of dollars the sugar and pharmaceutical companies spend in advertising and outright ownership of media channels. As they say, our news venues today have nothing to tell and everything to sell and none of them want to offend their advertisers. The two largest streams of cash come from pharmaceutical companies and their many subsidiaries, and the sugar (candy, cokes, pastries), refined and junk food product distributors. In a relationship like that, freedom of the press cannot exist. Airing a story exposing the ill health effects of products that are produced by a large corporation that spends millions of dollars yearly in advertising will never happen. Especially since these products are the ones that are being advertised on the same network. It's simply not good business; it makes everyone look bad. Mark Twain once said, "If you don't read the newspaper, you are uninformed; if you do read the newspaper, you are misinformed." This is the void in which most Americans live if they rely on mainstream TV and newspapers for information for use in lifestyle decisions or to form opinions of world events.

Children need to be taught how to survive in this toxic world. They need an environmental education so that they will be inspired to participate in reversing the toxic damage that is harming and polluting their bodies and environment. They need a truthful education that exposes the poisons so that they know what to avoid. They need to be taught these fundamental life management skills because they promote reverence for our bodies and for the world we live in, which will serve to keep them alive and well in today's industrial jungle. Today, it is not a tiger chasing you that can kill you; it is poisons called food and drugs called medicine. Without the skills to recognize the difference between poisons called foods and dangerous drugs called medicine, the most prestigious college degree available will do nothing to enrich people's lives and keep them healthy so they can enjoy life. Lack of an education exposing the world they truly live in and life management skills developed from that knowledge is precisely why so many thirty- and forty-year-olds are falling apart at the seams mentally and physically. No college education or achievement means anything without your health, and none of it will prevent you from suffering the negative impact on your physical and mental health if you fall victim to the poisons called food or drugs called medicine our society is being fed.

The best intervention is to learn that to avoid addiction we must break away from many ideas on which we were raised. Sugar could very well be the parent of all addictions and fast foods poison the body. For the sake of our children, we need to intervene between them and the products being marketed today that are likely to one day put them in rehab or on anti-depressants (or both), or cause them to be plagued with one or many of the thousands of disorders and diseases becoming epidemic in today's world. We can protect the young and innocent: those growing up in today's world, which pushes that which we know causes addiction and addictive biochemistry.

The canvas of our lives should be composed like an inspired painting: with vibrancy, color, meaning, inspiration, balance, and harmony, and with purpose expressed in every stroke; so when they blend together they tell the tale of a beautiful life which mirrors our true divinity. Poor life management skills, especially when they affect health, will

make that impossible. Therefore, the first priority must be to find and practice the methods that bring about sound physical and mental health, so that you will achieve a healthy and balanced state of mind. This will naturally bring about a healthy interest in all the meaningful things in life such as spirituality, friends, family, and personal interests and evolvement. Once we have achieved this, we must educate our children as to how to paint this picture for themselves.

We need to start living the way we were meant to live.

The laws of health are not negotiable!

Chapter Two

What Makes Addictive Body Chemistry Different

When health is absent
Wisdom cannot reveal itself
Art cannot manifest
Strength cannot be exerted
Wealth is useless and reason is powerless.
--Anonymous

So far this text has established that you have a metabolism disorder due to nutritional deficiencies if you are addicted to alcohol. To understand why it requires orthomolecular treatment to fix it, it is necessary to know how and why it was broken in the first place. Becoming acquainted with your specific body chemistry will also give you a clear idea of the exact nature of the challenges ahead, and make you better prepared for the journey to liberation.

Brain Chemistry
Mental Health and Problem Drinking
Introduction to Neurotransmitters

Mental health relies on neurotransmitters and hormones being produced, utilized, and metabolized properly in the right amounts, at the right times. Neurotransmitters are chemical messengers that provide information between nerve cells via their receptors; hormones are chemicals produced by the endocrine glands that travel through the blood to relay messages to and from every organ of the body. Hormones are primarily responsible for establishing the 'directives' required to maintain the perfect balance the brain seeks in order to function healthily. It is extremely important that the brain functions properly, since every organ in the body, down to each and every cell, is under the control of the central nervous system (CNS). Thoughts can create dis-ease or health for the body and mind because thoughts create neurochemicals in the

body, which determine how the cells will function by giving the orders: healthy or unhealthy.

Alcohol metabolism impairs physical and mental health by destroying and exhausting the vital nutrients and biochemical processes required for neurotransmitters and hormones to function properly. This makes it impossible for them to carry out their purpose in establishing healthy brain chemistry and homeostasis, or maintain a stable, balanced environment throughout the body. Hormones and neurotransmitters govern every aspect of our living bodies. They govern brain activity: our moods, emotions, behavior, and sleep patterns, as well as every aspect of our physical health. The diminished availability of just one neurotransmitter or a disruption in its path can adversely affect every aspect of life and health. Each neurochemical pathway relies on the accurate bioenergetics of all the others to function properly. These biochemical pathways keep all neurochemicals reacting in accordance with the needs of the brain to constantly stay in balance. The disruption in production or utilization of just one neurotransmitter can lead to a change from a positive to negative attitude overnight, making the world appear lifeless and painful.

The amino acids in the proteins we eat are the building blocks for neurotransmitters. Metabolizing alcohol and its associated sugars, and detoxifying its poisonous metabolites, exhausts the body's supplies of amino acids, vitamins, minerals, and fatty acids. With these nutrients being used for alcohol metabolism and detoxification; they are not available to produce a healthy supply of neurotransmitters. Without proper amino acid conversion to neurotransmitters, the resulting imbalanced brain chemistry will begin to reveal itself through mental distresses like anxiety, depression, mental fatigue, low self-esteem, and varying degrees of social disinterest.

An example of one altered biochemical process in the brain affecting all others is the use of Zoloft for depression. Zoloft is an anti-depressant medication belonging to a group known as SSRIs (selective serotonin reuptake inhibitors). Serotonin is one of the inhibitory, 'feel good' neurotransmitters sent out by the brain. Zoloft blocks the serotonin molecules that have been released into the system from being drawn back into the nerve vesicle, so that they stay in the system longer and hit

more receptors than they usually would. It forces these molecules to send their feel-good messages more times before being enzymatically ingested, in order to combat depression. On the surface, this sounds wonderful, but it really isn't. This artificial way of addressing depression further disrupts brain chemistry and causes its own health issues as a result due to causing further imbalances in brain chemistry. Drugs do not carry with them the intelligence of nutrients. They do not work *with* the body; they attempt to *control and manipulate* the body. Haven't we learned by now that you can not control nature?

There are many side effects from using this type of drug. Severe side effects may include bizarre behavior, pounding in the chest, chest pain, and muscle disorders. Common side effects may include weight loss, failure to ejaculate, dry mouth, increased sweating, drowsiness, tremor, tiredness, general pain, stomach pain, loss of appetite, constipation, diarrhea/loose stools, indigestion, nausea, agitation, sleeplessness, decreased sex drive, abnormal skin sensation, rash, gas, vomiting, hot flashes, anxiety, nervousness, sore throat, changes in vision, dizziness, and headache. Other side effects may include painful erection, increased appetite, back pain, weakness, general body discomfort, weight increase, muscle pain, yawning, sexual dysfunction, runny nose, and ringing in the ears.

All of these symptoms are neurotransmitter related, indicating the ill effects and further damage being done to brain chemistry. This is the result of manipulating just one biochemical process of one neurotransmitter. These side effects are just a sample of the possibilities since everyone is different. Also, as with any other drug, the brain will develop a tolerance to antidepressants. Once that tolerance is met there will be yet another dependency to address, and further damaged brain chemistry.

Neurotransmitter Effects on Psychological Health

Below is a list of the major neurotransmitters that are profoundly affected by alcohol and excessive refined / simple carb consumption, and their pro (normal, healthy states) and con (addictive, disruptive states) effects on psychological health.

Serotonin

Serotonin deficiency is directly related to simple carb cravings and compulsiveness – two hallmarks of alcohol addiction. Medical research is now beginning to unveil that low serotonin levels are linked to most, if not all, obsessive and compulsive behaviors as well.

Serotonin and beta-endorphins are neurotransmitters essential for the feelings of joy, well being, and peace of mind in various emotional and psychological centers of the brain. In order for a neurotransmitter to transmit its message it must be released into the synapse (gaps between nerves), where it will bind with its counterpart receptor and transfer its information. Problem drinkers have very low levels of these neurotransmitters and higher levels of their corresponding receptors; this is defined as "upregulated" brain chemistry. It is commonly due to either genetic or acquired damage to the functional HPA (hypothalamic, pituitary, adrenal) axis due to environmental influences such as high sugar diets, malnutrition, or toxicity.

Here I will provide a very high-level explanation as to how brain chemistry becomes upregulated, which will explain how those with addictive biochemistry are different than those who do not possess addictive biochemistry.

Upregulated brain chemistry is a result of the brain being unable to provide the number of neurotransmitters required to meet the demands of a healthy number of its corresponding receptors. If there isn't a large enough beta-endorphin and serotonin supply, the body will create more serotonin and beta-endorphin receptor sites in a chemical effort to find and bind with what little serotonin and beta-endorphin neurotransmitters there are available. When people with this kind of brain chemistry drink alcohol, they experience a far more euphoric response to the alcohol than people with balanced brain chemistry do because the upregulated beta-endorphin and serotonin receptor sites cause a saturated infusion of the incoming neurotransmitters docking on them. Combine with that the fact that alcohol promotes the release of excess beta-endorphins, and the sugar associated with alcohol prompts a quick, spiked release of serotonin and you get a very pronounced response to alcohol. One of the reasons serotonin levels spike like this is because simple carbohydrates, such as alcohol and sugar, help the tryptophan

(which is a precursor to serotonin) in the blood pass the blood brain barrier while blocking other amino acids from crossing. Once across the barrier, the tryptophan is converted to serotonin. These new neurotransmitters will then flood their eagerly awaiting receptor compliments. To make matters worse, another biochemical process is occurring at the same time: the byproduct of alcohol metabolism, acetaldehyde, combines with dopamine and serotonin to form salsolinol and beta-carboline. Salsolinol and beta-carboline produce tetrahydroisoquinolines (THIQs) which are morphine-like molecules that fit into beta-endorphin receptor sites, and provide an even greater euphoric experience making them extremely addictive.

During extended periods of alcohol abuse, this process of flooding beta-endorphin and serotonin receptors sends signals to the brain that the receptors are satiated. This signals the brain that there are plenty of beta-endorphins and serotonin, in which case the brain diminishes or discontinues production of these neurotransmitters, causing a shortage of natural feel-good neurotransmitters in the body. While the initial ingestion of alcohol causes a flood of serotonin to be released thus activating the relaxing, inhibitory GABA neurotransmitters, the elevated amounts of acetaldehyde in the body caused by excess alcohol intake will place increasing demands on serotonin by binding with it to form beta-carboline; this will also make the serotonin unavailable to bind with its own receptors. The symptoms of this condition goes unnoticed while the intense euphoric effects of THIQs are present, but the next day the diminished levels of beta-endorphins and the emptying out of serotonin will produce the many symptoms with which problem drinkers are all too familiar.

This cycle of neurotransmitter depletion and displacement is worsened by the malnutrition caused by alcohol toxicity and the typical refined carb diets that problem drinkers tend to adopt. If there is a lack of the specific amino acids and vitamins and minerals required to produce feel-good neurotransmitters, the dependency on alcohol to provide replacements becomes progressively worse.

Autopsies performed on people with a history of alcoholism have shown that those who were actively drinking, and those who were recently abstinent, had very little

serotonin in their brains. When you stop drinking, the time it takes for your withdrawal to subside is a good indicator of how much damage your brain chemistry sustained in this area. The process of withdrawal involves the symptoms of the exogenous (external) chemicals emptying out, and the brain recognizing the resulting chemical imbalance (withdrawal stress and discomfort) and signaling the body to renew the natural feel-good neurotransmitters as medication for the symptoms. Withdrawal begins to subside as the brain responds with its own feel-good neurotransmitters, and disappears when it has successfully achieved a healthy balance known as homeostasis. Depending upon how recovery is approached, this process can take an extremely long time. If the recovery process doesn't address your nutritional deficiencies, and assist your body in providing the nutrients required to produce the necessary neurotransmitters, your malnourished system won't have the means to provide these natural feel-goods in the proper quantities for quite some time, if ever- especially if you dive into the sugar bowl and coffee cup. The result of this is the many symptoms the biologically damaged dry drunk continues to suffer and is the number one reason for relapse; in a desperate attempt to self-medicate and reintroduce feel-good neurotransmitters into the brain, you will seek relief in the most effective way you know. On the flip-side, healthy brain chemistry can be quickly re-established when one approaches recovery by infusing the body with the absent nutrients required for healthy amounts of feel-good neurotransmitters and general neuroendocrine repair and rejuvenation.

Do not underestimate the biochemical strength and psychological influence that sugar and alcohol addictions have in a person with upregulated brain chemistry. Those empty serotonin and beta-endorphin receptors are desperately seeking their biological mate, and if they can't find them naturally they will instruct you to find them elsewhere. These cravings and desires are strong and deep seated because they attract you both psychologically and physically, urging you to use chemicals that interfere with and replace biochemical processes that are vital to your health and well being while worsening your addictive, upregulated brain chemistry. The immediate, exaggerated effects that a

damaged brain chemistry will get from these substances include a short-term rise in self-esteem, energy, perceived happiness, relaxation, physical and emotional pain relief, optimism, and confidence. These fixes are extremely appealing to a person who is experiencing the symptoms caused by unhealthy brain chemistry. The only way to eliminate that dangerous appeal is to naturally heal the symptoms.

Whether related to diet or a family history of sub-optimal endocrine performance, the fact is that those with upregulated, damaged serotonin and beta-endorphin brain chemistries are known to possess "addictive biochemistry" because they have demonstrated the ability to become addicted more quickly, with less exposure to the addictive substance, and in life-debilitating ways that reach more deeply into mental and physical health than those who do not have the condition.

Signs of Optimal Serotonin Levels

- Serene
- Inspired
- Optimistic, positive attitude toward difficulty
- Joyful, happy
- Able to concentrate
- Creative
- Focused, mentally sharp
- Intuitive
- Mentally "relaxed"
- Active rather than reactive; solution oriented
- Responsive
- Caring, volunteer oriented

Signs of Low Serotonin Levels

- Depressed
- Compulsive; unable to resist temptation or stick to behavioral modification decisions
- Short attention span
- Seeking quick, short lived forms of stimuli (eg, coffee, gambling, shopping, etc)
- Mentally foggy, unable to concentrate or stay focused on a task or goal
- Emotionally unstable; mood swings

- Suicidal
- Anxious
- Reactive
- Craving sweets (eg, cokes, candy, etc)
- Craving simple and refined carbohydrates (eg, pastas, cereal)
- Craving for alcohol

Beta-endorphins: The Morphine Within

People who have a predisposition for addictive biochemistry are insufficiently medicated with healthy levels of natural endorphins and enkephalins. Research has established that low basal-endorphin and enkephalin production from the hypothalamus for any reason, including genetic / epigenetic influences including excess alcohol use, is a strong indication of addictive biochemistry.

Beta-endorphins and enkephalins are opioids whose functions in brain chemistry are as physical pain relievers and psychological and emotional calming and euphoria agents. Endorphins are essentially the body's natural morphine. In some circumstances, endorphins are considered stress hormones much like cortisol and the catecholamines: dopamine, epinephrine, and norepinephrine (adrenaline, noradrenalin). Stress hormones are released in response to psychological or physiological pain; cuts, broken bones, intense exercise, excitement (good and bad), anxiety, inflammation, cold, extreme heat, or hemorrhage – basically anything causing an extreme response (either good or bad) from the body.

Endorphins are polypeptides and enkephalins are pentapeptides. Enkephalins are found in the beta-endorphin chain and are specifically responsible for managing pain and psychological distress. While endorphins and enkephalins are both produced by the hypothalamus, only endorphins are found to be produced by the pituitary as well, which gives this neurotransmitter substantially more "play time" in the endocrine system. For instance, endorphins are simultaneously released with ACTH from the pituitary in response to stress. ACTH releases cortisol from the adrenals to assist serotonin levels in easing the effects of the stressor, while endorphins do their part activating other biochemical pathways that reduce psychological and physical pain.

The most popular understanding of beta-endorphins is that they are responsible for the euphoric high you get when you jog: the "runner's high". To mediate the heightened pain and discomfort caused by the use of excess resources for running over extended periods, endorphins flood the brain and provide the euphoric feeling athletes get from the activity. The body is truly a self-contained survival mechanism; it knows what it needs to do to stay mentally and physically healthy. That is why The 101 Program concentrates on providing the body with the means to do what comes naturally instead of medicating it with prescription drugs that further destroy its ability to heal and care for itself.

Endorphins are also responsible for reducing your perception of stress by providing a natural sense of well being and a centered disposition that "all is well" in the world. Endorphins and enkephalins help reduce the reaction to disappointment by giving you the neurochemical ability to "let things go", turn reactive into active (prompting you to do something about a displeasing situation rather than existing in anger and helplessness) and maintain the attitude that "this too shall pass". In an endorphin-starved brain, such as that of a chronic or problem drinker, small nuances can be magnified into explosive, life-threatening, cataclysmic disasters, which the sympathetic nervous system will respond to as strongly as it is capable of doing via the fight or flight response. This response drains your internal resources, impairs your immune system, and fatigues your neuroendocrine system. It is unproductive and problematic, since it intensifies the original displeasing event and draws upon and wastes even more life essence. Reactive states like these will send a person straight to the bar to find relief from life situations in general, and the painful symptoms that small events can bring on; the next broken pencil while writing a note can easily result in another hangover when one is depleted of the natural "feel-goods".

Achieving and maintaining healthy endorphin and enkephalin levels is necessary to cure alcoholism and is crucial in being biochemically capable of responding to difficult circumstances in a non-reactive way.

Signs of Optimal Beta-endorphins/Enkephalins Levels

- High pain tolerance
- Pleasant disposition, feeling light throughout the day
- Sensitive, sympathetic
- High self-esteem
- Compassionate
- Connected and in touch
- Hopeful, optimistic, euphoric
- Positive attitude
- Emotionally positively energized
- Indifferent attitude toward sweet foods and alcohol
- Solution oriented

Signs of Low Beta-endorphins/Enkephalins Levels

- Low pain tolerance
- Tearful, reactive
- Small tasks seem to require too much effort
- Low self-esteem
- Uninspired
- Aggressive
- Depressed, hopeless
- Craving sugar
- Emotionally and psychologically overwhelmed
- Feelings of isolation

Enkephalins ("in the head")

As mentioned in the previous section, research has repeatedly established that low enkephalin levels in the brain, which are produced by the hypothalamus, are a key marker of both genetic and acquired addictive biochemistry. In laboratory tests, rats that were deprived of enkephalins drank extensively while rats bred with healthy concentrations of enkephalins had absolutely no interest. The next logical step is extremely important in healing addictive biochemistry: if low natural levels of opioids create a desire or need to drink, wouldn't healthy levels dismiss it? Yes, they do.

Enkephalins are actually distributed throughout more areas of the brain than endorphins, so their deficiency can adversely affect more areas of an individual's mental health. Enkephalin deficiency is the underlying cause of many of the symptoms problem drinkers use alcohol to self-medicate:

incompleteness, lack of fulfillment, inability to participate in activities and experience any gratification or enrichment to the point that they become disinterested in things they once enjoyed or lack any motivation to do new things, inferiority complex, feelings of inadequacy, fearfulness, and insecurity. A shortage of enkephalins can essentially cause a person to feel empty inside, worthless, and unable to find self-gratification in personal interests or ineffectual as a person. Healthy enkephalin presence in the brain, however, produces a natural sense of well being, calm, an almost spiritual peacefulness and joy, healthy self-esteem, confidence and even euphoria.

A key feature of The 101 Program is that it brings the neuroendocrine system to such a healthy state that the function of the HPA axis is repaired to the degree that the hypothalamus is able to produce and store a healthy level of enkephalins. The use of supplements first accelerates the healing process, removing the toxic damage that impaired brain function; then nutritional support and herbs stimulate endorphin and enkephalin production, while also preserving what is produced by inhibiting premature reuptake. While these treatments are taking place, you are taught how to integrate other lifestyle activities and employ the benefits of mind/body energy healing to stimulate healthy, natural endorphin and enkephalin levels. This is a very important feature of The 101 Program's success because it is necessary for a chronic drinker to be able to maintain healthy enkephalin levels in order to dismiss the desire for alcohol. Here the phrase, "follow your bliss" has true sound, scientific biochemical meaning; doing things you enjoy raises endorphin and enkephalin levels in the brain!

There can be a number of reasons for low enkephalin levels; reasons that are common for most neurotransmitters.

- Malnutrition or toxicity cause a lack of sufficient amino acid precursors and their nutritional cofactors, which means the brain does not have the ingredients to produce enkephalins.
- High concentrations of enkephalinase, the enzyme that metabolizes endorphins and enkephalins, removing them from the synapse where they are active (other

neurotransmitters have their own respective digesting enzymes)

- Damaged or functionally deficient hypothalamus (which can be healed).

Dopamine

Dopamine is a neurotransmitter involved in controlling movement and posture, modulating mood, and playing a central role in positive reinforcement as well as addictive behavior resulting in dependency. This neurotransmitter plays an important part in signaling reward in the brain. For example, pleasurable events such as eating, drinking, and having sex are all associated with increased brain dopamine levels, while individuals who are experiencing depression or anxiety may have lowered brain dopamine levels. Many drugs that provide pleasurable or calming effects either stimulate dopamine levels in the brain, mimic it, or, such as in the case of cocaine, inhibit the re-uptake of dopamine. The result is increased dopamine levels for longer periods of time, which causes the euphoric, pleasure seeking, alert, inspired / ambitious (albeit short-term) effect of the drug.

Dopamine is also associated with the reward system in the brain in that the pleasure a person gets from the memory of how an event, person, or drug made them feel stimulates dopamine in the associated reward center of the brain and encourages them to seek out that pleasure or feeling again.

Prolonged alcohol abuse can cause low dopamine levels, rendering one incapable of feelings of pleasure unless they are provoked by events or activities. Dependency on a drug to provide pleasure means that dopamine levels are being artificially over stimulated, which raises the expectations in the brain: from that point on higher dopamine levels will be required to produce a significant pleasurable response. Once the bar has been raised, the dependent brain will now find it extremely difficult to satisfy the requirements for experiencing pleasure in activities that were once greatly enjoyable. This is because dopamine receptors are downregulated (fewer produced) due to extended periods of overproduction of the neurotransmitter, which creates a requirement for more dopamine to stimulate the same sense of pleasure that they once received from the "simple things" in life. A new biochemical scenario is created, where the reward system's new threshold for excitement or pleasure is raised

above what regular life has to offer. Someone who has experienced artificially produced exaggerated dopamine levels over a long period of time can become desensitized to the environment, events and moments that once provided pleasurable effects of happiness, fulfillment, and self-gratification.

Biochemically, The 101 Program will show you how to naturally increase dopamine levels if yours are low; however, it is also important for you to re-engage in your interests until you begin again to receive the joy and pleasure you once did, or to find new interests or pleasurable activities. The bottom line is that finding sources of self-gratification, pleasure, and joy also helps to fix imbalanced biochemistry, but it takes time. Inspiration or satisfaction from the activity will not typically happen right away; damaged brain chemistry needs time to re-adapt to pleasure, just as it did to alcohol. But it will happen.

In the initial stages of The 101 Program, dopamine precursors are included in the therapeutic protocol to assist the body in producing healthy levels of the neurotransmitter, so that the body and mind may begin experiencing the benefits of naturally produced dopamine quickly. Providing one is faithful to a condictive diet and the sugar and refined carb restrictions that someone with addictive biochemistry must maintain, a former problem drinker will quickly overcome the damage from alcohol toxicity and be able to produce healthy levels of dopamine and other neurotransmitters naturally.

GABA

GABA (gamma-aminobutyric acid) is the most abundant inhibitory neurotransmitter found in the brain. Inhibitory neurotransmitters prevent post-synaptic firing (electrical pulses) and are associated with calm, relaxed, and pleasurable states because they manage the excitatory neurotransmitters and prevent over activity in the nervous system. GABA is widely distributed in the neurons of the cortex and contributes to motor control and vision. It also regulates anxiety, and is an important player in inhibiting stress signals and calming the mind in upsetting situations.

Alcohol and sugar are known to increase GABA levels; conversely, levels drop during hypoglycemic periods when the body is low in blood sugar, causing hyper excitability during

these episodes. Clinical studies of alcohol dependence have shown that GABA levels are also significantly low during alcohol withdrawal and protracted abstinence (the initial withdrawal period after the cessation of drinking, which is when a person is especially vulnerable to relapse). Alcohol produces many of its intoxicating effects through over expressing GABA. Problem drinkers have shown that they have more GABA in the brain while drinking, with a dramatic decrease when they stop. The rise in GABA is partly due to the quick rise in serotonin (a GABA modulator), caused by alcohol. During alcohol metabolism, the serotonin binding to its receptor on the GABA molecule activates GABA, initiating the relaxed and calm states associated with initial alcohol intake.

The ability of the brain to produce GABA diminishes over time in long-term problem drinkers, so that when GABA levels drop too low in response to low blood sugar episodes or prolonged alcohol abuse, there becomes an imbalance of GABA/glutamate during non-drinking hours. The relative rise in the excitatory neurotransmitter, glutamate, produces the anxiety that problem drinkers are known to try and drink away.

Since GABA is always substantially depleted during withdrawal, GABA and its nutriceutical cofactors that help it over the blood brain barrier are included in the Krispy Klean Detox formula. The use of therapeutic dosages of niacinamide, inositol, and C in the formula will help reduce the anxiety typically experienced during withdrawal, since this combination creates molecules that attach themselves to the GABA-benzodiazepine receptors and induce a calming effect without the use of alcohol.

Glutamate

Glutamate is the most abundant excitatory neurotransmitter in the body, and is associated with learning and memory. An excitatory neurotransmitter is one that causes postsynaptic cells to fire. These are normally balanced by GABA and other inhibitory neurotransmitters like glycine and serotonin.

While alcohol will initially increase GABA, providing the relaxing effects of drinking, in cases of long-term alcohol abuse GABA is severely depleted; in the absence of alcohol this causes glutamate levels to become relatively high (over

expressed). Upregulated glutamate levels can be responsible for mental withdrawal symptoms like anxiety, fear, tremors, and paranoia. Excess glutamate in concert with extremely low levels of GABA (inhibitory neurotransmitter) is also responsible for the more severe symptoms of withdrawal where the central nervous system becomes dangerously over excited and causes convulsions and delirium.

The over expressed glutamate and under expressed GABA condition is also a primary cause of the uncomfortable symptoms such as anxiety, nervousness, paranoia, frustration and feelings of being overwhelmed that problem drinkers experience during the day before they start to drink. These symptoms also intensify when the individual tries to quit. Over expressed glutamate levels and toxicity are also the two major causes of cell death in the brain.

Norepinephrine

Norepinephrine is a neurotransmitter associated with the sympathetic nervous system that is important for attentiveness, quality of emotions, sleeping, dreaming, and learning. Low levels of norepinephrine are known to contribute to depression. High levels are known to cause anxiety, agitation, irritability, chronic fatigue syndrome, and even bipolar disorder. In the case of depression, which is common to alcohol abuse, there is a biochemical chain of events that dictates this: when an individual meets with stress, norepinephrine rises, prompting serotonin to be released which then signals the hypothalamus to release CRF (corticotrophin release factor) which ultimately produces cortisol.

In a healthy person's response to stress, serotonin levels are raised because it is required to mediate the over expression of norepinephrine and bring brain chemistry into balance to reduce the effects of the stress. Over expression (excessive release of a neurotransmitter from cells) of a neurotransmitter always depletes its stores within cells, so when the stressor goes away, norepinephrine will rebuild stores and serotonin will regain its healthy levels. However, when a person is under prolonged stress and the body is not provided an environment to rebuild healthy levels, serotonin and its precursors are "emptied out" due to the constant demands in mediating the norepinephrine response, thus causing a biochemical environment primed for depression due

to low serotonin and high (unmanaged) norepinephrine. This exact same chain of events is played out in prolonged alcohol abuse to a far greater degree. A common condition in problem drinkers is one of serotonin being chronically low during alcohol-absent hours of the day, allowing norepinephrine to rise because due to fatigued adrenals there is also a lack of cortisol needed to convert it to epinephrine for use in raising blood sugar levels during hypoglycemic periods. The individual will begin to experience extreme nervous-related and emotionally uncomfortable symptoms from anxiety and panic attacks, to hypertension and emotional outbursts originating from low blood sugar as well as unmanaged excitatory neurotransmitters. These symptoms provide a fertile environment for addiction to alcohol to develop.

Epinephrine (adrenaline in Europe)

Epinephrine is the body's fight-or flight-hormone and is produced by the body to prepare you to either protect yourself or get out of harm's way. Epinephrine is produced in the adrenal medulla and is found in the sympathetic nervous system. When it is released throughout the nervous system it produces states of heightened awareness (alertness) and energy to provide everything necessary to survive threat. It is also released during periods of emotional upset, physical or emotional trauma, any type of actual or perceived threat; and the hypoglycemic episodes that alcohol abuse is known for.

The Key Biochemical Factors of Alcohol Addiction & Addictive Biochemistry

The neuroendocrine system is the "home" of addictive and addicted biochemistry because the genesis of addictive biochemistry is an imbalance of neurotransmitters and hormones caused by a deficiency in one or a combination of these neurochemicals. This imbalance results in the body's inability to sufficiently medicate itself in a natural way. Any external substance that a person experiences which produces and activates the neurochemicals that are absent will tempt that person to use it repeatedly to self-medicate the symptoms experienced by the absence of healthy, balanced brain chemistry. Those who inherit a neuroendocrine system unable to produce a balanced, sufficient supply of serotonin, GABA, dopamine, norepinephrine, enkephalins, endorphins, or

acetylcholine may possess addictive biochemistry and are
candidates for addiction to sugar, alcohol and other
substances.

Following is a list of symptoms and side effects of additive
biochemistry. It's easy to notice that the foundation for each
symptom is found to be in the endocrine system.

- Poor blood sugar management – most of the time the person
  is hypoglycemic or sugar sensitive.
- Weakened or damaged adrenals and pancreas, possibly
  noting a family history of an unmet need for brain glucose;
  results in general compromised endocrine function and
  digestive disorders.
- Upregulation of serotonin and beta-endorphin receptor sites
  in the brain (because not enough of the neurotransmitters
  are being produced). Low serotonin creates under
  expressed GABA (inhibitory) activity, which can cause a
  number of uncomfortable excitatory (over expressed
  glutamate) symptoms which alcohol efficiently medicates.
- Craving for sweets from birth; this is a product of low
  serotonin levels and poor endocrine function.
- Low dopamine levels
- Over active sympathetic nervous system caused by an
  imbalance between the inhibitory and excitatory
  neurotransmitters, leaning heavily toward the excitatory
  side. This condition can cause mental disorders in
  childhood such as ADD and ADHD, and may lead to using
  alcohol in an attempt to release and activate calming,
  inhibitory neurotransmitters such as serotonin, GABA,
  endorphins and dopamine to bring down the excitatory
  neurotransmitters and mediate the symptoms of the over
  active sympathetic nervous system.
- Tendency toward insulin resistance, which leads to more
  internally produced alcohol in the body from unused carbs,
  thus producing more highly addictive, brain-altering
  THIQS. THIQs occupy endorphin receptors and can cause
  reduction of endorphin production, promoting self-
  medication. Insulin resistance also adversely affects the
  delicate balance of the neuroendocrine system and has a
  tendency to create intense cravings for simple/refined carbs,
  perpetuating the habit of "mainlining" with sugary

industrial foods, a habit that underwrites alcohol addiction in adulthood.

- Poor pancreatic function, which causes the digestive process to prefer simple/refined carbohydrates over complex carbs, proteins, and fats. This condition causes the body to seek simple carbs for energy, and leads to malnutrition and compulsive behavior.

- Low enkephalin storage and availability in the hypothalamus, possibly due to extreme fluctuations in blood sugar from adrenal fatigue and the pancreas overreacting to blood glucose levels. Also, since proteins and good fats are required for enkephalin synthesis, the anti fat and high sugar/refined carb diets adopted by those with addictive biochemistry provide little to produce healthy enkephalin levels.

- Chronic, high glucose levels make it impossible for the delicate workings of the hypothalamus, pituitary and other regions of the brain to function properly due to glycosylation; cross-linking of sugar, fats, and proteins of the cells which harden their membranes. This process is similar to that of basting a turkey.

- Underdeveloped or injured hypothalamus or pituitary

- Efficient alcohol metabolism combined with inefficient acetaldehyde metabolism.

Addicted Biochemistry

- Acquired addicted biochemistry is caused by any brand of lifestyle that involves prolonged use of a substance (legal or illegal) that causes the body and mind to become dependent on it to feel right; due to the neuroendocrine system being damaged to the point where it can no longer provide or utilize the neurochemicals required to feel good naturally.

- Excessive simple carb diet causes aggravated hypoglycemia and creates symptoms that the person is driven to satisfy or medicate.

- Alcohol metabolism produces THIQs (morphine-like neurotransmitters that bind with beta-endorphin receptors) in such abundance that the body's own production of endorphins is cut down.

- Overall diminished performance of the neuroendocrine system results in the brain's inability to produce its own

feel-good neurotransmitters, causing depression and a plethora of mental and physical disorders.

- Acetaldehyde toxicity leads to liver, brain, gastrointestinal, adrenal, thyroid, and pancreatic damage. This depletes numerous nutrients and undermines vital biochemical processes and leads to tissue damage, metabolic disorders (addiction), and dis-ease.
- Liver becomes progressively less able to properly detox; more acetaldehyde exposure for the brain accelerates the brain damage and addictive capacity.
- Alcohol and excessive refined/simple carb diet causes chronic high insulin levels, which lead to suppression of the endocrine system by diminishing many key hormones such as HGH (one reason why problem drinkers age quickly).
- Advancing injury to the neuroendocrine system due to continued use of alcohol and simple / refined carbs causes the addiction and its symptoms to seat deeper into the biochemistry, causing one to become progressively more dependent.

Breaking Down the Damage

Below are conditions caused from alcohol toxicity damage, and inherent metabolic disorders that are associated with and contribute to addictive biochemistry and alcohol abuse. Keep in mind that genetic tendencies do not rule your destiny-epigenetic influences (diet, lifestyle, attitude, perspective) on the body are the key to health or dis-ease and need to be corrected so that the genetic tendencies toward addictive biochemistry never have the opportunity to express themselves.

Just because your mother or father may have been a junk food junkie, or heavy drinker, and therefore passed on a deficient neuroendocrine system does not mean that you are destined to follow their ways. You can heal your neuroendocrine system by providing it an environment that promotes healing and health.

The HPA Axis

The HPA axis is where the endocrine and central nervous systems interact in the brain, and is responsible for the regulation of every biochemical function of the body down to

the performance of every cell. Any hypothalamus, pituitary, and adrenal dysfunction leads to deficient provision of the neurotransmitters and hormones required by the neuroendocrine system to produce sound mental and physical health- a result of homeostasis. This dysfunction shows itself as an imbalance in the HPA axis, and more importantly, in a plethora of mental and physical illnesses, including addiction. The cause can be genetic/environmental or acquired; the end product is the brain failing to produce sufficient natural feel-good neurotransmitters. The ensuing neurochemical imbalance encourages an individual to seek relief through outside sources. When those sources are toxic, the condition becomes worse and intensifies the addiction. The art of healing this condition resides in removing the toxic substance, healing the damaged organs, and then assisting the neuroendocrine system in producing sufficient feel-good neurotransmitters naturally until you heal to the point where you can produce your own feel-good neurochemical supply from faithfully following a condictive diet and practicing a healthy lifestyle.

Brain Chemistry

- Serotonin depletion and neurotransmitter/receptor imbalance
- Beta-endorphin depletion and imbalance and the effect on dopamine release
- Enkephalin depletion and imbalance
- Inflammation causing poor circulation, biosynthesis of key neurotransmitters and hormones, and poor communication between neurons
- Over excitation of sympathetic nervous system
- Profound negative effects on brain chemistry from fatigued adrenals
- Tolerance increases and withdrawal intensifies over time, encouraging daily use of alcohol

Endocrine System

- Hypoglycemia/sugar sensitivity
- General suppression of the endocrine system
- Adrenal fatigue
- Pancreatic injury

- Low thyroid function
- Compromised hypothalamus function
- Compromised pituitary function

Liver

- Alcohol metabolism byproducts, inefficient acetaldehyde metabolism
- Efficient alcohol metabolism
- Nutrients exhausted from metabolizing alcohol and detoxing its byproducts
- Inadequate protein synthesis
- Metabolic poisoning
- Liver damage

Gastrointestinal System

- Gastrointestinal damage, malnutrition
- Carbohydrate metabolism

Acetaldehyde Damage to the HPA Axis

- Acetaldehyde toxicity
- Acetaldehyde addiction
- Sources of acetaldehyde
- Candida Albicans

The Home of Alcoholism in the Body and Mind

As stated, addictive or addicted biochemistry is essentially the body's inability to adequately self-medicate with natural neurotransmitters like serotonin, GABA, dopamine, endorphins, and enkephalins. This inability predisposes an individual to seek relief from the resulting symptoms in external ways such as alcohol. Low GABA, serotonin, dopamine, endorphin and enkephalin levels mean that excitatory neurotransmitters such as glutamate, norepinephrine, and epinephrine are not properly managed, causing an overactive sympathetic nervous system. This overly sensitive nervous system leads to symptoms that problem drinkers are known to self-medicate. These symptoms, along with the nutritional deficiencies that create them, are the bedrock of the progression of alcoholism in

active drinkers because the longer one drinks, the more damage is done to the neuroendocrine system, intensifying the problem and causing the person to drink more and more. This vicious cycle continues to apply to the former problem drinker since they will self-medicate with caffeine, excess simple and refined carbs, or cigarettes all of which promote release, for a short period, the naturally deficient feel-good neurotransmitters while they continue to damage the same organs in the same way, creating more symptoms to medicate.

Research has concluded that the 'home' of alcoholism is in the HPA (hypothalamus, pituitary, adrenal) axis of the neuroendocrine system. The neuroendocrine system is the sum total of the nervous system and endocrine system. The endocrine system is the network of glands in the body comprised of the hypothalamus, pituitary, pineal, adrenals, thyroid, parathyroid, and sex glands that release hormones in response to stimulation from the nervous system. These glands secrete hormones that travel through the blood to the organs of the body, carrying messages with the intention of keeping an organ regulated and healthy, essentially functioning as it should. A hormone's message will stimulate, suppress, or maintain functional cell or tissue activity of the organ by which it is received.

Armed with the knowledge of the markers of addictive chemistry, scientists have developed sophisticated tests, which monitor the performance of this axis by measuring dopamine, serotonin, GABA, glutamate, epinephrine (adrenaline), norepinephrine (noradrenalin), cortisol and DHEA which are the primary neurotransmitters and two key hormones affected by alcohol metabolism. These tests provide invaluable information for evaluating the breadth and depth of addiction in an individual, as well as for targeting the specific needs for therapeutic nutriceuticals to balance brain chemistry and dismiss the addiction.

The hypothalamus is the centerpiece of the endocrine system and is located in the middle of the base of the brain. The hypothalamus' ultimate purpose is to establish and maintain balance, or homeostasis, within the body while adapting to the external environment. It regulates functions of the autonomic nervous system such as breathing, heart

rate, hunger, thirst, sex drive, sleep, urination, and metabolism including blood sugar control.

The hypothalamus houses connections to hormones from the endocrine system and neurotransmitters from the nervous system. It utilizes the information it receives from these systems to control and balance the CNS and endocrine system and to establish healthy brain chemistry and nervous system function. It communicates with both systems to correct hormone and neurotransmitter imbalances by either slowing production of what is in excess, ingesting or degrading specific neurotransmitters faster, or in cases of deficiency, producing and releasing them as required.

The door to addictive biochemistry and imbalanced brain chemistry opens when either the hypothalamus or one of the organs that report to the hypothalamus is injured, dis-eased, or malnourished. In any one of these conditions the entire system will fall off the "point zero" (homeostasis) that the HPA system tries to maintain, and the door for addictive biochemistry is opened. Addictive biochemistry and full out alcoholism are associated with over expression of the excitatory neurotransmitters. This over expression indicates low levels of the inhibitory neurotransmitters: serotonin and GABA, the neuromodulator dopamine, and the opioids, endorphins and enkephalins. In the case of alcohol addiction, excessive use results in various nutritional and chemical deficiencies that render the hypothalamus incapable of doing its job and providing the necessary inhibitory neurotransmitters on its own- it essentially becomes burned out. Over time, these nutritional deficiencies will result in actual damage to the brain, endocrine system, and other key organs that are taxed by the metabolism of alcohol. Do not despair, this damage can be healed and you can actually grow new brain cells!

The pituitary gland is located below the hypothalamus and is directly connected to it via nerve and circulatory pathways. The hypothalamus regulates the function of the pituitary gland, which in turn controls hormonal secretions of all other glands. The pituitary gland controls the adrenal glands and signals for the release of cortisol, epinephrine, and norepinephrine in response to low blood sugar which is very common in problem drinkers. The pituitary secretes

adrenocorticotrophin (ACTH), which controls the adrenals and their release of cortisol. Adrenal release of epinephrine and norepinephrine is also triggered by corticotrophin releasing hormone (CRH) and signals from the sympathetic nervous system (SNS). In the case of cortisol release, when the hypothalamus registers low blood sugar it will send CRH to the pituitary, which then releases ACTH, causing cortisol to be secreted from the adrenals. This chain of events will also cause the release of epinephrine and to a lesser degree norepinephrine. Prolonged increased levels of epinephrine leads to insulin resistance and lowered serotonin, endorphin, enkephalin, and GABA levels. This translates into impaired HPA function and increased compulsive and addictive behavior.

The adrenals sit on top of the kidneys and are directly controlled by the pituitary gland and signals from the sympathetic nervous system. The adrenals are comprised of two sections; one is the medulla, which is the inner core, and the second is the adrenal cortex, which is the outer layer. The medulla relates to the sympathetic nervous system and produces the catecholamines epinephrine and norepinephrine. The adrenal cortex produces sex hormones, aldosterone, and cortisol.

Chemical messengers (hormones) that are received from the pituitary, and signals from the sympathetic nervous system, determine the timing and quantity of hormones to be released from the adrenals. If they are injured, diseased, or fatigued they will not be able to keep up with the demands for production, and mild to severe mental disorders will surface as symptoms of compromised adrenal health.

Although it is hard to imagine because they are docked on our kidneys, adrenal health is fundamental to our mental health. Proper levels of cortisol, epinephrine and norepinephrine are crucial to mental well being, so concentrated focus needs to be applied to their health when healing addictive biochemistry and alcohol addiction.

How They All Work Together

These organs are not only your adaptation headquarters which assist you in maintaining a harmonic existence with your environment; planet earth and the

universe which is your fundamental key to survival, but they help control your response to situations that are stressful, upsetting, or threatening. They can also be the path to addiction through excess alcohol use. During periods of acute stress special serotonin receptors on the hypothalamus are stimulated causing the hypothalamus to produce CRF (corticotrophin release factor). The CRF is sent directly to the pituitary, where it causes ACTH to be sent to the adrenals, triggering the release of cortisol. Cortisol is sent throughout the body on a number of different missions, with the primary one being to reduce the stress by stimulating serotonin (inhibitory neurotransmitter) release in the amygdala, as well to stimulate other helpful neurotransmitters to mediate the effects of stress on the body. The amygdala is directly connected to the hypothalamus and is a component of the limbic area of the brain where processing of emotions, fear, panic, and long-term memories happen. The serotonin has an inhibitory effect on the amygdala's glutamate receptors (excitatory neurotransmitter) and acts to calm you down so that you can think with a clear mind in stressful situations. If you can not calm down, the amygdala will sound alarms of panic and fear and you will go into cortical inhibition. Cortical inhibition is a result of the actual danger alarms going off and initiating the body's fight or flight mechanisms. One of the tasks of this mechanism is to redistribute blood flow and energy to the muscles and extremities where energy is needed for survival (such as fighting or running) which robs blood flow from all functions that are not immediately necessary for survival such as the frontal lobe of the brain and digestion (which is a primary reason why over-stressed individuals experience digestive disorders). When blood flow and energy are redistributed away from the frontal lobe, the person experiences cortical inhibition which dramatically diminishes the reasoning, visionary, thinking, executive, and problem solving area of the brain. One should never attempt to go into problem solving mode with someone in this condition because it is simply impossible to reason with them. Humans learned long ago that they couldn't talk a lion out of its hunger or shift its attention to a nearby rabbit, so this area of the brain through evolution has been turned off in a survival crisis – even if it is only a "perceived" and not actual threat to their survival.

Excess alcohol use damages the adrenals leaving little cortisol to respond to these situations and empties serotonin and GABA out of the amygdala making the brain incapable of remaining calm even while reading disruptive emails, much less an actual threat to survival. Yes, when a person has developed a blunted response to stress because they are chemically and nutritionally deficient, they begin responding to even small disappointments in a hyper-reactive way which many times sets off the survival mechanisms. Many forms of depression, anxiety, and panic disorders originate here due to low serotonin levels, and the ensuing over expressed glutamate and other excitatory neurotransmitters.

The HPA and Addictive / Addicted Biochemistry

The markers in the brain chemistry that spell genetic addictive potential are the same as those of a person who earned the condition through alcohol abuse; they are low endorphin, enkephalin, GABA, serotonin, and dopamine expression. These always result in the same chemical situation: the over expression of the sympathetic nervous system through the excitatory neurotransmitters; glutamate, epinephrine, and norepinephrine. The condition does not always involve all of these neurotransmitters; the deficiency or imbalance of just one or two of the inhibitory neurotransmitters which takes the brakes off the excitatory ones can initiate the practice of self-medicating once a person is exposed to a substance that helps bring up their inhibitory neurotransmitter deficiencies. The symptoms suffered by people with an inherited potential for addictive biochemistry, when it is being epigenetically aggravated, that are not actively drinking are not as pronounced as those of the active drinker; however they are debilitating and extremely mentally and physically uncomfortable which is why they typically fall into some form of addiction be it alcohol, excessive sugar/refined carbs, anti-depressants, or any of the street or OTC drugs that answer to their discomfort.

Symptoms can vary depending on the exact neurotransmitters involved, but they can include everything from depression, emotional instability, hyper-reactivity, mental and physical fatigue, and cravings for simple carbs to low self-esteem or confidence, low-grade to chronic to acute anxiety, panic attacks, inability to relax, insomnia, social

withdrawal, and nervousness. Alcohol can fix all of these in just a couple drinks because it immediately raises the levels of all of the deficient neurotransmitters. The price is high though, because on the other end, with withdrawal, comes the bottoming out of the already-low levels of neurotransmitters which magnifies the original symptoms.

What happens within the body of a person who has been abusing alcohol for a while and has damaged their neuroendocrine system is this: while the person is drinking, GABA, endorphins, dopamine, and serotonin are over expressed. This causes relaxation and soothing of the symptoms from which they had been suffering. However, this expression of inhibitory neurotransmitters causes a depletion that leaves stores empty the next morning when the person wakes up, causing the symptoms that accompany the over expression of glutamate and catecholamines. Similarly during drinking, endorphins and enkephalins are over produced and emptied out, causing a lack of natural pain killers available to mediate the condition and the person will need to have alcohol again to provide opioids, dopamine, serotonin, and GABA to help kill the pain and achieve a comfortable state of mind.

The internal scene of a person who rarely drinks excessively is quite different; this person has ample healthy stores of serotonin, dopamine, GABA, endorphins, and enkephalins that will quickly rise to the job of rebalancing brain chemistry. In the long-term drinker this is impossible because their body's stores and ability to manufacture and replenish healthy levels of these neurotransmitters has been diminished from the damage of alcohol toxicity and the resulting malnutrition.

Once damage is established in the HPA system by long-term drinking, the cycle becomes deeply embedded in a person's biochemistry. This condition renders the person entirely dependent on alcohol to achieve chemically provided peace, relaxation, a sense of happiness, and the natural euphoria of life; they can no longer achieve these states naturally, within a reasonable amount of time, and not without going through a severe withdrawal period.

Long-term Alcohol Abuse and Stress Disorder

Due to alcohol toxicity damage, extreme daily blood sugar fluctuations, and malnutrition, the adrenals become fatigued causing low cortisol output, which leads to high norepinephrine levels (over expressed). The reason for this is that cortisol is required (along with SAMe) to produce epinephrine from norepinephrine. When this doesn't occur, norepinephrine is over expressed while epinephrine and cortisol are diminished. Note here that cortisol is also required in some areas of the brain to activate serotonin, so that when it is low, serotonin expression is also inhibited. This condition of elevated norepinephrine with decreased serotonin delivers a person into the "alarm" stage for stress disorder, characterized by extreme anxiety, panic attacks, paranoia, insomnia, aggression, irritability, hypertension, and even bipolar disorder.

Philosophy and Science Join to Explain the Existential Effects of Alcohol Addiction

The conscious is the communication center between the soul and the physical world, and vise-versa – a mission control that reads information from our senses, feeds it to our esoteric body, and then responds according to our spiritual blueprint. It is a labyrinth of roadways housed inside the brain that provide a means for energy to convey information in the form of electrically charged pulses, from the "esoteric body" and the physical world down to every cell in the body. Problems arise when these roadways and tunnels are blocked, damaged, or forced into detours. More problems occur when these roadways are littered with vehicles (molecules) that cannot make the trip and are breaking down due to environmental assaults or lack of proper fuel and maintenance. Discord and chaos ensue when the information for which each vehicle is responsible misses its destination; communication is lost. As these chemical "vehicles" break down and drift around aimlessly, they cause traffic jams, accidents, and distractions on the roadways of the mind while picking up dangerous hitch hikers. When life-sustaining information cannot be expressed – either through directives from your DNA, which stores the cell renewing information of our species, or through the quantum field embodying your

mind/body/environmental relationship – it becomes disconnected from the universal laws that sustain and generate life. The vibrancy and light of life fades and separation and chaos cloud your perfect expression of self.

The chaos and discord in your cellular body out-pictures itself in a number of physical, emotional, psychological, and situational distresses. The macro mirrors the micro: as it is above, so it is below. Perspective becomes distorted and you lose contact with the better side of yourself when constant intoxication damages the vehicles and roadways that facilitate communication between the higher self and physical existence. You become a chaotic swirl of nervous impulses, constantly reacting to circumstance because neurological damage from alcohol toxicity and the amped-up existence caused by excessive sugars have disconnected you from your higher self and removed you from the driver's seat. You become more energy and compulsiveness than thought. In this state it is easy for you to lose your direction in life and find that you are no longer able to take charge of events and circumstances. You no longer hear the music your biochemical rhythms are supposed to dance to, feel the higher vibrations your life energy is supposed to align with, or see the world you live in through the crystal clear understanding the eyes of one who is spiritually present does. Losing this higher vision disrupts your view of the world and your understanding of your place in it; you incorrectly react to circumstances and events in life and as a result, become mentally and physically exhausted by your struggles by the end of the day.

Essentially, a disruption in this self communication means that we lose our grace and biochemical rhythm in the cosmic harmonic dance that celebrates health, because the grace and beauty of that dance is expressed in the choreography of the mind and body communicating as they were designed to. As deities created in the "image of God", our perfection is unable to express itself when our intuitive understanding of the world becomes blocked or distorted by the physical separation and chaos caused by toxic substances that poison the paths between our spiritual and mind/body communication systems. The supreme intelligence of God can no longer harmoniously integrate our DNA with our environment to keep us healthy in mind and body and give life to our creative forces because

they are at odds. DNA is the blueprint of life and toxicity in its environment disrupts its paths of regeneration and renewal; it is its antithesis. These two very different systems of information interacting create chaos. Our creative energies are the entitlement that separates us from all other creatures on Earth, the gift that allows us to consciously create our day, ultimately making us masters of our reality and images of God. They are impaired by the disconnection to the master plan; the vibrational blueprint of our existence which channels the crystalline creative energies of the universe through our consciousness is lost as sheaths of foreign substances distort their path and we lose touch with the creative forces which define us as the "image of God".

The result is that the body's higher intelligence and instinct for living can no longer keep the physical body healthy or give life to its creative forces. Thus, we become unable to mold energy in our lives into a healthy, happy environment and become instead victims of random circumstances. The clear channels of peace, intuition, inspiration, joy, guidance and sense of well being that bring us naturally to happiness and accord are replaced by fear, anguish, anxiety, depression, and lack of healthy desires. This is when circumstance, stress, toxic thoughts, and addiction begin to rule us instead of our better judgment and the higher laws of the supreme intention. The enlightened information required for sound judgment, higher thinking, insightfulness, and guidance is not being received because our brains become like radars with low power supplies tuned to the wrong frequencies. We begin responding to our surroundings in an inaccurate way, without focus or healthy intentions. This internal disharmony leads to matching disharmony with the outside world. The disharmony with your environment is a result of the disharmony within your body. The laws of balance in the universe are not negotiable. Your external life becomes progressively messier as it adapts to your chaotic internal world. You become cut off from "the universe that provides" because the universe doesn't know what you need, since your "transmitter" has been shut down by addiction, which diminishes the expression of your "Chi" - Life Energy – the umbilical chord that connects you to the abundance of the heavens that is your rightful inheritance as a child of God. The stronger your chi is, the brighter your

light; and the closer and more open you are to the flow of energy that operates on the frequencies of the universal laws that express health. In order to have a healthy relationship with the world, you must build a healthy vessel through which the energy of life may flow and open a path for your divine inheritance.

Physiological health has a profound effect on mental health and vice-versa. It is possible to modify genetic expression (DNA) with focused thoughts and beliefs, so it is extremely important to maintain a healthy frame of mind; thoughts, beliefs, and expectations will reflect themselves in physical health down to each and every cell, experiences, and environment.

The beauty of all this is this that there are many ways in which you may reestablish accord with your divinity by clearing the roadways and building vehicles fit for the trip. In addition to treating the body like the temple that it is, you must also treat your mind like the temple's garden and plant loving, appreciative, beautiful thoughts in it as well by creating a holy space within through meditation and prayer. This provides a wonderful destination for your vehicles with enchanting roadways and scenery. By practicing the principles that bring you back to the vibrancy where the laws of mental and physical well being operate in accordance with the divine laws that created the physical world, you will once again find the sense of spiritual connectedness that has been lost.

The spirit is always present; it's the awareness of it and how it is integrated in your experiences in life; and the enchanting gifts of holistic, noetic perception; understanding, and vision that is removed from your awareness and experiences by the effects of alcohol toxicity. Through focused concentration on bio-repair and mental hygiene the flow of these laws' vibrancy and perfect instruction returns; abundance flows once again and life becomes the very enchanting journey it is meant to be.

Endocrine System

Hypoglycemia and Alcohol Addiction

Most problem drinkers are hypoglycemic, meaning they experience low blood sugar episodes throughout the day which cause fatigue, cravings and many psychological and

emotional symptoms. The rest are at least sugar sensitive, meaning that they experience a distinct high when they have sugar and a distinct low when they don't. Hypoglycemia and its' causes play an important role in the root of addiction and addictive biochemistry. On the surface, hypoglycemia appears to be a rather simple condition to review. But extreme fluctuations in blood sugar throughout the day set in motion a very serious chain of events that strongly contributes to addictive biochemistry and other health issues. Left unattended, these issues frequently result in numerous physical and mental dis-eases.

A child can be born with hypoglycemia or a precondition that will result in hypoglycemia if not managed with a proper diet. An adult can also drink their way into the condition. Habitual alcohol consumption can create hypoglycemia by continually triggering insulin, coritsol, and epinephrine reactions, thereby exhausting the pancreas and adrenals. Damage from the very toxic acetaldehyde also plays a major role in injuring these two organs and diminishing their functions, which will eventually render the problem drinker hypoglycemic.

Insulin initiates a number of metabolic processes associated with addictive biochemistry, making it a key player in the development of addiction. When you drink alcohol, the sugars it contains are absorbed immediately into the bloodstream and quickly send your blood sugar up to abnormal levels. In response, those who are sugar sensitive or hypoglycemic overproduce insulin to deliver the glucose into cells and bring blood sugar levels down. Because the pancreas over reacts the high insulin brings glucose levels down to unhealthy levels, resulting in low blood sugar. When the glucose-starved cells aren't getting the fuel they need, they begin sending out distress signals, some of which cause very uncomfortable symptoms. You can become irritable, shaky, easily overwhelmed, depressed, fatigued, 'low', headachy, and fearful. In the absence of another drink, the adrenals and the pancreas will release epinephrine and glucagon, which will counter low blood sugar by triggering the release of the body's stored glucose from the liver in the form of glycogen which will ease the symptoms. As the damage continues and blood sugar dives lower and lower, that step will no longer satisfy the body's glucose needs and it will

begin tapping the adrenals for cortisol. This is the common cycle early in the addiction, however, this quickly exhausts the adrenals and eventually there won't be enough cortisol released to satisfactorily raise blood sugar, nor mediate the effects of the increased norepinephrine caused by lack of cortisol to convert it to epinephrine; the resulting anxiety, inability to relax, and a host of other symptoms will add to the person's dependency on alcohol to reduce those symptoms, and increased alcohol consumption follows.

In the early stages of addiction, the common physiology of those who can drink all night is due to the elevated cortisol levels, caused by the adrenals being in a constant adaptation phase, and SAMe in the brain converting norepinephrine into epinephrine; the increased levels of the three stress hormones wakes the person up. These are the drinkers that become energetic after a couple of drinks, and because of this characteristic in their metabolism they are encouraged to drink themselves to sleep. Trying to stop during the middle of this cycle would cause them to feel wide awake, yet at the same time experience the crash of their declining blood sugar levels physically and in mental capacities such as anxiousness and restlessness. Combined with the fact that rapidly falling blood sugar levels will cause serotonin to empty out, these symptoms cause tremendous cravings for another drink. Remember, low serotonin equals carbohydrate cravings plus compulsive behavior. This is why it is so hard to "just have one"! Especially when your good judgment not to is impaired by inebriation.

This process takes only a short time to damage the pancreas and adrenal glands, causing more severe alcohol-induced hypoglycemic symptoms like emotionally charged mood swings and the 0 to10 explosive reaction to confrontation and difficulty that problem and heavy drinkers are known to have made an art form. Keep in mind that on a much smaller scale this same blood sugar roller coaster exists for caffeine and sugar junkies; however, their episodes are not as colorful since they do not have the intoxicating effects of alcohol reducing their inhibitions.

There is a huge difference between someone who is ***curing (correcting their metabolism)*** his or her addiction with The 101 Program and someone who is *treating* it using traditional methods which do not address their alcohol-

induced and/or genetic and environmental (epigenetic-nutritional) disadvantages. Remember, there is no profit in curing a disease in the eyes of pharmaceutical companies, there is only profit in *treatments*. And if you are one of the very common people who try to quit drinking and exchange sugar, caffeine, and a high refined carb diet to replace alcohol, then use their pills to mask the symptoms caused by this common mistake, you're heading for trouble. As the resulting hypoglycemic symptoms and effects of the neurotoxins typically found in high caffeine/refined/simple carb diets intensifies, the damage from former alcohol abuse combined with that which these substances inflict will continue to progress under the surface, causing you to suffer a plethora of symptoms. Everyday reality will become frustrating and difficult when seen through the lens of the mental incapacities caused by these symptoms. You can become easily overwhelmed as the day's events mount on top of compromised physical and mental health, inundating you with psychological and physiological struggles. The body prompts you more and more urgently to relieve your symptoms with sugars, caffeinated beverages, and refined carbohydrates. These will ease the symptoms, since they will promote some energy and release a little serotonin and endorphin to help medicate you; however, when the short-term effects wear off, the same cycle will repeat itself.

Empty carb diets like this continue the damage to the neuroendocrine system, and also "empty the tank". Over time there is less serotonin and endorphin to be released, reducing the small yet rewarding pleasures you received from simple/refined carb substances to energy lifters only that offer next to none of the psychological and emotional relief they once did. Without the relief you once gained from the neurochemical reactions these "foods" caused, you will be prompted to search for relief somewhere else. The addiction to alcohol can never be healed while a low blood sugar appetite is being maintained by a diet and lifestyle that continue the damage to the body, mainlining with another form of the same substance that created the appetite and damage in the first place.

The detox and healing within the practices and guidelines of The 101 Program rid you of those symptoms and impulses in a healthy way, since they will cure the hypoglycemia by

establishing healthy blood sugar levels throughout the day. You will eat to nourish the brain so that you have plenty of the right nutrients to help you feel great naturally throughout the day. You will cure one of the key causes of the addiction, instead of feeding or masking it for a few hours with coffee and donuts. Since hypoglycemic symptoms are a key cause of alcohol addiction and relapse, this condition absolutely must be addressed to free you from the symptoms.

The Sugar Connection to the Addiction to Alcohol

The sugar associated with alcohol plays a very big role in the appeal of and addiction to alcoholic beverages. If your biochemistry is naturally sugar sensitive, the habit of drinking simply for the enhanced effect sugar/glucose has on a serotonin/beta-endorphin-starved brain chemistry is easily fostered. An upregulated brain chemistry (more receptor sites than neurotransmitters to bind with them) is a strong marker for a predisposition to addictive biochemistry, which is in turn a symptom of an imbalanced neuroendocrine system. The power of sugar addiction is every bit as powerful as that of alcohol. Godiva chocolate stores are as appealing to a sugar addict as the dealer's house is to a junkie because of the manner in which its products are experienced in a beta-endorphin- and serotonin-affected upregulated brain chemistry. For sugar-sensitive people, sugar produces a milder, yet similar, euphoric high as that of opium or morphine. This is because their beta-endorphin/serotonin-starved brain cells have an army of receptor sites waiting to collect as many of the beta-endorphin and serotonin molecules released from the metabolism of sugars as possible.

Compare this to the more balanced neurotransmitter-to-receptor count in non-addictive, non –sugar-sensitive people. There is much more of a rush feeding the starving receptor sites than there is feeding the balanced receptor sites. The quest for that euphoric feeling will send addicted people rushing to the nearest liquor store day-in and day-out or for sweets in the absence of alcohol, without blinking an eye. The urge to reach for a beer comes from the same place as the urge to order pie after dinner, or even have pie for dinner.

In many respects, alcohol and sugar travel through your system in the exact same manner. They create the same

endocrine, brain chemistry, and digestive imbalances, and they are both carbohydrates with zero nutritional value. They feed upregulated serotonin and beta-endorphin conditions in brain chemistry, negatively influencing a number of other metabolic functions and affecting other neurotransmitters, while reducing internal production of natural enkephalins, beta-endorphins, and serotonin. It is this distortion of the brain chemistry, in particular the disruption of the serotonin process, that creates intense cravings for sugar and alcohol. Specifically, low serotonin makes you crave sweets and other carbohydrates, thus giving you the feeling that it's either time for snacks or for drinks. The main difference is that with alcohol you get a second level of chemically induced euphoria; the metabolism of alcohol and sugar turned acetaldehyde produces high levels of THIQs that mimic beta-endorphins and other opioid-type neurotransmitters. While excess sugars can ultimately be turned to alcohol and then acetaldehyde in the body, drinking alcohol provides a very strong dose of THIQs which will provide a far more profound response.

Low serotonin levels are directly linked to compulsive disorders, and addiction is a compulsive disorder. When it comes to alcohol, the compulsive disorder translates into not having the internal control to resist an urge, desire, or temptation to do something you know to be unhealthy, and not being able to stop the repeated behavior. The temptation creates an impulse and you, who are supposed to be the one in control, are not present or "vocal" enough to intervene. In the heat of the moment, how much strength do you have against reaching for that donut or beer? Why is the temptation or desire so strong in the first place? When it comes to alcohol or sugar, the presence or absence of mental fortitude in the face of temptation is directly related to the availability and utilization of serotonin in the brain. With adequate serotonin, beta-endorphin, and enkephalin biosynthesis, you are able to feel good naturally with or without a drink, so the desire for alcohol is not experienced as a physical and mental craving. Moderate drinkers drink because they enjoy having a drink or two with friends, not because it will make them feel better or give them relief from an emotional or psychological symptom. Although it will provide relaxation and give them a slight

buzz, it is not essential, since they feel good inside their own skin anyway.

Since compulsiveness is one of the symptoms of an addicted biochemistry, when you add the mental, emotional, and physical symptoms suffered by problem drinkers, there is not much standing between them and answering the call to self-medicate those symptoms. It is natural to seek relief from mental and physical pain; it is a survival mechanism. Compulsiveness means that there is no 'off' switch to help someone maintain control in the face of those urges. So the goal must be to heal the root cause of the symptoms so that you are no longer carried by compulsiveness to engage your inherent sense of survival through self-medication with harmful external substances.

Hypoglycemia and Dry-Drunk Symptoms

Another obvious indicator that ties hypoglycemia and alcoholism together is the identical symptoms experienced in the absence of sugar or alcohol. They are a direct result of the imbalanced brain chemistry caused by beta-endorphin, enkephalin, GABA, and serotonin deficiencies.

Hypoglycemic and dry-drunk symptoms may include:

- Depression
- Anxiety, constant worrying
- Fear
- Nervous exhaustion
- Phobias, paranoia
- Inability to concentrate
- Mental and physical fatigue
- Suicidal tendencies
- Insomnia
- Excitability, irritability
- Frustration
- Confusion, lack of mental clarity
- Crying spells
- Asocial/antisocial behavior
- Short attention span
- Lack of follow-through
- Mood swings, emotional instability
- Stomach problems
- Internal trembling

- Nightmares, night terrors
- Night sweats
- Faintness, dizziness, tremors, cold sweats
- Heart palpitations
- Numbness

A brilliant endocrinologist, Dr. Tintera, after years of research, concluded that even recovered problem and chronic drinkers who have been sober for many years continue to suffer the symptoms of hypoglycemia. He asserts that the treatment of alcoholism "centers essentially on the control of hypoglycemia... by far the most important part of the physiological treatment of alcoholics is the complete restriction of easily absorbed carbohydrates." He also states, "If hypoglycemic alcoholics stop drinking but continue to consume large amounts of caffeine and refined sugars, the outbursts of irritability and sudden anger will continue. These symptoms will disappear only when brain glucose levels stabilize."[4] This is true for all the other symptoms of the dry drunk as well. When a recovering drinker gets off the hypoglycemic cycle and stops replacing one source of sugar for another, the cravings and urges go away. "...for many years, he [Bill Wilson] suffered from depression and other hypoglycemic symptoms. He also consumed huge amounts of sugar and caffeine. Finally, by eliminating sugar and caffeine and making other dietary changes, he stabilized his blood sugar and achieved a sense of well being."[5] Bill Wilson has been reported as being severely depressed for years after he quit drinking. One of the most evident symptoms of hypoglycemia is depression. When Bill learned that quitting sugar and caffeine would rid him of his depression he did so and found that he stabilized his blood sugar and "achieved a sense of well being". This is why heavy drinkers, after not drinking for years, go back to alcohol during low blood sugar cravings. When they return to drinking, they are replacing the sugars and refined carbohydrates such as cokes, candies,

---

[4] Joan Mathews-Larson, Ph.D. Seven Weeks To Sobriety. New York, NY: Fawcett/Columbine, 1997; 122.

[5] Joan Mathews-Larson, Ph.D. Seven Weeks To Sobriety. New York, NY: Fawcett/Columbine, 1997; 121.

muffins, donuts, pastries, chips, empty carb snacks, and other junk foods on which they relied for relief during sobriety. This behavior is reversed when they try to stop drinking; they will eat refined, simple carbohydrates and drink cokes and coffee to replace the blood sugar levels alcohol provided. Alcohol and sugar are interchangeable substances that answer to the same neurochemical addiction. Low blood sugar symptoms are actually distress messages that precede full-blown withdrawal if they are not answered. This cycle will continue until the addictive biochemistry is healed. Until then, in order to feign off withdrawal, you will continually cater to the strong sugar and alcohol (i.e., endorphin and serotonin) craving, be it dry or drunk.

This process of replacing one for the other is also the premise of the well-known progression of alcohol addiction even in the absence of alcohol. The root of the addiction is continually worsened and progressively more deep-seated in the biochemistry by sugar products, in the same way as it was with alcohol. Sugar causes identical imbalances in brain chemistry, and damages the neuroendocrine system; the damage is just progressing slower when sugar is taking the place of alcohol. When you approach recovery with a treatment that heals you as opposed to just trading one harmful substance for its cousin, your success will not center on your will power because there will no longer be a battle to fight. When you successfully maintain healthy blood sugar levels with a condictive diet, and end the feeding of the monstrous simple carb appetite of a distorted biochemistry, the desire for alcohol will fade and so will the battle.

It is no wonder that almost everyone at AA meetings covets that coffee machine at 9:00 at night and consumes sugary snacks that are provided. While they think they're doing the right thing by giving up alcohol, they're actually continuing that harmful attachment to both sugar and alcohol. By quitting drinking, they are now enduring all the suffering without any of the benefits of self-medicating with the potent version of their biochemical attraction. This is sometimes so physically and mentally debilitating that it drives people into deep depression, isolation, and suicide. While their outward symptoms such as drunken behavior and missed days at work are gone, the personal suffering is still there.

In this situation, it is very easy for you to believe that you have a disease to battle with for the rest of your life. As long as you are simply replacing alcohol with sugar, you will suffer from these extreme blood sugar fluctuations and resulting symptoms, and will be tempted to start drinking again. You are maintaining addictive biochemistry when you answer with a coke the same symptoms you once answered by going to the bar after work.

Caffeine, sugar, and cigarettes all raise glucose levels, providing quick, short-term energy, pleasure, and mental acuity. These substances temporarily elevate serotonin and beta-endorphins levels and provide sober hypoglycemics the sense of well being that their mind and body crave in the absence of alcohol. Those that try to quit drinking, yet adopt the habit of mainlining simple sugars and caffeine to self-medicate their symptoms, are not getting off the hypoglycemic roller coaster or stopping the addictive behavior that continues their suffering. Carb- and sugar-dense diet choices and their resulting symptoms adversely affect all other areas of your life, many times leading you to develop an addictive personality that affects your relationships with other people as well. Essentially, your relationships with all the people, events, and products in the environment become absorbed by the quest to ease your symptoms via any means available. Aggravated addictive biochemistry typically carries with it obsessive/compulsive disorders that can reach into nearly every aspect of one's life. An imbalanced biochemistry will out-picture itself in an unbalanced lifestyle.

Suppression of the Endocrine System

Why Drinkers Age so Quickly

When insulin is constantly being over produced to counteract spikes in blood sugar, another health issue arises: after it is done delivering the available glucose into the cells, insulin hangs around far longer than the sugars that triggered it. The endocrine system is a very complicated network of checks and balances; when one process is unstable, the others are sure to suffer as well. An equally disruptive process begins in response to the over abundance of insulin in the blood: the body produces another hormone called somatostatin, which suppresses insulin release. At the same

time, it suppresses HGH (human growth hormone) release and hormone production throughout the endocrine system. This process is a contributing, if not key, cause of hypothyroidism and the pre-aging that afflicts many problem drinkers. Long-term suppression of HGH promotes rapid aging (drinkers lose their glow quickly and are easily identified in their 30's because of this), increased body fat, reduced energy levels, reduced lean tissue, diminished bone density, cognitive impairment, poor sleep, and decreased sexual interest.

Because the endocrine system relies on a second by second series of checks and balances to maintain healthy levels of neurotransmitters and hormones to meet with the needs of its environment, one imbalanced condition such as too much insulin which leads to unhealthy levels of somatostatin can become the genesis of many hormonal and neurotransmitter health issues. Women are particularly at risk during perimenopause and menopause; an imbalanced and suppressed endocrine system will certainly complicate and aggravate the physiological process of menopause and vise-versa.

Another reason problem drinkers age so quickly is that the process of metabolizing alcohol produces acetaldehyde and other associated toxic metabolites which create extremely harmful amounts of free radicals that contribute to accelerated cellular cross-linking and aging. Cross-linking is when cells bond together, making them denser. This is one reason why those who smoke and drink lose the elasticity in their skin quickly. Cross-linking, for example, is the process responsible for windshield wipers hardening and having to be replaced periodically ... not good for those wishing to maintain a youthful, healthy glow.

Hypoadrenocorticism

Hypoadrenocorticism is the medical term for fatigued adrenals and is one of the key causes that render the body unable to maintain healthy blood sugar levels.

The adrenals are a key player in blood sugar management and their compromised health is at the very root of addictive biochemistry. Research has established that alcohol addiction's home address resides in the dis-eased, imbalanced functioning of the HPA axis, and adrenal fatigue lives in that

home. An imbalanced neuroendocrine system, in the case of addictive biochemistry, over expresses the excitatory neurotransmitters that feed the sympathetic nervous system, which then produces the symptoms and health issues related to the condition. Herein lies what is broken and herein lies what needs to be fixed.

Those with inherited inadequate adrenals characteristically show a decreased metabolism and typically possess cravings for simple/refined carbohydrates from birth, which is a sign of upregulated brain chemistry. Fatigued adrenals cause upregulated brain chemistry because they can't adequately meet the demands of the system to stabilize blood sugar, resulting in prolonged low blood sugar episodes.

The adrenals produce cortisol to bring blood sugar up during low blood sugar episodes, but this should happen only occasionally; it should be the exception, not the rule. There should be an intermediate step between low blood sugar and adrenal activity; it is the glucagon step. During this step, glucagon is released from the pancreas to stimulate glycogen release from the liver, which will be converted into glucose. However, when alcohol has been in the picture, sugar sensitivity or hypoglycemia will develop, and insulin will drive blood sugar down much faster and lower than it should. This causes the glucagon step to cycle through much more quickly. When glucagon stores are exhausted, the endocrine system triggers the adrenals for cortisol.

This example assumes that there were adequate glucagon stores available in the first place. If the pancreas is damaged or fatigued, sufficient stores of glucagon will not be made available for the glucagon step, and the body will go directly to the adrenals for help. This process takes long enough that once blood sugar has dropped so low as to require cortisol from the adrenals, you are already making yourself a drink or are in the refrigerator fetching a beer. If you have quit drinking, you are heading for a soda or cup of coffee.

When the pancreas does not function properly, your internal ability to manage blood sugar before it falls too low is diminished, and as it diminishes you will be prompted to seek external methods. The more you rely on external methods, the closer your diagnoses for diabetes and a number of other illnesses becomes, while also advancing addictive

biochemistry causing you to become increasingly more compulsive.

Chronic, extreme blood sugar fluctuations throughout the day can ultimately harm the entire neuroendocrine system, because every organ in this delicately balanced network is directly responsible for maintaining healthy blood sugar levels. Chasing blood sugar levels up and down all day long is extremely taxing on the organs of the HPA axis. Low blood sugar signals the hypothalamus to secrete CRH (corticotropin-releasing hormone), which then signals the anterior pituitary cells to secrete ACTH (adrenocorticotropic hormone), which then signals the adrenal cortex to secrete cortisol to raise blood glucose. In problem drinkers, especially those who are sugar sensitive or hypoglycemic, this cycle occurs numerous times each day, giving life to the term "blood sugar roller coaster" and fatiguing everything involved in its maintenance. As the adrenals become more stressed from trying to keep up with daily blood sugar fluctuations, they get progressively slower in responding to descending blood sugar, and symptoms become more severe. A person suffering from these symptoms begins to seek anything that will feed the need for immediate glucose throughout the day. This may be caffeine, cigarettes, cokes, simple carb meals, or alcohol. Though the pathways are multiple, the end destination is the same: constant blood sugar fluctuations will fatigue and eventually injure the adrenals. The more overworked they are, the more inefficient they become at responding to the body's blood sugar regulation requirements, and low blood sugar symptoms are worsened and continue to feed addictive biochemistry.

Hypoadrenocorticism and the Angry Drunk

Over time, the constant demand on the fatigued adrenals to respond to high and low blood sugar levels takes its toll, and the natural ability to physically, emotionally, and psychologically handle stress diminishes. When exhausted by continuing demands for epinephrine and cortisol, the adrenals no longer have the ability to respond properly; they no longer have the ability to protect you from stress. When the adrenals are so weak that they can no longer provide a sufficient supply of stress hormones, you can no longer respond calmly or think clearly in times of difficulty. The

result is usually anger, frustration, anxiety, or emotional instability.

Hypoadrenocorticism combined with the lowered inhibitions of alcohol can bring on periods of uncontrollable anger, for which many long-term heavy drinkers are well known. In a milder scenario, the failing adrenal glands and lack of stress hormones can have daily low-grade psychological effects. These include worry, agitation, paranoia, anxiety, fear, and the artificial feeling that something is wrong. Because failing adrenals adversely affect brain chemistry and the body's ability to produce, store, and regulate the release of stress buffers and feel-good neurotransmitters, one can become over-sensitive and begin distrusting people and situations, causing them to live defensively and migrate toward complete isolation. They tend to have outbursts, create arguments, and become emotionally distraught and over reactive in response to mild disruptions. A brain low on glucose and lacking in calming neurotransmitters is not capable of rational thought, which renders a person progressively more unable to control their irrational thinking. Left untreated and with alcohol in the picture, this lifestyle can cause them to quickly spin out of control and fall into a life-debilitating downhill spiral. Jobs, lovers, family members, and friendships are lost and children are often verbally and physically abused. Ultimately, lives are disrupted or even damaged as a result of the destructive personalities that these drinkers develop. Through their own actions they become isolated and are left to drink themselves to death while they become angrier and angrier at the world.

Adrenals and Sleep Patterns

Coritsol levels are usually higher in the morning and gradually decline; just before sleep they should be at their lowest. If cortisol levels are high at night, it can be difficult to fall asleep; if they are too low in the morning, it can make it difficult to even think about getting out of bed.

Long-term problem drinkers usually experience insomnia when they first stop drinking. This is because in the absence of alcohol, blood sugar will remain very low for the first few days, until it stabilizes naturally. During this time, in a continuous effort to bring blood sugar up, cortisol will be released throughout the day which then lingers in the system,

making it hard to fall asleep at night. Long-term drinkers also usually suffer from lowered serotonin levels. Since serotonin is the precursor for melatonin (induces sleep), serotonin precursors must be supplemented in the diet to prompt serotonin and melatonin release. Once blood sugar stabilizes, serotonin is made available, and cortisol resets for the natural sleep patterns, called the circadian rhythm, and the person will experience a good night's sleep.

How Stress Contributes to Addictive Biochemistry

Initially, when you are under a lot of stress, your adrenals raise cortisol and the catecholamines; norepinephrine and epinephrine. If everything in your body is working well, these levels will return to normal once the stress is gone or reduced. If you are exposed to a moderate or significant amount of stress over an extended period of time, cortisol levels can remain elevated. This will result in fatigued adrenals. Diminishing cortisol supplies from fatigued adrenals can offer up several symptoms that include anxiety, extreme mental and physical fatigue, nervousness, and restlessness; symptoms that you will be compulsively driven to self-medicate.

Problem drinking alone creates both physical and psychological extended periods of stress causing excess stress hormones to be continually secreted. However, no matter the source of the stress, if it is chronic, the result will be production of excess stress hormones, which will deplete the body's resistance and can lead to many illnesses, addictive biochemistry, and alcoholism.

The Biochemical Physical and Mental Roadmap

This is how and why, from a biochemical standpoint, alcohol negatively impacts cerebral function, mood, attitude, perception, and behavior through the damage it causes to the physical body. Essentially, alcohol metabolism places extreme demands on the body. It exhausts vitamins, minerals, and essential fatty and amino acids, thus creating deficiencies in the biochemistry and negatively impacting each and every organ and cell in the body. It is extremely important for anyone suffering from this condition to

remember that much, if not all, of their negative thinking is a result of the physiological damage caused by alcohol, and when that damage is gone the negative thinking will go with it.

A general review of conditions that cause psychological illness as a result of alcohol abuse is:

- The HPA axis is the intersection of the central nervous system and the endocrine system. When nutritional deficiencies or actual injury keep the hypothalamus from balancing these two systems and maintaining homeostasis within the body and brain chemistry, mental capacity is diminished in all areas of the human psyche. Any combination of a number of symptoms may have opportunity to manifest. One of the symptoms of an imbalance in the HPA axis is addictive biochemistry, which, given the opportunity, can lead to alcoholism. In essence, if the body cannot properly medicate itself thru the HPA axis, it will instruct you to do so on your own using external substances.
- Alcohol damages the organs of the digestive system including the stomach, gastrointestinal system, liver, and pancreas. Without a healthy digestive system it is impossible for you to get an adequate, balanced supply of vitamins, minerals, and fats from the foods you eat. If you lack this nutrition you cannot produce the neurotransmitters and hormones needed for brain and general health. This condition inevitably results in malnutrition, disease, and contributes to addictive biochemistry.
- Toxins and free radicals produced during the breakdown of alcohol in the system kill cells in every organ of the body. Organs that suffer the most initial cell damage are the brain, liver, pancreas, adrenals, stomach, and gastrointestinal system. This promotes destruction of key biochemical processes required for a healthy metabolism. These free radicals also cause hardened arteries, prematurely aged skin, degenerative diseases, and cancer.
- Alcohol is a depressant that drains serotonin levels from the brain. As you continue to drink, your life begins to suffer; opportunities are missed and healthy avenues of gratification, relaxation, pleasure, fulfillment, and sources

of natural joy and happiness are lost. The result is a life that becomes progressively more centered on alcohol to supply these sensations, which perpetuates the cycle of serotonin deficiency. Alcohol-induced depression due to low serotonin levels is a very serious issue. Autopsies reveal that those who have drunk themselves to death or committed suicide have very low serotonin levels in the brain.

- Alcohol metabolism exhausts and destroys vitamin B stores in the body, resulting in health problems such as fatigue, depression, anxiety, stress, obesity, and weakened adrenals.

- Alcohol damages and suppresses the endocrine system, causing conditions such as hypoglycemia, hypothyroidism, adrenal fatigue, low HGH, and the inability of the pancreas to produce necessary enzymes for the breakdown and utilization of foods, particularly protein and fat. Inability to break down protein and obtain amino acids for the body's biochemical processes makes it impossible for the body to manufacture healthy levels of neurotransmitters.

- Heavy alcohol use destroys the availability of acetylcholine, a neurotransmitter essential for memory, general nerve health, and neurotransmitter transmission.

- Alcohol disrupts the inner wisdom of the body, which is designed to carry out genetic / environmental processes to establish healthy, balanced brain chemistry. This disruption surfaces in many active problem drinker and dry drunk symptoms such as depression, fatigue, nervousness, anxiety, mental collapse, outbursts, emotional instability, and paranoia.

- Elevated norepinephrine, typically caused by low cortisol in problem drinkers, creates over excitement and symptoms like anxiety, nervousness, impatience, aggression, and hypertension.

- Alcohol consumption over a long period of time causes constant, elevated levels of insulin in the body, which lead to suppression of the endocrine system. This results in conditions such as hypothyroidism, hypoglycemia, and compromised pituitary and hypothalamus function. Elevated insulin levels also provide an environment for accelerated aging.

- Long term alcohol abuse essentially empties out serotonin, beta-endorphins, and GABA which causes an imbalance

between these inhibitory neurotransmitters and glutamate, the most abundant excitatory neurotransmitter. This is the fundamental cause for the over excited nervous system that develops and its many symptoms that strongly encourage the problem drinker to use alcohol to calm down.

Peripheral Damage That Contributes to Alcohol Addiction

Acetaldehyde Toxicity - Neurotransmitters and THIQs

The body produces an average of one ounce of alcohol a day from unused carbohydrates. A body that is constantly being fed excessive amounts of sugars will produce even more. Both internally produced alcohol and ingested alcohol are metabolized into acetaldehyde by alcohol dehydrogenase. From there, it is converted into acetate (vinegar), and is dismissed from the body through the bile or urea. The liver is the organ in charge of executing this process. If the liver cannot keep up with the amount of acetaldehyde being produced, and it is not efficiently detoxed, the unmetabolized acetaldehyde will travel through the blood, adversely affecting everything with which it comes in contact. In the brain it combines with beta-endorphins to produce THIQs, which have morphine-like qualities and fit into the opiate-type receptor sites meant for beta-endorphins, thus giving you a euphoric response to alcohol. This is also very dangerous because acetaldehyde is more toxic than alcohol and is the major cause of brain, liver, pancreatic, adrenal, and gastrointestinal damage and disease in problem drinkers. It will also be interesting to note that alcohol dehydrogenase, which breaks alcohol down into acetaldehyde, is found in the stomach and small and large intestines. This could give an indication of why a large percentage of alcohol-related diseases originate in the GI (gastrointestinal tract). Excessive acetaldehyde levels over time will damage cells, generate scar tissue, and cause a high production of free radicals, ultimately resulting in accelerated cell death and disease.

Since THIQs feed all of the eager upregulated beta-endorphin receptor sites, an individual with imbalanced brain

chemistry will achieve a more intense morphine-like response to alcohol. High production of THIQs equals a high risk that the individual will choose to drink because he or she enjoys it that much more.

This arm of the addiction cycle looks like this: you drink excessively because you like it more than most if you have upregulated beta-endorphin and serotonin brain chemistry. As the alcohol slowly begins to adversely change your body chemistry, THIQs replace the few beta-endorphins that were being produced by the body, further decreasing their production and utilization. You begin to feel daily low-level anxiety, fatigue, depression, and frustration. Progressively, small things begin to frustrate you more and big things weigh heavily in the absence of alcohol. Ultimately, you become chemically depressed and suffer a number of psychological and emotional disorders, resulting in the inability to function healthily in the world. Alcohol becomes your only answer, since it leads to production of THIQs to fill the endorphin sites, making the world seem livable again.

Excess sugars and simple carbohydrates promote the same premise of addiction as alcohol does, since they too stimulate serotonin, endorphins, and dopamine on one end and empty them out on the other, and they both produce acetaldehyde. This is why pasta, donuts, coffee, breads, ice cream, candy, and refined/simple carbs will defeat rather than help a person trying to quit alcohol.

Acetaldehyde toxicity cannot be discussed without including mention of hangovers. Hangover symptoms are caused from a number of neuroendocrine changes, and free radical and dehydration effects on the body. But the sensation of extreme nausea is due to acetaldehyde poisoning and that of another by-product of alcohol metabolism: malondialdehyde. The harmful effect on the body from this substance is similar to that of radiation poisoning.

Sources of Acetaldehyde

Acetaldehyde toxicity is present in high levels in the environment, slowly poisoning the public's minds and bodies. Acetaldehyde toxicity is a strong contributor to alcohol and sugar addiction; it is also likely to be a key one for nicotine addiction, and a contributing factor for why some people like to smoke only when they drink. Cigarette smoke produces

acetaldehyde, which temporarily increases THIQ production and intensifies the euphoric experience from the alcohol. Chronic acetaldehyde exposure increases your propensity for addictive biochemistry because it diminishes natural endorphin synthesis, and binds with serotonin further depleting its availability causing you to seek the THIQs produced by acetaldehyde and serotonin produced by the sugar more urgently and consistently.

Due to the many environmental toxic assaults in today's industrialized world, including acetaldehyde exposure, it is wise to do an environmental detox a couple times a year.

Common sources of acetaldehyde are:

- Alcohol
- Cigarettes
- Candida Albicans
- Excess / unused carbohydrates
- Car and diesel exhaust
- Perfumes, drugs, lacquer, varnishes, synthetic flavoring substance, food preservatives and fragrance
- Residential fireplaces, wood stoves, bushfires, and agricultural burning

Tolerance

When receptors are flooded with too much of a specific neurotransmitter, the body will begin to downregulate, meaning fewer receptors will be made available to receive the corresponding neurotransmitter. This is the brain's effort to regulate and balance its chemistry. A tolerance to a drug or alcohol means that it takes more of that substance to achieve minimal results, due to fewer receptors being available to receive and activate the substance's effect.

Withdrawal

The brain requires a steady flow of specific amino acids and other nutrients to produce neurotransmitters. These nutrients become exhausted by the demands of metabolizing alcohol and its byproducts, and over producing the inhibitory neurotransmitters while drinking. In most alcohol abusers it is rare that the appropriate nutrients are in the diet to begin

with, making metabolism and detoxification of alcohol even more inefficient and malnutrition a strong candidate for the person's addictive biochemistry. Consistent alcohol use also begins to replace the brain's natural neurotransmitters with those produced by alcohol, which will trigger the brain to increasingly slow production of the natural chemicals. These factors lead to the brain failing to have the necessary neurotransmitters available to produce healthy moods and mediate emotional and physical pain naturally.

When you stop drinking, withdrawal is the discomfort you experience between the time when the brain registers the need for inhibitory and feel-good neurotransmitters, and the time when it actually manufactures them in adequate amounts. This time frame depends on a number of factors, mostly based on the general health of the digestive system, endocrine system, and liver, and the availability of the required nutrients needed to produce serotonin, beta-endorphins, enkephalins, dopamine and the relaxing GABA.

Digestive System
Alcohol Metabolism in the Liver

The liver is the organ primarily responsible for converting alcohol into acetaldehyde. The liver converts much of the acetaldehyde into a neutral substance called acetate (vinegar). In some individuals alcohol changes very quickly into acetaldehyde, and the acetaldehyde is converted much more slowly into acetate. This provides increased opportunity for addiction and damage to vital organs like the pancreas, adrenals, brain, gastrointestinal system, and heart.

Those who are extremely efficient at metabolizing alcohol into acetaldehyde have an enzyme called alcohol dehydrogenase II, which can process alcohol up to 40% more efficiently than the standard alcohol dehydrogenase enzyme. People who have this enzyme have a natural ability to drink large amounts of alcohol without becoming intoxicated. This is very dangerous; if you are able to drink more than the average person, and choose to do so because you like it, you are producing more THIQs, thereby draining serotonin and beta-endorphin from the brain and causing neuroendocrine damage at a higher rate. This will more quickly bring the body to rely almost entirely on THIQs to feel good, which reinforces the addiction.

In short, if you're 120 pounds and can drink most people under the table without becoming intoxicated, when normal drinkers would be calling random people out of the telephone directory in the wee hours of the morning, nip it in the bud now. Anyone who can drink at that rate needs to learn to manage their body chemistry. Chemistry such as that, left unmanaged, usually leads to alcohol addiction.

Gastrointestinal Damage and Malnutrition

The heavy drinking that poured excess amounts of sugar into your system for years has also made your body dependent on simple carbohydrates for energy. If you abuse alcohol for a substantial period you lose the ability to efficiently break down the complex carbohydrates, proteins, and fats in the foods you eat. The inability to break foods down leads to a lack in the building blocks necessary to produce hormones and neurotransmitters. One night of heavy drinking can damage the lining of the stomach and intestines, which is why problem drinkers consistently demonstrate mild to severe gastrointestinal damage that interferes extensively with digesting nutrients. Due to this damage and the standard 21st-century diet, which is heavy in simple carbs and hydrogenated fats, long-term drinkers do not have the enzymatic fortitude to get through the tougher digestive jobs with complex carbs, proteins, and fats; therefore, they cannot benefit from the nutrition they need from the foods they eat.

Lifeless foods provide energy, but not nutrition. There is good energy and there is amped-up, running from a tiger energy. The body should be fueled by nutrition that feeds the parasympathetic nervous system; the natural, peaceful, long-lasting, focused, and centered source of energy. It should not be fueled by jolts of energy derived from nearly pure glucose being shot into its veins and setting off its biochemical alarm system throughout the day. Excess ingestion of this "wired", raw energy over activates the sympathetic nervous system and forces it into a "fight or flight" chaotic swirl of nervous impulses all day.

In regards to malnutrition, this is how the cycle goes: alcohol damages the pancreas, reducing its ability to produce and release the enzymes needed to extract amino acids from the proteins and synthesize the fatty acids from fats (lipids) we eat. The gastrointestinal tract suffers its own list of

damages caused by metabolizing alcohol. Assuming you have a decent diet (which a majority of heavy drinkers don't), this damage interferes with your ability to digest and utilize the nutrients in the foods you eat. When your body is not provided with the proteins, complex carbs, fats, vitamins, and minerals it requires to function healthily, or cannot digest them regardless of how much food is eaten, it becomes malnourished. This is extremely serious; in the view of orthomolecular medicine all disease, when traced to its origins, is caused by some form of malnutrition. Weakened immune system, semi-starvation neurosis, disease, various forms of psychosis, mental distress, fatigue, depression, and addiction are just a few of the ways in which malnutrition manifests itself. Further, when a body is malnourished it cannot detox efficiently because it does not have the necessary nutritional tools to do so. Cell function is further damaged and destroyed by the prolonged levels of toxins in the body, which aids and abets the progression of more diseases.

In conclusion, malnutrition results from alcohol-inflicted gastrointestinal tissue damage, the exhaustion of nutritional resources, the taxing nature of free radicals produced by the process of alcohol metabolism, and the damaging effect of toxins building up and recycling throughout the body.

The only way to accurately address malnutrition and the damage it causes is through a highly nutritious diet and therapeutic supplementation. It is extremely difficult to derive adequate amounts of nutrition from today's foods; even harder for someone who is recovering from malnutrition and also has the challenge of healing from long-term alcohol abuse. To heal, you must meet one extreme, alcohol toxicity, with the intelligent tools of the opposite extreme, targeted therapeutic nutrition.

Carbohydrate Metabolism

Given time, alcohol and refined carbohydrate diets will injure the pancreas and create a preference for digesting and using simple carbs for energy. An overworked and undernourished pancreas under attack from acetaldehyde poisoning will release inadequate levels of pancreatic enzymes into the small intestine. Because the body is being told that "it needs energy now, please raise blood sugar" the pancreas will use its resources to make and secrete amylase

(carbohydrate) enzymes over trypsin and lipase, the protein and fat enzymes. When there is a deficiency of these enzymes, complex carb, protein, and fat nutrients are not adequately broken down or absorbed, resulting in malnutrition and spiked blood sugar from the metabolism of empty carbs only.

This simple carbohydrate digestive preference is a contributor to insulin resistance because it causes chronic high levels of insulin. Just as receptors in the brain will downregulate in response to too many neurotransmitters, insulin receptors do so in reaction to the chronically high insulin levels that are experienced as a result of problem drinking and excessive refined carb diets. Due to this insulin resistance and deficient pancreatic function, problem drinkers tend to have higher blood glucose levels after a meal and in response to alcohol than the non-addictive person; if insulin is ineffective in delivering glucose into the cells of the body, the glucose remains in the blood and continues to rise.

Those with healthy diets and digestive capabilities would not have the same elevated blood sugar levels; the work it takes to break down and digest fats, complex carbs, and proteins slows the conversion of these foods into glucose, and their entry into the bloodstream. In addition, what little refined / simple carbs are present in a healthy diet would need to compete with the complex carbs, fats, and proteins in the digestion process, which also slows the simple carb's entry into the blood system. This ensures balanced blood sugar levels, and healthy levels of insulin.

Candida Albicans

Candida Albicans is a microscopic yeast/fungal infection, similar to molds that live in damp areas, and can be a lethal production house of acetaldehyde. It is one of the most commonly encountered human pathogens, causing a variety of conditions that range from mucosal infections in generally healthy persons to life-threatening systemic infections in individuals with impaired immunity. Oral and esophageal Candida infections are frequently seen in AIDS patients. Those with a history of long-term problem drinking are easy candidates for Candida infections that are often localized, such as vaginal and oral infections, and cause considerable amounts of discomfort. In some patients with

severely compromised defense systems (AIDS, burn and leukemia patients, prematurely born infants, those suffering from long bouts of emotional or physical stress), the yeast of Candidas can turn into a deadly pathogen and cause systemic infections. Few classes of drugs are effective against these fungal infections, and all of them have limitations with regard to efficacy and side effects.

Candida Related Complex can also be caused by excessive sugar intake. Excessive sugars in the diet, addiction to junk foods and simple/refined carbs, drug and alcohol addiction, and excessive use of broad-spectrum antibiotics are causing Candida cases to grow at an alarming rate in the modern world.

Those with mild to moderate Candida growth tend to get it under control naturally during the 8-week Krispy Klean detox, making additional nutriceutical supplementation unnecessary if they are faithful to the rest of the Program. However, anyone who experiences lingering health issues after their detox should look up Candida's many symptoms and if they suspect they may have it, get tested. You may contact our support line at support@the101program.com for assistance finding a qualified holistic healthcare practitioner that specializes in Candida.

Progression of Addicted Biochemistry

Alcoholism is commonly referred to as a "progressive" disease. This term promotes the idea that as a recovering drinker, you can never have another drink. The common belief is that because it is progressive, the dis-ease only gets worse, so a drink will always equal a drunk, for the rest of the recovering drinker's life. Conversely, the biochemical processes and the resulting damage that created the addiction can be completely healed and reversed in most cases. Using orthomolecular corrective practices and the present knowledge of the fundamental influences that affect the cells and create addictive biochemistry; the genetic potential and the environmental influences and conditions that bring life to the addiction, we are now able to successfully restore healthy cell bioenergetics and correct the addictive metabolism.

The conventional approach toward recovery which includes the absence of taking the initiative to heal alcohol's damage with targeted nutritional therapy (TNT), as well as removing

the environmental (diet and lifestyle) influences that caused the addiction, the progression theory is absolutely right; the condition is progressive and having just one drink is dangerous.

Many people would gasp at the idea of a former problem drinker being able to become a moderate drinker, but that is because – until recently – the process of actually healing the addiction was never offered. However, through the art and science of actually healing addictive biochemistry it has been demonstrated that if the once problem drinker addresses the damage before it is permanent, then moderation can be an option *for some*. Long-term alcohol abusers are capable of successfully completing The 101 Program and remaining abstinent, with no desire to return to drinking, while leading healthy and happy lives. Some have chosen drinking in moderation after completing the full program, and are able to do the same: lead healthy and happy lives, unencumbered by a battle with addiction. This program heals the addiction, returning the choice to drink or not to you… you are put back in the driver's seat when you heal your compulsive behavior and alcohol addiction. Complete abstinence or moderation are personal options that you must explore for yourself. One person who drinks to the point of such mental and physical damage that they can't achieve a complete cure does not dictate the lives of everyone who has ever abused alcohol.

Moving Forward

It is paramount to address your specific healthcare requirements as a former problem drinker. You have specific healthcare requirements that you need to implement in your recovery in order to cure the addiction which goes beyond just stopping the drinking. You need to heal the damage that has been done and balance your neuroendocrine system so that you can enjoy healthy brain chemistry. This will enable you to enjoy sobriety and live and cherish a full life, not endure it as an unending battle with addiction.

Roadmap to the Cure

- Withdrawal – the condictive diet and nutriceutical protocol provided in the appendix will get you through the initial

stages of detox with minimal discomfort. The majority of the symptoms will subside within a week.

- Detox – the Krispy Klean 8-week detox is the most comprehensive, aggressive detox for addiction and addictive biochemistry. It aids in clearing symptoms and accelerating the healing process. Many ailments that people did not even realize were alcohol toxicity-related disappear during this time.
- Therapeutic supplements aggressively correct cellular composition as well as biochemical deficiencies created by epigenetic influences and the damage caused by alcohol.
- The Program will heal the adrenals, GI, pancreas, thyroid, pituitary, and hypothalamus, and optimize the neuroendocrine system, which all work together in balancing brain chemistry.
- Correct hypoglycemia and sugar sensitivity and banish low blood sugar symptoms; curing cravings for sugars and refined carbohydrates.
- Adjust dietary practices to heal and avoid addictive biochemistry.
- Provide the nutritional components required by the organs to achieve optimal mental and physical health, via healthy levels and usage of all key neurotransmitters and hormones.
- Encourage natural endorphin and enkephalin production through nourishing the pituitary and hypothalamus and reducing enzymatic ingestion of these key neurotransmitters.
- Heal and regenerate the liver.
- Identify the metabolic disorders created by alcohol toxicity and learn how to use the tools that will heal them.

Healing and Curing the Addiction

What You Can Expect to Heal in Addition to the Addiction

- Hypoglycemia
- Brain and brain chemistry; mental disorders like anxiety, depression, despair, mental fatigue, mood swings, emotional instability, learning impairment, memory problems, hypertension, and paranoia.

- Heart disease and high blood pressure
- Hypothyroidism
- Accelerated aging process
- Diabetes
- Liver disease
- Skin disorders and eczema
- Impaired immune system
- Kidney, pancreas, adrenal, cerebral, intestinal and stomach damage

What Can Be Gained by Doing The 101 Program

- Freedom from addiction and addictive personality disorders
- Excellent health
- A sense of well being
- Elimination of cravings for alcohol and sugar
- Inspiration
- Optimism
- Energy
- Clarity
- Peace of mind
- Natural euphoria and joy
- Cerebral retention
- Weight loss and control
- Neurological health
- Focus

Goal: A Life Lived to the Fullest

Understanding the biochemical mechanics of addiction and knowing how it operates is a tremendous advantage for you in recovering your health and curing an addiction to alcohol. The 101 Program also gives you the opportunity to turn your problem drinking into a blessing that will set the stage for a happy and full life; a life lived unencumbered by addictive biochemistry or the social politics of alcohol abuse. Managing addictions requires an enormous amount of energy – energy that would be better spent participating in productive and fulfilling activities and making life more enriched and enjoyable. The process of healing this condition will deliver you to a state of enhanced health that most people never experience; this challenge can truly be a blessing. Millions of people live their lives only halfway because they don't

recognize that they are suffering from various mental and physical ailments; their mild condition never culminates in a way that is life or lifestyle threatening. Since their condition is not life threatening, they never respond to it or realize how much better life could be. These people live in a sort of purgatory, thinking that what they feel is normal because they can function in an outward way and appear to be fine on the surface. However, just underneath the surface lies despair, a feeling of being disconnected from others and the world, the inability to really open up to, and enjoy, life and most likely a lot of doctor visits. Clearly, they are not living to their full potential and embracing all the splendor of life.

Successful completion of The 101 Program will provide the opportunity to live your life to its full potential and experience the whole of the magnificent world in which you live.

Naturally Cleaning Up Your Life through Your Body

A depressed mind void of hope, joy, and peace will make choices and create situations in life that will serve only to reinforce the anguish, pain, loss, hopelessness, and misery in which it believes is its destiny because it can't see a way out beyond its present circumstance. It will leave behind a trail of missed opportunity; a result of a life half lived because you were too poisoned to see and manifest a better future. One who is chemically poisoned cannot achieve harmony with other people or their environment. The result is further anguish, anger, distress, emotional and physical pain, suffering, panic, destructive behavior, and disease. But when the poison that has been damaging your social and personal relationships and circumstances is removed, you will naturally choose healthier, more fulfilling ways of communicating and managing your interpersonal relationships. You will be one hundred percent capable of getting on the path to healthy relationships and personal success.

What you expect out of life and circumstances is the vehicle that will carry you through your journey in life and will deliver you to the destinations your belief system has mapped out for you. Thoughts and the belief system play a defining role both consciously and unconsciously in the experiences you choose and what you get out of them. Your

innermost thoughts create your expectations, expectations govern your behavior, and behavior creates the experiences you draw from what life has to offer, both good and bad. If you clean up your thoughts and open up your awareness and higher consciousness through healthy brain chemistry, you will naturally clean up your life.

A balanced mind and body chemistry is the foundation of the inspiration, strength, focus, and peace of mind that will keep you on your path to a healthy, joyful, and productive lifestyle. If you started drinking early in life you may not have experienced a balanced, healthy lifestyle as an adult. You may not have a mental picture of what you are like unencumbered by addiction. In this case, you will have an exhilarating experience as you come to know the life within you. The energy and inspiration that has been lying dormant will begin flooding into you as you progress through this program; you will come out of the fog of addiction feeling reborn. Those who do have memories of a vibrant time in their life have those memories to refer to for inspiration: times of health and the inspiration that comes with it, of close friendships, lots of fun and activity, good relations with family, witnessing goals come to fruition and desires manifest, personal and career objectives being met, and peace of mind. Everyone will discover a positive, inspired zest for life. As healing begins, your spiritual awareness will open and life will present itself in the majestic manner in which it was meant to be experienced.

Chapter Three

The 101 Program

Overview

Healing in Three Phases

The 101 Program is divided into three phases, which serve the healing process through detoxing, elimination and cleansing, nourishing, healing, and curing.

Phase One

The Krispy Klean Detox is an 8-week aggressive detoxification program that initiates the healing process that will ultimately cure the addiction. The fundamental components are a detoxifying condictive diet, and an aggressive targeted nutritional therapy (TNT) formula that will assist all biosystems in minimizing withdrawal symptoms, detoxifying every organ, providing the brain an abundance of the precursors required for healthy levels of key neurotransmitters known to be deficient in problem drinkers especially during detox, and maximizing nutritional composition to feed the enormous appetite of the healing process.

Phase Two

The Ark will take anywhere from 10 to 18 months. After a thorough detoxification, The Ark focuses on healing the organs that were damaged by alcohol toxicity, particularly those of the neuroendocrine system, and addressing epigenetic influences that set the stage for you to become addicted in the first place. The nutriceutical supplements required are significantly reduced when transitioning to The Ark stage of the program. During this phase, HPA axis testing is used to measure neuroendocrine function, and specifically brain chemistry (neurotransmitter and hormone levels), to provide information required to develop highly accurate targeted nutritional therapies that will directly address deficiencies in neurochemical levels that prevent healthy brain chemistry and bioenergetics. The Ark is

finished when you are able to produce healthy neurotransmitter levels on your own, and the endocrine system shows itself to be healed.

Phase Three

The Preserve & Protect phase is the maintenance program that starts after The Ark has been successfully completed. This is where the health you have created is maintained per your specific biochemical requirements and addictive biochemistry and alcohol addiction is a memory.

Phase One: Krispy Klean

The Krispy Klean Detox uses diet, nutriceuticals, exercise, and mind/body energy healing such as yoga and meditation to detox the body and mind. The goal is to heal the liver, ease withdrawal, establish healthy blood sugar, cleanse toxins from the bowel, blood, and GI, begin to balance the neuroendocrine system, and establish optimum brain neurotransmitter production and utilization. This is an extremely aggressive program that delivers you to the 'other side' of addiction quickly; generally participants lose all desire to drink within one or two weeks, and begin in that short period of time to feel better than they have felt in years, sometimes decades.

The Krispy Klean Detox includes a one-week "prep" period, a six-week detox (flush) period, and then a one-week deep detox (snow white). During this time, you will find yourself healing ill health conditions you would have never thought were due to alcohol damage and toxicity.

The Krispy Klean diet, therapeutic supplements, and exercise guidelines are specifically designed to:

- Minimize withdrawal.
- Provide a thorough deep tissue detoxification with focus on liver cleansing and support, and brain and endocrine system health.
- Begin healing the mind and body from the damage of long-term alcohol toxicity through practicing a condictive diet and employing targeted nutritional therapy (TNT). Mind/body energy healing techniques are explored per the interests of the program participant once healthy biochemical function is re-established.

- Heal the gastrointestinal tract; maximize thorough digestion and absorption of the complex carbs, proteins, and fats included in the diet.
- Cleanse the bowels by encouraging healthy elimination of waste; this minimizes opportunity for diseases and other ill-health conditions to manifest.
- Nourish and heal the pancreas, adrenals, pituitary, and hypothalamus.
- Obtain and maintain optimum stable blood sugar levels, to heal hypoglycemia and many other illnesses caused by elevated insulin.
- Begin to heal the known biological markers of addictive biochemistry in the brain, liver, and endocrine system.
- Balance the neuroendocrine system. Optimize brain chemistry by correcting damaged neurotransmitter and hormonal bioenergetics.
- Provide optimum conditions and precursors for natural production of neurotransmitters and hormones.
- Teach the practices of healthy dietary habits that must stay with you for a lifetime. Dietary guidelines are designed for optimum health, specifically meant to let the adrenals, pancreas, and liver rest, heal, and stabilize brain chemistry.
- Cure alcohol abuse and "dry-drunk" symptoms such as mental / physical fatigue, anxiety, poor cognitive performance, emotional lows and instability, depression, paranoia, agitation, nervousness and insomnia, in addition to the craving to drink.
- Encourage healthy spiritual, mental, and emotional existence.

Should you opt to enlist the services of AAAA and utilize the Comprehensive Services Package, during the Krispy Klean Detox you will also take the CBC Complete Blood Count which includes tests for kidney, thyroid, electrolyte, liver, cardiovascular health (cholesterol, triglycerides, and blood sugar); an FDLP test (Functional Liver Detoxification Profile); and the HPA brain chemistry test (Hypothalamus, Pituitary, Adrenal, which includes adrenal fatigue). These tests will help to pinpoint the specific organs and systems that have been most damaged and are in need of healing or correcting. They also provide functional neuroendocrine

performance information regarding neurotransmitter deficiencies and excesses so that an evidence-based targeted nutritional therapy can be provided that will quickly balance brain chemistry and correct metabolism disorders.

Phase Two: The Ark

The Ark module continues to optimize brain chemistry, heal the physical and mental damage caused by alcohol, correct errors in general metabolism, rebuild and strengthen the liver, and reverse addictive biochemistry.

This phase continues where The Detox left off, lasting anywhere from 10 to 18 months, and provides the body with all the essential nutritional support it requires in milder therapeutic quantities to continue nourishing and balancing the neuroendocrine system. Use of supplements are diminished to a very targeted few that address only the exact deficiencies found in brain chemistry, liver, and blood testing. As the body heals and the condictive, whole foods, nutrient rich diet is practiced, the brain is provided all the necessary nutrients and conditions to begin producing healthy brain chemistry which translates to healthy states of mind and freedom from addictive biochemistry, therefore supplementation can be reduced to answer only to the fine tunings required as exposed by the tests.

Fish, meat, and dairy that were restricted during the detox are allowed back into the diet at this time if you choose, however all sweets and refined carbs are generally avoided, being enjoyed in extreme moderation.

Components of The Ark include:

- A personalized Ark TNT protocol
- Protein shake
- Continuing with the dietary guidelines of the Krispy Klean diet, with the optional addition of fish, lean meats, and raw dairy foods.
- Liver health – continued renewal of the liver
- Nutritional focus on brain and endocrine system – healing organs of the neuroendocrine system and balancing the HPA axis, so eventually the brain is entirely capable of naturally balancing itself.

- Correcting addictive brain chemistry -- providing all nutritional precursors required for optimum neurochemical health while the neuroendocrine system heals and stabilizes
- Continued stabilization of blood glucose levels
- Cardiovascular health
- Continued healing of all physical and psychological symptoms that result from long-term alcohol abuse
- Enhanced general physical, psychological, and emotional well being

NOTE: While alcohol detoxification and the initial stages of healing can be generalized for most everyone during the Krispy Klean Detox unless there is a specific health issue to address, the Ark phase should be personalized for maximum efficacy. It is highly suggested that if you didn't do The 101 Program Comprehensive program that you have a metabolic panel, Pyroluria, and HPA brain chemistry test done so that you may have a personalized, supremely effective protocol created for you.

Healing is absolutely enhanced and accelerated with the use of targeted nutritional supplementation. If you have been suffering alcohol addiction for any substantial length of time, you are in a healing crisis and your neuroendocrine system and other supportive organs are in a state of deficiency in dire need of the nutrients required for it to heal. And since your deficiencies are unique, your nutritional therapy should be as well to address those areas that need the help the most, in an aggressive way that will pull you out from under the oppression of the addiction as quickly as possible. Having the tests done and a personalized protocol prepared not only accelerates the healing process by ensuring deficiencies are being addressed and damage is being healed, but serves to save money in the long run because targeting your specific condition will mean that you save time and money that might have been wasted on unnecessary supplements. The efficacy of your treatment is enhanced considerably because you are benefiting from supplements that answer directly to your nutritional requirements which are validated through testing. Targeted nutritional therapy during the Ark phase is key in reaching the ultimate goal of changing the fundamental body

chemistry from an addictive one to a non-addictive, healthy one.

A minimum of 10 months is recommended for The Ark module; any extended stay in this phase is an individual choice. The degree of your physical and mental damage, and the depth of alcohol involvement in your lifestyle, is what you must take into consideration when determining how long to stay on The Ark. How long, how much, and how often you drink, how much damage you have to heal, how difficult withdrawal was, how strong your association to alcohol is, and how your body processes alcohol and simple carbs are all factors that must be weighed when establishing a realistic individual timeline for The Ark module. You should establish that your endocrine system is healed and that you have naturally balanced brain chemistry before moving on to the maintenance phase. This could be established by HPA testing or by discontinuing all supplements and monitoring mental function and mood. If all is well, then one can confidently move on to the Preserve and Protect maintenance phase.

Everyone must employ the methods The 101 Program promotes to heal the physical and psychological damage inflicted by alcohol, since that damage is the one thing that all problem drinkers share. Alcohol's method of injuring critical organs and biosystems to cause the addiction and the illnesses that follow is not selective. However, recovery and reaping the benefits of the enhanced health The 101 Program encourages has a different physical, emotional, mental, and spiritual time frame for everyone. Over the years, as alcohol embeds itself into your daily routine, it becomes your "go to"; you gradually stop turning to the activities you once did for enjoyment, relaxation, and fulfillment. The habit of going to alcohol for relaxation, good and bad times, or to occupy idle time needs to be replaced with the personal activities you enjoy and by which you are enriched. You also need to allow yourself the time to learn how to manage your biochemistry and build a healthier lifestyle, and to then embed that healthiness in your lifestyle as alcohol was once embedded. Staying on The Ark phase for 10 months after the detox phase is a good minimum for a person who feels that alcohol is a moderate problem. But this stage can take up to 18 months for the person who has been fostering a chronic problem for

some time, and is experiencing moderate to severe alcohol toxicity-related illness.

Going into the Ark phase, many adverse health conditions that you might have been experiencing should have disappeared entirely or be rapidly subsiding. Most people have no idea that alcohol toxicity could be the genesis of their daily aches and pains, as well as hundreds of other serious health conditions. The standard Westerner does not see the link between diet, toxic assault, and health, so they consider it to be a miracle when disease and discomfort suddenly disappear due to a simple correction in the diet. The beginning of The Ark phase is a good time for you to take inventory of your physical, psychological and emotional health. If you feel that you have lingering health issues in any of these areas that need to be addressed, you might want to move forward in finding a holistic or integrative practitioner for help. However, if health issues have begun clearing up as a result of detox, you will most likely heal entirely given adequate time in The Ark.

Phase Three: Preserve & Protect

Upon completion of The Ark, the body and mind are in excellent condition, addictive biochemistry is healed, symptoms are gone, and only a maintenance program is required to maintain health and protect you from recreating addictive biochemistry. This maintenance program is the Preserve & Protect phase. The Preserve & Protect module is simple: you continue to employ the mechanics of the healthy lifestyle that you've created for yourself while staying on the condictive biochemistry diet of predominately whole foods and taking a few supplements that will preserve and protect the enhanced health you have achieved. Because the Ark phase has accomplished so much healing, your biochemistry has changed and is now non-addictive and in good shape, so another HPA and metabolic test should be taken to adjust your TNT. Unless there is an unrelated health issue or something outstanding that requires special attention, supplementation should be reduced to general good nutrition (multi vitamin, natural minerals, fish oil, and excellent anti-oxidant support), liver support and protection, and blood sugar regulation.

Preserve & Protect supplements provided in a TNT protocol provide a broad-based nutritional program styled to maintain enhanced health for those that have demonstrated addictive biochemistry. A full-spectrum, food-based multivitamin should be provided because even those with excellent dietary habits get into ruts, eating similar foods over long periods, which potentially causes nutritional deficiencies. Also, due to commercial farming methods that no longer focus on maintaining the structural and nutritional integrity of produce much of the nutritional value of foods has disappeared and been replaced with toxins that further deplete the body which justifies a multivitamin supplement. A full-spectrum, naturally balanced, bioavailable mineral supplement is necessary for the same reasons a multivitamin is, and because due to the fact that we bath in chlorinated, denatured water (as opposed to lakes rich in minerals); most of us don't drink from wells anymore, and the soil used to grow produce is depleted by pollution, pesticides, and not being rotated properly, all of us suffer various degrees of mineral deficiencies. Fish oil is necessary because the Omega 3 to 6 ratios are dangerously imbalanced in industrial nations and the benefits of Omega 3 oils are a must for one that has demonstrated addictive biochemistry for brain, liver, and general health. Anti-oxidant support is included because no matter how well you take care of yourself, unfortunately, we still live in an environment which causes us to absorb and ingest not only hundreds of pollutants every day but the cross contamination factor once they are in our body is alarming. Anti-oxidants fight the good fight, keeping cells protected from an overload of free-radicals that deplete the cell's vitality while damaging and ultimately killing them.

This is the time during The 101 Program in which you can, if you want, test drive drinking in moderation. It is also the time when you may begin to occasionally have a dessert if you wish, or try coffee with prudence. I advise against including any potent mind altering substance such as sugar or caffeine in your diet daily because of the adaptation / addiction potential it poses, so only one cup of coffee should be enjoyed a couple of times a week or every other day in the morning on a full stomach. Coffee is extremely hard on the endocrine system, and particularly the adrenals; healthy adrenals are paramount in maintaining a well-earned non-addictive

biochemistry so it is important to be extremely prudent with stimulants.

Preserve & Protect Formula

A targeted Preserve & Protect formula is prepared to:

- Provide continued support for detoxing and eliminating endogenous and exogenous toxins (including environmental pollutants) to avoid the health issues that can manifest from toxic buildup.
- Encourage regeneration of liver cells by providing particular support for the liver.
- Target the known metabolic weaknesses of those who have a predisposition for addictive biochemistry, and ensure that they are properly nourished in order to maintain optimum endocrine function, nutrient utilization, and brain chemistry.
- Apply particular support for sufficient endorphin and serotonin levels.
- Help gently feed and balance brain chemistry through encouraging synthesis of serotonin, beta-endorphins, GABA and enkephalins and maximizing their effectiveness through inhibiting enzymes known to digest them.
- Provide general health nourishment so that this is the only supplement program needed.
- Stimulate the immune system.
- Help maintain healthy blood sugar.

Three Ways to do The 101 Program

- The 101 Program Comprehensive Services Package
- The 101 As Is Method
- The 101 Custom Services Package

Please see chapter 6, Krispy Klean Detox Instructions, for detailed, week by week, directions for completing the initial two month Krispy Klean Detox.

The 101 Program Comprehensive Services Package

Please contact info@the101program.com for more information on this very valuable resource.

Note: Details of all blood, urine, and saliva tests taken are found in Chapter Five, "Lab Tests". The tests are a very exciting element of The 101 Program because they expose exact values from liver, brain, and endocrine functions that provide concrete evidence regarding the extent of damage you suffer in these areas as well as the functional health of these organs. The information these tests provide is used to develop a personalized, informed, and accurate targeted nutritional therapy that directly addresses your specific requirements for healing the damaged organs and their metabolic functions. These tests are also exciting because they take the mystery out of the process and give you very real, evidence-based, information regarding your health and what must be done to be healthy again which includes achieving freedom from addiction.

Should you choose to enlist AAAA's services and pay the tuition for The 101 Program Comprehensive Services package, AAAA will send out the Functional Liver Detoxification Profile (FLDP), and HPA (hypothalamic/pituitary/adrenal) test collection kits and the Krispy Klean Detox formula supplement package for the 8-week detox. AAAA will also locate a nearby lab and arrange to have a blood draw done for the Complete Wellness – CBC blood test at your convenience. AAAA will email intake forms to inquire about your health history, drinking habit, current symptoms, and family health. After the intake forms are completed and returned, an initial phone consultation will be scheduled. The result of this consultation is a personalized "roadmap" similar to The 101 Program Roadmap to Recovery given in this chapter; however, this one will be personalized with specific instructions for moving forward providing for personal health and dietary issues, or lifestyle requirements. Many long-term problem drinkers are on antidepressants and since they are toxic drugs that harm physical and mental health and actually stand between you and the type of enhanced mental and physical health The 101 Program promotes, we will work with you to personalize your program,

depending on which drugs you are on and how long you have been on them, to safely discontinue them during the beginning stages of the detox. This program is so accurate in aggressively balancing brain chemistry naturally that when provided the extra layer of care required to get off of anti-depressants, most participants are stabilized by the third week of their program, and begin enjoying natural healthy states of mind and perspective.

Once the initial consultation and roadmap to recovery are provided, you will determine a start date, which is when you begin the 101 Prep Week. During the third week of the program, after your Complete Wellness and FLDP results are in, you will be contacted for a second consultation. This consultation is provided to share the results of the tests and the insights they provide toward your health and, if necessary, modifications that should be made to favorably respond to the results. These modifications are made because potential health issues learned from the test results may require immediate attention and cannot wait until the CBC and Functional Liver Detox Profile test results are ultimately used in combination with your HPA test results after the detox to design your personalized nutritional protocol for The Ark module.

At the end of the Krispy Klean Detox, after the Snow White fast, you will discontinue all supplements and reintroduce organic, lean meats, fish, and dairy into your diet. On the eighth day, you will take the HPA test (saliva and urine) and send the results in. After AAAA has received the results, you will receive notice that your HPA test has been evaluated, and a personalized nutritional protocol prepared answering to excesses and deficiencies exposed in your CBC, FLDP, and HPA tests. This personalized nutriceutical protocol addresses all information gleaned from your intake forms, symptom charts, consultations, progress, and from the tests regarding neuroendocrine, brain chemistry, liver, metabolic, and cardiovascular health. At this time you will also receive a detailed report exposing the results of your HPA test regarding dopamine, glutamate, serotonin, GABA, norepinephrine, epinephrine, cortisol, and DHEA levels. A complete explanation of the results and their impact on your physical and psychological/emotional health is provided. This customized protocol will address all deficiencies and

conditions that warrant concern found in these results, focusing specifically on healing addictive biochemistry and curing alcohol addition. A final consultation will be scheduled when the protocol has been prepared, to go over results, provide directions for the personalized Ark protocol, and answer any questions you may have regarding results or the program going forward.

The 101 Program Comprehensive Services Package includes:

- Initial phone consultation
- Complete 8-week Krispy Klean Detox Formula Package
- FLDP test (Functional Liver Detoxification Profile)
- Complete Wellness (CBC) blood test
- Second phone consultation to translate Complete Wellness (CBC) and FLDP test results
- Third consultation to prepare you for the fast and for your brain chemistry (HPA) test.
- HPA test (serotonin, dopamine, glutamate, GABA, norepinephrine, epinephrine, cortisol, and DHEA); includes Adrenal Fatigue testing (cortisol)
- Fourth phone consultation to translate HPA and Adrenal Fatigue test results. Full disclosure of test results and their impact on your health and the part they play in your symptoms and addictive biochemistry is provided.
- Personalized Nutriceutical Protocol that is prepared for the 10- to 18-month Ark module.
- Free download of Genita Petralli's lecture "Addictive Biochemistry: The Biochemical Solution for the Biochemical Epidemic."

The 101 As Is Method

Another option is The 101 As Is method. Choosing to do the program in this way, you will follow The 101 Program Roadmap to Recovery provided in this book, forgoing the benefits of laboratory testing, nutritional and program counseling, and personalized therapeutic nutritional therapy (TNT). The instructions for the Krispy Klean Detox are provided in detail in Chapter 6 so that anyone using the As Is method can successfully complete the basic 101 Program on their own.

Approximately a week before you plan to begin the 7-day Prep Week of the Krispy Klean Detox, you will have to purchase the Krispy Klean Detox Formula supplements. Information regarding purchasing supplements for the 8 week detox is provided in The 101 Program Formulas section below.

The Custom Services Package

AAAA offers HPA (brain chemistry), metabolic, functional liver, histamine, pyroluria, and other addictive biochemistry profile testing to obtain health information required to prepare personalized targeted nutritional therapies (TNT). This option allows you to pick and choose among the services offered in The 101 Program Comprehensive Services package. Many who suffer from any addiction (including sugar and carbs), depression, bipolar disorders, anxiety and panic attacks, and even schizophrenia have used these services to balance brain chemistry, correct their metabolism, and free them from their suffering permanently. We also help patients get off of psychotropic drugs (antidepressants), anxiolytics (anxiety meds) and stimulants (Ritalin etc.). Because we are passionately and politically opposed to their use, the pharma-cartel that is producing them, and the white collar drug pushers prescribing them, we do this at a minimal fee. If you are interested in this service you should contact AAAA at info@the101program.com to speak to a Program Coach about scheduling an initial consultation to determine what services you should consider and a roadmap to recovery for your specific needs. This service also includes those psychotropic medications given to children and even deeper discounts are provided for parents helping their children off of them.

The 101 Program Formulas

The Krispy Klean Detox formula for The 101 Program is included in The 101 Program 8-Week Comprehensive Services Package. If you choose to do the As Is method it may be purchased prepackaged at http://the101program.com/KK_detox.html. You may also purchase the supplements at most health food stores or on the internet. The current formula and its corresponding dosage chart is in the appendix. However, it is strongly advised to purchase them through AAAA.

AAAA and The 101 Program are key contributors to the research that is further developing the effectiveness of orthomolecular treatments and work intimately with the scientific community to stay current with their latest research. AAAA is always researching methods to minimize the amount of supplements (capsule count) and maximize efficacy with advances in research, supplement combinations, use of herbs, as well as ways to use liquid supplements as they are developed. The 101 Program Krispy Klean Detox formula will be modified as the most recent research dictates, so that program participants will be receiving a therapy based on the most advanced findings and clinical studies. For this reason, contents and pricing may vary. You will receive the most up to date protocol and its corresponding dosage chart and directions with your AAAA order.

AAAA does not mark the items up, we simply do not pass the wholesale 10% discount we receive on to the participant in order to pay the counselors who order, package, and ship your program products to you. AAAA provides this service to make the program as easy as possible for you to get started.

Therapeutic Nutriceuticals

The Krispy Klean formula is an aggressive therapeutic formula, which requires many nutrients. It provides the depth of nutritional support needed by those addicted to alcohol for an efficient detox with minimal symptoms, stabilized blood sugar, support for a severely compromised neuroendocrine system, and achievement of the healing that The 101 Program provides. This will quickly get you "on the other side" of your addiction, and functioning in a healthy manner. The time frame by which this program provides these rewards is phenomenal. The Krispy Klean Nutritional Protocol is a scientifically developed, intelligently targeted nutriceutical protocol that effectively addresses each biosystem that has been damaged by alcohol abuse. Since alcohol damages the liver, brain, endocrine, and cardiovascular systems, the initial detox and healing supplement protocol requires nutritional supplements to answer to the extensive damage therein, and particularly to the neuroendocrine system; the home of the addiction. For this reason, the Krispy Klean Detox formula is quite

comprehensive requiring many products which all work together toward the same biochemical goals.

A personalized Ark module supplement protocol is typically 60% to 75% smaller in capsule count than that of the Krispy Klean, because after the detox your nutritional support no longer requires minimizing withdrawal and assisting efficient radical detoxification. The Ark specifically focuses on correcting brain chemistry, uprooting addictive biochemistry, and replacing it with healthy biochemistry.

Personalized Ark and Preserve & Protect formulas are about equal to the number of supplements a health-conscious person living in today's world would consume daily. The difference is that these nutrients are designed specifically to heal and balance the neuroendocrine system of someone who has demonstrated addictive biochemistry with alcohol, and to continue healing and protection of all the biosystems known to suffer from alcohol damage.

About Supplements

As with any product, there are great, good, and mediocre supplements available on the market. Also, different forms of the same supplements provide different results and facilitate different biochemical responses. It is important to avoid modifying the recommended supplements unless instructed to do so by a *holistic* professional trained in addictive biochemistry and the use of nutritional supplements for healing.

The number one thing you must be concerned with when purchasing supplements is to be sure you are not purchasing them from a company owned in any way by a pharmaceutical company. Pharmaceutical companies have been very unethical competitors of supplement companies and figured out a while ago that while they wait for their influence in government to have your right to supplements taken away from you, the best way to win the war on health would be to buy the supplement companies. Now this sounds fairly benign on the surface, however, it is suspected, and it would not be beyond their history of unethical activity that they are weakening the strength of their supplements and using fillers etc. that ultimately make the supplement entirely ineffective. This is a wonderful strategy for them because they get top dollar for crude product, while at the same time are tainting

the reputation of holistic medicine and targeted nutritional therapy for healing dis-ease. No one is going to get better taking these products so they will discontinue use, lose faith in targeted nutritional replenishment for dis-ease, and run off to the doctor for their toxic drugs. So before you buy your next bottle of supplements, do your homework and make sure that the company demonstrates ethical political involvement in the holistic industry, is using the best sources of nutrients available (organic, virgin sources), and their product regularly goes through independent testing. I've included a few good companies that not only provide excellent nutritional products, but are very politically active in protecting your rights to their use and holistic medicine.

You should not go to a pharmacy or supermarket to buy supplements. You don't want to give them your money; they have been making a lot of money peddling products that cause dis-ease and death for quite some time, and you don't want to reward them for this with your hard earned cash and continue feeding the pig that is inhaling our health and lying to the public to accomplish that. In fact, now that people are becoming wise to the lies and the threat their products impose on our health, and have begun to stop buying their weapons of mass destruction, drug companies are having laws passed to force their drugs into our bodies!

On the interpersonal level, a pharmacy is not as fun or educational as shopping at places like Whole Foods, Wild Oats, Erewhon, or any of the local or mom-and-pop health food stores; along with the supplements, places like this offer the organic whole fruits, grains, and vegetables you should be eating. These stores also post community activities that may interest people pursuing a healthy lifestyle and offer ways of finding others to enjoy it with. It is an entirely different experience shopping at a health food store than a supermarket or pharmacy, and I strongly recommend that you learn to enjoy exploring these venues.

While whole foods and organic produce can be slightly more expensive (depending on how you shop), and the supplements will increase the weekly food budget, the money you save on alcohol will null that cost, if not actually save you money. Regarding the cost of organic foods, I would like to note here that a recent study was done on the cost of buying organic verses commercial "food" (industrial denatured

products) by a naturopathic student, and she actually saved $1.22 feeding her family of three for a week (please visit www.mercola.com for full story). She did price comparisons for 3 meals a day and 2 snacks, serving for serving; ounce for ounce. One important fact that was not brought up in this study is that those who eat whole foods eat less calories because they do not suffer from "false hunger" produced by low blood sugar and insulin resistance- so you will save even more while enjoying the health that comes with eating fewer calories naturally without dieting and those calories coming from nutrient rich sources.

Regardless of the money you save not buying alcohol, shopping wisely, and eating less, sometimes the fact is that in this day and age health can be expensive. The government subsidizes dis-ease because there is money in treating it and the government is run by companies that profit from those treatments. Health, on the other hand is expensive because it is not subsidized by the government because there is no profit in it, and so it nearly always must come out of pocket. Health also leads to you enjoying more years on social security which is a big problem for the government's profit machines. Also, please keep in mind that there is no profit in a cure for any disease so that is not the focus of mainstream medicine which is run by pharmaceutical companies. There is profit only in treating disease, not curing it and those treatments are now being recognized to be more often the cause of death than the disease itself.   Treating is nothing more than a very expensive stroll to the cemetery and this has even been recognized by many doctors and prominent members of the AMA! Iatrogenic illness (illness resulting from medical treatment such as pharmaceutical/psychiatric drugs, hospitalization) is the leading cause of death in America. "In the Journal of the American Medical Association, Dr. Barbara Starfield wrote an article revealing that from conservative estimates the practice of medicine is responsible for the third leading cause of death in the U.S. Because this was a conservative report, Gary Null (www.garynull.com) and a team of doctors decided to make a complete listing of all the deaths that arise from medical treatment. He found that rather than it being the third leading cause of death, iatrogenic illness is the first leading cause of death with over three quarters a million people dying a year from medical

treatment. Why this is relevant is because what this really reflects is a point of logic; if medicine really knew what it was doing, it wouldn't be that lethal" [6]

Preventative costs are never as expensive as the cost of the diseases that result from drug and alcohol abuse and bad, denatured diets. You can't put a price on enhanced health, and all the opportunities a healthy mind and body will create. Eating healthy means you are re-purposing the money you were once using to slowly kill yourself to now enjoying life with excellent health and foods that are good for you and taste great, so you should not resist this program or the health edicts it rests upon because of cost. You will be getting the most out of life because you feel great, and will have that much more of it to enjoy in your later years. No one can put a price on another day, year, or decade of quality life.

---

[6] Dr. Bruce Lipton, Ph.D., The Wisdom of Your Cells. www.soundstrue.com

Chapter Four

Detoxifying and Healing the Liver

The liver has two ways of detoxifying and removing unwanted toxins from the body; they are referred to as Phase I and Phase II. Phase I involves chemically altering harmful toxins through oxidation, hydrolysis, or reduction processes to make them less harmful. The result of these processes produces free radicals that must be nullified and removed from the liver by Phase II. If there is not a sufficient supply of antioxidants such as vitamin C, E, NAC, catechins etc. to efficiently carry out Phase II detoxification, serious health issues can arise. The toxic chemicals that free radicals can produce while awaiting removal from the liver by Phase II can be converted into far more harmful substances than the original toxin, such as cancer-causing carcinogens. However, far before cancer becomes a problem, the toxins or their metabolites that are not efficiently broken down and modified for removal via the bile will negatively impact the function of cells, injure tissues, or possibly damage RNA and DNA. All of these effects can and usually do result in many other illnesses and dis-eases throughout the body.

Phase II alters the toxin by utilizing the conjugation pathways, which adds a small molecule to the toxic compound. In order for these two processes to work efficiently, though, adequate key vitamins, minerals, amino acids, and EFAs must be available to assist each step involved in the process of detoxification. Important molecules for Phase II conjugation include glutathione, sulphate, glycine, acetate, cysteine, and glucuronic acid.

Phase I and II Detox

Combined, Phase I and II reactions make the toxin more polar, or water-soluble so that it can be easily excreted through the urine or bile. This biotransformation process is required for numerous toxins, including:

- Enterotoxins (potentially toxic chemicals endogenously generated by gut bacteria)

- Endobiotics (intermediate/end products of normal metabolism/hormones, enzymolysis etc.)
- Exotoxins (ingested, inhaled, and absorbed toxic chemicals – commonly known as xenobiotics)

Your ability to efficiently detox these chemicals and toxins depends on your diet, environment, emotional/psychological health, lifestyle, and genetic strengths and weaknesses. Biochemical detoxification pathways can be enhanced, slowed down, or even disabled depending on many environmental and nutritional factors. Beyond genetic influences, lifestyle, nutritional composition, and regular detoxification are key factors in determining someone's ability to efficiently rid the body of externally introduced toxins and built-up metabolic waste. Regular detoxing ensures that these pathways are "cleaned out" and waste is removed on a deep cellular level.

Balancing Phase I and II

It is extremely important that you detoxify your body efficiently, intelligently, and safely. The key to accomplishing this is balancing Phase I and II pathways.

Phase I and II run at different speeds
- If Phase I is too slow, the individual will experience a buildup of toxic waste in the blood, which will be distributed to all organs of the body.
- If Phase I is too fast, there will be a buildup of toxic intermediaries in the liver. This can lead to accelerated cell damage in the liver and is a very dangerous condition.
- If Phase II is too slow, which is usually a result of shortages of sulfur, N-acetyl cysteine, methionine, and other key cofactors, a buildup of toxins will occur in the liver, creating similar unfavorable conditions and health risks as those associated with Phase I functioning to fast.

Different toxins must be broken down and eliminated via different detoxification pathways. In order to do an intelligent and efficient liver detoxification, it is absolutely necessary to get a Functional Liver Detoxification Profile test. This test will "challenge" the six primary liver detox pathways with substances that test their specific abilities by measuring what is present in the saliva and urine after

taking the challenge substances. The test results provide the crucial information required to determine the exact nutritional and dietary support you will need to efficiently and safely detox and heal your liver.

It is not wise to do a detox without this information, and can actually be harmful. For instance, green tea, a popular detox aid, will induce Cytochrome P450 enzymes, causing Phase I to function faster. If you are deficient in any amino acid or co-factor vitamin required for efficient Phase II function, you could be causing more damage than good since toxic intermediate metabolites will build up in the liver. Conversely, if your Phase I detoxification is too slow already and you use cayenne pepper as a detox aid, or allow it in your diet, you will further inhibit Phase I and cause it to function even more slowly. This will cause toxins to re-circulate throughout the blood and wreak havoc on all vulnerable tissues and organs in the body.

For this reason, everyone doing The 101 Program is encouraged to get the FDLP test done to ensure a safe and supremely effective detox. See Chapter 5, "Lab Tests", for more details.

Phase I Too Slow

If Phase I detoxification is too slow, toxins will accumulate in the bloodstream and cause cellular damage in any vulnerable areas they find. Oral contraceptives, heavy metal exposure, large amounts of sugar, and hydrogenated fats will slow Phase I down. These substances actually change the DNA of the liver cells, causing reduced production of the detoxification enzymes. This slows down and in some cases halts the process of breaking down and eliminating harmful toxins. Some substances that can slow Phase I are glycoside (found in grapefruit juice), antihistamines, capsicum (substance in hot peppers that makes them hot), any drug containing anti-depressants and Valium, cloves, and turmeric.

Phase I Too Fast

If Phase I breaks toxins down too quickly for Phase II to properly rid the body of the intermediates produced, a buildup of toxic intermediates will develop, generating free radicals.

These toxins can be more dangerous than the original toxins. The two organs that are initially most vulnerable to the damage inflicted by these intermediate molecules are the liver and brain. Alcohol, cigarettes, and other carcinogens are known to speed up Phase I without having the same effect in Phase II detoxification pathways. These carcinogens also re-circulate toxic poisons throughout the liver, blood stream, and other vital organs (no wonder smokers' and drinkers' skin wrinkles prematurely and the aging process is accelerated).

Combining alcohol with other drugs is extremely dangerous and harmful to the liver. An example is when alcohol (which speeds up Phase I) is combined with a commonly used and seemingly harmless drug, acetaminophen. During this combination, a dangerously toxic intermediate compound is created during Phase I called n-acetyl-p-benzoquinoneimine (NAPQI). If Phase II is slow to react, this intermediate toxin sits in the liver for an extended period of time, potentially causing serious damage.

Substances that induce Phase I include St John's Wort, Echinacea, licorice, HRT, and green tea (the catechins in green tea are extremely powerful antioxidants). Alcohol and cigarettes also induce Phase I, so those with sluggish Phase II detoxification pathways are at a greater risk for accelerated liver damage if they use these substances.

Seriously compromised Phase I and II liver function accompanies heavy alcohol use, so it is very important for you to get tested so that both phases can be nutritionally assisted and regulated with an evidence-based protocol, effectively removing the toxins and their intermediates, while healing damaged cells and generating new cell growth.

Liver Detox Pathways and Supportive Nutrients Phase I Regulation

Below are the primary nutritional constituents of the Phase I detoxification pathways in the liver. Liver function may be impaired if any one, or a combination of these, are not available. I have adapted this list from Dr. Sandra Cabot's information-rich website, www.liverdoctor.com.

- B2, B3, B12, and folate
- Glutathione (glycine, glutamine, and cysteine or NAC)

- Branched chain amino acids (leucine, isoleucine, and valine)
- Selenium
- Vitamins C, E, and Coenzyme Q10
- Bioflavonoids (quercetin, green tea catechin, silymarin, and Ginkgo)
- Naringenin is used to slow Phase I if it is too fast.

Intermediate Stage

The intermediate stage between Phase I and II is extremely important to support. It is always a good idea for you to provide your body with ample antioxidants to minimize free radical damage and support the system in case processes aren't functioning at their best, even if they seem to be healthy. These antioxidants will help prevent liver cellular damage caused by the free radicals produced between Phase I and II. Helpful antioxidants include Vitamins A, C, and E, Coenzyme Q10, zinc, selenium, magnesium, and manganese.

Phase II Regulation

Impaired Phase II functions will provide ample opportunity for free radical damage within the liver, making it extremely vulnerable to cellular damage and disease. This also provides opportunity for many illnesses, since all organs depend on a healthy liver for proper functioning. Decreased energy levels are a common symptom of impaired Phase II.

Below are the primary nutritional constituents of the Phase II detoxification pathways in the liver. If any one, or a combination of these, are not provided in necessary quantities, liver function will be impaired. I have adapted this list from Dr. Sandra Cabot's information-rich website, www.liverdoctor.com.

- Glutathionation – N-acetyl cysteine, glutamine, and glycine produces glutathione in the body. Selenium, B6, B12, folate, Carnosol, camosic acid (rosemary), curcumin (may inhibit phase I- use only when phase I is normal), and Indole-3-Carbinol
- Sulphation – sulphur-containing amino acids (cysteine, cystine, methionine, and taurine), vitamin A, protein rich diet, garlic, onions, and sodium sulphate

- Glucuronidation – calcium d-glucerate, magnesium, and essential fatty acids
- Glycination – glycine, glutamine, gluceronic acid, ornithine, and arginine
- Glycine - glutamine, arginine, ornithine and taurine

NOTE: Methyl donors (methionine conjugation) such as TMG, folic acid, and adenoslcobalamin support biotransformation of homocysteine into methionine.

Gastrointestinal Restoration

Everyone accumulates waste and needs to detox. The amount of waste and bacteria someone has built up over the years depends on their diet, lifestyle, the conditions of their environment, and the extent of their drinking habit. Accumulated harmful amounts of waste inhibit efficient absorption of nutrients and proper elimination, and cause bacterial overgrowth and possibly leaky gut syndrome. Bowel cleansing is a required process of The 101 Program for this reason; no detox will be successful without a thorough cleansing of the lower intestines and the bowels.

The basic ingredients required for two bowel cleansings are provided in the Krispy Klean Detox Formula; one takes place during the second week of the program, and one during the eighth week.

Colonic Irrigation

While doing The Krispy Klean Detox, you should also begin a series of three colonics, beginning in the third week of The Program at the start the parasite cleanse. One colonic a week for three weeks will achieve the best results. Adhering to a cleansing diet at the same time means you will meet with even greater success in achieving a deep cleanse, detoxification of the bowels, and removal of dead parasites, fungi, and bad bacteria from the body.

For a visual of how impacted and toxic the intestines and bowels can become from bad diets, accumulated waste and sedentary lifestyles go to http://curezone.com/image_gallery/bowelcleanse.

Parasite Cleanse

A parasite cleanse will begin on the first day of the third week of the Krispy Klean Detox. It is essential that you do this, since it is estimated that 80% to 95% of people in the USA have parasites. Parasites are energy suckers, increase appetite, are the cause for many ailments and illnesses, encourage addictive biochemistry, and increase cravings for sweets and simple or refined carbs. Below are the ingredients required for the parasitic cleanse.

- Clove
- Black Walnut
- Wormwood
- *Arginine
- *Ornithine

Dr. Clark of http://curezone.com has prepared a liquid tincture of clove, black walnut, and wormwood for the parasite cleanse she recommends. The recommended extra strong Clarkia tincture can be purchased at http://drclarkia.com. Dosage instructions can be found at http://drclarkia.com/dosage.asp. The best way to go about doing the cleanse is with the 14-day method of progressively increasing the dosage to 20 drops three times a day, and then maintaining 20 drops three times a day until the tincture runs out, up to three weeks. On the first day of the sixth week, you will begin your liver flush and should discontinue the parasite tincture. Information about parasites and the importance of getting rid of them can also be found at Dr. Clark's parasite cleanse link at http://curezone.com/clark/parasites.asp.

Liver and Gallbladder Stone Flush

Immediately following the parasite cleanse, on the first day of the sixth week, you will begin the liver and gallbladder stone flush. This process takes two days only, and the benefits are innumerable. People are always surprised at how many stones they release. Stones in the liver and gallbladder inhibit proper function of these organs, and can accumulate to the point of causing serious health issues in addition to the common gallbladder infection. Many times,

gallbladders are removed due to accumulation of stones: an unnecessary process, since a stone flush can be performed in combination with the right diet and select nutritional support, in order to bring the gallbladder back to healthy functioning. Cleansing the liver of stones dramatically improves digestion, which is fundamental to excellent health.

For the problem drinker, stones are extremely dangerous; they block bile flow and prevent it from removing the excessive toxins created by the metabolism of alcohol. Left to increase in size and accumulate waste in the liver, the stones will accelerate damage and the onset of inflammation. Hepatitis and many other undesirable liver conditions like a sluggish and fatty liver can lead to cirrhosis.

For complete instructions on the liver and gallbladder stone flush, go to http://curezone.com/cleanse/liver/default.asp. Throughout the day before the liver flush, you should drink five glass of water with a tablespoon of Bragg's apple cider vinegar to help soften the stones.

Ingredients for the liver and gallbladder stone flush include:

1/2 Cup Olive Oil Extra Virgin (1.25 dl)
*3 lemons
4 tablespoons EPSOM salts ($MgSO_4 + 7H_2O$)
3 cups water (750 dl)

*On the http://curezone.com website grapefruit and freshly pressed apple juice are suggested as options along with lemon. While taking part in a detoxification program, you should use lemon or apple juice. Grapefruit is an excellent fruit to have in your diet once you are healthy; it has many beneficial, cancer-fighting properties and is helpful for some liver functions. However, it is not recommended during a detox program.

Those who stay with a healthy diet after the program, which is crucial to continued success in remaining addiction free, should only need to do a liver and gallbladder flush once every year or two.

Chapter Five

Lab Tests

The best detox plan is always an individual one, and the best approach to full recovery is the same. Everyone's body is different, and each person has their own inherent strengths and weaknesses. Acetaldehyde poisoning can lead directly to liver cancer in some, and in others the most vulnerable and damaged area will be the brain. The tests associated with The 101 Program are scientifically developed to evaluate and address the known vulnerable areas of the body and brain chemistry, and determine to what degree they have been injured. These tests take out the guesswork; they will provide the concrete facts regarding the condition of your liver, neuroendocrine system, brain chemistry, cardiovascular, and kidney health so that you may move forward with critically important information about your health and have a nutriceutical protocol developed to target your specific needs. This process will enhance your recovery and health goals. You will also be able to monitor your progress along the way, providing you full confidence in the effectiveness of this program and your ability to succeed. These tests expose the degree to which you are addicted, your propensity for alcohol addiction, and the damage that alcohol has done. They will also give you an opportunity to address abnormalities in your blood, urine, and saliva tests that may not have surfaced as symptoms yet, but pose a potential or present health risk as a result of lifestyle or various health issues in your family's history.

These tests include a Complete Blood Count (CBC): Thyroid Profile with TSH, Lipid Profile, Liver Profile, Kidney Panel, Minerals and Bone, Fluids and Electrolytes, and fasting blood sugar; the Functional Liver Detox Profile (FLDP) to measure the liver's ability to detoxify harmful substances in the body, and the HPA test to detect neurotransmitter and hormone values directly associated with alcohol abuse, addiction, and addictive biochemistry. The results will provide a scientific basis on which you can establish an intelligent, targeted, and measurable method for approaching your recovery from alcohol addiction and quest

for enhanced health. The effectiveness of this program, with this foundation, is awe-inspiring.

AAAA will send the collection kits for the FLDP and HPA tests, which are done at home, and will arrange a blood draw at a lab near you for the Complete Blood Count (CBC).

	CBC — Complete Wellness Profile	Functional Liver Detox Profile	HPA
Series I: Pre Krispy Klean	☼	☼	
Series II: Post Krispy Klean			☼
Series III: Post The Ark	☼	☼	☼

Test Series I and II are included in The 101 Program Comprehensive Services Package. It is strongly suggested that you retest at the end of the Ark phase to be reevaluated for a modified Targeted Nutritional Therapy for the Preserve & Protect phase. Healing changes biochemistry and serves to dramatically reduce and sometimes entirely eliminates the need to continue with supplements targeted for addictive biochemistry and bio-repair from alcohol related damage.

Krispy Klean Series I Tests

The pre-program tests are used to evaluate the level of damage caused by alcohol, expose any health risks, and target your biochemical strengths and weaknesses. AAAA does not typically prepare custom protocols for the first 8-week detox beyond the standard Krispy Klean Detox because everyone, unless they have special conditions like current disease or illness, must detox in the same manner. Detoxing and cleansing is universal for the majority of people. Should you have special circumstances, contact AAAA to have the detox

modified to meet your particular needs dictated by those circumstances.

Complete Blood Count (CBC)

The CBC blood test consists of the following panels, with details below:

Complete Blood Count (CBC)
Thyroid Profile with TSH
Lipid Profile
Liver Profile
Kidney Panel
Minerals and Bone
Fluids and Electrolytes
Fasting Blood Sugar

Functional Liver Detox Profile (FLDP)

Efficient liver function is necessary for the processing and elimination of endotoxic toxins (internally produced), and exotoxic toxins (drugs, chemicals, pollution, and food additives), which are commonly referred to as "xenobiotic" chemicals. Inefficient liver function can lead to "metabolic poisoning" which refers to the buildup within cells, tissues, and organs of unprocessed toxic metabolites. These metabolites alter the pH gradient and the electrolyte profile within cells, and can serve as competitive enzyme inhibitors and ultimately interrupt effective bioenergetics within the cell. The symptoms of an elevated level of metabolic poisoning include fatigue, digestive disorders, hypotonia, and brain biochemical disturbances. Recent studies have reported a relationship between this impaired detoxification capability and mitochondrial dysfunction and chronic fatigue syndrome (CFS). These reports suggest that oxidative damage to the mitochondria due to impaired detoxification processes is itself a fundamental mechanism in the development of CFS. Well-recognized examples of metabolic poisoning include the symptoms of uraemia or hepatic encephalopathy; both of which are associated with fatigue and central nervous system disturbances.

The FLDP is a non-invasive challenge test that assesses the efficiency of the liver's ability to detoxify and eliminate toxic chemicals. Multiple detoxification pathways are assessed by using challenge substances such as low oral doses of caffeine, aspirin, and Paracetamol (acetaminophen). Saliva and urine samples are collected at home during timed intervals, and sent to the laboratory for analysis. An injured liver will show deficiencies in one or more of its six major detoxification pathways. If this is the case, free radical damage is being allowed to proliferate throughout the liver and other organs, causing illness. Since the FLDP test exposes exactly which pathways are deficient, specific nutriceutical therapies can be recommended to assist and heal the injured areas of the liver. This test provides crucial information that can be used to inspire cell rejuvenation and regeneration processes; healing the liver and providing a long-term protocol for excellent liver function and support. Results are also used to correct any imbalances such as fast Phase I and slow Phase II liver function.

Series II Tests
Post-Krispy Klean Tests

After the Krispy Klean Detox your approach toward healing and recovery is personalized by doing the HPA test. The HPA test is extremely important because it provides information regarding the 'home address' of alcohol addiction in the hypothalamus, pituitary, and adrenal axis. The CBC and FLDP test results are combined with the results of the HPA test to provide an extremely accurate targeted nutritional therapy (TNT). This will include a supplemental therapeutic nutritional protocol to address your specific nutritional requirements and accelerate healing of all injured tissues and organs. The HPA axis test is the most valuable tool used to measure the damage done to the brain and endocrine system, since it provides the indisputable concrete evidence necessary to determine what is required to heal and balance it, and uncovers influences that may have encouraged the addiction.

The HPA axis test measures:

Neurotransmitters:

- Serotonin
- GABA
- Dopamine
- Glutamate
- Epinephrine (adrenaline)
- Norepinephrine (noradrenaline)

Hormones:
- Cortisol
- DHEA

*Details about these hormones and neurotransmitters can be found in Chapters 2 and 9.

Adrenal Fatigue

Despite the fact that the adrenals are possibly the first organ to be depleted by alcohol, sugar, and junk food, little attention is given to the rising epidemic of adrenal fatigue found in both adults and children. Healing the adrenals is given special attention in The 101 Program specifically because they do tend to be so heavily effected by alcohol; the adrenals and the pancreas are hit the hardest initially by alcohol, especially if a bad diet accommodates heavy alcohol use. Depending on lifestyle, they are always injured to some degree by long-term alcohol abuse.

Adrenal fatigue alone can cause a vicious cycle that encourages alcohol addiction. As the adrenals fatigue they become deficient in their release of cortisol, norepinephrine, and epinephrine. These are stress hormones produced to help you through extreme emotional, psychological, and physical demands. The extreme blood sugar fluctuations a chronic drinker experiences will diminish the health of their adrenals, which will then produce less and less stress hormones, especially when needed. When this happens, any kind of stressor is perceived as more profound since the problem drinker is ill equipped to deal with it. The intensified perception of stress will cause a higher demand for stress hormones from the adrenals, injuring them still further. If this cycle is allowed to perpetuate over a significant period of time, the individual will fall into a "stress syndrome", and will be vulnerable to stress-related health issues like compromised

immunity, accelerated aging, and a plethora of mental and physical discomforts and diseases.

Symptoms of adrenal fatigue are:

- Sugar and alcohol cravings
- Mental and physical fatigue
- Decreased physical performance or ability
- Anxiety
- Frustration
- Nervousness
- Apprehension
- Increased reactions to allergies
- Recurring colds or infections
- Hair loss
- Depression
- Being easily overwhelmed
- Feelings of being emotionally "taxed"
- Decreased libido

Obviously, it's possible for adrenal fatigue to account for many of the symptoms experienced by an active or former problem drinker. Adrenal health is a primary focus of The 101 Program, and as a result individuals on the program quickly find relief from these symptoms.

Series III Tests
Post-The Ark Tests

Whether the standard or individualized version of The 101 Program was used, after completing The Ark you should discontinue all supplements for a week and take the Series III tests (HPA, FLDP, and CBC). Having these tests done at the end of The Ark phase means that after all the health issues associated with alcohol abuse have been addressed, you can develop your maintenance strategy and directly address your personal to-date nutritional requirements. You will also be able to see in black and white the phenomenal success that you have achieved in curing your addiction and regaining your health.

The Series III tests will provide information for long-term personal care that intelligently accommodates your specific requirements. Once the damaged biochemistry and

metabolism, tissues, and organs are healed, therapeutic supplement dosages are no longer necessary, and you may enjoy the simplicity of a nutritional protocol that an average health-conscious person practices, with the exception that yours will be a TNT which addresses your personal health goals, protection from the unfortunate fact that we live in a very toxic, polluted environment; and neuroendocrine health which is crucial in maintaining an addictive free biochemistry. Now is the time when the body and mind are entirely capable of staying healthy and engaging the physician within as necessary, so long as you maintain a healthy diet that provides the necessary nutrition it needs to do its job.

Heavy Metal Toxicity

This is an optional test that can be arranged. Testing for heavy metals helps to determine the condition of the thyroid and other glandular tissues. Mercury fillings, environmental pollutants, and cigarette smoke are key contributors to metal toxicity. Cigarette smoke is considered to be one of the highest sources of cadmium poisoning exposure.

Information about this test is included because heavy metal toxicity is epidemic, and most people do not even realize that they could be suffering from it. Heavy metal toxicity symptoms are nearly always misdiagnosed in conventional medical diagnostic procedures; conventional practitioners never consider it to be the possible underlying root for neurological disorders, cardiovascular dis-ease, fatigue, and cancer. It can also be a key contributor to addictive biochemistry. If you are or have been a smoker, lived with second-hand smoke, or have mercury (amalgam) fillings, you should suspect heavy metal toxicity and be tested for it.

Mercury fillings and vaccinations are the two leading causes for mercury poisoning, which has been shown to be a key, if not primary cause, for many mental disorders and other diseases. There is growing speculation that the increase in breast cancer may be related, in part, to mercury poisoning from dental (mis)care. Additionally, leading nutritional psychiatrists and scientists have shown evidence that children who were given vaccinations that had Thymerasol (a mercury-based preservative) in them acquired serious health conditions like autism, ADD, depression, and

even death. Once these and other health effects were shown as results of Thymerasol, the federal government mandated that it be removed from vaccine preparations. However, there are reports that some pharmaceutical agencies are still using this deadly toxin in their vaccines. To learn more about this immoral behavior on the part of pharmaceutical companies that produced the vaccines children were forced to be injected with, please visit http://www.mercola.com/2004/sep/22/blaylock_vaccine_coverup.htm. There is also a KPFA broadcast on the subject with Robert Kennedy Jr. at http://www.kpfa.org/archives/index.php?arch=8933.

If you suspect mercury poisoning in yourself or your children visit www.greenbodyandmind.com for assistance in finding a nutritionally trained healthcare professional that specializes in mercury detoxification. Detoxing from this substance is an important step required to re-establish healthy brain chemistry and other metabolic functions.

Amalgam fillings are suspected to be at the root of some forms of depression, aggression, declining mental faculties, and addiction, depending on the level of toxicity and the person's sensitivity. If you decide to get the amalgam removed from your mouth you should go to a dentist who specializes in the proper method of removing the amalgam and chelating the mercury out of your system. A full metal toxicity panel will test your individual reaction to all metals so that you and your dentist may choose the least reactive material for new fillings.

Do not dismiss the serious health risks associated with mercury poisoning. People have literally reclaimed their lives and recovered from many mental disorders, digestive problems, cardiovascular illness, and other health issues by having their amalgam fillings removed and chelating mercury from their system.

Chapter Six

Krispy Klean Detox Instructions

The Holistic Detoxification Manual

The 101 Program Supplements
Disclaimer- Please read carefully.

All information within Alcoholism: The Cause & The Cure is provided for general information only. It should not be treated as a substitute for the medical advice of a doctor or healthcare professional. Neither AAAA nor Genita Petralli is responsible or liable for any diagnosis made by the reader based on the information provided in Alcoholism: The Cause & The Cure.

AAAA is not liable for the contents of any external internet sites listed, nor does it endorse any commercial product or service mentioned or suggested on any of the sites. A qualified healthcare provider should always be consulted if you are in any way concerned about your health.

! If you are on prescription drugs, MAO inhibitors, diabetic, or have high blood pressure or any other known or suspected health risks, it is strongly advised that you seek a healthcare provider educated and trained in the use of nutriceuticals (naturopath, integrative physician) before taking these supplements.

! No one should take the amino acid L-phenylalanine if they are on MAO inhibitors. People taking monoamine oxidase (MAO) inhibitors, commonly prescribed for depression, should not take any supplements containing L-tyrosine, as it may lead to a sudden and dangerous rise in blood pressure.

! No one should take these supplements while breast feeding or pregnant.

Note: A heavy, chronic drinker who suffers from seizures or any other symptoms that could jeopardize life,

cause injury, or extreme discomfort, should not attempt doing this program without supervision provided by a trained holistic detox healthcare professional to assist them through the initial week. You may request supervision from The 101 Program Alliance of Orthomolecular Addiction Treatment Professionals by writing support@the101program.com

PLEASE READ BEFORE TAKING FORMULAS

The formulas should be taken only as directed. All the individual supplements are interdependent on each other to achieve very specific results. The 7-day 101 Prep Week must be completed to prepare one's system for the dosage requirements this program suggests. It is strongly advised that you consult a holistic healthcare provider before beginning this program. The doctor should be well educated in orthomolecular medicine and biochemistry. Many conventional doctors, however good they may be with a knife and bottle of pills, simply don't understand how to assist the body in awakening the physician within by providing the nutrients in which it is deficient and letting it heal itself. But because more people are moving away from invasive approaches to complimentary, integrative, and holistic healthcare, many good doctors are obtaining naturopath, nutrition, and homeopath degrees and integrating holistic methods into their practices. Those with AMA-accredited medical degrees, who have successfully completed their ND (naturopathic doctorate or other alternative medicine degrees), are called integrative or complementary physicians.

Getting Started

You have already begun the journey to true liberation because this book has provided you with the truth and concrete science embodying the information and the guidance you require to address your specific needs if you possess addictive biochemistry or are addicted to alcohol. And it's true: *the truth will set you free.* You will now be able to

engage the most advanced information known to "fix" that biochemistry and release yourself from the compulsive desire to drink, while curing numerous health issues that are related to alcohol toxicity. You have in your hands the holistic detoxification "operations manual", for alcohol dependency and it is far more effective than any conventional in or outpatient program in minimizing withdrawal, accelerating detoxification, and repairing alcohol's damage to the body and mind. Orthomolecular medicine is also the only treatment model that offers a cure!

Intelligent detoxification, with the appropriate nutritional support, can rid a person of alcohol cravings in four to seven days. Within a couple of weeks you can expect to no longer crave the simple carbohydrates and sweets that are avoided on The Program. This is extremely important for you to remember while you are going through the initial withdrawal. This is not going to be like previous attempts; the supplements are going to ease the symptoms of withdrawal and the combination of the condictive diet and nutriceuticals are going to have you feeling great in just a week or two. There is a tremendous reward on the other side of this process and it doesn't take long to start reaping the benefits.

If you consider yourself a problem drinker, and are ready to do the work that will finally liberate you from the bonds of chemical dependency, you should prepare for a journey that will both enlighten and engage you in a healthy lifestyle. A healthy biochemistry will support you in creating a lifestyle that will become the pillar of your recovery, inspire you, replace despair with hope, make your dreams feel tangible, and empower you to face whatever challenges lie on the road to success. You will find that you are no longer powerless; that you are powerful, and can use this new can-do attitude to alter all challenging situations to your favor.

Orthomolecular medicine will become more widespread as people become aware of it and learn to trust that when you live in compliance with the natural laws and provide what the body and mind require to function as they were intended to, the physician within can heal and correct the destruction caused by alcohol and rid the body and mind of addictive biochemistry. Orthomolecular treatment statistics lead all other methods by a 75 to 82% margin, with success rates in the 85% range; conventional treatments and AA are hard-

pressed to claim 3% today, and never bring a recovering drinker anywhere near the enhanced state of health that provides the quality of sobriety achieved with The 101 Program.

There is something wonderful happening on the horizon of healing addictions and you are now part of it. Welcome everyone to the winning team.

Module 1 - The Krispy Klean Detox

The detailed instructions for the Krispy Klean Detox follow, along with a current dosage chart for the protocol at the time of this writing, in the appendix.

The 101 Program Meal Planner for the Krispy Klean Detox, and the condictive diet guidelines practiced after the detox, can be found in Chapter 7, "The 101 Program Condictive Diet".

As previously mentioned, there are three methods for approaching the Krispy Klean Detox. All three of these methods are explained in Chapter 3, "The 101 Program". A high-level overview of The 101 Program process is provided in the Roadmap to Recovery below.

The 101 Program Roadmap to Recovery

Note: Complete instructions for the Krispy Klean Detox can be found in Chapter Six, "Krispy Klean Detox Instructions".

The 101 Program Comprehensive Services Package	AAAA will: • Send the Krispy Klean Detox formula supplements. • Send the FLDP and HPA specimen collection kits for the tests. • Arrange for a blood draw at a local lab for your CBC and Complete Wellness tests. • Email intake forms. • Schedule an initial phone consultation, upon receipt of these forms. • Please note: The comprehensive services is designed to coach you throughout the

	process. AAAA provides 4 personal consultations during the detox and email support is provided throughout the 8 weeks by AAAA's addictive biochemistry counselors. Prior to or during the Prep Week, you will take the Complete Wellness (CBC) and FLDP tests.
The 101 As Is Method	Purchase Krispy Klean Detox formula supplements at least one week before you plan to start The 101 Prep Week. This formula can be purchased prepackaged at http://the101program.com/formulas.html, or you can use the list of supplements for the formula in the appendix and purchase them at your local health food store or online.
The Custom Services Package	Contact AAAA at info@the101program.com to correspond with a program coach.
Suggested Items	
	Juicer
	Personal Blender from Tribest at http://personalblender.com
	Stevita (Stevia) is a natural sweetener made from a Brazilian plant and is 50 times sweeter than sugar. It is suggested for sweetening herbal teas, etc, and has no glycemic value so that it does not raise insulin or fuel the blood sugar roller coaster.
Prep Week	
	You should reduce drinking by at least 50% to help minimize withdrawal during Week 2. A chronic, excessive drinker who suffers any kind of severe shaking, delirium, or even mild seizures upon quitting should use caution and seek a doctor's assistance at http://alternativementalhealth.com.

	Purchase the parasite cleanse and liver detox flush items required. A 2-oz bottle of the parasite tincture can be purchased at http://drclarkia.com. Directions for the parasite cleanse are found in the 'Parasite Cleanse' section of Chapter 4, "Detoxifying and Healing the Liver". You may purchase the liver and gallbladder stone flush items from a local grocery store. Directions and ingredients for the stone flush are provided in the 'Liver and Gallbladder Flush' section of Chapter 4, "Detoxifying and Healing the Liver".
	Remove all disallowed food items from the house.
	Begin Prep Week supplements
	Begin morning protein shake.
	Commit to an exercise routine.
	Two days before Week 2 (Flush week), begin pancreatin enzymes.
Week 2 (flush)	
	Stop drinking.
	Begin The Flush phase of the detox
	Begin full dosages of supplements.
	Begin bowel cleanse. (Super Highway)
	Throughout the week, drink the puréed version of 101 Fasting Broth.
Week 3	Parasite Cleansing
	Begin parasite tincture (see ch. 4)
	Discontinue Super Highway bowel cleansing product.
	Begin suggested series of three colonics.
The 101 Program Comprehensive Services Package	A phone consultation will be scheduled to discuss the results of the CBC and FLDP tests. Any serious conditions found will be addressed immediately. Questions, concerns, and progress will also be addressed.
Week 6	Liver and gallbladder stone flush

Week 7	
	If you are not doing the comprehensive program, now is the time to seriously consider getting an HPA (brain chemistry) test done so you can be provided with a TNT that will accurately address your needs for the healing and restorative phase of this program Balancing brain chemistry is key in uprooting addictive biochemistry so it is my strongest recommendation that you be tested so that you may be provided the exact support you require in establishing healthy brain chemistry that translates to healthy, non-addictive states of mind.
Week 8	Snow White fast
	The first five days are the same as Week 2 (second bowel cleanse, the super highway, is begun). On the sixth day all supplements will be discontinued, and the Snow White fast will begin. The fast will last for a minimum of two, preferably three, days.
Week 9	
The 101 Program Comprehensive Services Package (or doing any post-Krispy Klean Tests)	Reintroduce healthy lean meats, game, fish, and dairy into diet. **HPA testing** – You will discontinue all supplements for seven days, and on the eighth day begin your in-home HPA test (urine and saliva). The specimens should be sent to the address provided in the kit. You will take a basic maintenance protocol for nutritional support for the 12 to 16 days following these tests; this is how long it will take to receive and evaluate your results in order to provide a custom nutriceutical protocol for your continued recovery throughout The Ark module.
The 101 As Is Method	Reintroduce healthy lean meats, game, fish, and dairy into diet.

	Begin supplements provided by qualified practitioner.
Week 11 The 101 Program Comprehensive Services Package	A phone consultation will be scheduled to translate the results of the HPA and Adrenal Fatigue tests. A complete explanation of the results and the insights they provide toward your physical and emotional health is provided. A personalized nutriceutical program for The Ark is also provided at this time, with directions. The personalized protocol will reference all blood, urine, and saliva tests taken for liver, brain, and endocrine function during the Krispy Klean Program. The protocol will maximize your body's ability to balance the neuroendocrine system, heal the liver, and support ongoing healthy brain chemistry.

Weekly Breakout

Krispy Klean Detox Weekly Instructions

This is a high-level, quick-guidance chart; more discussion regarding instructions follows.

The 101 Prep (Week 1)

		Morning	Midday	Evening
DI ET		Protein shake – mix one scoop of powder with 12 to 14 oz of rice or almond milk. Drink half with breakfast and the other half with lunch.	Be sure to drink plenty of water throughout the day. Lunch with second half of protein shake.	Dinner

K K F O R M U L A	Acidophilus, upon rising Begin taking full dose of multivitamin only. Two Days prior to beginning Week 2 (Flush), begin taking pancreatic enzymes with breakfast, lunch and dinner.	1 Tbsp of acidophilus between breakfast and lunch Pancreatic enzymes	1 Tbsp of acidophilus between lunch and dinner Pancreatic enzymes
A C T I V I T Y	Meditation/ prayer/yoga deep breathing/chi kung; routine should be at least 20 minutes in the morning, afternoon and again in the evening. Begin a suitable exercise routine that includes aerobic and anaerobic activities.	Take a 20-minute midday break to meditate, relax, and do deep breathing exercises. If unable to do this due to work, etc. take a walk after lunch.	Hot bath (with mineral salts), sauna, or steam at least three times a week Deep breathing /chi kung, Yoga, or walking

Prep Week Notes

- Two strongly recommended companions are a juicer and a good juicing book. A quick and easy way to get the protein required when having juice is to enjoy a handful of nuts. This will help maintain the goal of an insulin-sparing diet.
- Prepare the menu for weeks 2 through 8 with the help of the 101 Meal Companion. We have also provided videos at http://the101program.com to help you shop and cook for a Condictive Diet. During weeks 2 through 8, adhere strictly to the Krispy Klean Detox diet presented in Chapter 7, "The 101 Condictive Diet".
- Organic green tea is strongly recommended – one or two cups a day; should be caffeinated if Phase I is slow and decaf if it is fast. Be sure to steep leaves, do not use bags. Do not use

green tea during the detox if you have not had your liver tested and are sure you do not have a fast phase I and slow phase II.

- Homemade almond milk made from organic almond meal is recommended.
- Making a larger protein shake to consume over breakfast and lunch sometimes helps those on the go meet their protein needs during the workday.
- Acidophilus is not shipped with supplements; the suggested brand is Nature's Life – non-flavored (refrigerated section of health food stores).
- During this week you should begin weaning yourself from refined carbohydrates and sugars – this will help ease the crash during Week 2.
- Freshly juiced carrot and pineapple or papaya juices are very good for the gastrointestinal tract, and are strongly recommended especially during the Prep Week. Do not prepare more than one day's supply at a time. Juice 4 to 6 ounces and be sure to have a protein source such as nuts with your juice.
- A heavy drinker should use this period to cut back on their drinking to help reduce withdrawal intensity during week 2. The supplements will help tremendously, but this is a good opportunity to minimize the various symptoms the body may go through while adjusting to the new regiment.
- It's important for you to put a little time aside every day for yourself, even if it's only to lay down for 15 minutes to collect yourself and reduce midday stimuli. Use this time to relax the mind, and concentrate on breathing. Meditate or do Qi Qong breathing exercises just before bed.
- Internal and external exercise must be done every day. You may change and individualize the plan, but you should maintain one internal and one external exercise routine daily. Balance and moderation in all things is the focus for your new, healthy lifestyle. Above all, meditation should be included; meditation is key to neuroendocrine health and "rewiring" your brain for a healthy lifestyle.
- It is important to get into the habit of taking time to relax and re-center in the middle of the day. Studies have proven that those who do this regularly are actually more productive throughout the day and maintain better energy levels throughout the evening.

Krispy Klean 7-Day Prep Week

Detailed Instructions

The prep week supplements are intended to prepare the body for the high-density nutrients you will soon be introducing into your diet, and to maximize absorption and utilization of the supplements.

During the 7-Day Prep you will begin:
- Consuming a protein shake with a light breakfast
- Taking the Acidophilus
- Begin taking pancreatin enzymes two days before The Flush (Week 2)
- Taking the recommended multivitamin in the protocol
- Drinking 8 to 12 cups of water a day

Removing all food items that are no longer allowed from the home is strongly recommended at this time. It is also necessary if you are a heavy drinker to cut down on your alcohol intake during this week to help minimize the withdrawal symptoms you may experience in Week 2 when you stop drinking. It's a good idea for a moderate yet consistent drinker to cut down as well. Depending on your condition, you may suffer some uncomfortable symptoms for the first couple of days during withdrawal, even with the nutritional support. Cutting down during this 7-day preparation will make the transition more tolerable.

At least 30 to 60 minutes a day should be set aside for exercise. Going to the gym several days a week, taking a jog outside, hiking, bicycling, tennis, or racket ball are all healthy options; do what you enjoy. For lighter days a simple 30 to 60 minute walk is completely adequate. Oxygenating the organs and stretching the muscles is absolutely necessary.

You should also take time to meditate reverently, visualizing your goals coming to fruition, and yourself as a vibrant and radiant person who enjoys life. Blessings should be counted daily and kept at the forefront of your thoughts throughout the day. For those unfamiliar with meditation, find a yoga studio and ask them if they teach meditation and if not, if they could refer you somewhere. There are also many transcendental meditation clinics throughout the world.

Go online and check for clinics in your area. Meditation will ground you, boost your immune system, help you relax, and keep you focused and "fluid" throughout the day. Meditation done properly also stimulates endorphin release in the brain, which is very important for reducing stress and healing addictive biochemistry.

During the 7-day prep week you should design a plan for getting back into the Big World and living large. You should decide on some new activities that do not include television or a drink. If all of your friends drink heavily and party excessively, you will need to figure out how you're going to go about making new friends. After the first few weeks on this program, contact with moderate drinkers is okay, especially if you plan to moderate your own alcohol consumption after completion of The Ark. Moderate drinkers tend to be those people who have a proven ability to make good choices in life when it comes to managing potentially dangerous substances in their environment. They demonstrate this by practicing a balanced lifestyle and not allowing themselves to be distracted by irresponsible use of substances that disrupt their health, relationships, or goals in life. A recovering drinker can learn a lot from people like this about how to deal with stress, emotional issues, and disappointments, and how to spend free time constructively, enriching their lives.

Some ideas for getting back into the Big World include a class in something that interests you, be it physical such as dance, or academic like astronomy; joining a health club, painting, rollerblading, skydiving, surfing, or bicycling. Anything that serves your personal or creative interests and puts some fun in your life is a good plan. No one should spend their free time in isolation, or in front of a TV; you need to engage yourself in life. Although you may not feel up to it at first, if you put your first foot out there and force yourself to follow it, anything will become an enriching experience as you bond with it and the people sharing the activity with you. A heavy drinker's senses are a little numb, and it will take some time to get out of the initial depressed and uninterested mood; the best way to do that is to get out there and do something. A healthy lifestyle centers on engagement in wholesome, stimulating activities and the enjoyment and gratification they provide. These activities will also help to heal addictive biochemistry through stimulating the feel-good

neurotransmitters and providing you a healthy source of connection with others.

Krispy Klean Flush (Week 2)

Weeks 2 and 8 are the same, except that on the sixth day of week 8 you will begin the first day of the detox fast, Snow White. During weeks 2 through 8, the Krispy Klean Detox diet presented in Chapter 7, "The 101 Program Condictive Diet" must be strictly followed.

Important!

Begin the Super Highway bowel cleansing product provided in Krispy Klean Detox formula per instructions on label. This will be done for weeks 2 and 8 ONLY!

Please read the notes provided with the dosage chart in the appendix for how and when to take the Krispy Klean supplements.

	Morning	Midday	Evening
	Upon waking: 1 Tbsp Acidophilus Thistle Cleanse (let rest under tongue for 30 seconds). **This product is used for week 2 and 8 only!** Start first round of Super Highway (bowel cleansing product). Use per directions on label. **This product is used for week 2 and 8 only!**	Thistle Cleanse – one hour before lunch 1 Tbsp Acidophilus	Thistle Cleanse – one hour before dinner. 1 Tbsp Acidophilus
D I E T	Half hour later – prepare protein shake with one scoop of powder and 12 to 14 oz of rice or almond milk. Drink half with breakfast and second half with lunch. Take pancreatin enzymes	Lunch with protein shake Take pancreatin enzymes	Take pancreatin enzymes
K K F O R M U L A	Full morning doses (MD) of Krispy Klean – with meal Dissolve one B12 tab under tongue.	Noon doses (ND) of Krispy Klean	Evening doses (ED) of Krispy Klean Melatonin as needed for sleep

Weeks 2 through 8 Notes

For Weeks 2 through 8, until the fast, eat only organic produce, nuts, fruits, and grains listed in the 101 Meal Planner, fermented soy products (miso, natto, and tempeh), seaweed salads and soups, and legumes (beans). Consume absolutely no dairy, meats, fish, or sugars/sweeteners. Olive oil (cold pressed, extra virgin) is the absolute best for daily use and I encourage its consumption. Coconut and sesame oils (moderately) will also provide health benefits and flavor. Sprouted or whole food breads made of gluten free seeds that emulate grains such as millet; quinoa, buckwheat, and amaranth are your best choices. The recent focus on low-carb breads has produced many good seed and whole grain breads from which to choose. Choose breads with no sugar or soy content, and use even these very good breads in moderation.

Eat as may cruciferous vegetables as possible (eg, cabbage, celery, broccoli, cauliflower).

This week may cause some indigestion and stomach discomfort depending on how nutritious your former diet was. The acidophilus and pancreatin enzymes are included in The Program to address this, as well as for other health reasons. It should take no more than 7 to 10 days to adjust. Enzymes are suggested from the sixth day of the Prep Week, through week 2 (first week of Flush). By the end of the second week your system should have adapted to the new, healthy diet and be working efficiently, producing adequate digestive enzymes to properly digest the protein, good fats, and complex carb-rich foods you now enjoy. If not, it is safe to take the enzymes until you have adjusted.

Some people may experience intermittent sleep patterns for 3 to 5 days after beginning Week 2. This is because the body has become accustom to having alcohol to relax and settle into sleep, and blood sugar levels are lowering and stabilizing. Use the melatonin per the label or an additional tablet to achieve sleep. Do not take any other drugs or sleep aids. The body will correct itself and produce the right hormones and neurotransmitters for sleep naturally. If your circadian rhythm is off due to fluctuating cortisol levels throughout the day, and other neurotransmitter / hormone imbalances, it will take 3 to 5 days typically to stabilize blood sugar and reset the circadian clock.

As soon as you begin to sleep well naturally, you will awake relaxed and peaceful and this feeling will last throughout the day.

Krispy Klean Flush (Weeks 3 through 7)

CLEANSE and FLUSH   Weeks 3, 4, 5, 6, and 7

	Morning	Midday	Evening
D I E T	Upon rising- ½ lemon in 8 oz spring water. Prepare protein shake with one scoop powder and 12 to 14 oz of almond milk. Drink half with breakfast and second half with lunch.	Lunch with protein shake	Dinner
K K F O R M U L A	Morning doses (MD) of Krispy Klean – with meal Dissolve one B12 tab under tongue. Discontinue Super Highway and thistle cleanse products. Take pancreatin enzymes and acidophilus for an additional week (after week 2) if still experiencing stomach discomfort or indigestion.	Noon doses (ND) of Krispy Klean	Evening Doses (ED) of Krispy Klean

Krispy Klean Flush (Weeks 2 to 8)

Detailed Instructions

After the 7-day prep you will:

- Stop drinking completely.
- You should start your detox on a Friday evening, so that by Monday you are in fair shape for the demands at work. An

even better solution would be for you to take a day or two off after the weekend.

- Start the 101 Krispy Klean full strength supplement protocol.
- Continue drinking the protein shake with breakfast or half with breakfast and half with lunch. Start the Super Highway bowel cleanse.
- Drink 8 to 10 glasses of water a day (this is a standard for a healthy lifestyle, and should be incorporated into your daily routine for life).
- Drink a pureed version of the fasting broth (see 'Snow White' section) during the first week of the Krispy Klean Flush phase (second week of the program). Essentially, the preparation is the same as in the fasting broth recipe, the only exception is that you will not strain it for just the broth; you will put the entire mixture in a blender, puree it, and then water it down (1/2 broth and 1/2 water), so that it may be consumed easily. Drink the broth during the day for the entire week. No fasting is suggested at this time. Have the broth with meals and in between.
- Begin a good exercise program built around your time allowances and interests at this point. It's extremely important for you to exercise as much as possible during the first week. Exercise is a primary factor in detoxification and getting on the other side of addiction, feeling great, and improving health quickly.
- Take hot baths or go to the gym and get in the sauna several times a week. An excellent product for detoxification and absorbing much needed minerals is soaking in Dead Sea Mineral Baths.
- Review and practice the condictive dietary guidelines in 'The 101 Krispy Klean Meal Planner' section. It's important for you to become thoroughly educated about the components of a healthy lifestyle, which begins with what you put in your mouth.

Note: If your stomach gets upset because of the vitamins, you should cut the dosages in half for a few days and build up to full dosages.

If you are a chronic, problem drinker you should not detox alone. If you have ever had Grand Mal seizures or become

extremely shaky, sweaty, or panicky when you go without alcohol, a holistic doctor's supervision is strongly advisable. The degree of withdrawal symptoms you experience when quitting is also a good gauge to use when judging how long you should stay on The Ark program which follows the detox.

The first few days may be a little rough; alcohol has entered your life on a cellular level, and it won't leave quietly if it has been a resident for awhile. Initially, you may feel like you have crash-landed into a pool of quicksand. The feeling will quickly reverse itself. Typically within just a few days you will begin to feel surges of well being, enjoy restful sleep, and have unlimited energy that does not come from high anxiety or adrenaline. You will begin to feel inspired, optimistic about life, and peaceful. This part of The Program is one of the most important; it gets you quickly to the other side, removing much of the depression, anxiety, and craving. It gives a jump start toward healthy living, and experiencing results in such a short period of time will increase your confidence, instilling conviction in what you are doing and fuel your spirit for the demands of completing The Program. That conviction will soon be rewarded by all the benefits of health and happiness and a new healthy cycle will be brought to life!

During the first week of The Flush you should give yourself that time for the withdrawal period. You should make no social plans, focusing instead on your health, and getting plenty of rest and quiet time. Soon after that it will be time to engage in the plans made during the 7-day prep period, and initiate some healthy and exciting activities. You should get into the Big World as quickly as possible, but the first week is for personal recovery and focus. No extra curricular engagements should be planned during the first week if they are stressful or strenuous in any way. Quitting sugar and alcohol cold turkey is extremely hard on the body for the first few days, so you should prepare yourself by maintaining your inner strength: plenty of rest, pampering with long walks and soaking baths, reading uplifting and empowering books, and doing nothing emotionally or mentally strenuous. Health is more important than anything else, especially at this stage.

Week 3: Begin Parasite Cleanse & Colonics

For complete instructions, refer to the 'Parasite Cleanse' section in Chapter 4, "Detoxifying and Healing the Liver".

Arrange for a series of three colonics, once a week for three weeks.

Week 6: Begin Liver and Gallbladder Stone Flush

For complete instructions, refer to the 'Liver and Gallbladder Stone Flush' section in Chapter 4, "Detoxifying and Healing the Liver".

Snow White Fast (Week 8)

Go by the guidelines in this chart for the first five days, then prepare the Fasting Broth as instructed and consume only that, water, and herbal non-caffeinated teas of your choice for Days 6 and 7. If you can do a three-day fast, the extra day is recommended. It is important to remember to discontinue all supplements on Days 6 and 7 for the fast.

For the first five days of this week, resume your Super Highway bowel cleansing and thistle cleanse products per instructions on label and dosage chart.

	Morning	Midday	Evening
W **e** **e** **k** **8**	Upon Rising: Thistle Cleanse per label. 1 Tbsp acidophilus (upon rising)	Thistle Cleanse – One hour before lunch 1 Tbsp acidophilus	Thistle Cleanse – one hour before lunch 1 Tbsp acidophilus

D I E T	Prepare protein shake with one scoop powder and 12 to 14 oz of rice or almond milk. Drink half with breakfast and second half with lunch.	Lunch with protein shake	Dinner Start second round of Super Highway (bowel cleansing product included in detox package). Use per directions on label until you begin the fast.
K K F O R M U L A	Morning doses (MD) of Krispy Klean – with meal Dissolve one B12 tab under tongue.	Noon Doses (ND) of Krispy Klean	Evening Doses (ED) of Krispy Klean

Snow White (Week 8) Notes
During this week until the fast begins, it is extremely important to stay away from hot peppers (including black pepper) and grapefruit. Also important is to eat as many vegetables as possible from the cabbage family (eg, cabbage, celery, broccoli, cauliflower). Include as much onion and garlic in meal preparation as is possible and appealing.

Week 8: Snow White Fast -- Deep Detox

Detailed instructions

The first part of Week 8 is the same as week 2 (Flush), until the last two or three days when the fast begins. The fast should be done for a minimum of two days, ideally three. It will be done using the fasting broth (recipe provided in 'Fasting Broth' section in this chapter), which will literally

wash out cells, rejuvenate them, "tune up" bioenergetics, and help the body eliminate toxins from deep within. The fasting broth provides the system with the specific nutrients necessary to maintain the baseline nutrition it needs to function healthfully; it will also stimulate detoxification processes and aid in efficient elimination of toxins, which is extremely important while fasting. Fasting done without this very important elimination support can actually do more harm than good because it will cause ancient, built-up toxins to break loose and recirculate throughout the body, causing cell death and metabolic havoc.

- Beginning on the first day of week 8, and up until the fast begins, you will do another bowel cleanse using the Super Highway product.
- Extreme heat-type hydrotherapies and strenuous exercise are not advised during fasting.

Days 1 through 5
- The diet is the same as it was for the last six weeks, minus nuts. Essentially, focus on small amounts of fruits and generous amounts of vegetables, seeds, and legumes. Seaweed salads and miso soup are excellent at this time for thyroid support.
- Continue with the Krispy Klean supplements.
- Start the second round of the Super Highway gastrointestinal cleanse.

Days 6 and 7
- Sip on Fasting Broth throughout the day. Preparation instructions for the fasting broth follow this section.
- Drink the recommended 8 to 10 glasses of spring water daily. Herbal teas and strained broth count as water. Do not drink carbonated water during a fast.
- Discontinue Super Highway product
- Discontinue Krispy Klean supplements
- Light exercise is beneficial. Bicycling, walking, Tai Chi, Yoga, deep breathing, or rollerblading are excellent during this time.

Fasting

Fasting is an important element of The 101 Program. It is the key to awakening the physician within and opening the

door to a powerhouse of natural healers within the body. It must be done intelligently, purposefully, accurately, and with the reverence that all but Western cultures give to it. Fasting provides a deep cleansing of organ tissues, rejuvenates the bioenergetics of cells by removing toxins, and will clear out old metabolic waste from the intestines and bowels that have been resident for some time. This built-up waste has been linked to a number of health issues, as well as the bacterial overgrowth that some researchers believe may encourage addictive biochemistry.

Evart Loomis M.D., considered in many circles as the father of naturopathic medicine, summarized the miraculous benefits of fasting when he wrote: "Fasting is the world's most ancient and natural healing mechanism. Fasting triggers a truly wondrous cleansing process that reaches right down to each and every cell and tissue in the body. Within 24 hours of curtailing food intake, enzymes stop entering the stomach and travel instead into the intestines and into the bloodstream, where they circulate and gobble up all sorts of waste matter, including dead and damaged cells, unwelcome microbes, metabolic wastes, and pollutants. All organs and glands get a much needed and well-deserved rest, during which their tissues are purified and rejuvenated and their functions balanced and regulated. The entire alimentary canal is swept clean. By rebuilding immunity, health is naturally restored and disease disappears. If health and immunity are thereafter conscientiously maintained, the individual is no longer vulnerable to disease and dieting becomes unnecessary. Surely one of the most overlooked and yet most valuable modes of healing that will be rediscovered in the future of the new medicine is the fast. This is because of the increasing interest in looking to oneself for healing powers. For the fast is an inward process and cannot be entered upon only from an outer approach with any expectation of a lasting benefit. The person must invariably be involved with the overall results. This therapeutic encounter is in direct contrast to the usual non-involvement

in the physician-directed, disease-oriented medical practice of today." [7]

Benefits of fasting include:

- Promotes detoxification. As the body breaks down its fat reserves, it mobilizes and eliminates stored toxins.
- Accelerates detoxification deep within cell tissue, and rids metabolites and other toxins that inhibit proper cell bioenergetics.
- Gives the digestive system a much-needed rest. After fasting, both digestion and elimination are invigorated.
- Promotes the resolution of inflammatory processes, such as rheumatoid arthritis, hepatitis, pancreatitis, and gastrointestinal problems.
- Clears the skin and whitens the eyes. It is common to see skin eruptions clear while fasting. The whites of the eyes never look so clear and bright as they do after fasting.
- Accelerates the healing of health issues and illnesses.
- Quiets allergic reactions, including asthma and hay fever.
- Corrects high blood pressure without drugs. Fasting followed by a whole foods diet will normalize blood pressure.
- Helps to reduce the priming conditions those with addictive biochemistry are known to possess in the brain; upregulation of serotonin and beta-endorphin receptors.
- Stimulates the endocrine system and causes the pituitary to release healthy levels of Human Growth Hormone (HGH).
- Eases the way to overcoming bad habits and addictions. Fasting rapidly dissipates the craving for nicotine, alcohol, caffeine, and other drugs by quickly removing the toxins that are inhibiting healthy cell bioenergetics, and causing the distortion of the metabolism that creates alcohol dependency.
- Restores appreciation for wholesome natural foods. Natural foods will begin to burst with flavor.
- Quickly reduces desire for sweets (again, due to the effect on brain chemistry).

---

[7] E. Loomis, Return of the Priest Physician: Medicine for the Twenty-First Century, (Hemet, CA)

- Uproots addictive biochemistry and compulsivity.
- Restores an enhanced sense of one's self.
- Extremely effective method of balancing the neuroendocrine system.

The 101 Program Fasting Broth

This is a must in any healing, detoxifying program, because it will flush out toxins, poisons, and unhealthy salts and acids. It will also provide a baseline amount of vitamins and minerals required to keep organs functioning, and efficiently ridding the body of the toxins you are releasing from cells and the digestive tract. During The Program you should make a large pot and keep it refrigerated for up to one week. For week 2 (Flush) you will puree the vegetables for the broth. For the week 8 fast, you will make another batch, but drain the broth from the vegetables and use only the broth. The vegetables can be put aside to be enjoyed after the fast is finished.

Fasting Broth Recipe

Fill a large pot with:
- 10% potato peelings
- 30% carrot peelings and whole chopped beets
- 25% chopped onions
- 35% celery and broccoli
- Add 20 cloves of garlic (minimum). Buy whole garlic to peel, since the ready-peeled garlic has lost some of its healing qualities as it sits in the jar and is exposed to oxygen, which sets off enzymatic activity.
- Pour in enough distilled water to cover vegetables, plus 7 inches.
- Simmer on very low temperature for 2 to 3 hours. Strain and refrigerate.

*Use only organic produce.

Depression

Most of the people who follow this program leave their depression behind in the first few weeks of the detox phase, because the condictive diet, exercise, and supplements are the

pillars of healthy brain chemistry. However, your brain chemistry and nervous system, under the assault of alcohol toxicity, may have suffered more extensive damage that requires more aggressive assistance. This assistance is provided for in the Krispy Klean Detox formula through the use of the natural serotonin precursors, 5HTP and tryptophan, to help brain chemistry achieve optimum levels of serotonin until it can do so on its own. These amino acid supplements should be taken on an empty stomach, 30 to 60 minutes before the lunch and evening meal, with 1 oz of freshly squeezed juice in a glass of water.

At the end of the Krispy Klean Detox, the tryptophan may be discontinued. If you are able to maintain a positive attitude and states of psychological well being, then obviously your brain chemistry has begun to balance and won't need further healing assistance. If your frame of mind and mood deteriorate after discontinuation, then that indicates that your brain chemistry has suffered extensively, and you should resume use while on The Ark supplements, checking once a month to see how you feel without it.

Vitamins B3, B6, C, and the amino acid tyrosine, are cofactors for serotonin synthesis. While on the Krispy Klean supplements there is no need to purchase these separately since they are included in the formula.

For political reasons, which are designed and carried out to serve pharmaceutical cartel profit interests, tryptophan was taken off the market and made unavailable at health food stores for many years. Although thousands of people were successfully using it for conditions like depression, it was taken off shelves as a dietary supplement just as many of the anti-depressants were being developed and promoted in the media and through extremely misguided medical practice. The pharmaceutical companies wanted tryptophan off the market; it was inexpensive, available at any health food store, and extremely effective, causing no side effects. It created intense competition for their drugs, which were causing nausea, sexual dysfunction and a plethora of other symptoms indicating dis-ease.

Please go to this link http://www.lef.org/fda/fdaban95.html to read the truth behind this scandal, which essentially led to people being poisoned and refused known effective natural treatments. FDA officials were paid to get tryptophan off the

market so that pharmaceutical companies could force those suffering from depression into using their extremely toxic, harmful and expensive products.

The good news is that the FDA woke up and lifted their ban on L Tryptophan for adult consumption and pharmaceutical-grade tryptophan is now available through a limited number of suppliers designated by the FDA. The bad news is that through the influence of pharmaceutical companies, the cost has not gone back down to where it was before being banned. In this round-a-bout way the pharma-cartel ensures their drug-based profits, since that cost will force many people to unwillingly use and then become addicted to their anti-depressants.

If low serotonin is the cause of your depression, tryptophan, when complimented with all the nutritional cofactors necessary to accomplish the biotransformation to serotonin, will relieve your depression naturally. While tryptophan and its complementing co-factors required for serotonin synthesis is the absolute most common cause of depression in long-term, heavy drinkers, it isn't the only cause. There are other chemical imbalances such as low norepinephrine that can cause depression. Both of these pathways to depression are addressed in the 101 Program Krispy Klean Detox formula since low norepinephrine is an indicator of low thyroid and adrenal function very common in long-term problem drinkers. Testing your levels of serotonin, GABA, glutamate, dopamine, norepinephrine, epinephrine, cortisol, and DHEA will yield significant results that AAAA can use to develop a scientifically validated, highly effective targeted nutritional therapy (TNT) that will help balance your neuroendocrine system, heal your depression, and tremendously improve your quality of life in all areas, not just mental health. This process makes anti-depressants unnecessary (not that they were ever really necessary), saving you from the health risks and side effects they are known to pose.

Smoking

If you are a smoker, now is the time to put some serious effort into quitting that habit as well. Detoxing provides an excellent opportunity to quit, since the nicotine withdrawal fades quickly during this process. The 101 Program

accelerates the release of nicotine from tissues, eliminating cravings far more quickly than quitting while pounding down burgers and fries. Quitting is strongly recommended, but if now is not the right time, cut down as much as possible. A cleaner body will reject inhaled smoke more and more; it will begin to cause nausea. That feeling can be used to help you quit whenever you feel ready.

In addition to the many health risks smoking causes, another extremely important reason to quit smoking is that smoking produces acetaldehyde, which has been discussed as a key factor in the addiction to alcohol. The body needs to clear this out of its system to heal the addictive biochemistry and thoroughly cure the addiction.

Relapse versus Process

Most program participants are successful the first time they go through The 101 Program. However, slipping does happen with some problem drinkers seeking to cure their addiction. The relapse is not ever caused because they craved alcohol, quite the opposite; it was brought on because they thought they were totally healed during the 2 month Krispy Klean Detox. One of the side effects of this program is that you will feel so healthy, happy, and vibrant, with absolutely no desire for alcohol by the end of the detox, that you will feel totally cured and think that you can drink moderately. What you're feeling, though, is a symptom of healing but not yet the cure. Completely rooting out addictive biochemistry takes more time than that. It took years to become addicted, and healing has its own time frame as well; expecting to heal within two months after ten years of drinking is not reasonable.

For those who begin The Program and then interrupt it with a drinking spell, relapse is not as severe nor does it become the debilitating event it is known to become for those who are not healing the addiction by repairing what years of alcohol had done to their body and health. Relapse simply does not have the same depths of despair for the person who knows how to get back on track nutritionally; who knows how to eat right to minimize the horrific symptoms that a bad diet can add to alcohol abuse detox; who knows how to detox with minimum symptoms; who has spent time learning how to maintain healthy blood sugar levels; who has begun the

biochemical healing process and who has memories of how great they felt without alcohol while formally on the program as opposed to suffering through the dry-drunk symptoms of their sobriety while replacing alcohol with sugar and caffeine.

Viewed as a process, which is exactly what healing is, there is no relapse. A practicing drinker doesn't become a tee-totaling square just because they miss a day of drinking. And if you drink before the time frame that you have set for yourself for abstinence, that doesn't make you an "alcoholic" drunkard. Be kind and forgiving with yourself; each day on The Program builds healthy brain chemistry and helps balance the neuroendocrine system, which widens the gap between a you and alcohol. Each drink you choose not to drink is a success, and brings you that much closer to regaining your health and a balanced lifestyle, free of addiction.

xSugar - Don't stray!

Sugar and refined/simple carbs is the enemy here. You must accept this truth and stay true to your diet. Healthy eating and avoidance of sugars and toxins should be embraced as a lifestyle and practiced every time you raise a fork to your mouth. In addition, you must absolutely dismiss any notion of ever using an artificial sweetener!

The political, criminal, and misleading propaganda and advertising campaign tactics of the multi billion dollar sugar and artificial sweetener death industry is all designed to keep you ignorant about the real consequences of these products, so you will continue to ingest the poison regardless of its proven ill effects on your health and quality of life. The crimes of the sugar and sweetener industry and the product's effect on your health is far too immense a subject for me to give any justice to in the framework of this book, however an excellent resource to get an honest and informative exposé of these lethal denatured and synthetic substances is Dr. Mercola's book, _Sweet Deception_. A better explanation of the large role that sugar plays toward developing cancer, diabetes, arthritis, addiction, etc., and to get an introduction to what's behind the political and propaganda campaigns the sugar and artificial sweetener industry imposes on our society to protect its interest (despite evidence of the lives these products destroy and the deaths they cause) while keeping you ignorant about

its threat to your health, can be found in this book. The book is truly educational and enlightening, and will certainly feed your conviction in staying away from sugar and artificial sweeteners, and keeping it away from those you care about. Refined sugar and its cousins such as high fructose corn syrup are not food; they are drugs and are killing more people every day than any other single drug in the legal and illegal markets.

Why Food Consumption Has Become Such a Science

It's a fact that healthy eating and lifestyle have become a science. The reason behind this is that when science feeds our bodies, we need to use science to protect our bodies in return because science used to try and control or manipulate nature has a tendency to really mess things up. In today's industrialized societies the public eats from the "fruit" of knowledge wrongfully used by profit-driven companies who use science to produce man-made, denatured substances that don't even resemble food. These companies use addictive substances, convenience, and false advertising tactics that claim or imply health benefits to make it extremely easy to obtain their "foods" quickly while convincing people that not only can they eat and drink these products without being harmed, but that it is healthy for them! This practice is killing thousands of people every day.

Since more than 95% of the food items at the market these days has in some way been poisoned or processed to the point of having the nutritional value of cardboard, you must be able to make educated, conscious decisions regarding what you put into your body, to avoid these lifeless, adulterated, and poisoned substances and to maintain your health. You need to qualify what you consider to be food by its nutritional value and service to the body, and then use an educated response to filter anything that doesn't fit out of your diet. That is why diet has become such a science; people need to actually define what is and what isn't food today because what they are being fed in the media is lying to them. It's really no different than the hunter/gatherers that had to learn what organisms were poisonous in nature and to avoid them. However, in today's industrialized societies we actually have companies and their advertisers using healthy looking people to promote products

known to cause disease and death with standard pitches such as, "here, eat this... you'll be cool, healthy and have tons of energy!" Our ancestral hunter/gatherers were saved from this thank goodness, or we probably wouldn't be here today. And God only knows how long we're going to be able to continue like this before we mutate or die out as a species.

It has also become a science because people don't want to accept the laws of health; they are trying to justify the consumption of junk and lifeless foods by adding fruits and vegetables or in some other way creating a balance act between what they want to eat and what they should eat. Diet is not a science in regards to natural food; if all you ate were organic fresh vegetables, fruits, legumes, and grain (in moderation), healthy lean and clean meats, fish, seeds, and nuts, there would be no balancing act or quantity to think about. There would be no labels to read; no opportunity for poisoning, denaturing, or processing. But because people have been trained, cultured, and even lied into eating processed, poisonous, addictive, denatured foods, they consume products of unethical science and must become educated as to who the ethical food *handlers* (not processors) are and who aren't, and what to look for to determine that. I say food handlers because you don't want to be eating anything from food processors. Processed foods always come with some form of adulteration. Food handlers are your local farmers and all you need to do to determine which of those to purchase from is to establish that they are organic and ethical about it. Also, if you are insistent on eating unethically handled and processed food, it will become a science trying to decipher what all those words mean on the labels and how to balance them in a way that will allow you to at least minimally function with the fewest side effects until you develop a dis-ease as a direct result of their consumption. The only reason why food consumption has become is science is because people are attempting to balance what they *want* to eat with what they *should* eat. There is absolutely no need to diet when you consume only what the human body was designed to consume and you do not eat addictive drugs called food such sugar and refined carbs.

Now we have to use knowledge in the interest of our health and survival to combat irresponsible industrialized "food" distributors and protect ourselves from knowledge

being used for the sole intent to profit from addictive substances. For example, why must there be sugar in canned kidney beans? To continue to cultivate our, and our children's, taste expectations for the sweet addictive substance. Furthermore, reading labels does not necessarily mean you're going to be any more educated about what you are eating. In Kevin Trudeau's best-selling book, <u>Natural Cures "They" Don't Want You to Know About,</u> he reveals that these irresponsible food distributors have gone to Congress and have won the right not to disclose at least 1,500 food additives on their product labeling. You know these can't be chemicals that are good for you. He also claims that companies put additives in foods to actually cause hunger so that you will eat more and they will generate more profit. MSG is purposely used in foods because it is addictive. Because of this food adulterating insanity and the role it plays in addictive biochemistry, I have made it a point to provide a starting education on what the food and pharmaceutical industries are really all about. This education is crucial for protecting yourself and living a full, healthy life with some longevity.

You absolutely must care for yourself; I guarantee you these companies could care less about your health or what you want or don't want in your food. An example of this is the introduction of cloned animal meat into the commercial food chain and it being distributed in supermarkets. Because the commercial farms know that the average American is repulsed with the idea of eating cloned animals (for good reason, the health and DNA mutation risks for those, and their offspring, that eat these products is off the charts and extremely alarming), they won the right from the FDA to not have to disclose on the package that it is meat from cloned animals!

Mankind was given perfection, and it is being destroyed (in the corner supermarket anyway) through the actions of those who thought they could improve on God and / or control nature. There is nothing anyone can do to make natural foods healthier for the human body. Our earth has been polluted to the point that it can no longer provide a high level of nutrition in our food as it once did (at least not where and how it is currently being produced). The blind consumption of pills that mask rather than heal is slowly driving people crazy

while killing them, because they are not willing to accept the fact that the "foods" in those colorful packages are at the root of their psychological and physical distress. Profit over health has poisoned the public's food and minds, and for the sake of convenience and to feed an abnormal cultivated taste for what is offered, people are willing to believe the lies of irresponsible food distribution companies. These companies push sugar, hydrogenated fats, genetically modified products (real scary implications for the entire human race with this one), hormones, pesticides, toxic preservatives, addictive substances, neurotoxins and excitotoxins that destroy brain chemistry, and cardboard as foods, that people accept as food because a diet based on the truth is too inconvenient to practice. This immoral use of knowledge focused on profit with no reverence for health is robbing people's quality of life via the nagging day to day mental and physical health issues they cause, while ultimately creating dis-eases that cause extreme suffering our loved ones endure until they are prematurely delivered to their grave. There are no longer nutritious, natural foods rich in all the vitamins, minerals, EFAs, and amino acids required for healthy minds and bodies conveniently within reach. Good foods that do not possess the desired profit margin due to their short shelf life do not find themselves in the supermarket in today's industrialized nations.

Now, you must use science to do the right thing in a society where unethical businesses are using science to focus on their bottom line with no regard to your health or immediate and long-term impact on our planet. You absolutely must eliminate the middleman and filter out any products produced by scientific knowledge used for the wrong reasons, such as shelf life and promoting addiction and other physical and mental disorders, so that you may reclaim your health and mental well being.

The Premiere Side Effect of The 101 Program: Enhanced Health

Having suffered the effects of excessive alcohol for so long, the adventures associated with learning to treat yourself well, love yourself, and have patience and forgiveness with yourself are exhilarating. The better you feel the happier you become. The happier you become, the more choices you see opening up

in the world, and the more inspired you are to choose to engage with these opportunities. As you release addictive biochemistry, you will also release an addictive personality; you will begin to naturally make better choices. You will suddenly find the energy and desire to do the things that you couldn't follow through on before, and see these projects to completion. Contentment will be found once again in the simple things in life when you feel at peace with the world; the small things will explode with meaning because you will actually be present for them and not desensitized by the fog of addiction. Just a few weeks into The 101 Program, you will begin to feel like a kid again; as you re-sensitize, the world will look fresh and new, with the glow you remember. The baggage that a polluted brain and body chemistry carries will disappear, and be replaced by your ability to enjoy life.

The misery of alcohol withdrawal will quickly turn into a sense of enthusiasm, inspiration, and well being during the detox process of The 101 Program. Most people are astonished at how they feel in an incredibly short period of time. Do not jeopardize the healing process by listening to that little voice telling you that you can drink healthfully and moderately because you feel healthy again. True change and physical healing take time. Feeling great is a side effect of healing; it does not mean that healing is completed. Reversing addictive biochemistry takes time; if it took years to become addicted, depending on the extent of damage, it may take a year or two to heal and replace that addictive biochemistry with a healthy one. You simply must give your body and mind the time to heal and rewire your brain's neuro-net with the new, healthy cells you are producing, and the damaged ones you are healing. The good news is that while this miraculous event is taking place and the bio-repair and healing brings you back to your original self, life will begin to be perceived as the precious gift it is, which leads to natural euphoric states of mind, an appreciative heart full of joy, and the blessings of enhanced health. It's an enchanting journey; so relax and enjoy it.

Chapter Seven

The 101 Program Condictive Diet

Addiction to various drugs (legal and illegal) and alcohol has risen in close proportion to the consumption of fast / junk food, sodas, coffee, refined/simple carb snacks, sweets, and sweetened foods. Alcoholism is just one of the extremes that people may fall into when they develop addictive biochemistries as a result of consistent over-consumption of these substances. Food, sugar, opiate, amphetamine, and alcohol addiction; gambling, and smoking... the genesis of all obsessive/compulsive disorders can be found in the underlying biochemistry of long-term malnutrition and continuous mainlining of refined and simple carbs.

A protein, good fats, complex carb, low glycemic, insulin sparing, organic condictive diet focused on stabilizing your blood sugar and providing your body with the nutrients to heal and protect your specific biochemistry is a lifestyle change that must be permanent in order to cure addictive biochemistry. A permanent change in your diet is fundamental to your success in curing alcohol addiction, and is a responsibility that must be taken seriously.

A condictive diet must be followed to first heal the addiction, and then it must be continued to protect you from relapse. Using known "food" substances that re-create the biochemical damage that causes the symptoms of depression, anxiety, fatigue, and mental and emotional disorders that encourage self-medication will promote addictive biochemistry and the monstrous appetite for food and drug medications that goes with it.

A condictive diet focused on healing addictive biochemistry must address:

- Insulin response, glycemic index of foods
- Insulin resistance
- Hypoglycemic symptoms
- Healthy adrenaline/cortisol levels throughout the day
- Efficient liver support, protection, and daily detoxification
- Proper protein/complex carb/good fats ratios
- General endocrine health to assist optimal brain chemistry, which is fundamental to excellent general health.

- Energy levels
- Cravings/Priming - stopping the process that causes the brain to continue upregulating serotonin and beta-endorphin receptors, which is a key premise of the addiction.
- Providing the brain with the nutrition and toxicity-free environment required to produce healthy amounts of the neurotransmitters and hormones required by the HPA network to maintain neuroendocrine health.
- Maintaining healthy neuroendocrine function -- preserving the feel-good neurotransmitters for longer periods of time by inhibiting the reuptake of serotonin, GABA, endorphins, and in some cases dopamine, through the use of herbs; bio-available vitamins, minerals, amino acids and essential fatty acids; and specific foods known to be natural MAO inhibitors.

Basic Guidelines for an Addictive-free Biochemistry

This section will provide the condictive dietary guidelines for The Krispy Klean Detox, The Ark, and the Preserve & Protect modules. The dietary requirements are basically the same for the three modules, with the exception being that during the Krispy Klean Detox you must exclude all water, air and land animal products: meats, broth, dairy; and refined sugars and carbs. Graduation to The Ark means you have the opportunity to reintroduce organic animal products into your diet such as meat, fish and dairy. During both the Ark and the Preserve & Protect module, you may have a healthy, non-refined desert occasionally; you should, however, always avoid using any type of refined or synthetic sugar-type sweeteners. There are a few very wholesome, natural products such as agave and yacon that can be used to prepare wholesome deserts. Wholesome deserts can also be purchased from bakeries that use these non-refined natural sweeteners. These two do trigger an insulin response; however, used occasionally they do not pose a problem. Stevita is an excellent, natural sweetener that does not trigger insulin because it has no glycemic value, making it a good choice for sweetening teas, etc. The fundamental idea here is to again, eliminate the middle man by entirely avoiding refined sugar, and instead, occasionally enjoy desserts prepared with

wholesome sweeteners in their natural form. Be very diligent about not fooling yourself with even the natural sugars and thinking it is okay to use them excessively because they are natural and organic. Agave and yacon are natural sugars with some health benefits; however, used irresponsibly they can disrupt brain chemistry in the same way as refined sugar.

I would also like to add here that a dessert is defined by a natural, wholesome prepared pie, ice cream, or cake type product that is occasionally enjoyed after a nutrient rich dinner. Donuts, candy bars, cokes and other "convenient" items which are essentially reduced to pure sugar are to be avoided always. They are markers of an unhealthy lifestyle; an unhealthy lifestyle that could get you in trouble with addictive biochemistry again. Also, you want to be sure that you enjoy wholesome desserts *occasionally;* never every day, and should it become a focus in your life, it is time to take a break.

Some basic guidelines to follow are:

It is very important that you include protein and a little healthy oil with every meal and snack. Proteins and fat slow the digestion of the carbohydrates and will therefore slow and reduce the insulin response, promoting stable blood sugar levels throughout the day. This method of eating will also minimize the stress placed on the adrenals.

It's important to know that even among complex carbohydrates and proteins there are good, better, and best choices. For example, in general, red meat has greater amounts of undesirable fat than do chicken or fish. Non-organic chicken and beef is typically loaded with exogenous estrogens and antibiotics, and fish may have heavy metal contaminants. It is not possible on our planet to eat without pollution. It is possible, however, to choose carefully and pray for the best. For a complete list of safe and unsafe fish to eat visit http://www.thegreenguide.com/gg/pdf/fishchartissue97.pdf. Something else to realize is that in most cases low fat or non-fat is not preferable to regular fat. When the nonfat or low-fat option is created by adding an assortment of other undesirables, you are better off choosing the real thing. For example, butter is a much healthier choice than atomized

olive oil, margarine, or other vegetable spreads because they are full of hydrogenated/heavy "trans" fats.

The addition of fiber from whole grains, fresh vegetables, and water-soluble fiber supplements such as psyllium, guar gum, xanthum gum, and agar-agar promotes good intestinal flow. This will also stimulate and enhance digestion, and prevent the reuptake and recycling of deleterious waste products.

Steaming, poaching, baking, and broiling are preferable to frying.

A very good general rule to follow: If bacteria doesn't want it, neither should you. Eat live foods!

Glycemic Index and Glycemic Load

The Glycemic Index (GI) is a measure of how fast a carbohydrate is broken down into glucose, which is what determines how fast blood sugar will rise. Foods with a high glycemic index cause blood sugar to rise quickly, which then causes insulin to do the same, and in greater quantity. In hypoglycemic conditions, insulin overshoots the mark, producing way too much for the job at hand. This in turn causes blood sugar to drop dramatically, creating the well-known low blood sugar symptoms that have caused problem drinkers to make self-medicating an art form.

The glycemic index of food is also determined by four other factors.

- Processing: Grinding, stoning, smashing, or any other manner of processing food essentially begins the breaking down process and does the work that the stomach is supposed to be doing. The degree to which the food has been processed determines the loss of nutrients and leads to the higher glycemic index. This is why whole foods are always preferable over any kind of processed grains.
- Cooking: During cooking the starch granules in foods absorb water, swell, and rupture; this is called gelatinization. Gelatinized starch is quickly broken down by digestive enzymes and absorbed, causing a "spike" in blood sugar. Processed grains have less fiber and absorb more water; therefore they gelatinize more than whole grains.

- Fiber: There are two types of carbohydrates in any given food item; one is digestible and the other is not. The indigestible carbohydrate is called fiber, which is used to determine the "net carbohydrates". More fiber in a food means less digestible carbohydrates, and a lower glycemic index. For instance, brown rice (unprocessed) has more fiber than white rice (processed) and a much lower glycemic index.

- Fat and protein: These nutrients slow the rate by which carbohydrates are digested, thereby slowing the carbohydrate-to-glucose conversion.

The glycemic index values of various foods can be obtained at http://www.glycemicindex.com.

Glycemic Load (GL): Once the glycemic index of a food item is known, one can determine the glycemic load. Multiply the GI value of a food by the amount of carbohydrate per serving and divide the result by 100 to determine the glycemic load of any given food.

Example: An apple has a GI value of 40 and a serving contains 15 grams of carbohydrate. The glycemic load of an apple is then calculated like this: (40 times 15) divided by 100 = 6. This means apples are an excellent food item during the Krispy Klean Detox because a good rule of thumb for those healing addictive biochemistry is to pursue numbers like GI 50 / GL 10 and below through The Krispy Klean Detox, and rarely above GI 60 / GL 15 during The Ark. These values are set for complex carbs, not refined simple carbs; refined simple carbs such as cokes, candy bars, protein bars, etc. are avoided entirely on The 101 Program. They are not considered food; they are pure energy void of nutrition, which will in turn fuel compulsive behavior and addiction.

When you move on to the Preserve & Protect phase, you will maintain focus on organic whole foods that are low to medium on the glycemic load chart. However, at this time it is assumed that you are healed and your "window" of error is far more forgiving should you enjoy a favorite food or desert a few times a week that is outside of the suggested glycemic load ranges. The key is to not slowly introduce simple/refined sugars into your diet by having it here and there every day. Nothing with such an impact on glucose levels and brain

chemistry should be in the diet every day because this will trigger the adaptation mechanism and begin the process of creating addictive biochemistry again.

Starches and the Glycemic Index

Starch is a form of glucose stored in plant foods; it is formed by thousands of glucose molecules that are strung together in chains, which is why starch was considered a complex carbohydrate until recently. New research has found, however, that there are two different starches, amylopectin and amylose, which have two very different effects on blood sugar.

Amylopectin's glucose chains branch out individually and are easily broken down by digestive enzymes. White rice and potatoes have high amounts of amylopectin and are easily digested, causing a rapid rise in blood sugar. Amylose's glucose composition consists of strings of long, tightly packed glucose molecules that are harder to digest and will cause a slower, more gradual rise in blood sugar. Foods such as basmati rice and beans are high in amylose and are preferable to those with elevated amounts of amylopectin.

It is advisable for you to study the glycemic index of foods, and how it is affected by food preparation. For instance, if you overcook your vegetables, the glycemic value rises. There is much to be learned about food preparation, so I strongly suggest you study the holistic practices shared in the suggested books and links that I have provided in the appendix.

Good Fats versus Bad Fats

Recommended reading on this subject includes <u>Healthy Healing</u> by Linda Rector-Page for the specifics on fats, and <u>The Omega Rx Zone</u> by Barry Sears for a thorough education on essential fatty acids (EFAs) and their crucial contribution to good health. In general, good fats help to keep you alive and happy, bad fats can depress and kill you. Good fats stimulate the formation of good eicosanoids and prostaglandins, which support immunity and communication between cells, control inflammation, and inhibit the over production of thromboxane. Over production of thromboxane and narrowed arteries, clogged by cholesterol, can lead to a

heart attack. Good fats reduce serum cholesterol. Bad fats, on the other hand, rot inside your body, clog your heart, diminish brain functions and meaningful benefits of circulation, and lead to sickness, aging, and death.

The order of preference for fats is (from best to worst):

- Monounsaturated
- Polyunsaturated (Omega-6 to -3 intake should be 1:1 to 4:1)
- Saturated (only allowed sparingly)
- Hydrogenated, or Trans-Fats (never)

An important fact to remember with fats is that they all oxidize and become rancid with heating or cooking, and produce high levels of free radicals during the cooking process. For this reason, the good fats are at their best in their natural or cold pressed forms. The three fats that are most resistant to heat oxidation and are therefore advised for cooking are coconut, olive, and sesame.

Omega-3 and -6 are called "essential fatty acids" because the body requires them for many healthy biochemical functions and they must be provided for in your diet; the human body does not produce them on its own. Without them in your daily diet, you will become deficient in these important fatty acids and as a result become vulnerable to chronic physical and mental illness. Due to the modern methods of preparing foods for the supermarket though, the public's food choices lean heavy on the Omega-6 side. It is estimated that today's average adult diet is a ratio of 20:1 to 30:1 Omega-6 to Omega-3, when it should be 1:1 to 4:1. For this reason, it is a good idea to make olive oil and Omega-3 oils the preference for salads, etc., and use Omega-6 oils sparingly. For more information on essential fatty acids, please see Chapter 9, "The Cure".

Good Fats	Fats to be avoided
Raw vegetable fats such as olive oil and avocados Coconut Oil	Saturated fats – Animal fats (with prudence)
Omega-3 EFAs	Canola Oil (unless you are

These are good for you cold pressed only- Do not cook with these oils: Cold water fish oils Borage Walnut oil Evening primrose oil Flax oil Wheat germ oil Pumpkin Cod liver oil	absolutely certain it is organic and not genetically modified! Palm kernel Hydrogenated fats including soy and vegetable Margarine Most margarine-type spreads (read the labels) Found in: Pastries and cakes French fries Doughnuts Cookies / biscuits Chocolate Margarine Shortening Fried chicken Crackers Potato chips
Omega-6 oils **Sesame** **Peanut** *These oils should only be used occasionally- see below	Omega-6 oils that should be avoided: Sunflower oil (polyunsaturated) Safflower oil (polyunsaturated) Soybean (polyunsaturated) Corn oil (polyunsaturated)

Important- The Right Oils to Cook With!

Olive and coconut oil are very good for you and should be included in a healthy diet.

Olive oil is best used on salads and cold food preparations. Do not cook with olive oil! All the health benefits of olive oil are nearly completely destroyed when cooking, frying or baking with it. The process of heating poly and monounsaturated oils can cause the fats to become carcinogenic; which means they promote cancer! Heating causes enzymes to be destroyed, proteins are denatured, fats

become carcinogenic, carbohydrates (sugars) become caramelized, and vitamins and minerals are destroyed. Essentially, the heating turns a medicine into a poison.

Organic, non GMO coconut oil is the absolute best for cooking. And despite the urban legend that it is a saturated fat and because of that, it is bad for you, nothing could be farther from the truth! Coconut oil is extremely good for you and everyone should consider including ½ to an ounce of it in their daily diet. It can be added to smoothies, shakes, etc... It has also been found that coconut oil reduces cholesterol and actually raises the metabolism and helps you lose weight. Please see Dr. Mercola's website (http://mercola.com) for a rich source of information regarding this health elixir.

Peanut oil is relatively stable and, therefore, can be used for cooking in low temperatures such as for stir-frys on occasion. However, due to the high percentage of omega-6 found in peanut oil it is a potential danger, so use it with prudence.

Sesame oil is similar in composition to peanut oil, however, it is much safer for frying, baking, and sautéing because it contains unique antioxidants that are not destroyed by heat. Due to its high concentration of omega 6 oils, sesame oil should also be used only occasionally.

Removing Pesticides from Produce

You should ideally purchase organic produce for their superior health benefits over conventionally grown food. However even organic produce can be exposed to toxins and bacteria during shipping and handling, so cleaning it is always advisable. An excellent way to wash vegetables is to fill the kitchen sink half way with water and add a half-teaspoon of salt mixed with the juice of a lemon. This method will also help to keep them fresh and crisp longer.

Microwaves

Warning: Do not use plastic or recycled products in microwaves. Known toxic carcinogens in plastics called dioxins, which are extremely harmful, are transmitted into the food when it is microwaved in plastic containers. Not only do these toxins dismiss your efforts at detoxing, they can also cause serious health problems and lead to the cancers they

promote. Microwaves are an extremely unhealthy way to heat food and liquids all together and you should consider discontinuing cooking with microwaves.

The Krispy Klean Detox

The 101 Program Meal Companion

The Krispy Klean Detox Diet

Up to this point, the general guidelines for The Ark and Preserve & Protect dietary practices have been covered, so you have an idea of how diet fits into the big picture, and where you're heading with The Program. Following is the more restrictive detox dietary practices and instructions for the Krispy Klean Detox that will be maintained for seven weeks after the 7-Day Prep.

Review of healthy condictive dietary guidelines

- During the Krispy Klean Detox absolutely no refined sugars, carbs, meat, fish or dairy is allowed.
- As in the Ark phase, whole grain breads and grains should constitute no more than 10% of your diet. Rich sources of complex carbohydrates such as vegetables, and protein from natto, miso, tempeh, beans, nuts, and seeds should be your main food sources. Fruit may be enjoyed in moderation.
- Eat real, whole foods. Eliminate the middleman and any technology, except for what it takes to organically grow it, pick it, transport it, and package it when necessary (whole frozen foods).
- Practice an insulin-sparing diet: 30% protein, 30% fat, and 40% complex carbohydrates.
- Establish a diet around foods that have a 50 GI / 10 GL for the Krispy Klean Detox and a 60 GI / 15 GL thereafter. Look up the GI and GL of foods at http://www.glycemicindex.com.
- Eat and use only the good fats suggested in the Good Fats / Bad Fats chart in Chapter 7, "The 101 Program Condictive Diet".
- Stay away from hydrogenated fats – all of them. Check for these fats on food labels.
- Coffee should be consumed with extreme prudence during the Ark phase and never more than a cup a day on a full stomach, or as a daily habit; and never more than 3 cups a

week. Cultivating a taste for green tea in place of coffee and enjoying a variety of non-caffeinated herbal teas throughout the day is a better option. The endorphin-stimulating teas listed in the Meal Planner section are a good first choice.

- Eliminate industrial simple sugars and refined carbohydrates from the diet (eg, candy, cokes, pastas, pastries, flours). Fruit is good in moderation; fruit with nuts is an ideal snack. This helps toward reducing a sharp rise in insulin and provides for longer-lasting energy.
- Clean foods before they are consumed.
- Eliminate all processed foods – they are normally found in boxes, bags and cans. The box has to appeal to the eye because the lifeless, cardboard-looking contents certainly would not be purchased off the shelf.
- Avoid all soy products except fermented soy items like tempeh, natto, and miso. Use fermented soy powder only for protein shakes. After the detox, I suggest the Whey Healthier protein shake. I do not suggest fermented soy protein shakes for long-term use; fermented soy protein powder is best used for animal product restricted detoxes only, such as the Krispy Klean detox.
- Seek the most nutrition per mouthful. Eat nutrient dense foods.

Krispy Klean 7-Day Prep

- Drink 8 to 10 glasses of spring water a day.
- Cut down on drinking.
- Stock the kitchen with items that will be needed during the 7-week detox.
- Remove all junk food.
- Eat sensibly and reduce sugar and caffeine.
- Begin recommended supplements for The 101 Prep week.

You should begin cutting way down on all the things that you will be required to avoid during the Krispy Klean Detox. If you are a heavy drinker, you should cut your drinking down to 2 or 3 drinks an evening. This will help minimize what could be very uncomfortable withdrawal symptoms. It is extremely important that you taper off during the 7-day prep to avoid the misery of physical and mental withdrawal that can occur during the first few days of your total abstinence

program. The supplements in the Krispy Klean Program will relieve much of the withdrawal misery, but the process will be easier if the drinking has slowed down.

It is also important for chronic problem drinkers to cut down because their withdrawal could send them to the hospital. If you feel that you may need a healthcare provider's assistance, you should seek one immediately. It is best to get through the first few days without the help of drugs because this will get the body working in its natural, healthy state and at peak performance as quickly as possible. Drugs always come with their own list of setbacks. If you decide to seek a healthcare provider's assistance, you should select one who is friendly with the holistic arts and will only use drugs as a very last resort. No-one who has worked with AAAA has required drugs to get through the first few days. Through thorough testing and individualized preparation, AAAA is able to prepare severe cases with a very specific protocol to address withdrawal anxiety, panic attacks, tremens and seizures; this way a recovering drinker is able to get through this time with minimal discomfort.

You should also use some time during this week to try new dishes and fill your refrigerator and cupboards with only the items that are allowed during the detox. Once you graduate to The Ark, you should add only organic, unadulterated meats, fish and dairy into your kitchen, leaving no temptations sitting around. You should also resolve never to bring food imposters into the home or body again. This is a comprehensive change of lifestyle.

Resolutions that should be made when The 101 Krispy Klean Detox begins include eating foods bought from venues (organic farms or health food stores) that do not poison the produce, and complete elimination of flours, refined carbs, industrial sugars, synthetic or refined sugar sweeteners, and boxed or canned processed foods. This is a dramatic change for most people, so you should prepare in advance. Use the Krispy Klean Detox Dietary Guideline chart along with the allowed foods list, and prepared foods and recipes resource links provided in this chapter, to get started in writing out a personal menu for the 7-week detox and cleanse. A great resource is our free video series on Shopping and Cooking for a Condictive Diet which can be found at http://the101program.com. There you can find of what to and

what not to buy as well as videos of our featured Organic Chefs preparing easy to make meals for both the Krispy Klean Detox and the Ark and beyond phases. The book, _The 101 Program Condictive Diet,_ should be considered your culinary bible for healing and avoiding addictive biochemistry. You need to be entirely prepared for the dietary changes you are going to establish for those seven weeks. The detox period is especially restrictive since it is meant to rid the body of poisons that have been accumulating for years and blocking the healthy cellular bioenergetics required to uproot addictive biochemistry. This phase will take particular concentration and planning.

While a new diet may be difficult at first, as you heal, your taste for sugar, sweets and junk food will disappear and you will begin to find enjoyment in healthy foods. There is a wide range of delicious, wholesome, real food out there that has been neglected because you have been cultivated to eat industrial products. It takes only a little time and study for you to reacquaint yourself with natural foods and regain the forgotten world of fresh, vibrant, and nourishing earthly cuisine that explodes with taste.

Coffee should also be slowly reduced during the Prep Week. Liver, adrenal, pancreatic, and intestinal health is extremely important toward healing the addiction to alcohol, and caffeine is extremely taxing on all of these organs. It also aggravates low blood sugar conditions. With confirmation through liver testing that your phase II liver function is good, a cup a day of green tea is recommended as a good tonic for the liver during and after the detox. Although it contains some caffeine, research indicates that it does not have the same over-stimulating effect on the adrenals as coffee. Please refer to http://greentealovers.com /wordpress/2005/08/08/is-caffeine-in-green-tea-all-bad/ for information regarding the benefits of the small amount of caffeine in green tea. Green tea has another important advantage over coffee: it contains theanine, which has a calming effect that counteracts the stimulating effects of the caffeine. Theanine helps to transport GABA over the blood brain barrier, a tribute that is extremely beneficial for the former drinker.

Green tea contains cancer-fighting catechins, which are powerful antioxidants that help to protect and detox the liver; this makes it an excellent tonic for the livers of people

recovering from years of alcohol abuse. These and other health benefits derived from drinking green tea make it a choice that should be enjoyed by everyone. For a deepened understanding of the history, health benefits, and uses of green tea, please visit http://teaforhealth.com and http://www.greenteahaus.com. Some of the highest quality and most nutritionally potent green tea can be purchased from Dr. Lee at http://teaforhealth.com. Quality green tea should always be purchased in bulk form rather than in bags.

Krispy Klean Flush (Weeks 2 through 8)

The detox diet is simple: remove all meats, dairy (i.e., all animal products), flours, added sugars, synthetic sweeteners, industrial sugary products (candy, "fitness" drinks, protein bars, etc.), bad fats, coffee, and refined carbohydrates.

Week 2

- Stop drinking.
- Eat only the foods outlined in the Guidelines chart for the 101 Krispy Klean Detox (below).
- Have a morning protein shake. Prepare the shake and have half in the morning and half for lunch in addition to the breakfast and lunch meals. Also, while frozen organic fruits or freshly juiced organic juices may be used for the protein shake during The Ark, while in the Krispy Klean module of the program almond milk should be used instead, to help regulate blood sugar levels.
- Pineapple, apples, or papaya should be juiced daily. Have one 4- to 6-oz. serving per day of any one of these. Lemon is an excellent addition for adding zest to any of these juices. These juices should always be consumed with a protein source such as nuts or with a protein rich meal.
- Drink 8 to 10 cups of water a day.
- Do not eat or drink anything with sugar or sweeteners of any kind, including honey, molasses, high fructose corn syrup, etc. If you are thirsty, drink water. About 99% of flavored drinks on the market are sweetened and contain more carbohydrates in one bottle than is healthy for an entire meal.
- Stevita is an excellent product for sweetening. It is 50 times sweeter than sugar, and has no glycemic value, so it won't raise blood sugar. You should disassociate yourself

from industrial sweet foods and drinks to acquire a healthier taste for foods; however, if you must use a sweetener, Stevita is your best option. Not only does it naturally sweeten drinks and foods but it has actually been found to be good for you!

- Do not eat walnuts; they are hard on the liver due to the molds they contain that are known to be carcinogenic (cancer causing). During the detox the three best nuts to use for a source of protein are hazel, brazil and almond. All seeds are good; sunflower seeds are great in salads and provide a rich source of vitamin B6 required for neurotransmitter synthesis.
- The best sources of protein for this period of time are the protein shake, natto, miso, tempeh, legumes, nuts, and seeds.
- The goal should be to eat whole foods the way the earth put them together. Minimize the human handling of the food selected; the more directly a food comes from natural sources, the better. It is best to avoid machine handling, additives, canning, and processing.

Krispy Klean Detox Dietary Guidelines

Source	Unacceptable	Acceptable
BEVERAGES	Alcohol, coffee, "fitness" drinks, pasteurized/sweetened juices and fruit drinks, soda, and caffeinated tea.	Herbal teas, freshly juiced vegetable/fruit juices, unsweetened almond or rice milk.
DAIRY PRODUCTS	ALL	
EGGS	ALL	
FISH	ALL	
FRUITS	Canned, bottled, or frozen fruits or juices, with sweeteners added	Fresh organic fruits, or purchased frozen or dried without sulfites, preservatives, or sweeteners

GRAINS	ALL flour products (cereals, pastas, baked goods, crackers, breads, muffins) and white rice; anything that has been processed to the point of becoming flour is not allowed during the detox. Gluten containing grains: such as oats, wheat, rye, and barley.	• Whole grains, which are low on the glycemic index, and products containing whole grains; however, these should be kept to a minimum and represent no more than 10% of the diet. • No soy breads or sprouted soy products. • A list of suggestions can be found in the Meal Planner Guide.
MEATS	ALL; also avoid anything with broths or flavored with meat products.	
BEANS	Canned beans with preservatives, sugar, or meat broths; frozen beans. Tofu, Edamame, soy burgers and soy milks; all unfermented soy products.	• Beans listed in the bean section of this chapter that are cooked without animal fat. • Miso, tempeh, and natto of the soybean family only. These are fermented soy products.
OILS	ALL Saturated fats (animal products), hydrogenated oils, margarine, refined and processed oils, shortenings, hardened oils Most polyunsaturated fats including soy bean oil	ALL organic, cold-pressed olive, sesame, coconut, and omega 3 fats listed in fat section.
VEGETABLES	ALL canned or frozen that include salt and preservatives or additives	• Organic raw, fresh or frozen • Seaweed • Non-starchy, low glycemic index is preferred. • See vegetable section.

SOUPS	• Canned soups made with salt, preservatives, MSG, or fat stocks; all creamed soups with dairy • Read labels for chicken, pork, and beef stocks.	• Preservative-, sweetener-, saturated fat-free soups • Bean, lentil, vegetable, barley, and onion soups
SEASONINGS	Black or white pepper, cayenne, salt, hot red peppers	Garlic, onions, all herbs, dried vegetables, dulse and kelp (good salt substitutes), apple cider vinegar, and miso.
ZERO Sweets	• White, brown, or raw cane sugar, corn syrups, processed chocolate (the "candy" preparations), sugar candy, fructose (except from whole fruit), all syrups, all sugar substitutes, (Equal, NutraSweet, Sweet & Low, Aspartame, Xylitol), and jams and jellies made with sugar; barley malt or rice syrup, honey, maple syrup, and molasses • Raw chocolate is not only allowed, but advised. Please see 'Chocolate' section in this chapter for details.	

It will be nearly impossible for you to eat at any restaurants unless they offer organic produce. For the most part, you will have to eat in for the seven weeks of the Krispy Klean Detox. If you do go out, you should eat before going, and then take healthy organic snacks with you.

The Best Choices
Complex Carbohydrates and Vegetables

Seaweed is a nutritionally potent sea vegetable and should be a new regular in your diet. The best way to enjoy it is in miso soup, seaweed salads, or added to land vegetable salads. Seaweed and kelp are rich in vitamins B1, B2, B6, B12, vitamin K (aids in regulating the adrenals), Lignans (fight cancer), amino acids, and minerals. Trace minerals such as calcium, zinc (neurotransmitter co-factors), iodine (boosts thyroid function; required due to the many suggested cruciferous vegetables in the diet), iron, and magnesium (depleted by alcohol; crucial for healthy neurotransmitter production) are also found in seaweed. Seaweed is an excellent natural detoxifier, and is a truly medicinal vegetable for everyone, particularly those healing addictive biochemistry.

Preferred vegetables include:

- Cruciferous: broccoli, cauliflower, celery; red, green, and yellow peppers
- Chinese cabbage
- Spinach
- All salad types of lettuce: romaine, endive, red leaf
- Bell peppers: orange, green, red
- Zucchini and summer squash
- Mushrooms
- Cucumber
- Tomatoes
- Beets
- Artichokes (reduce insulin response)
- Garlic and onions

These are all non-starchy vegetables. Starchy vegetables are usually root-type vegetables like carrots and potatoes. Cruciferous vegetables are the best: broccoli, Brussel sprouts, cabbage, turnip greens, mustard greens, collard greens, Daikon, radishes, turnips, kale, kohlrabi, cauliflower, and celery. Red and green vegetables are excellent. Sulfur-containing vegetables are excellent for detoxification, so include lots of onion and garlic in meal planning. Prepare vegetables with tempeh, natto or the suggested grains or legumes.

Whole Grains

- Pearled barley
- Bulgur
- Spirali, durum
- Buckwheat
- Brown rice (occasionally, not as a staple)
- Basmati
- Wild rice
- Millet
- Amaranth
- Quinoa (highly suggested)
- Sprouts

Brown rice, basmati, and wild rice are acceptable in moderation. However, white or processed rice products such as rice cakes, rice breads, and pasta should be avoided; they are very starchy and therefore have a high glycemic value.

Breads

- Sprouted, seed, bean, whole grain, or freshly ground whole grain breads that contain no refined, enriched, or processed flour.
- High protein / low carb breads – typically made from beans and seeds.
- Breads made from gluten-free whole grains such as millet, amaranth, and buckwheat are highly recommended.

Cereals

- Gluten free organic Oat bran, raw
- All bran
- Some Muesli's (research brands on the Internet to get the glycemic load)

Beans / Legumes

- Butter beans
- Black beans
- Pinto beans
- Lentils
- Kidney beans
- Garbanzo beans (hummus)
- Green beans
- Split peas
- Sprouts

Garden burgers (not tofu or soy burgers) made with legumes, vegetables and grains are a good source of protein. Do not make sandwiches with them since the grain in the burger itself is enough; it is important to keep bread and grain intake to a minimum, eating only whole-grain or sprouted, low carb, and sugar/honey-free breads on occasion. Burgers can be spiced up with a variety of enjoyable sauces.

Note: Unfermented soy such as soy milk and tofu should not be consumed by those on a program correcting neuroendocrine health, and I strongly suggest unfermented soy products be entirely removed from the diet.

I strongly discourage consumption of unfermented soy products for anyone, especially babies (soy formulas) and children (I know I just made a lot of kids happy out there) for many reasons that do not pertain to addictive biochemistry and many that do. Unfermented soy is counterproductive for those healing neuroendocrine function and works against your goal for enhanced health. The only truly healthy soy products are fermented soy like miso, tempeh, natto, soy sauce, and fermented soy protein powders. Unfermented soy contains trypsin inhibitors, which block protein digestion; it is also high in phytates, which are organic acids that block the uptake of iron, magnesium, calcium, and zinc. This is harmful to former heavy drinkers attempting to correct brain chemistry for many reasons; however, one major concern is the risk of zinc deficiency caused by unfermented soy products. Zinc is a *key* nutrient cofactor required for neurotransmitter synthesis, and is emptied out of the system by heavy alcohol use, rendering active and former heavy drinkers zinc deficient and vulnerable to pyroluria and many other psychological and physical health issues. Unfermented soy products such as soy milk and tofu not only block absorption of key minerals, but will exacerbate the existing compromised mental health of former heavy drinkers trying to heal and correct their brain chemistry by further depleting already low levels of this much needed mineral.

Consumption of soy increases the body's needs for vitamin B12 and D. Vegetarians are typically known to be deficient in vitamin B12 already, since the primary source for this vitamin is meat products, so consumption of soy only increases this deficiency. B12 is crucial for methylation processes, which are involved in detoxification, feel-good neurotransmitter synthesis, and in keeping homocysteine levels down.

Unfermented soy is unhealthy for the thyroid because it inhibits T3 and T4 release by binding with iodine. Inhibition of these hormones can cause thyroid abnormalities such as hypothyroidism, goiter, and autoimmune thyroiditis. The production of soy milk removes trypsin inhibitors, but at the expense of denaturing the proteins, which makes them indigestible. The bottom line is that soy was used for years as a cheap protein substitute; however, today it is no longer

cheap, and we know it to actually inhibit protein absorption and utilization, while causing multiple mineral deficiencies.

Soybeans also contain hemagglutinin, which causes red blood cells to coagulate.

Fruits

All fruits except grapefruit may be consumed during the detox. Grapefruit and grapefruit juice inhibit the cytochrome P450 enzymes that are required for Phase I detoxification. If you are having a piece of fruit as a snack, you must be sure to have a small amount of nuts, seeds, or other protein as well.

The fruits lowest on the glycemic index are:
- Cherries
- Figs
- Apples
- Olives (improves insulin sensitivity)
- Avocado (improves insulin sensitivity)
- Pears
- Grapes
- Oranges
- Strawberries
- Plums

Liquids

Water should be your main source of liquid; you should drink at least 8 to 10 glasses of water a day. Proper hydration is necessary for a healthy mind and body; nothing tops it and nothing should replace it. You should never drink tap water, especially during a cleanse.

Anything other than freshly squeezed fruit juices or juiced vegetables found in a store should be avoided. Canned and commercially bottled juices are pasteurized, and this process renders them little more than sugar water by the time they get to the consumer. When doing the juicing yourself, you should juice what you need first thing in the morning and drink the juice throughout the day; this way you get the benefits of the live enzymes and its full nutritional value. It is not advisable for you to drink more than 8 oz of fresh fruit juice per day during your detox due to the effect on the adrenals and blood sugar when consumed in excess.

However, one or two 8-oz servings of vegetable juice a day are encouraged. Lemon will also add zest to any fruit or vegetable drink.

Nuts / Seeds

- Hazelnuts
- Almond
- Brazil
- Peanuts (if not allergic)
- Macadamias
- All seeds

Oils

- Extra Virgin Olive oil for salad dressings and other raw food preparations
- Refined Olive oil for cooking
- Sesame oil
- Coconut oil

Coffee Substitutes

- Teechinoo http://www.teeccino.com/ (creamed with almond milk, hot or cold, makes an ideal coffee substitute)
- Kaffree roma (instant)
- Twig teas: kukicha and bancha
- Roastaroma tea
- Uncle Lee's snappy ginger tea
- All herb teas

Condiments

Braggs makes an excellent amino acid dressing. It helps pick up the flavor of salads and sautéed vegetables, and is also good with tempeh and natto dishes.

Brown Rice Butter is a good alternative to animal fat and soy butter. Make sure it does not have hydrogenated fats or is supplemented with soy.

Herbs and Spices as Condiments

All herbs and spices: rosemary, thyme, basil, mint, dill, cilantro, curcumin (turmeric), ginger, paprika, curry, cinnamon, Italian seasoning, etc.

Use sea salt with prudence; and vinegar, soy sauce, and all the natural herbs as often as desired.

Medicinal Qualities of Raw Chocolate (Cacao) for Healing Addictive Biochemistry

A small handful of cacao nibs a day is a good tonic for the brain chemistry of those healing addictive biochemistry, and it's also great for anyone in excellent health. Of all the things you have been consuming to get yourself into trouble with addictive biochemistry, chocolate in its original form isn't one of them. Raw chocolate (cacao), *without* the added fat, sugar, and caffeine, is actually healthy, and even more mood enhancing than the sugar industry's products.

For the purposes of this study, this section will highlight some of the known benefits achieved from the organic composition of cacao. However, for a full disclosure of all cacao's nutrients specific to healing addictive biochemistry, as well as for other enjoyable life-sustaining and enhancing purposes, see Naked Chocolate by David Wolfe and Shazzie. Copies are available at http://naked-chocolate.com. Beyond the health aspects of the cacao bean, Naked Chocolate provides a history of the commercial, political, and ethereal aspects of chocolate. The book is as enchanting as its subject. It is also a full-color, enlightening testimony to how the for-profit sugar industry has taken a gem of the earth that provides well being and pleasure and translated it into obesity, disease, and addiction. They have perfected the art of transforming something that heals into something that kills, and misuse of the cacao bean crowns this achievement.

This is yet another example of the necessity for filtering out the middle man to find a delightful food and medicine.

Cacao:
- Stimulates endorphins and enkephalins
- Boosts many feel-good neurotransmitters, including anandamide and serotonin
- Is a natural MAO inhibitor (prevents early reuptake of the feel-goods, including the "blissful neurotransmitter" anandamide)
- Reduces anxiety
- Is high in antioxidants
- Nourishes and stimulates the hypothalamus, pituitary, thyroid, and adrenals

While the cacao bean contains hundreds of nutrients known to the vitamin, mineral, amino acid, EFA, polyphenol and enzyme families, we can only report on the ones we know how to test for. There is something about chocolate that is beyond what we can intellectually understand because none of the ingredients in the cacao bean are in high enough doses to justify the response that we experience from it. Apparently it is Earth's proprietary blending of the natural chemicals in cacao that provides the mild euphoria and healing properties for which it is famous. In truth the mystery seems to add to the pleasure.

There are a great number of chemical compounds in the cacao bean, in very small amounts, which trigger hundreds of healing processes in the human body that scientists are just beginning to understand. For this reason it seems natural to view the cacao bean as a homeopathic tonic to help heal addictive biochemistry by encouraging natural neurotransmitter production and balanced HPA axis function. Homeopathic medicine is the art of providing a small amount of a given substance in order to stimulate the body's natural resources into mimicking the healing properties of that natural chemical. The chemical composition of the cacao bean does exactly that in multiple biochemical pathways, thus encouraging the body and mind to correct imbalances and weaknesses throughout the complex labyrinth of human physiology.

If the kingdom of heaven can be found in the mustard seed, the cacao bean is the limo that can take you there.

After The Krispy Klean Detox

After the detox, when you may again include meat, fish, and dairy in your diet, there are a few healthy tips that should be considered.

Meats

Purchase organic, free-range, unprocessed (not pre-basted, marinated, or smoked) meats and poultry that do not contain added or fed hormones, drugs, antibiotics, pesticides, or preservatives. The best meat sources are wild game and organic pasture raised farms, which can be found at butcher shops, health food stores, and on the web. A good place to

begin your education regarding these healthy alternatives to conventional poisoning of our meats is http://www.eatwild.com. There is a wealth of information at Eat Wild, as well as a list of companies that will ship healthy meat to you if you can't find it locally. The meats from grass-fed cows and other pasture-type animals are best because grass, not grain, is their natural diet; they are healthier and develop the way nature intended them to if they are fed this way. The Omega-6 to -3 EFA ratios they pass on are also far healthier; grain-fed animals can have a 20:1 to 30:1 Omega-6 to Omega-3 ratio, which is unhealthy for you, and was unhealthy for the animal as well. Human diets should be at about 4:1 to 1:1. Anything beyond 4:1 will encourage a list of diseases and illnesses, particularly in the inflammatory, degenerative, cardiovascular, and mental health categories. The standard diet today is far too Omega-6 heavy, which explains the genesis of many of the diseases that were rarely heard of 100 years ago and are epidemic today.

Be sure to include a lot of wild fish (not farmed) in the diet. Always buy and cook fresh; fresh fish is far better than fish sticks, crab cakes, etc. Farmed fish are not provided their natural food sources and does not contain the concentrated amounts of Omega-3 EFAs that makes wild fish a healthy source of protein and Omega-3 oils. The currently popular farmed salmon is full of synthetic coloring that has been added to entice people into buying it. Carotenoids and astaxanthin are the pigments and antioxidant that produce the red color of wild salmon, caused by eating the crustaceans, algae, and other naturally occurring foods in their indigenous habitat. Fish farmers know that consumers expect this red color in salmon (focus groups have actually been conducted), and since the diet they provide the salmon (often soy based) does not produce the rich natural red color, they must inject synthetic coloring into farmed fish to sell it. Neither the diet nor the synthetic, man-made colorings are able to produce the anticarcinogenic, EFA, and antioxidant health benefits of wild salmon. When a farmer has to color your salmon to coerce you into buying it, because they did not provide a natural environment of rich nutrients that would give the salmon its natural color, you can only imagine how unhealthy the environment was that the salmon lived in, and what it was fed. Add to that synthetically produced anything

and you've got another recipe for disease-causing, for profit-not health, industrial products- not food.

Fish farmers have begun to feed their fish soy which completely negates the health benefits of eating fish because it is the natural diet mentioned above that produces the high density nutrients and protein that natural fish provides. The absolute best, clean, line caught, flash frozen, fresh fish can be purchased at www.vitalchoice.com at very reasonable prices. This company is run by Alaskan locals that operate a sustainable fishing business, care about the planet, and your health.

Dairy

It is important to purchase only organic dairy items. Dairy products from conventional farms are dangerous because the pesticides, hormones, drugs, and antibiotics that are given to animals in conventional animals-for-food farms are stored in the fat. This means that they are passed on to anyone who eats the meat or drinks the milk. Organic raw milk and raw milk products such as butter are best. Do not purchase yogurt products with fruit or jellies in them unless it is clearly stated that it is fresh, organic, unsweetened fruit. Plain yogurt can be mixed with diced apples, bananas, and oranges, and sprinkled with almonds, sunflower seeds, goji berries, and cinnamon. This is just one idea for being creative and healthy with yogurt, dried fruits, and berries.

Natural, organic butter is always better than margarine or other spreads with hydrogenated fats.

Eggs

When buying eggs, look for eggs from chickens that are organic-*grass* fed, free-range, and raised without hormones and antibiotics.

Krispy Klean Foods

Single food items that can be considered staples are:

- Vegetables
- Fruits
- Nuts and seeds
- Vegetarian soups and chilis

- Miso, natto, tempeh – these are fermented soy products, and are healthy protein sources when they are a member of a diet based on a variety of good protein sources such as nuts, seeds, and legumes. Later in the Ark phase fish and organic, pasture raised meats and diary made from the same organic sources are also advised.
- Canned organic beans without sugar, fats, or meat/broths
- Unsweetened almond milk
- Sprouted, seed or whole grain breads. Look for high protein and the fewest carbs. Millet, quinoa, amaranth, and buckwheat (grain-like seeds) are preferred over grains containing gluten. Due to the low-carb boom in the media, good low carb/high protein breads are becoming popular.
- Organic frozen fruit – great for tossing in a blender and making a protein shake or smoothie with almond milk
- Kelp and seaweed for use in miso soup and making salads
- Brown rice butter (make sure there are no hydrogenated fats used in the product)
- Gluten free steel cut oats
- Peanut butter
- Fruit jams and jellies that do not contain any added sweeteners
- Falafels
- Burritos – use crisp lettuce for wraps as opposed to flour/grain tortillas.
- Bragg's Liquid Aminos is excellent for aiding digestion and "picking up" a salad.

Krispy Klean Recipes

Meal Prep Guide for the Krispy Klean Detox

Calorie counting is for people who are trying to get away with eating as much junk as possible. When you eliminate industrial processed and refined products in favor of wholesome foods, and attain healthy, stable blood sugar levels, your appetite will naturally adjust to nourish your body and request only the calories it needs.

Migrating into a healthy lifestyle begins with what you eat and drink. As you embrace this new lifestyle, you will find that there is an abundant selection of organic, delicious, nutritious, and healing foods for you to enjoy. It is a world far too vast and ultimately too personal for this text to do any justice to it by attempting to provide an education regarding its products and nutritional and healing value. The links provided below and in the Resource section will direct you to people who specialize in this kind of education. These resources will serve as excellent guidance and a beginning education in selection and preparation of foods that serve health and healing, which is not only extremely important, but also very interesting. This world will be a leap from what people have been raised in and made accustomed to, and it will take some time to absorb and understand it. For this reason, this transition should be considered a new hobby for a few months while you focus on finding truly healthy and enjoyable foods and learning how to prepare them. A good start that will get you well educated in what to look for in food choices and their preparation for maximum benefit is The 101 Program Condictive Diet Meal Companion. The Condictive Diet is not a diet in the traditional sense of the word, it is more a food plan because when you eat only those foods the body is meant to eat there is no need to diet.

David Wolfe is well respected as an expert whole and raw food advocate and practitioner. There are three very valuable websites that contain his wealth of knowledge and just about every resource required for natural food selection, education, purchase, and recipes, as well as their medicinal qualities.

http://www.rawfood.com

http://www.thebestdayever.com
http://davidwolfe.com

David's sites and guidance are useful to people following The 101 Program because he is a true "purist". While many vegetarian sites will use sugar, bad fats etc., David's recipes are all 100% Krispy Klean Detox user friendly.

Some other helpful sites include:

http://www.thevegetariansite.com/index.htm
http://www.rawfoods.com (different website than http://rawfood.com)
http://www.rawgourmet.com/
http://www.living-foods.com/
http://vegweb.com/recipes/raw/

These sites provide recipes, educational resources, articles, newsletters, book links, community services, restaurant guides, chat lines, notifications about lectures and other events, and mail-order healthy foods and snacks.

After graduating the Krispy Klean Detox module, you will simply add meat, fish and dairy to the cleansing diet you have been on if you choose to do so. Many people adopt the raw food lifestyle as their new way of life due to the miraculous healing transformation that they experience during the detox, and others enjoy meat and dairy only occasionally. Once the healing powers of healthy foods have been experienced by someone who has suffered from any illness or disease, this usually becomes their new way of life- it is simply too profound an experience to fade from their lifestyle. A positive experience that propels a person toward their health goals is always the genesis of true transformation.

To give you a head start while becoming familiar with how to eat properly, the following are some staples for the Krispy Klean Detox.

Protein Shake

During the Krispy Klean Detox: unsweetened almond milk and fermented soy protein powder (no sugar). You may add vanilla and cinnamon, or get creative and use other spices that you enjoy.

After the detox and only if you know that you don't suffer adrenal fatigue, you may have an organic frozen or fresh fruit protein shake prepared with plain organic raw yogurt, spring water, vanilla extract, cinnamon, and whey protein powder in the morning with a small breakfast. If your adrenals are still healing, it is best to use home made almond milk with vanilla and cinnamon instead of the fruit. I recommend the *vanilla* flavored <u>Whey Healthier</u> protein powder at this time, since this is the only flavor that does not have xylitol in the ingredients. I recommend Whey Healthier because the whey protein is derived from organic fed, pasture and humanely raised animal sources. Should you wish to explore other whey protein sources just be sure they are organic. I strongly advise that you do not use the other flavors by Whey Healthier because I do not endorse using xylitol.

Morning Meals

Protein Shake with:

Oatmeal (gluten free steel cut) – dress with almond milk, flax seed, and cinnamon. Sprinkling flaxseed meal on the oatmeal will add omega EFA benefits and flavor.
Or,
A medley of fresh cantaloupe, orange, apple, berries, or banana (essentially any fruits except grapefruit).
Or,
Ezekiel whole grain cereal dressed with almond milk.

NOTE: You can make your own almond milk (highly suggested) by putting about a half cup in a blender and once they are good and crunched up, add about 15 parts water for 1 part almond paste and blend that for a few minutes. Strain it through cheesecloth and you have a really tasty, high protein, good for you drink! Add cinnamon, nutmeg or vanilla per taste.

*You can also purchase organic almond meal that is already powdered at <u>http://www.almonds-from-california.com</u>

*Soaking the meal or homemade paste overnight brings more almond flavor out.

Afternoon / Evening Meals

Note: Be sure to recognize the difference between a garden burger and a protein burger. A garden burger can sometimes be predominately grains and vegetables and is considered a complex carbohydrate source. A protein burger will be primarily vegetables and legumes and is considered primarily a protein source – both are good. Labels will tell whether a burger is more protein or carbohydrate, and whether it contains soybeans or tofu, which should be avoided.

Salads

Salads should include an assortment of standard and exotic vegetables; lots of spinach, red leaf lettuce, red cabbage, broccoli, celery, onion, tomato, carrots, cucumber, cauliflower, artichoke, and avocado. Add seaweed, sprouts, seeds, or nuts to the salad for protein. Garbanzo, red kidney, and other beans are also excellent protein-rich additions to salads. There is a full-spectrum, nutrient rich world of flavors in the vegetable kingdom, explore your choices and include as many as you like in your diet.

Experimenting with different fresh herbs and homemade dressings can provide change and variety.

Steamed Vegetables and Garden Protein Burger

Steaming vegetables: Steam until hot (do not overcook, keep them crisp) lemon and salt to taste, and garnish with parsley, basil, etc. Use olive oil for taste and health benefits.

Choose a bean, vegetable, or whole grain garden burger (no soybeans, hydrogenated fats, etc.) topped with Tahini sauce, mustard or marinara, and seasoned to taste. No buns or bread.

Steamed Spinach and Garden Burger

Steam a generous amount of spinach with onion and garlic. Salt to taste. Spray with olive oil, and sprinkle with sesame seeds. Enjoy with a protein-rich veggie burger.

Steamed spinach (as above) added to a variety of beans for protein can constitute a meal in itself.

*An olive oil pump is a good way to get an even spray of olive oil on salads and steamed vegetables. They can be found in specialty cookware stores or on Amazon by doing a search for "stainless-steel olive oil pump". They should always be stainless steel rather than aluminum.

Miso Soup

Miso soup (without tofu) should be a staple during the detox due to its many healing and detoxification properties. Add lots of kelp (wakame) or other seaweed vegetables and shitake mushrooms. Season to taste.

Seaweed Salads

See links provided in appendix for a variety of recipes for seaweed salads.

Natto

Natto is a fermented soy product that is a rich source of protein, vitamin K, magnesium, copper, iron, and manganese. Natto's health benefits are innumerable for those healing from addictive biochemistry.

Natto is traditionally served as a topping for brown rice, in miso soups or salads, or added to steamed or sautéed vegetables.

Tempeh burgers with salad

Tempeh is a high-protein food source made from fermented soy. You can make the burgers yourself or purchase them on the web or at health food stores. They range from very good to low quality; with some experimenting you can find the tempeh burger preparations that you enjoy. Tempeh burgers should be prepared in the same way as a garden burger, dressed with a condiment such as mustard or marinara. They also make great sandwiches prepared with tomato, lettuce, onion, and almond cheese. For more tempeh recipes visit http://www.tempeh.info

Almond-Green Bean Salad

3/4 pound green beans in 1 1/2-inch pieces
1 cup halved cherry tomatoes
1/3 cup sliced red onion
2 Tbsp balsamic vinegar
1 Tbsp olive oil
Salt to taste

Torn lettuce leaves
½ cup sliced almonds, toasted
Steam beans for five minutes or until crisp; rinse under cold water.
In a bowl, toss beans, tomatoes, onions, vinegar and oil.
Season to taste.
Line plates with crisp lettuce.
Top bean mixture with raw, slivered almonds.
Recipe makes three servings.

Protein Salad

For the dressing, use twice as much extra virgin olive oil as lemon juice, and add sea salt and pepper, whisking mixture into a smooth, creamy dressing.

Add ripe, sliced tomatoes, chopped basil, mint, and thyme. Allow the tomatoes and herbs to marinate in the dressing while preparing the rest of the salad. Chop greens: baby spinach, mesclun, baby lettuces, romaine, or butter; and add them to the mixture. Chop cucumbers, mushrooms, celery, broccoli, cauliflower, red cabbage, onion, and radishes into bite-size pieces. Add a mix of assorted Greek, or other olive oil-cured olives. Add natto and sprouts.

Soups

Lentil
Black Bean
Split Pea

Select an organic bean or combination of beans and soak per the package.

Amounts of the following are added to taste and depend on the amount of beans involved. Keep in mind the 30/30/40 protein/fat/complex carb ratios. Using olive oil, lightly sauté as much of any of the following as desired: garlic, onion, broccoli, green bell pepper, celery, or zucchini.

To get the suggested levels of monounsaturated fats per meal, eat half of an avocado or some olives with a bowl of soup. Olive oil may also be added to the soup when it is finished cooking.

Rinse soaked beans and add to a large cooking pot. Add sautéed vegetables, and then add water to about three inches over ingredients. Cook down to desired consistency. Season to taste.

Vegan Refried Beans (for burritos)

1 cup dried black pinto beans
2 Tbsp olive oil
2 to 3 stalks of celery, finely chopped
1 green pepper, finely chopped
Half of a small onion, minced
4 to 5 cloves of garlic
Dash of (each) salt, thyme, marjoram, dried parsley flakes

Prepare the beans by inspecting them for stones and dirt. Rinse, then soak overnight and then rinse again. Cook them in a saucepan until done, then lightly mash.
Sauté the celery, onion, and garlic. Add the spices and cook for five minutes.
Add the beans and 2 cups of water to mixture. Cook uncovered until the water reduces. Add 2 cups of water, and reduce again.

To avoid flour tortillas as a wrap for your burritos, you can use crisp lettuce halves.

Note: This recipe yields two servings.

Snacks

Snacking can get you into trouble if you're not prepared with some Krispy Klean-friendly items immediately accessible when the urge hits. It can also be a little difficult to find the right foods to snack on while maintaining the goal of balancing your neuroendocrine system. A list of resources for healthy snacks can be found at http://101programsnacks.wholefoodfarmacy.com. Phi Plus, TropiPhi, and Vichyssoise V-8 Creamy Bean Soup are the three snacks that are most highly recommended during the detox. After that you can get adventurous and explore the other healthy whole foods offered on the site. The Farmacy has many other items that will also compliment a new healthy lifestyle.

A few items that can be put together from produce available at health food store are:

- Peanut butter spread on apple
- Peanut butter spread on celery sticks
- Home-prepared trail mix (made of selected nuts and seeds from the "Best Choices" list), goji berries, raw cacao beans, and dried raw coconut shavings
- A small smoothie of blended fresh or frozen organic berries, goji berries, mango, fresh-squeezed orange juice and ice (remember to have some nuts/seeds with it)
- Flaxseed crackers with Hemp Seed butter, topped with a natural, sugar-free preserve or jelly
- Raw vegetables and nuts/seeds
- A piece of fruit with some nuts/seeds
- Sliced cucumbers are an excellent, healthy replacement for chips when enjoying dips such as hummus.

Important! It's absolutely necessary that you enjoy the food that you're eating. These are some long-time staples for the Krispy Klean Detox Diet, but you should expand your horizons and find a groove that fits your own palette. You should use the resources provided here to do that, keeping in mind that during the Krispy Klean Detox you will have to choose recipes that do not include meat or dairy. And since soybeans are still popular with vegetarians and other people who are seeking meat alternatives for various reasons, it's still pushed in the health-based venues, and will have to be avoided.

Some tips to follow during detox are to become very low maintenance and avoid putting high expectations on dietary requirements. There are a lot of other things going on at the same time, like bowel cleansing, stone flushing, work, parenting, etc., so it's easiest for you to find a few standard things that you enjoy for each meal and rotate them. Soups and vegetarian chilis are great because you can make a lot over the weekend and have it ready and waiting during the week. A half sandwich or garden burger with a cup of soup or chili makes an excellent meal.

Dietary Guidelines for the 101 Ark

10 to 18 months

- If you are having your brain chemistry and adrenals tested (HPA axis tests), and it is highly suggested that you do, you will discontinue all supplements for one week after the detox and on the eighth day, take the test. You will then resume only the multi vitamin, cod liver oil, and antioxidants suggested for the Krispy Klean Detox until you receive your targeted nutritional therapeutic (TNT) protocol for the Ark phase. The supplement requirements for this phase are *significantly reduced.* During the Ark phase you will typically be taking the amount of supplements that most health conscious people consume to protect and encourage their health today; however, your nutritional program will be justified and validated by extremely accurate scientific testing, and will target and accelerate your demonstrated requirements for healing provided by these tests.
- Introduce clean, lean organic meats and dairy, if desired. You may also include organic, natural honey at this time. Manuka honey is best. Do not use anything but organic honey from a reputable bee farm. Many conventional bee farms, again in the name of profit, are now giving sugar to the bees to speed production, reducing one of nature's medicines to a harmful, denatured product. Organic, raw honey actually has health benefits when used in moderation.
- Continue to include a protein shake with the morning meal. I suggest organic whey protein after the detox. Be sure the whey is derived from organic sources and has no artificial or refined sweeteners. This includes alcohol sugars such as xylitol, sorbitol and mannitol. The vanilla flavored *Whey Healthier* product is a good organic whey protein powder. Be sure to use only the vanilla flavor because the strawberry and chocolate are sweetened with xylitol. Whey Healthier can be purchased from Dr. Mercola's site at www.mercola.com
- Continue drinking plenty of water.
- Consider taking pancreatic enzymes for a week or two into The Ark module of the program to help digest the animal products that have been reintroduced.

If you are a meat lover you should continue to do your best to avoid red meats for general health reasons. If you must have red meat, be sure that it is organic, pasture raised or wild game, and enjoy it only a couple times weekly. The rest of the week you should enjoy a variety of leaner meats such as chicken, lamb, fish, and foul.

Everyone must continue to stay away from all sweeteners during this time (except honey, agave, yacon, and Stevita). Reading labels, being aware of labeling that is not 100% straight in exposing every ingredient, and watching for "natural flavors" and "natural seasonings" is very important. Many times this means that sugar and other unhealthy items are being hidden under general terms. MSG is a huge problem when it comes to manufacturers being deceptive with exposing it on their labels. MSG is a neurotoxin that is extremely disruptive to the neuroendocrine system, and is not always disclosed as an ingredient on labels. It can and does promote addictive biochemistry, as well as many other nerve and brain chemistry health issues. More information on the misleading terms that food distributors use to avoid disclosing MSG as an ingredient in their products can be found at http://www.truthinlabeling. org/nomsg.html.

During the Ark and Preserve & Protect modules of the program, you will be able to have a dessert occasionally after a healthy, balanced evening meal, but must stay away from cokes, muffins, candies, donuts, and other pastries. These foods only do harm, and are the markers of a very irresponsible lifestyle that can get you in trouble again.

Preserve & Protect

Your diet should remain 95% healthy simple carb (fruits), complex carbs, good fats, and protein from healthy sources. It is only human to be adventurous and indulge in an old favorite every so often; this does not make a lifestyle- so have your fun with deserts made from food sources (not refined junk food) occasionally. Healthy food sources would be considered baked cherry/apple pie, ice cream made from organic dairy or coconut; carrot cake and mousses etc. that have been made with coconut, honey or agave- not refined sugar. A diet without any junk food is required not only for personal health but to avoid addictive behavior and chemistry

as well; this diet will also help future generations of your family. Sugar, excess simple carbs, refined carbs and junk food in general are not only your enemy, but your offspring's as well.

- Continue with the protein shake.
- Seek to pack ultimate nutrition into every bite. Avoid lower quality (filler) foods.
- Drink only fresh juices from blended frozen fruits, freshly juiced fruits, or the many freshly juiced vegetable combinations that provide exquisite health benefits. If you are not making them at home, be sure they are not pasteurized!
- Continue drinking plenty of water.
- Continue with the excellent dietary habits that were cultivated during the detox and Ark phases.
- Instead of coffee, have a cup of green tea daily or try hot drinks such as Teecchino. A cup of coffee a couple of times a week is fine; however, coffee should never become a daily habit again.

Chapter Eight

Addictive and Addicted Biochemistry

The Cause

Inherently compromised biosystems in endocrine and brain function when complimented with enabling environmental triggers (malnutrition, chronic stress, trauma, abuse, lack of an empowering and nurturing environment, parental influence etc..) is the genesis of the known markers of addictive biochemistry.

Regarding malnutrition, the inability of the body to regulate brain glucose can be caused by a family history of high simple/empty carbohydrate diets, as well as certain dietary amino acids, vitamins, EFAs, and minerals not being provided adequately, which can stunt the development of the brain and endocrine system. These contributing factors usually happen concurrently since long-term empty carbohydrate diets will assuredly create malnutrition. There are early signs that will show your capacity for addictive biochemistry; if they are recognized and properly addressed, it can be successfully addressed before addiction ever becomes a problem.

The over stimulating poisoned, processed, empty carb/excessive refined sugar diets combined with the nutritional deficiencies they cause, produce an upregulated endorphin/serotonin receptor count in the brain, which leads to an over reaction to any substance that produces endorphin/serotonin release. This over reaction provides increased and exaggerated sometimes euphoric-like, pleasure which relieves the symptoms of upregulated brain chemistry. There is also a biochemical chain of events that stems from this damage that produces the symptoms of alcoholism like compulsive behavior (addiction). This chain of events, and the process of correcting the metabolic patterns of addiction, is the topic of the following chapters on "The Cause" and "The Cure".

Alcohol Addiction Review

As defined in Chapter One, addicted biochemistry (and addiction) is caused by severe nutritional deficiencies. These deficiencies originate from the inability to digest and utilize nutrients, and from stores of nutrients being exhausted by the requirements of metabolizing alcohol, toxins and denatured foods. Various minerals, vitamins, EFAs, and amino acids are required to manufacture neurotransmitters for healthy biochemistry. When these building blocks are missing, all biosystems suffer, and essential neurotransmitters for healthy body and mind states are not made available. Over time, the addictive byproducts of alcohol metabolism such as THIQs begin to replace the brain's natural feel-good neurotransmitters, while malnutrition makes it next to impossible to produce them in healthy quantities, causing you to develop a dependence on alcohol to feel "right". Since compulsiveness is the parent symptom of addiction, it is nearly mentally impossible for someone to resist the strong urges to drink as a means of self-medicating the resulting symptoms of this condition.

In this state, the body and mind's metabolism has lost its "inner wisdom" due to prolonged toxicity and malnutrition. Until that "inner wisdom" is re-established, through detoxification and provision of the "tools" (nutrients) for healthy bioenergetics, the person will remain addicted.

Due to not having the bio-friendly molecules required to communicate with the body and maintain homeostasis, xenobiotics such as alcohol and psychiatric drugs do not possess the intelligence to "seek balance" that natural pleasure-giving neurochemicals do. As a result exaggerated states of euphoria are produced by the chemical, emptying nutritional reserves needed for the creation of natural neurotransmitters and hormones responsible for pain relief, pleasure, and well being which causes symptoms to develop. When the chemical is absent, withdrawal ensues. This is because the body needs time to register the need for its own feel-good natural chemicals and initiate their production.

This "error" in neurotransmitter production and communication is the root cause of the addiction because it results in mental anguish, depression, emotional distress, mental fatigue, anxiety, and other mental and physical discomforts that prompt you to self-medicate. Seeking relief

from pain is a survival mechanism that is unavoidable. Seeking this relief in toxic substances, however, is a very popular yet misguided and uneducated method of survival.

The life-renewing / repairing response to this problem would be to heal the cause of the discomfort and cravings, not medicate or mask it which provides the opportunity for dis-ease to progress as well as new ones to develop. Symptoms are the first indication that dis-ease is in progress. Symptoms are signs that organisms within your body are detaching from the biochemical grace that defines health; they are detaching from how the whole organism (your body) is supposed to function as a whole to maintain universal wellness within and harmony with its environment. Symptoms are literally a sign that cells are dysfunctioning and dying. Symptoms are a blessing because without them, we would all just walk around until we shut off with no opportunity to correct what has begun to go wrong before it's too late. Only by healing the root cause and relieving the symptoms can you end the directives from the brain that have been etched into our survival mechanisms since the beginning of our cellular development to end the discomfort. You can not fight 3 million years of evolution and the survival mechanisms developed in that time to stop pain and to adapt; the most fundamental means to heal and protect the survival of the organism. Just as naturally as a wound heals, your mind seeks to heal and utilizes these survival tactics built into our brain to do so. We should refrain from both the temptation to think that we can control nature by manipulating and silencing it, and being audacious enough to attempt to usurp the wisdom that our cells have collected while not only surviving, but flourishing for 3 million years. We will never succeed at attempts to manipulate, control, or silence our symptoms as a strategy to heal. That is simply not how it works; you must listen and respond; not silence and ignore them.

To the reptilian brain all pain, fear, and the stimuli generated from stress (even just perceived stress- it doesn't have to actually exist) is ultimately interpreted as impending death/danger, so it engages its survival mechanisms when it senses it is endangered, and its influence on the rest of the brain takes priority because all other issues line up behind the first primal one to survive. So rational, conscious thought disappears and compulsivity enters to make way for pure

action focused on reducing discomfort (threat of impending death). This is why conventional methods at treating addiction fail; they are built around trying to control or manipulate survival systems embedded in our biochemical processes and the wisdom of the cells since the beginning of time, instead of working with them and assisting the natural healing process involved in curing the root cause that produces the symptoms. You can't usurp these survival mechanisms; you can only heal what is engaging them! Trying to usurp survival mechanisms within the body is against nature, destroying every healing mechanism developed over eons to maintain life, and that is where additional dis-eases will be given a rich environment to proliferate. The only way a genuine transformation from dis-ease to health, from disorder to grace, can occur is by assisting the biochemical processes designed by the cell's successful record at surviving through getting out of its way (removing toxins), and then providing the tools it needs to do what it does best- keep you alive and well! Let me stress: *you can't fight 3 million years of evolution! Our number one health risk is our audacity in all respects; our most recent history is drenched with medicine and technology that attempts to control or manipulate nature. Not only will this strategy never heal dis-ease, it causes us to suffer the consequences that follow the resulting denaturing of our bodies and our planet. These are misguided and extremely dangerous tactics. Nature sustains us, without it, we die- it is as simple as that- and that nature needs to be recognizable to the cell and can't be so void of its original integrity or reorganized (GMOs) that it offers very little or nothing for the cell to use for its survival. You can't put a pharmacist in a biochemist's lab and expect much to get done.*

When it comes to the psychological / physical symptoms experienced that encourage someone to self-medicate with alcohol and/or sugar, it is typically the result of chronic over neuro-excitation from the diet and emotional, psychological, and physical environments that lead to over excitation of the sympathetic nervous system and the person attempts to use alcohol, sugar, and legal and/or illegal drugs to silence the symptoms of over stimulation. This includes the stimuli produced from low blood sugar which also initiates a survival mechanism to raise blood sugar (find food and eat) from the

reptilian brain. Initially, the symptoms of over excitation will be managed by the limbic areas of the brain which will redirect its neurotransmitter and hormone resources to try and maintain calm (homeostasis) in the face of chronic stimuli. However, if the dietary and/or environmental stimulus is not reduced, you will soon run out of the resources required to produce the neurotransmitters and hormones that maintain calm and peacefulness and your adaptation mechanism will begin to fail causing the stimuli to strike the reptilian area of the brain directly.

The reptilian brain has two functions with one common goal; to find food and to keep you from becoming food = survival. Over excitation is perceived by the reptilian brain as life threatening because this part of the brain does not know it is just an angry email that you're reading; or that someone just cut you off in traffic; or that you are stressed *thinking* about how you are going to come up with your car payment next month. This type of stimuli is perceived and responded to the same as if a tiger were chasing you because this part of the brain does not know the difference between a threatening email and a tiger; it only experiences the threatening stimuli; it is not concerned with the why, who, what, where and when. This part of the brain was not given the faculties to sit and have a discussion with the tiger to see what was bothering it, or to try and talk it into a rabbit for lunch. This part of the brain is built for action and action only because in the case of true danger you want ALL your resources focused on actions required for survival and that is to get out harm's way or cancel what is threatening you. We probably learned long ago that you can't negotiate with a hungry tiger! When engaged for survival, the reptilian part of the brain actually shuts down many areas of the limbic and neocortex in order to stop you from interfering with its mission and to free up resources to focus on getting out of harms way. This is one of the reasons why it is entirely impossible for someone to be in solution mode and threatened at the same time. Areas of the brain that provide reason and negotiation are shut down when a person feels threatened; this is called cortical inhibition and people jacked up on sugar, coffee, and are suffering hangovers and the effects of long term drinking (over expression of sympathetic nervous system) suffer chronic cortical inhibition. They are not being

chased by a tiger, but their sympathetic nervous system certainly thinks it is, and all of the physical and psychological resources are responding as if it is.

So, if the stimuli is relentless and the limbic part of the brain has lost its ability to naturally self-medicate you by providing plenty of inhibitory and feel-good neurotransmitters to maintain homeostasis with its environment, and the reptilian brain figures it can't get out of harm's way, the next survival mechanism is engaged; to cancel the threat.

We give this process a horrible label such as "addiction", but really it is a survival mechanism to try and reduce pain / discomfort with external methods when the internal ability has been exhausted. The survival mechanism turns self-destruction mechanism when the inappropriate method is chosen and you respond to the symptoms with legal/illegal drugs and alcohol. Of course, these are extremely appealing to the reptilian brain because it will seek the quickest method to reduce pain in the absence of rational, conscious thought.

Once the limbic and neocortex systems are exhausted, and the reptilian survival mechanisms are engaged, not much thought is entertained while seeking relief. Instead of changing our lifestyle, and adopting healthier practices that would restock our nutritional and life essence stores and restore the resources for our internal physician to do its work, and re-establish calm, tranquility and the feeling of being at peace with and in the world (safe), people tend to choose the fast method. This usually involves drugs that temporarily quiet the pain. However, once the drug wears off, you will be even further depleted of the natural resources that produce physical and mental health and will gradually need more and more of the drug to achieve the desired effects. Regular ingestion of a toxic substance will initiate the adaptation survival mechanism because that is exactly what the body is designed to do; adapt to its environment and when you provide it something regularly that "something" becomes a part of its environment. Adaptation is at the very core of our survival as a species. Our cells have learned how to adapt as a way of surviving the changes in our environment. However, when this mechanism is activated by toxic quantities of any substance, it actually turns on us because the work and resources absorbed by the task of trying to adapt to the substance drains our resources far faster than we can make

the changes required to adapt to and survive its effects on our bodies. The body expends all its resources detoxifying and metabolizing the substance, leaving little to none for repair and regeneration of cells, and the organism as a whole (you) begins to waste away and die.

When the body is producing symptoms, it is telling you that it is having difficulty either repairing or creating new cells. When you don't listen to the symptoms and respond with a method that will help it correct what is going wrong and reestablish its ability repair and replicate itself, and you instead respond by using a toxic substance daily to silence its communication with you and its community of cells, you engage adaptation to the toxic substance and the result is "addiction". Once the body and mind have adapted to the substance, withdrawal will be experienced when it is discontinued until the body and mind can once again create homeostasis and sufficiently self-medicate with ample amounts of its natural "feel good" neurotransmitters as requested by your internal and external environments. Anything you give the body regularly will cause it to adjust its internal environment to accommodate it, as well as its external environment through pursuing a lifestyle around fulfillment. Addiction is at its core, a product of internally and externally adapting to a toxic substance.

Any condition that detaches a cell or a group of cells from the parent organism that they serve is the genesis of dis-ease. Symptoms are the communication system used to advise the parent organism that something is wrong with some of its cells and it needs help. Silencing symptoms and the malnutrition that ensues as a result of energy and nutritional resources being depleted by the demands of toxin metabolism and detoxification processes are two of those conditions. When you use a drug to silence your discomfort, the body actually mimics your response to it- you sow what you reap. It stops "listening" and "responding" to its needs. The result is the original problem progressing while also suffering the effects of the toxic substance you use to silence the symptoms. Not only is absolutely no healing accomplished, but even more distress is put upon the body and mind, detaching more and more cells from the bioenergetics of the parent organism (your body and mind), and dis-ease is given an environment to flourish.

People today develop many addictions in addition to alcohol such as psychiatric drugs because conventional medicine is not focused on listening to the patient and the patient's symptoms in a quest to find the genesis of why the person is suffering, and then assisting the repair and cell renewal processes required to make the body whole again. Conventional medicine is focused on *silencing* the physical and mental pain, not *listening and responding to it using human parts to repair the human organism.* This is why any medical treatment, especially psychiatric drugs, which prescribe toxicity for an organic health crisis will never produce health.

The Biochemistry of Addiction – How the Major Organs are Afflicted

The major organs that are most affected by addiction are:
- Gastrointestinal tract
- Liver
- Endocrine system
- Brain and nervous system

Gastrointestinal (GI) Tract

The small intestine is the organ where most nutrients are absorbed into the bloodstream. Alcohol causes interference with absorption of nutrients via the GI tract and stomach. It can also interfere with enzymes needed for digestion, the transportation of nutrients from the intestines to the bloodstream, and the enzymes needed to metabolize drugs and other foreign organic substances in the gut. This last side effect is especially dangerous because the gut is the "first pass" area for detoxification. If the gut is doing its part in metabolizing a portion of the toxins ingested, the liver is not loaded down with added responsibility and can work more efficiently. Further, the damage alcohol inflicts on the stomach and GI tract increases health risks related to ingestion of bad foods, toxins and drugs, as well as internally produced toxins and free radicals.

Alcohol can cause mucosal damage (ulcerative lesions on the intestinal walls) even in healthy people, during a single episode of over consumption. It can also cause erosion and

bleeding. Free radicals, inhibition of prostaglandins, and cytokine accumulation have been credited to alcohol-related mucosal damage. These are all conditions that further prevent the proper absorption of nutrients, creating a malnourished state even in individuals who have healthy and nutritious diets. Even the finest super foods and organic produce on the planet will be mostly useless given to a body that is unable to digest and utilize them.

Alcohol decreases the muscle movements in the stomach. This causes the stomach to retain food longer than it should, giving it time to increase production of bacteria; conversely, it speeds the transit time of food through the small intestine, which prevents it from being thoroughly digested. This may cause increased sensitivity to foods with high sugar content (easily digested) and decreased digestion of foods high in proteins that need more time for digestion. These types of foods will not be properly broken down, and the amino acids they contain will not become available to the body or mind for healthy cell bioenergetics.

Alcohol causes an increase in intestinal permeability, meaning that large molecules that would normally be contained within the intestinal walls are allowed to get through, into the body. This creates a portal for bacterial disease and increases the transport of toxins across the intestinal walls, increasing the risk of liver injury.

Endotoxins (internally produced toxins), created by metabolic discord, intestinal damage, and over production of bacteria both released from and resident in the intestines, can induce the release of cytokines and interleukins from certain white blood cells and Kupffer cells in the liver. These cytokines are known to play a role in the development of alcohol-related damage to the liver and other organs.

The metabolism of alcohol actually begins in the stomach and small intestine as well as in the liver when the enzyme alcohol dehydrogenase (ADH) converts alcohol to acetaldehyde. The second stage of metabolism is carried out by aldehyde dehydrogenase (ALDH), which converts the toxic acetaldehyde into harmless acetate. The amount of alcohol that is metabolized in the stomach and small intestine is subject to much controversy and research. The initial introduction of alcohol into the system will demonstrate its addictive propensity in you with high concentrations of ADH

available to convert alcohol to acetaldehyde in the stomach, small intestine, liver, and bowels. A higher concentration could be why some people convert alcohol far more quickly than others. This has in turn been a leading characteristic attributed to people with a predisposition to addiction.

Alcohol is also metabolized into acetaldehyde by bacteria in the large intestine; this provides more opportunity for the production of acetaldehyde and gives it more opportunity to find its way to the brain. Once in the brain, acetaldehyde combines with dopamine and serotonin to create THIQs; morphine-like chemicals known to be extremely addictive and given credit for many of alcohol's addictive properties.

In summary, alcohol-related GI damage can manifest in the following ways, all of which can lead to serious health issues, disease, and ultimately death.

- Mucosal injury – inhibited production of prostaglandins
- Malnutrition – alcohol interferes with absorption and enzymatic function designed for breaking down food substances, and enzymes involved in detoxification of endotoxins and exotoxins.
- Increased permeability
- Acetaldehyde toxicity
- Free radicals damage
- Increased bacterial overgrowth
- Inflammation
- Production of cytokines
- Tumors

GI-related cancers and other GI related health issues are responsible for approximately 20% of the mortality rate in people who abuse alcohol. While many who drink excessively fear cirrhosis, symptoms such as gas, abdominal pain, difficulty swallowing or digesting, ulcers, and inconsistent stools should be investigated thoroughly by a physician for alcohol-related GI disorders, since those are a serious danger to the chronic drinker.

The Liver

When the liver is overwhelmed and cannot efficiently remove toxins and their metabolites, they are recycled and re-circulated through the blood stream and body tissues. They

interfere with the body's "inner wisdom", poisoning the mind and body and leading to both physical and mental disease. Efficient liver function is the most fundamental contributor to overall health; when liver health is compromised, all other vital organs will suffer in varying degrees. The liver is the law giver for the rest of the body's functions. Alcohol-induced liver damage can result in illness and disease anywhere in the system, caused by the free radicals from endogenous and exogenous toxins that are not being efficiently eliminated and which cause metabolic disorders and cell death.

The damaged physiological mechanisms discussed in the following sections combine and interact to influence the progression of addiction and disease.

Liver Function

The liver performs over 500 biochemical processes. The major processes impaired by alcohol abuse are:

- Energy balance and regulation
- Blood protein synthesis - metabolizing carbohydrate, fat, and protein
- Immune modulation
- Converting ammonia to urea, which is filtered by the kidneys and excreted through urine
- Producing bile to transport waste through the intestines to excrete it via the bowels.
- Filtering of the blood: detoxification, processing and excretion of endotoxic (internally produced toxins) and exotoxic (external toxins; environmental- xenobiotics) chemicals

Inefficient or afflicted liver

- An afflicted liver will not process and excrete metabolites efficiently, and can lead to metabolic poisoning caused by a buildup of metabolites in the blood, and within cells, tissues, and organs.
- This buildup of metabolites and toxic substances alters and inhibits effective bioenergetics within all cells of the body.
- Left unchecked, altered or inhibited cell function advances from disrupting metabolic processes to illness and disease. The disease or illness that surfaces is largely dependent on accompanying lifestyle factors and genetics.

- Inadequate protein synthesis by the liver essentially starves the rest of the body, deepens the addiction, prevents efficient detoxification, prevents new tissue formation, impairs healing mechanisms, disrupts brain chemistry, and sets the stage for many toxic and malnutrition-centric illness and disease.
- Nutrients exhausted while metabolizing alcohol into acetaldehyde (AH) and AH into acetate are unavailable for other vital metabolic processes such as repair and regeneration, and providing precursors for healthy brain chemistry, which accelerates aging and slows physical, emotional and psychological healing.

Alcohol Metabolism in the Liver

Although alcohol is now known to be metabolized in the stomach, GI, bowels, and even pancreas, most alcohol is metabolized in the liver. The metabolism of alcohol occurs when ethanol (alcohol) is transformed into acetaldehyde through cytoplasmic ADH and through the proxysomal enzyme, catalase.

Acetaldehyde Metabolism

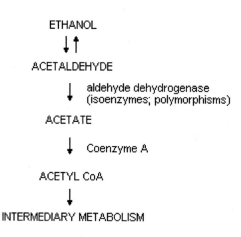

Causes of Liver Damage

- Acetaldehyde

- NAD deficiency, fat accumulation
- Excessive production of cytokines
- Scarring
- Malnutrition
- Other lifestyle factors that exacerbate the effects of alcohol metabolism and its toxic byproducts such as OTC drugs (including the popular use of acetaminophen), prescription drugs, hydrogenated fats, high simple carb diets, smoking, etc.
- Location (environmental toxins)

Acetaldehyde Toxicity

Acetaldehyde (AH) promotes addiction to toxic substances by altering normal brain function. This is because of its ability to combine in the brain with two key neurotransmitters, dopamine and serotonin. When AH and dopamine combine, they form a condensation product called salsolinol. When AH combines with serotonin, beta-carboline is formed. Salsolinol and beta-carboline are part of a group of interrelated compounds called tetrahydro-isoquinolines (THIQs). THIQs are closely related to opiates such as morphine in structure, function, and addictiveness. Since their structure is similar to our natural opioid neurotransmitters, endorphins and enkephalins, they mimic these chemicals and bond to the brain's opioid receptor sites, creating a far more enhanced euphoria than the natural molecules for which these receptors are meant.

Alcohol, car exhaust, cigarette smoke, Candida Albicans, and sugars either produce or are sources of AH. They all cause the same addictive bioenergetics in the brain chemistry. One of the reasons those suffering from Candida crave sugar is due to excess acetaldehyde being produced in their system from the yeast. This yeast starts the alcohol → acetaldehyde → THIQs chain, which causes an upregulated brain serotonin and beta-endorphin condition known to produce addictive biochemistry and sugar/simple carb cravings. People who are addicted to alcohol experience a compulsive disorder toward alcohol for the same biochemical reasons as sugar junkies do toward sweets. There is a traceable chain from sugar or alcohol, to acetaldehyde, to THIQs, which causes the upregulated brain serotonin and beta-endorphin condition known to lead to addictive biochemistry and alcohol, sugar,

and refined simple carb cravings. Candida sufferers, sugar
addicts, and problem drinkers all experience similar
symptoms of lethargy, compromised cognitive function,
anxiety, mental and physical fatigue, depression, apathy, and
agitation caused by the underlying biochemical similarities of
their compromised health and addiction. Another side effect
is that over time, the liver becomes "sluggish" due to cell
death, inflammation, fat deposits, and the ensuing
malnutrition. This causes a lag in detoxification, and allows
for even more acetaldehyde to recirculate through the blood
and find its way to the brain to cause serious damage and
increased addiction.

THIQ toxicity can be responsible for:

- Impaired memory
- Decreased ability to concentrate ("brain fog")
- Depression
- Decreased mental energy
- Paranoia
- Heightened irritability
- Anxiety and panic attacks
- Slowed reflexes
- Decreased sensory acuity
- Cell and dentrite damage, making it more and more
  difficult for neurotransmitters to communicate their
  messages
- Lethargy and apathy
- Increased tendency to alcohol, sugar, and cigarette
  addiction
- Decreased sex drive
- Increased PMS and breast swelling/tenderness in women

   Acetaldehyde is more toxic than alcohol; it is the key
addictive substance, and is created by the metabolism of both
internally produced alcohol and ingested alcohol. Everyone
knows the dangers associated with over consumption, but few
people understand that alcohol is also produced in the body as
a by-product of the bacterial breakdown of unused
carbohydrates. The healthy average person on a whole foods
diet produces about an ounce of alcohol a day. Those who
ingest denatured foods full of simple/refined carbs all day will

produce much more. Even higher amounts of acetaldehyde can be produced when insulin resistance is in the picture due to glucose not being able to get in the cells and be burned for energy, allowing it to build up in the blood and be converted into acetaldehyde. This sheds a lot of light on why those who quit drinking make a bee-line for the sugar bowl and live in it. They are creating biped breweries out of themselves and continuing the suffering and damage that alcohol started. Also, mainstream conventional treatments simply don't take into consideration how sugar consumption could be a key contributor toward the predisposition and continuance of addictive biochemistry; the extremely addictive THIQs are also being manufactured from the metabolism of internally produced alcohol. The amount of alcohol produced in the body is dependent on the following factors.

- Some individuals produce less gastric acid, which allows for bacterial overgrowth and proliferation in the stomach giving more opportunity for alcohol to be produced.
- Retention of food in the stomach for longer periods of time results in bacterial growth.
- The amount of unused carbs due to excess food and refined, simple carb/sugar ingestion affects alcohol production. This is one reason sugar is so appealing to improperly treated / untreated former problem drinkers; it encourages more internally produced alcohol.

Ingesting excess carbohydrates will produce more alcohol, and therefore more acetaldehyde; this encourages the addiction and further disrupts brain chemistry. Internally produced alcohol is metabolized in the same way as ingested alcohol. Therefore, a higher-than-normal resident amount of acetaldehyde is found in the body and brain chemistry of those who eat and drink too many sweets and simple carbs. Those with sedentary lifestyles are particularly at risk because they will have higher amounts of unused carbs, which will produce more alcohol, AH, and THIQs, making the body unable to detox the metabolites as efficiently. In these conditions, the "one drink, one drunk" scenario is true. The pre-condition for an enhanced response to alcohol is present in the upregulated beta-endorphin and serotonin brain chemistry, caused by higher-than-normal THIQ production on

one end and low blood sugar on the other end. One drink will have an extremely euphoric effect on people with this condition, and the relief it provides will encourage more drinking.

This is also a very strong indicator of why former problem drinkers find so much relief in sweets and simple carbohydrates in the absence of alcohol. On the biochemical level, the addictions to alcohol and sugar are interchangeable; they both produce the most addictive and most damaging toxin known to this type of addictive biochemistry, THIQs, and satisfy upregulated brain chemistry. If alcohol is taken out of the diet, sweets can step in and adequately satisfy the cravings in the short term created by its absence. However, responding to the alcohol withdrawal like this comes at a huge cost to the health of the person and delivers them to a state of perpetual withdrawal experienced daily which is why former drinkers who stop alcohol and dive into the sugar bowl are called "white knucklers". They crave alcohol daily because they continue to produce alcohol and THIQ withdrawal due to self-medicating the withdrawal with sugar which produces the identical low blood sugar symptoms, alcohol, and THIQ withdrawal that in many cases attracted them to alcohol in the first place.

Acetaldehyde's Contributions to Addiction and Liver and Brain Damage

Acetaldehyde toxicity is a primary cause of the diseases related to alcoholism because it damages tissues, kills cells, and exhausts the body's antioxidants and nutritional resources needed to detox, repair, regenerate, and nourish itself. This opens the door to a long list of health issues and mental disorders.

Acetaldehyde toxicity also creates deficiency in vital biochemical compounds such as thiamine, niacin, pantothenic acid, EFAs, and amino acids. These deficiencies can be directly linked to brain injury and imbalanced brain and body chemistry, which lead to varying degrees of underutilization of all vital biochemical compounds. It is this chain of damage that creates the error in the biochemistry and defines the symptoms and extent of the addiction.

Following is a breakdown of this damage and the ensuing conditions.

- Alcohol dehydrogenase, which converts alcohol to acetaldehyde, is found in the stomach and small and large intestines. This means that deposits of acetaldehyde can be concentrated in these areas during alcohol metabolism and before entering the blood stream. This also means that these organs are very vulnerable to damage and disease; it is probably the reason for the commonly inflamed state of these organs in problem drinkers. Alcohol dehydrogenase has also been found in the pancreas, bowels, and adrenal glands, making them other targets of acetaldehyde damage.
- Acetaldehyde induces a deficiency of Pyridoxal-5-Phosphate (P5P). P5P is the metabolically active coenzyme form of vitamin B6, and is the major coenzyme necessary to form virtually all major brain neurotransmitters. It is involved in all transamination reactions, whereby cells convert many different amino acids in order to satisfy their ever-shifting amino acid needs. P5P is necessary to convert essential fatty acids into their final use forms, as well as to turn linoleic acid into the key, nerve cell-regulating biochemical, Prostaglandin E1 (PEG1). Prostaglandin E1 is a key regulatory biochemical for both nerve cells and the immune system, controlling blood pressure, muscle contractions, and inflammation. It also regulates the production of the pro-inflammatory Prostaglandin E2. Prostaglandin E1 prevents excessive production of Prostaglandin E2 from the dietary fatty acid, arachidonic acid, which is abundant in meat, poultry, and dairy products.
- P5P is also needed for the production of GABA. The fact that AH induces a deficiency of this coenzyme explains why long-term drinkers develop anxiety, nervousness, and agitation; these are all symptoms that would be controlled by GABA.
- P5P helps regulate magnesium entry into cells. The level of excitability of nerve cells is strongly dependent upon their magnesium level.
- P5P is necessary to convert vitamin B3, niacin/niacinamide, into the active coenzyme form, NAD.
- Researchers in prostaglandin biochemistry have discovered that AH is a powerful deactivator of Delta-6-Desaturase. Delta-6-Desaturase is the enzyme that converts linoleic acid into gamma linolenic acid (GLA), which is nearly absent

from any typical diet. If the body can't produce its own GLA it will suffer from a deficiency, which has been linked to many physical and mental disorders.

- Suppressed GLA production leads to suppressed Prostaglandin E1 production. This condition "takes the brakes off" of Prostaglandin E2 production and that of a related compound, TXB2. High levels of Prostaglandin E2 and TXB2, coupled with low levels of Prostaglandin E1, have been shown in research to be a major causal factor in some forms of depression.

- Acetaldehyde reduces Acetyl Coenzyme A and impairs cellular energy production. Acetyl Coenzyme A, which is the active form of B5 combined with acetate, is necessary for the production of acetylcholine, the chemical responsible for memory, learning, and concentration. Acetyl Coenzyme A is perhaps the most pivotal single biochemical in all cellular biochemistry; both sugar and fat must be transformed into Acetyl Coenzyme A to power the Krebs' cycle, which produces 90% of the energy used by cells in the body. The lethargy associated with problem drinkers, adrenal fatigue, and poor cognitive skills are all explained by the diminishing stores of this vitamin.

- Alcoholism and Candida are the two conditions that generate the highest chronic AH levels in the body. The health issues related to AH are similar in both.

- Acetaldehyde promotes deficiency of vitamin B1 (Thiamine) because B1 is required to metabolize alcohol. B1 is critical to nerve function in the brain and to the metabolism of carbohydrates to produce energy. This deficiency is a characteristic in many mental diseases and disorders found in problem drinkers. Two very serious syndromes that can occur together or separately are Wernicke's and Korsakoff's syndrome; both due to the low thiamine levels found in problem drinkers. Symptoms of this deficiency include confusion, emotional instability, irritability, depression, fear, paranoia, fatigue, insomnia, and headaches.

Acetaldehyde and NAD Deficiency

Niacin (Vitamin B3) is present in the human body primarily in its coenzyme form, NAD. Acetaldehyde affects NAD supply in a number of ways.

- Acetaldehyde induces deficiencies of niacin and NAD. B3 is a cofactor in the metabolism of alcohol to acetaldehyde and ADH to acetate, and gets used up during this process, disabling many biochemical processes that require NAD to function.
- NAD is involved in burning sugar and fat for energy in all cells (glucose metabolism). Due to its key role in glucose metabolism, NAD deficiency will result in aggravated blood sugar fluctuations.
- NAD is normally the most plentiful vitamin coenzyme in the human brain; it is a catalyst in the production of many key brain neurotransmitters, including that of serotonin.
- NAD is the coenzyme that combines with zinc to activate alcohol dehydrogenase and aldehyde dehydrogenase - the enzymes that break alcohol and AH down. Since the need for NAD in all cells is great, yet the supply is limited, NAD is recycled continually during cellular energy production. But when NAD helps detoxify AH it gains hydrogen atoms and is converted to NADH; in this process the recycling of NAD is blocked and the altered form, NADH, accumulates. This accumulation interferes with and impairs cellular bioenergetics in many ways. It slows the Krebs cycle, causing a buildup of pyruvate and acetyl Co-A. The excess acetyl Co-A becomes a building block for fatty acids, which clog the liver and inhibit its function.
- Niacin is required in large amounts for optimal brain function. Niacin deficiency will first produce mostly psychological symptoms. These symptoms may include feeling fearful, apprehensive, suspicious, and worrying excessively with a gloomy, downcast, angry, or depressed outlook. Headaches, insomnia, depression, agitation, and inability to concentrate may also occur.

Cytokines

Acetaldehyde binds with cell membranes to form antigens that stimulate production of cytokines, posing serious health risks for the liver. This causes much of the damage that can lead to cirrhosis.

Cytokines are produced by cells of the liver and immune system, in response to infection or cell damage. Alcohol consumption increases cytokine levels, and cytokines produce symptoms similar to those of alcohol-induced hepatitis. Recent studies implicate cytokines in scar formation and in

the depletion of oxygen within liver cells; conditions that are also associated with cirrhosis. Each of the disease mechanisms and deficiencies described above contribute to the death of liver cells. The presence of damaged cells triggers the body's defensive responses, including the release of additional cytokines. The result is a vicious cycle of inflammation, cell death, and scarring.

Scarring

Scar formation is a normal part of the wound-healing process. But alcohol-induced cell death and inflammation can result in scarring that distorts the liver's internal structure and impairs its function. This scarring is the hallmark of cirrhosis. The process by which cirrhosis develops involves the interaction of certain cytokines and specialized liver cells (stellate cells). In the normal liver, stellate cells function as storage for vitamin A. Upon activation by cytokines, stellate cells proliferate, lose their vitamin A stores, and begin to produce scar tissue. In addition, activated stellate cells constrict blood vessels, impeding the delivery of oxygen to liver cells. Acetaldehyde may activate stellate cells directly, promoting liver scarring in the absence of inflammation; this is why heavy drinkers can develop cirrhosis insidiously, without pre-existing hepatitis.

Malnutrition

The body needs proper nutrition for energy production and to fight off disease, rebuild tissue, detoxify, and generally sustain life.

This chapter has already explained many nutritional deficiencies that excess alcohol consumption creates in the body, and the resulting physiological and psychological illnesses. There is no doubt that alcohol abuse, and even one night of over consumption, causes malnutrition in the body. In chronic, long-lasting states of malnourishment, such as that imposed by alcohol abuse, those biosystems that are the weakest will be the first to succumb to illness or disease. Below is a list of the common symptoms caused by malnutrition. However, if you ask any purist nutritionist, environmental or natural medicine physician, they would agree that on the cellular level all disease is caused by some form of malnutrition, because all diseases demonstrate a deficiency in one or more nutritive compounds and if they are

restored soon enough and a healing environment is established, the disease disappears.

- Anemia
- Diarrhea
- Disorientation
- Goiter (enlarged thyroid gland)
- Loss of reflexes and lack of coordination
- Muscle twitches
- Scaling and cracking of the lips and mouth

Malnutrition manifesting in the liver can produce:

- Chronic fatigue
- Digestive disorders, loss of appetite
- Nausea
- Abdominal bloating
- Intolerance to fatty foods
- Chronically recurring infections
- Multiple chemical sensitivities
- Hormonal imbalances
- Hypotonia (muscle weakness or pain)
- Chronic headaches
- Brain biochemical disturbances/disorders
- Uraemia (a toxic condition resulting from renal failure due to compromised kidney function and urea, a waste product normally excreted in the urine, is retained in the blood).
- Hepatic encephalopathy (complication of advanced liver disease caused by toxins in the bloodstream; clinically manifested by personality changes and impaired intellectual ability, awareness, and neuromuscular functioning).
- Inability to detox, which can result in symptoms manifesting throughout the body ranging from acne to depression, body odor, cancer, arthritis, and gout.

Physical manifestations of malnutrition can include:

- Fatty liver
- Hepatitis
- Cirrhosis

Lifestyle and Liver Disease
Drug Interaction (Recreational, OTC, Prescription)

Drug use is a key contributor to liver disease. Many people drink and use various other legal and illegal drugs at the same time. This is extremely dangerous because liver toxicity and the resulting damage is exacerbated, resulting in rapid deterioration of health and the onset of many physical complications. One common interaction that most people never think about is that between alcohol and acetaminophen; this interaction is very dangerous, and accelerates liver damage.

Location

Location is another underestimated contributor to liver disease and toxicity.

Heavy alcohol use, combined with a polluted environment, will further tax the liver and accelerate injury and other toxicity-related illnesses.

People should seek alternatives to jobs that unnecessarily expose them to pesticides and industrial toxins.

High-fat and high-sugar diets, along with exposure to environmental toxins, can leave the immune system weak and chronically stressed. That kind of chronic physical stress leaves one susceptible to illnesses, colds, and infections.

A helpful resource for investigating the sources of environmental toxins and learning how to avoid them to protect personal health and gene pool is http://cureresearch.com/risk/environment.htm.

To minimize exposure to toxic chemicals:
- Drink spring water.
- Eat organic produce and meat products.
- Do not use pesticides in the house or garden.
- Use environmentally friendly cleaning products.
- Check hygiene products for aluminum and other chemicals known to cause cancer and endocrine disorders.
- Don't put anything on your skin a health conscious person wouldn't eat.

Diet

It's been well established throughout this book that unhealthy diets can lead directly to addiction and disease. Excessive consumption of food, especially denatured, unhealthy food riddled with sugar and refined carbs, leads not only to obesity and addiction, but also to higher concentrations of pesticides, hormones, food additives, environmental toxins; and the cross contamination complications born of all of these interacting within one's system that can produce a long list of health issues. This will assist the onset of psychological and physiological disease and, in the meantime, place even higher demands on an already challenged liver.

Stress

By design, the human body's most potent stress hormones should only be produced in response to a real "fight-or-flight" situation; situations that are not supposed to happen numerous times each day. People are also not designed to eat foods that over feed the sympathetic nervous system (SNS) and make it dominant, even when there is no stress, over the more relaxed, bountiful energy source, the parasympathetic nervous system (PNS). Modern living and the excess stimuli people are exposed to through lifestyle and diet causes their bodies to produce more stress hormones throughout the day than is healthy and can be efficiently metabolized. This leaves these hormones floating around and causing havoc on your health. In addition, problem drinkers produce more stress hormones such as coritsol, epinephrine, and norepinephrine, because their release is prompted by alcohol consumption on one end and the ensuing low blood sugar episodes on the other, and the increased *perception* of stress the problem drinker develops. Exaggerated levels of stress hormones are also a key reason why it is so easy to upset a heavy drinker; hormonally they are in constant fight mode.

Adrenaline (epinephrine) affects the body by increasing heart rate, blood pressure, breathing rate, and muscle tension. The regular presence of excessive stress hormones harms you because it compromises the immune system, damages the cardiovascular system, disrupts hormonal balance, prevents healthy digestion, and places impossible

demands on the brain chemistry to provide endorphins, GABA and serotonin to mediate the over-exaggerated SNS. When these feel-good neurotransmitters become depleted, the problem drinker experiences the many symptoms I've mentioned throughout this book. This scenario is another support system for the addiction to alcohol, keeping the addicted drinker drinking every day; it's truly a Catch 22, where the more you drink the worse you feel, and the more profoundly you perceive stress. This perception produces more stress hormones that continue to damage the body and deplete the mediating neurotransmitters and hormones, further exacerbating how bad you feel physically, emotionally, and mentally. Naturally, this leads to more drinking.

This process further affects and damages the liver since it continues to be taxed from metabolizing the stress hormones and their byproducts, and dealing with the unhealthy activities in which a stressed person engages.

Fat Metamorphosis

When the liver can no longer metabolize fats, they begin to deposit in the liver and elsewhere. Alcohol metabolism results in NAD consumption and deficiency, which slows or impairs fat metabolism and causes accumulation of fat in the liver. The nutritional demands of detoxing and metabolizing alcohol and its byproducts, combined with alcohol's ability to impair normal metabolism, creates deficiencies of lipotropics, choline, alpha lipoic acid, methionine, and cystine. This contributes to fat buildup in the liver, with the added health complication of toxins being stored in that fat.

Brain Chemistry

Neurotransmitters and Neuro-active Peptides: The Communication System of the Brain

The movement of neurotransmitters provides communication of information between neurons across a gap called the synapse. Neurotransmitters are released from one neuron at the pre-synaptic nerve terminal, and cross the synapse where they can "activate" their compliment receptors on another neuron. The action that follows this activation of a receptor site may be either depolarization (an excitatory postsynaptic potential) or hyper-polarization (an inhibitory

postsynaptic potential). A depolarization makes it more likely
that an action potential will fire; a hyper-polarization makes
it less likely that an action potential will fire.

Some neurotransmitters are excitatory and increase the
likelihood that a neuron's signals are sent. Some
neurotransmitters are inhibitory and decrease the likelihood
that a neuron's signals are sent.

Neurotransmitter Bioenergetics and Alcohol / Sugar

The processes described below are demonstrative of the
effects sugar, alcohol, and any other drug will have on the
brain, through various chemical pathways. This sequence
will explain, in simple terms, how brain chemistry is altered
into an addictive condition. This is extremely important to a
recovering drinker because understanding the pathway to
addiction is the first step in understanding how to heal and
reverse it.

Normal, healthy communication via neurotransmitters
takes place when the brain has all the nutritional precursors
it needs for synthesizing the neurotransmitters and firing
them. The brain must also have the right amount of
complementing receptors available to receive these
neurotransmitters for further communication, and then be
able to metabolize them after they have served their purpose.

Because the brain always seeks balance, when it is
continuously exposed to a toxic drug like alcohol that over
stimulates release of serotonin, GABA, dopamine, and beta-
endorphins, its response will be to "downregulate". This
means that it will begin decreasing receptors sites because
they are being over satiated.

Downregulation is the catalyst of tolerance to drugs and
alcohol because with fewer receptor sites available, a larger
number of the feel-good neurotransmitters produced by the
drug will be required to supply the same sensation of
pleasure. A larger concentration of neurotransmitters will
increase the chances of the feel-goods finding and bonding
with the sparsely populated receptors. This is a very
precarious stage of addiction because this means that, in the
absence of alcohol, a large demand for beta-endorphins and
serotonin is placed on the brain chemistry for you to feel good,
and at this stage you are actually producing very few of these
chemicals naturally. This condition contributes to the

tendency of chronic drinkers to self-medicate the symptoms of low levels of beta-endorphins and serotonin with alcohol.

This is also why it is extremely important to seek out ways of naturally healing depression. All anti-depressants cause side effects and further disrupt brain chemistry; most cause downregulation, which leads to tolerance. Ultimately, any condition is worsened because the downregulation process has exacerbated the brain chemistry imbalance. It also causes the brain to accommodate to a foreign drug; what small amount of serotonin and endorphins being produced naturally will have little effect. At a certain point, tolerance will lead to the drug no longer being effective; the person will be faced with either finding a new drug or addressing both drug and alcohol addiction. Many people who quit drinking for years and go on anti-depressants (typically to deal with the depression of the continued dry-drunk diet) report a strong desire to resume drinking once they begin taking the drug. This is because the system is now producing even less serotonin, which is the condition that many times led to the alcohol addiction in the first place. When the brain responds to an anti-depressant by producing even less serotonin than before, that condition is made much worse. Low serotonin causes compulsiveness and sugar/carb cravings, which lead to addictive biochemistry and addiction. The end result is physical and mental illness and disease.

Upregulated brain chemistry means there are many more receptor sites than feel-good neurotransmitters with which they can bond. This condition is a key marker of addictive biochemistry, and is common in those with naturally low serotonin and beta-endorphin levels, such as hypoglycemics and problem drinkers. It's important to realize that you can be born with this type of addictive biochemistry even if there is no history of alcoholism in the family. A family history of high, refined grain, simple/refined carb, and junk food/candy/coke diets can be the cause just as easily as alcohol. If your mother was a severe junk food junkie and drank cokes and ate candy all day, you could have the propensity for the addiction due to compromised neuroendocrine function and the stress this diet, before and during pregnancy, can put on the fetus in addition to the underdevelopment of critical organs due to malnutrition.

Prolonged periods of excess insulin in the system can be a primary cause for low serotonin which will lead to upregulated brain chemistry. In the presence of chronic high insulin levels produced to counteract high blood sugar episodes throughout the day, the high insulin level is maintained long after the blood sugar has gone down, keeping blood sugar low. This makes it difficult for tryptophan (serotonin precursor) to cross the blood/brain barrier and be made available for producing serotonin, causing the system to upregulate in an attempt to find and collect as many of those feel-good molecules as it can.

This condition is very dangerous, and is also the hallmark of those who have been sober for years and return to serious drinking after just one drinking episode. The standard dry-drunk diet of simple carbohydrates, cokes, cigarettes, sweets, coffee, etc. aggravates and continues the same nutritionally taxing, low blood sugar conditions that cause low serotonin levels in the brain to grow even worse. Until the brain begins to downregulate serotonin receptors, the (short-lived) immense pleasure received from feeding the many vacant receptors with alcohol is hard to deny for anyone who suffers the symptoms of low blood sugar, serotonin, and endorphin levels. After the brain chemistry has downregulated serotonin sites, constant hunger (carbohydrate tolerance and addiction), and addiction to other substances such as alcohol increases.

Upregulated brain chemistry is a key addictive biochemistry marker because anyone with upregulated endorphin and serotonin sites will receive much greater pleasure from satiating them. This makes it pretty clear how standard industrialized diets which promotes this condition have produced so many mental and physical disorders over the past 70 years. This diet is truly responsible for "priming" people to become addicted to alcohol and other drugs of choice.

Today, it is common for upregulated brain chemistry to affect its victims throughout childhood and the teens. Once the nutrient void, sugar saturated, denatured food diet progresses to a drug addiction which typically begins when the person finds the symptom cancelling qualities of alcohol, prescription, or street drugs, it is only a matter of time before the brain chemistry will begin to downregulate causing a

tolerance and intensifying the use of alcohol (or the drug of choice) and the addiction's negative effects on the lifestyle and health of its victims.

Warning: Not staying on a condictive diet that addresses and prevents addictive biochemistry will worsen and aggravate upregulated brain chemistry. This is a condition that is progressive when not addressed, which is why alcoholism is perceived to be a progressive disease. When most problem drinkers quit drinking, they replace the alcohol with extremely unhealthy, refined/simple carbohydrate diets, sugar drinks, and coffee; in doing so, they maintain the same brain chemistry imbalances that got them in trouble in the first place. This continues to engrave the addiction deeper into their biochemistry just beneath the surface. They may not be drinking, but the addiction and all of the symptoms are still present; exaggerated inebriation is the only thing missing.

This is a very precarious and uncomfortable way to live; it is the premise of the progression of the addiction. The symptoms will continue to get worse, causing physical health conditions, mental health problems, disease, and relapse until the root of the addiction is addressed.

How Alcohol Affects Neurotransmitter

Function in the Brain

Key Neurotransmitters Affected by Alcohol

Synapses, neurons, and neurotransmitters serve as the communication channels that determine how you think and act, how you respond to those thoughts and actions, and how your body functions. The activity of each of the components listed below is dramatically altered by heavy alcohol abuse.

If neurons do not properly relay signals in a balanced manner (excitatory/inhibitory), or there are inadequate precursors for producing healthy levels of neurotransmitters, the result will be impaired brain function, mental disorders, disrupted metabolic processes, and ultimately disease of the mind and body. The specific illnesses, health conditions, and diseases that result will depend on your lifestyle, genes,

stress, diet, and other endogenous and exogenous
environmental exposures.

There are many neurotransmitters and neuro-active
peptides, but the ones most important in alcohol addiction are
those most affected by alcohol metabolism.

The major neurotransmitters affected are:

- Serotonin
- Acetylcholine
- Dopamine
- Norepinephrine
- Epinephrine
- GABA (gamma-aminobutyric acid)
- Glycine
- Glutamate

The major neuro-peptides affected are:

- Somatostatin
- Beta-endorphins
- Enkephalins
- GHRH (growth hormone-releasing hormone)
- Neuropeptide Y

Neurotransmitters: A Delicate Balance

In healthy biochemical conditions, there is a balance
between excitatory and inhibitory neurotransmission in the
brain. Periodic short-term alcohol use causes more inhibitory
activity by enhancing the expression of inhibitory
neurotransmitters and neuromodulators (serotonin,
endorphins, GABA, glycine, adenosine) thus decreasing the
activity of excitatory neurotransmitters (glutamate,
aspartate). Chronic alcohol exposure causes the brain to
attempt to counteract the inhibitory effects of alcohol (excess
GABA) to regain equilibrium, by enhancing excitatory
neurotransmission.

During alcohol withdrawal there is nothing producing
inhibitory functions in the brain; the ability to balance is void,
and the person experiences a constant state of excessive
excitatory function producing nerve excitation. This is the
genesis of hyper-excitability, the symptoms of which are

moderate to severe seizures, delirium, panic disorder, nervousness, and anxiety. Note that low-grade instances of this condition, caused by daily cases of mild to moderate withdrawal up until the problem drinker has their first drink of the day, manifest themselves every day. Problem drinkers' personalities actually begin to change because of these daily doses of the hyper-excitability of withdrawal. They gradually become more and more reactive, impatient, moody, angry, easily excitable or upset, and neurotic.

Neurotransmitter Classifications

Amines:
- Acetylcholine (Ach)

Monoamines / Catecholamines
- Dopamine
- Norepinephrine
- Epinephrine

Indoleamines:
- Serotonin

Opioids:
- Endorphin
- Enkephalin

Amines

Acetylcholine

Acetylcholine is the neurotransmitter responsible for mental clarity, concentration, learning, memory, focus, and assisting in transmission. Over time, alcohol will impair its usage in the brain and cause the neurotransmitter to become desensitized and depleted. This can in turn lead to difficulty in learning, memory, and lack of clarity even in sober states.

Monoamines – Catecholamines

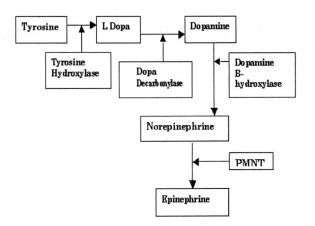

Flow chart Biosynthesis of Catecholamines

Alcohol's Effects on Dopamine

Dopamine acts as a potent and immediate stimulant. Too little dopamine has been linked to depression and too much has been associated with schizophrenia. For this reason, schizophrenia is treated clinically with psychoactive drugs that block the binding of dopamine to its postsynaptic receptor, shunting its effect on the brain and lessening schizophrenic states. Similar drugs are used to block the excess release of dopamine during alcohol ingestion, reducing the euphoric effect of alcohol. This thwarts the "reward" system with which dopamine is associated. Not only are drugs toxic, bringing with them many health risks, but they are not necessary. Orthomolecular medicine successfully treats these conditions naturally, producing enhanced health as opposed to further dis-ease and discomfort.

- Alcohol increases dopamine activity. Many people predisposed to alcoholism have lower-than-normal dopamine levels, making alcohol that much more rewarding (and tempting).
- Dopamine stimulates brain areas associated with reward (eg, nucleus accumbens), resulting in positive reinforcement

of the associated activity, and serving the association element of the addiction.

- Alcohol interaction with GABA and opioid peptide neurotransmitters deregulates the release of dopamine, causing excess supplies of dopamine in the system.
- The increase in dopamine release after alcohol consumption is much higher in those with addictive biochemistries.
- Problem drinkers given dopamine precursors in clinical trials reported fewer cravings for alcohol (this will be explored in more detail in Chapter 9, "The Cure").
- Alcohol metabolism over stimulates dopamine activity and causes downregulation over time. This contributes to tolerance.
- Effects are dose and region dependent. Over time, excessive alcohol use causes already-low dopamine levels to dip even lower. This contributes to the problem drinker's inability to find enjoyment in things he or she once did, or through normal, healthy activities. During sober hours, there is little dopamine to be stimulated through other activities. During this stage of the addiction, the problem drinker's primary path of reward becomes increasingly associated with drinking; it becomes the only activity associated with the pleasurable and rewarding effects of dopamine.
- Acetaldehyde binds with dopamine to make THIQs, which lodge onto opioid receptors and provide a far more intense euphoria than natural opioids do.
- Initially, high amounts of dopamine result in euphoric states. Over time dopamine receptors begin to downregulate in an effort to balance brain chemistry. Paranoia-type hangovers and worrisome, fearful general states of mind ensue.
- NAD is a precursor to dopamine; its depletion during the metabolism of alcohol and acetaldehyde is a possible contributing factor for why dopamine production is gradually reduced in problem drinkers. This reduction forces the brain to rely more and more heavily on the acetaldehyde and serotonin/ dopamine combinations of THIQs to create the sensation of feeling right and good. There are also phases of alcoholism referred to by those who experience it as "when drinking just doesn't work anymore". In this stage the euphoric feeling and relief of

symptoms can no longer be achieved through drinking. This is very likely due to serotonin and dopamine levels dropping so low that acetaldehyde can't bind to enough of them to create the amount of THIQs required to bring relief.

Norepinephrine (aka noradrenaline)

Norepinephrine is associated with attention, alertness, general arousal, and mental acuity. REM sleep states are achieved when norepinephrine is at its lowest. Due to the excess release of dopamine during alcohol ingestion (dopamine is a precursor to norepinephrine), many heavy drinkers 'wake-up' when they begin drinking. Chronic alcohol use can cause chronic high norepinephrine levels, and this is one reason why problem drinkers have difficulty sleeping for the first few nights after they've stopped consuming alcohol.

- Norepinephrine is depleted in situations of chronic or prolonged stress.
- It is the primary neurotransmitter in the sympathetic nervous system.
- Early in one's drinking habit, this is the neurotransmitter responsible for the enhanced alertness experienced by those with addictive biochemistry. Over the years, this reaction diminishes as brain damage and malnutrition causes less dopamine to be released.
- Norepinephrine is an "activating"-type neurotransmitter, responsible for promoting drive, ambition, alert mental functioning, and memory.
- Increased serotonin also increases norepinephrine levels.
- During initial abstinence, low serotonin and high norepinephrine aggravates withdrawal symptoms.
- During later stages of withdrawal, lowered norepinephrine levels contribute to lethargic mental symptoms of withdrawal until dopamine levels stabilize.

Epinephrine (aka adrenaline)

Epinephrine is both a neurotransmitter and a hormone. It is secreted from the adrenal medulla in response to low blood glucose, exercise, and various forms of acute stress.

Epinephrine causes several responses.

- It initiates the "fight-or-flight" response to fear, stress and emergencies.
- Converts glycogen from the liver into glucose
- Causes the release of fatty acids from fat tissue
- Triggers vasodilatation of small arteries within muscle tissue
- Increases the rate and strength of the heartbeat

Monoamines - Indoleamines

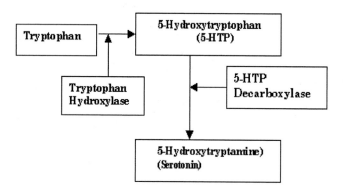

Serotonin

Serotonin acts in most cases as an inhibitory neurotransmitter and, like GABA, inhibits glutamate activity and neurotransmitter firing. Those predisposed to alcohol addiction have lower-than-normal serotonin levels, which causes upregulated receptor sites. Alcohol increases serotonin levels in the brain and will cause those sites to be temporarily satiated, enhancing the euphoric effects of alcohol and encouraging one to drink; people with addictive biochemistry get an added temporary high from drinking, and relief from low serotonin symptoms such as depression.

- Serotonin metabolites in the urine and blood increase after a single drinking session.
- During withdrawal, depression is common due to decreasing serotonin levels.
- Research has shown that problem and chronic drinkers have severely altered and/or injured serotonin systems.
- Injured serotonin systems can be healed.

Serotonin – Upregulation

Research shows that those predisposed to addictive biochemistry have naturally low levels of serotonin, making this yet another inherent marker known to encourage addictive behavior. This condition has early signs and, in most cases, becomes evident in one's food choices; you will initially seek relief from low serotonin symptoms at a young age through a diet that leans toward simple/refined carbs.

Whether this craving is inherited or earned through irresponsible lifestyle choices for extended periods, excess sugar or simple carbohydrates over time injures the neuroendocrine system and cause the brain's serotonin levels to drop to unhealthy levels sporadically throughout the day. Serotonin precursors are exhausted during the excess production of serotonin while mainlining sugar, so that when the initial thrust of serotonin dissipates there is nothing or very little left available to stabilize brain chemistry. In response, the brain will seek to balance by increasing serotonin receptors to try and find and bind with what little serotonin is left. This is called upregulation, and actually aggravates the condition of low blood sugar symptoms; in the absence of sugar or alcohol, even less serotonin is available for desired moods and energy and there are more receptors at large, seeking their complimentary serotonin. In this state, the unbalanced ratio has become even more pronounced and deep depression, anxiety, mood swings, distress, compulsivity, sugar cravings, and sleep disorders result.

Once an association has been established through food, sugar, cokes, or alcohol, in an effort to produce more serotonin, the brain chemistry will actually "instruct" the person to seek out and eat or drink what it has learned to be sources of the much-needed serotonin. This is the root of compulsive behavior and the mind-to-body "speak" that causes you to do things that you know to be harmful to your health. The relief you find is so rewarding that you cannot deny yourself; it speaks to a very primitive mechanism of human survival. It is far more powerful than any rational capacity because it is human nature to seek relief from pain. If you see relief in every coke, candy bar, bag of chips, or beer can, you will use it to get out of the uncomfortable symptoms caused by your low serotonin levels. However, this is short lived; the craving will only subside while those receptors are

getting their fix, which is for about an hour. Then the blood sugar will drop and serotonin will dissipate, causing the craving and compulsion to seek more "brain candy". This causes a vicious cycle of physiological and psychological addiction; you are finding only a temporary fix over and over again, with long-term serious health issues.

Serotonin and Sugar Addiction

Serotonin is the neurotransmitter that regulates sleep, reduces pain and appetite, and generally calms you down and improves your mood.

Simple sugars cause blood sugar to rise sharply, and those with addictive biochemistries have demonstrated that their blood sugar will rise higher with the same meal ingested compared to people with normal blood sugar metabolisms. The higher blood sugar will generate over production of insulin from the pancreas, which will lower blood levels of all amino acids except tryptophan. Normally, tryptophan must compete with other amino acids for entry into the brain. However, insulin eliminates the competition and helps tryptophan pass the blood/brain barrier, allowing tryptophan levels to rise sharply in the brain, where they are converted to serotonin just as quickly. The pleasurable effects of this cycle are well known and are the root cause for the epidemic of "junkfoodism" in our culture today. Within 30 to 60 minutes, when the insulin surge causes blood sugar to drop sharply, serotonin levels fall, with a corresponding crash in mood and energy.

Protein, on the other hand, raises the level of all large amino acids in the blood and does not spike blood sugar; it slows the digestion of simple/refined carbs. As a result, tryptophan is released in a steadier way into the brain and levels remain far more consistent throughout the day; ergo, serotonin levels do not rise and fall abruptly, and addictive biochemistry is not promoted. This is why a condictive diet must provide an adequate amount of protein and fats in every meal and snack. It is a way of regulating serotonin availability and usage, and preventing upregulation and the symptoms that go with it.

Serotonin / Melatonin

Melatonin is the hormone that induces sleep, and is manufactured from serotonin. When melatonin levels

increase, serotonin levels usually decrease correspondingly, since the serotonin is being converted into melatonin. In its role as sleep controller, melatonin is released in response to light and dark conditions; your exposure to light lowers melatonin levels, increasing serotonin levels. In the evening the reverse is true, and serotonin levels are lower while melatonin levels are higher, helping to induce sleep.

Many people who quit drinking have difficulty sleeping at first due to severely depleted serotonin levels brought on by malnutrition, alcohol toxicity and withdrawal. Low serotonin levels restrict melatonin synthesis, denying you your sleep.

Opioids

Beta-Endorphins / Enkephalins

- Beta-endorphins produce a sense of well being, reduce emotional and physical pain, ease emotional distress, increase self-esteem, reduce anxiety, and even create a sense of psychoactive euphoria.
- External opiate drugs, such as morphine are powerful and addictive drugs. They act on the same receptors as natural (internal) endogenous opiates like endorphins and enkephalins.
- Alcohol increases release of the natural opioids: endorphins and enkephalins, and produces excess amounts of powerful opioid type compounds called tetrahydroisoquinolines (THIQs), which dock on the endorphin and enkephalin receptors, and provide a pronounced morphine-like euphoric response to alcohol.
- Endorphins, enkephalins, and THIQs dis-inhibit the dopamine pathways, allowing more dopamine to be released into the synapses which engages the reward system with the use and feeling of alcohol.
- Elevated beta endorphins raise levels of norepinephrine and epinephrine.

Low Beta-Endorphin Symptoms

- Feeling tearful, isolated, depressed, and hopeless
- Having low self-esteem
- Feeling "done to" by others – no effect or control in life
- Having a low tolerance for pain (emotional and physical)

- Feeling emotionally overwhelmed
- Craving sweets

Endorphins are the controls on feelings of well being and euphoria. Alcohol increases levels of beta-endorphins in the hypothalamus and causes the "high" associated with it. The same chain of events that takes place in the brain, in regard to dopamine and serotonin up and downregulation, applies to the neurotransmitters in the opioid family.

Endorphins are substances containing various amino acids in peptide form. For example, one of these opioid peptides, enkephalin, consists of five amino acids. If levels of this neurotransmitter are low, it is a key contributor to the desire to drink, because enkephalin acts as an important inhibitory neurotransmitter responsible for stress reduction and natural physical and emotional pain management. Alcohol addiction has been linked to low opioid activity in the central nervous system, and experiments consistently support this theory. In one experiment, it was found that alcohol-preferring mice had whole-brain enkephalin levels that were significantly lower than the alcohol non-preferring mice.

When the supply of enkephalins is low, various psychological, physical, and emotional discomforts stemming from all neurotransmitter deficiencies are more pronounced. The enkephalin receptors send out messages asking for their complimentary molecules in an attempt to reduce these pronounced discomforts. The physical/psychological result is an increase in craving and desire for the substance that you have trained yourself to reach for in your quest for relief.

One key method in holistically treating alcoholism, balancing the brain chemistry, and healing addictive biochemistry is to supply enkephalin precursors through diet and nutriceutical supplementation so that more can be naturally synthesized. Nutrients known to inhibit enkephalinase, the enzyme that degrades and metabolizes enkephalin, should also be provided. This way, more enkephalins are being produced in order to meet the needs of healthy brain chemistry, and supplies remain available for longer since metabolism is not taking place as quickly.

People with adequate enkephalins in the brain do not prefer alcohol on the same level as those who have a propensity for the addiction. This could be for two reasons:

- There is plenty of enkephalin present for a natural sense of well being. Basically, this person's biochemistry provides a natural high and emotional/physical pain relief, making outside sources of relief far less appealing and unnecessary. People with adequate enkephalin levels are those known to "let things go" and are not gravely affected by life's normal bumps in the road.
- A healthy supply of enkephalins, balanced with an appropriate number of receptors, means there is less opportunity for the toxic and more addictive THIQs to lodge onto the receptors and displace enkephalin. This makes alcohol far less rewarding.

GABA

GABA is the most abundant inhibitory neurotransmitter in the CNS (central nervous system). Its function is to decrease neuron activity and inhibit the nerve cells from over firing. Alcohol's stimulation of GABA is implicated in the anxiety reduction, sedation, and motor impairment effects that you experience during alcohol usage. In the short term, alcohol increases GABA levels (decreases inhibition, promotes relaxation). However, after prolonged use, GABA levels decrease and the resulting symptoms of anxiety, nervousness, insomnia, and the inability to relax encourage alcohol use.

Glutamate

Glutamate is the most abundant excitatory neurotransmitter found in the brain. In the short term, alcohol reduces glutamate expression (decreased excitation), causing relaxation and sedation. However, after prolonged use, glutamate is over-expressed and GABA is exhausted, leaving glutimate to produce extremely uncomfortable symptoms including Alcohol Withdrawal Syndrome, and dangerous symptoms like seizures and delirium.

Impaired glutamate functioning results in:

- Cognitive impairment and amnesia, or blackouts (higher doses)
- Inability to learn new information (usually a result of prolonged consistent use of alcohol)

- Respiratory depression (very high doses)
- Lack of mental clarity

GABA and Glutamate: A Delicate Balance

Short-term alcohol consumption increases GABA activity, BUT prolonged drinking decreases GABA receptor levels and receptor sensitivity. Short-term alcohol consumption decreases glutamate activity; prolonged drinking increases glutamate activity. Results include:

- Excess glutamate levels are a strong contributor to Alcohol Withdrawal Syndrome and produce many of the more dangerous symptoms, such as seizures and delirium.
- The brain attempts to restore equilibrium after long-term alcohol abuse via compensating for the high GABA levels (depressive states caused by alcohol) by producing more glutamate. In this stage of the addiction, when alcohol is not present and there are high levels of glutamate in the brain, without the chemically induced high levels of GABA to reduce the excitatory nature of glutamate, one experiences anxiety, nervousness, agitation, frustration, and general over excitability. Biochemically, this is why long-term drinkers are known to be short tempered and over reactive.

Neurotransmitters: Disorders and Symptoms

Symptoms that you may experience due to neurotransmitter imbalance include:

- Alcohol addiction
- Migraine
- Anorexia Nervosa
- Panic attacks
- Anxiety
- Premenstrual Dysphoric Disorder
- Binge eating
- Mild-to-severe mental disorders including inability to focus, and inability to retain and utilize learned information
- Post-traumatic stress disorder
- Bulimia
- Sexual dysfunction

- Fibromyalgia pain
- Headache pain
- Social anxiety and shyness
- Irritable Bowel Syndrome
- Weight loss
- Fatigue, chronic muscle/joint pain
- Inappropriate hunger/food cravings (hungry all the time, or not hungry when you should be)
- Irritability, hostility
- Inability to focus or concentrate
- Depression or agitation
- Addictive behavior, addictive personality
- Anxiety
- Paranoia
- Worry, fear
- Excessive body fat
- Obsessive/compulsive behaviors
- Sleep disturbances
- Physical or emotional stress
- Recurrent diarrhea or constipation

REVIEW

Alcohol and the Brain
The Physiological to Psychological
Roadmap to Addiction

Alcohol...
- Increases release of serotonin, which over time downregulates receptor sites, causing depression
- Stimulates release of dopamine and endogenous opiates (beta-endorphins, enkephalins). This reinforces the reward system and pleasure seeking through repeated activity. Over time, the repeated use of alcohol downregulates the brain chemistry and causes a condition where more is needed to achieve desired results. This leads the problem drinker to drink more alcohol, causing more damage to the body and mind and advancing the addiction.
- Depletes stores of precursor vitamins, minerals, EFAs, and amino acids required to produce and utilize the neurotransmitters that provide healthy moods and emotions in the absence of alcohol's chemical contribution.

- Stimulates release of norepinephrine and epinephrine.
- Increases GABA expression (initially), which produces relaxation and decreased inhibition. Over time, however, GABA receptors will downregulate, contributing to the many anxiety disorders from which problem drinkers suffer, as well as social anxieties. At this stage, a greater amount of alcohol must be consumed before you can achieve even the slightest relaxation.
- In the later stages of alcohol addiction, to compensate for the inhibitory neurotransmitter effects of alcohol, more glutamate is activated. During this stage, when alcohol is removed, the resulting excess glutamate levels make you edgy, skittish, anxious, and generally over stimulated.
- Presence of THIQs fools the brain into thinking that it has plenty of natural endorphin and enkephalin present, so that it gradually diminishes production of these chemicals (negative feedback), forcing the problem drinker to rely more and more heavily on external methods such as drinking and other drugs to produce a sense of well being and pleasure.

Additional biochemical contributions to the addiction to alcohol include:

- Acetaldehyde binds with dopamine and serotonin to produce THIQs, which are potent morphine-like molecules that displace beta-endorphins and provide added intensity to the euphoric states provided by alcohol. Problem drinkers are known to metabolize acetaldehyde slower than non-addictive people, providing higher levels to accumulate in the body and more opportunity for THIQs to be produced.
- Alcohol is metabolized in two stages by the enzymes alcohol dehydrogenase and aldehyde dehydrogenase. In problem and chronic drinkers, the first stage of metabolism (from alcohol to acetaldehyde) is faster than in those not prone to abuse alcohol. The second stage reaction, involving the conversion of the acetaldehyde to acetate, is slower in problem and chronic drinkers, and gets progressively slower with age. The end result is an accumulation of acetaldehyde in tissues, particularly in the liver and brain which causes serious free-radical damage and deepens the addiction.

- Poor liver function causes inefficient protein synthesis, which translates into the brain being "starved" for the nutrients needed for healthy functioning; this allows for further damage to the brain.
- Deficiencies in vitamins B1, B5, B6, and in NAD cause impairment to all brain functions, including neurotransmitter production; this ultimately damages the brain in varying degrees of severity, and is a strong contributor to the psychological and emotional distresses problem drinkers endure.
- Alcohol suppresses the endocrine system, resulting in hypothyroidism, rapid aging, and promotion of mental disease.
- Nutrients exhausted by the extreme demands placed on the body during the process of metabolizing alcohol, combined with the damage alcohol toxicity inflicts, creates varying degrees of withdrawal throughout the day; the resulting symptoms encourage not only drinking, but other compulsive disorders as well.

Endocrine System

The endocrine system is a network of glands that regulates bodily functions via hormones secreted into the bloodstream. Hormones carry signals that are passed through the blood to arrive at a target organ, which has cells that possess the appropriate receptors for receiving that message.

Essentially the endocrine system is a closely interwoven network of interdependent communications centers. Each gland "speaks and listens" to the others to determine what the body needs to maintain health and survival. These communication centers (endocrine organs) each produce and regulate hormonal activity, sending out hormones that in turn act as "mission control messengers" for neurotransmitter synthesis. Alcohol suppresses and distorts the functionality of the endocrine system, preventing it from providing the messages required by the system in order to perform in a healthy manner which is harmonious with its environment.

The glands of the endocrine system, which will be explained in regards to addictive biochemistry, are:

- Hypothalamus
- Pituitary

- Thyroid
- Pancreas
- Adrenals

Hypothalamus / Pituitary Glands

The hypothalamus is a virtual hotbed when one is exploring addiction and addictive biochemistry. This is because this gland controls either the release or synthesis of serotonin, endorphins, enkephalins, and dopamine. As this book has demonstrated, those predisposed to addictive biochemistry display imbalances in all of these chemicals; they consistently display natural lower levels of serotonin, endorphins, enkephalins and dopamine. Low levels of these neurotransmitters lead to many of the psychological and physical symptoms problem drinkers tend to medicate with alcohol. Studies of problem drinkers have indicated serotonin levels to be 10% to 30% lower than normal, dopamine levels 20% to 30% lower, and D2 (dopamine-type) receptors to be 20% lower.

Research has provided many reasons for focusing on the hypothalamus when unearthing the root of alcohol addiction, since it is the hypothalamus' responsibility to synthesize and regulate the release of the neurotransmitters. We now know that low or imbalanced levels of neurotransmitters result in everything from physical and mental fatigue and joint pain to aggression, depression, and compulsive disorders. In fact, almost every condition covered in this book can be traced back to low or imbalanced levels of neurotransmitters, which is of course caused by nutritional deficiencies.

Some conditions known to affect the release of feel-good neurotransmitters from the hypothalamus are:

- GABA is produced by the hypothalamus and plays a key role in regulating dopamine and endorphin release from that gland.
- Serotonin, present in the hypothalamus, also regulates dopamine activity.
- Studies of strains of rats bred to prefer alcohol to water show that these alcohol-addicted rats have fewer serotonin-releasing neurons in the hypothalamus, higher levels of opioid peptides in the hypothalamus, more GABA neurons, in the nucleus accumbens, a reduced supply of dopamine in

the nucleus accumbens, and a lower density of dopamine
D2 receptors in certain areas of the limbic system when
compared to normal rats.[8]

- When drugs that stimulated serotonin release, or directly
  stimulated D2 receptors, were administered, alcohol
  consumption decreased, while the administration of D2
  dopamine-receptor antagonists increased consumption.[9]
  The observed increase in dopamine release after the
  consumption of alcohol is also much higher in alcohol-
  preferring rats than in non-preferring rats, suggesting that
  the brains of alcohol-preferring rats are much more
  sensitive to the effects of alcohol.[10]

- These findings have also been replicated to some extent in
  humans. Levels of serotonin metabolites in the
  cerebrospinal fluid of alcohol abusers have been shown to
  be lower than normal.[11] Problem drinkers given serotonin
  and dopamine precursors in clinical trials reported fewer
  cravings for alcohol, less stress, and had an increased
  likelihood of recovery and a reduction in relapse rates.
  Alcohol compensates for the same neurotransmitter
  deficiencies by stimulating the release of dopamine, as well
  as increasing serotonin, endorphin, and enkephalin levels,
  which is why it is so attractive with people suffering the
  symptoms of these neurotransmitter deficiencies.

Hypothalamus and Metabolism

The hypothalamus responds to elevated insulin by
secreting somatostatin. Somatostatin suppresses HGH

---

[8] Akino Irene Yamashita
http://serendip.brynmawr.edu/bb/neuro/neuro98/202s98-
paper1/Yamashita.html#note16

[9] Akino Irene Yamashita
http://serendip.brynmawr.edu/bb/neuro/neuro98/202s98-
paper1/Yamashita.html#note15

[10] Akino Irene Yamashita
http://serendip.brynmawr.edu/bb/neuro/neuro98/202s98-
paper1/Yamashita.html#note16

[11] Akino Irene Yamashita
http://serendip.brynmawr.edu/bb/neuro/neuro98/202s98-
paper1/Yamashita.html#note17

(human growth hormone) and thyroid stimulating hormone (TSH). Due to HGH's universal contribution to efficient functioning of cellular bioenergetics, this suppression adversely affects the thyroid gland and general health in many ways. One such consequence is that because HGH is directly involved in the aging process, lower HGH levels will lead to quicker aging, and a score of age-related health issues.

Suppression of HGH and TSH (thyroid stimulating hormone) contributes to addictive biochemistry by causing the system to become more sluggish. Thus, the body takes more time and effort to execute all functions of metabolism, including detox, tissue repair, fighting off disease, metabolizing fats/carbs/proteins, and manufacturing neurotransmitters. All of these functions, when compromised, will aggravate addictive biochemistry symptoms and add to its root causes in cellular deficiencies.

Low HGH conditions include:

- Higher propensity for general aches and pains
- Low immune system
- Loss of hair and hair color
- Wrinkles and cellulite
- Decreased bone mass
- Decreased exercise abilities
- High cholesterol
- Slow rate of healing
- Increased body fat
- Decreased energy
- Decreased sexual performance
- Decreased sex drive
- Decreased skin elasticity
- Decline in overall cognitive functions, including memory and ability to retain information
- Degradation of vision
- Decreased strength
- High blood pressure
- Poor sleep
- Joint pain

Hypothalamus and Neuropeptide Y

Peptides are a class of neurotransmitters. Neuropeptide Y (NPY) is the most abundant peptide and is involved in a variety of neurobiological functions, including feelings of anxiety, pain, memory, and feeding behavior. Researchers have found that a compound that blocks NPY activity decreases both the onset as well as the repetition of alcohol consumption. Interestingly, blocking neuropeptide Y will also decrease carbohydrate craving, again supporting the connection between the sweet tooth and the bar stool.

A group of nerve cells within the hypothalamus called the paraventricular nucleus (PVN) produces NPY, and appears to be the hub of carbohydrate craving; the more neuropeptide Y the PVN produces, the more carbohydrates one is driven to consume. Alcohol, being a naked carbohydrate itself, stimulates the PVN to produce high levels of NPY. This, in turn, will increase craving for simple carbs.

The next logical question is to ask what chemical messenger is stimulating the PVN to produce neuropeptide Y. Research seems to be pointing to the chemical byproducts that are created when carbohydrates are burned as fuel. As these byproducts accumulate, they send a chemical message to the brain that the carbohydrates are used up. The PVN responds to that chemical message by increasing neuropeptide Y production, making you hungry for carbohydrates to compensate.

Stress can also increase levels of NPY by increasing the production of the stress hormone cortisol. The main function of cortisol is to instruct the body to replenish carbohydrate stores; because of this, it too instructs the PVN to increase NPY production. Cortisol is also released from the adrenals during periods of low blood sugar. Hypoglycemic problem drinkers experience extremely low blood sugar levels throughout the day; one can expect heightened levels of NPY under these conditions, as well as the carb cravings and desire to drink that follows.

Research indicates that NPY is released during alcohol consumption in varying proportions, depending on the individual. How this translates to alcoholism and the propensity to addictive biochemistry is of particular interest, since the hypothalamus is the brain region in control of eating habits and NPY is associated with eating behavior and

repetition. When the same reinforcement is encouraged by alcohol (release of NPY), excessive use can be considered a disorder of consumption. In this case, it would be seen as inspired by a metabolic characteristic that was originally designed to keep humanity alive by encouraging us to eat; a characteristic that is now being usurped by alcohol. Essentially, it is possible that if you drink excessively for an extended period of time, your mind begins to think that it needs alcohol to survive, because of the consistent release of NPY in association with alcohol intake (established association).

Holistic practices that block NPY or minimize its release during alcohol consumption are a primary focus of research, due to their implications in addictive biochemistry. One holistic method for intercepting the production of NPY is to maintain healthy levels of serotonin. It has been found that adequate levels of serotonin in the brain will decrease NPY production by signaling the PVN to discontinue its production, thus turning off the carbohydrate and alcohol cravings.

Thyroid Gland

Suppressed Thyroid Hormone Release

Chronic elevated insulin causes an excessive release of somatostatin, which suppresses TSH. TSH is the hormone that stimulates release of thyroxin (T4) from the thyroid gland. Inadequate release of T4 leads to hypothyroidism, with which many problem drinkers are diagnosed for obvious reasons. In addition to the obvious connection to hypothyroidism, the thyroid's processes (or lack thereof) also affect the body's metabolism. Since the thyroid gland is charged with regulating metabolism, the extreme blood sugar fluctuations throughout the day tax the thyroid's capabilities, and exhaust its resources.

Symptoms of hypothyroidism are very similar to hypoglycemia and may be misdiagnosed. This is dangerous because thyroid medication can lead to more imbalance and dysfunction of the endocrine system and worsen hypoglycemia. Since The 101 Program targets the damage caused by alcohol abuse and in particular hypothyroidism, most clients who come into The Program on hypothyroid

medications are entirely off of them within six weeks of starting the program.

The Pancreas

The pancreas is a narrow, flat organ about 6 inches long, with a head, middle, and tail section. It is located below the liver, between the stomach and the spine, and is connected to the duodenum (first part of the small intestine). Inside the pancreas, small ducts (tubes) feed fluids produced by the pancreas into the pancreatic duct, which carries the fluids down the length of the pancreas, from the tail to the head, and into the duodenum. The common bile duct also runs through the head section of the pancreas, carrying bile from the liver and gall bladder into the small intestine.

The pancreas consists of two kinds of tissues:
- Exocrine/Acinar — make powerful enzymes to digest fats, proteins, and carbohydrates. The enzymes are normally created and carried to the duodenum in an inactive form, and activated as needed. Exocrine tissue also secretes bicarbonates.
- Endocrine/Islet — produce the hormones insulin and glucagon and releases them into the blood stream. These hormones regulate glucose transport into the body's cells and are crucial for energy production.

Excessive alcohol use is directly related to pancreatitis, a potentially fatal inflammation of the pancreas that is much like an inflamed liver. Symptoms can result from the blockage of small pancreatic ducts or from actual damage to pancreatic tissue by digestive enzymes. Byproducts of alcohol metabolism (acetaldehyde, free radicals) within the pancreas also damage the gland.

Damage done to the pancreas by alcohol toxicity is multi layered. Given time, it results in poor sugar regulation, indigestion, inflammation, disease, and in severe cases death. In short, there are two critical metabolic disorders related to alcoholism and hypoglycemia that present themselves as a result of a damaged pancreas. One is that the pancreas slowly becomes damaged and inflamed, rendering it incapable of secreting the enzymes necessary for healthy digestion in the small intestines. The other is under or over production of

insulin and / or glucagon. Both disorders cause numerous health issues that are categorized under malnutrition, diabetes and low blood sugar /hypoglycemia.

Exocrine/Acinar Cells

The three major origins of alcohol-related pancreatic injury to the acinar cells are:

1. Alcohol's effect on pancreatic enzymes: the acinar cells secrete the precursors to digestive enzymes. However, alcohol damage can disrupt this process by trapping the enzymes in the pancreas, leaving potential for the digestive enzymes to prematurely activate and begin digesting the acinar cells that produced them. This is termed "auto digestion", which is the pancreas literally eating away at itself. Auto digestion also causes the pancreas to progressively produce fewer and fewer digestive enzymes since the acinar cells are being destroyed.

- Digestive enzymes can be blocked from leaving the pancreas by protein plugs and/or inflammation and damage caused by acetaldehyde toxicity and metabolism.
- Lack of these enzymes results in malnutrition due to the inability to properly digest food and receive its nutritional benefit. Whether it is due to auto digestion, from enzymes never leaving the pancreas because of inflammation, or from tissue damage and/or protein plugs prohibiting an adequate supply of enzymes to the intestines, the effect is the same, and adversely affects the entire body. This condition will lower the pancreas' antioxidant fortitude within the cells and contribute to even faster cell death by oxidative stress.
- The acinar cells are also responsible for releasing bicarbonate, a substance similar to baking soda. This compound is released into the small intestine to maintain the relatively weak acidity levels required for digestive enzymes to do their job. Acid stomach and acid reflux can indicate problems associated with pancreatic malfunction.
- The result of these conditions imposed by alcohol toxicity means that long-term problem drinkers suffer from many digestive disorders.

2. Alcohol metabolism and free radical damage: the same enzyme that metabolizes alcohol in the liver, alcohol

dehydrogenase is found in the pancreas and is activated by excessive alcohol use. Research has shown that a significant amount of alcohol is metabolized in the pancreas during over intoxication, producing the same destructive compounds: acetaldehyde and free radicals. Recent research has also demonstrated that oxidative stress caused from these free radicals contributes to pancreatitis. Ultimately, these compounds seriously damage the pancreas in much the same way as they contribute to inflammation and damage of the liver.

3. Effects of toxic metabolites: as in the liver, acetaldehyde binds to proteins in the pancreas, triggering an immune response in which cytokines are dispatched to the area. Cells of the liver and immune system produce cytokines in response to infection or cell damage. Recent studies implicate cytokines in scar formation and in the depletion of oxygen within the cells they occupy, a condition that contributes to cell death. Since it is now known that the pancreas metabolizes alcohol and is producing acetaldehyde, we can assume the same damage is occurring there as is in the liver.

Endocrine/Islet Cells

The islet cells secrete insulin and glucagon from the pancreas. Insulin, released by the beta-islet cells, lowers blood glucose by delivering it into the body's cells via its receptors. Glucagon, released by the alpha-islet cells, is secreted to stimulate the liver to release stored glycogen, and helps to convert it into glucose when blood glucose levels fall below normal. It also releases fat from fat cells and converts that into glucose.

Over producing insulin helps to establish addictive or addicted biochemistry. There are many conditions that might be contributing to the cause behind a pancreas over producing insulin. However, the most common case is decreases in the hormones that oppose insulin.

Hormones that oppose insulin, and the conditions that cause lowered levels of these hormones (in parentheses), are:

- Glucagon (disease of alpha cells of the pancreas)
- Cortisol (eg, Addison disease, chronic stress, adrenal fatigue)
- Epinephrine (fatigued adrenals)

- GH (hypopituitarism)
- Thyroid hormones (hypothyroidism)

The endocrine system depends on a perpetual activity of checks and balances; each organ reacts to the information it gets from the others. It's hard to determine when the cycle starts; is the over production from an upregulated count of beta-islets the reason that you produce too much insulin in response to high blood sugar? Or is it insulin resistance (from downregulated counts of its receptors)? Or is it suppression of its counterpart, the alpha cells, in their secretion of glucagon, which is supposed to help keep insulin at healthy levels? Or do depressed quantities of any one of the hormones mentioned earlier cause the condition? The answer to this may vary depending on the individual. It seems logical to say that for most people the problem is in a combination of these factors. Everything comes down to the existence of compromised endocrine function, with a system that cannot properly respond to sugar and/or insulin- and it is certain that the problem is exacerbated as the health of those organs that produce the hormones that oppose insulin diminishes as a result of aging, malnutrition, and the toxic assault of alcohol. Just one imbalance, such as too many beta cells to produce insulin, or weak adrenals not producing enough cortisol, can throw off the delicate balance required by the endocrine system in order to function properly.

If you were born with a dysfunctional pancreas that over produces insulin or is deficient in producing adequate enzymes for digestion, you need to be extremely careful. Both of these conditions, to varying degrees, can be markers for a predisposition to addictive biochemistry; they both cause, among many other illnesses, imbalanced, neurotransmitter-deficient brain chemistry. Conversely, if you were born with a healthy pancreas but have subjected it to long-term excessive alcohol use, you might create the same damage, and cause the same symptoms and diseases.

The good news is the pancreas responds very well to targeted nutritional therapy, and it is possible to heal these conditions.

Alcohol, Pancreas, and Diet

Other avenues of pancreatic damage from alcohol abuse and its effect on the system include:

- Alcohol metabolites bind with proteins causing fibrosis.
- Acetaldehyde (AH) exhausts NAD and other nutrient stores required for fat, carb, and protein metabolism. Fat and toxic waste buildup interferes with cellular function.
- Primes islet cells to overproduce insulin
- Long-term over production of insulin can cause insulin receptor insensitivity, which develops into insulin resistance.
- Over time, alcohol can permanently damage islet cells, which leads to diabetes.
- Damaged cells encourage scar tissue formation by cytokines.
- Alcohol-induced free radical damage (oxidative stress), caused by a lack of available antioxidants in the pancreas for cleaning up after the metabolism of alcohol
- Pancreatic damage will also result in lower bicarbonate levels in the digestive tract. Lower bicarbonate levels, combined with compromised enzymatic activity, make digestion nearly impossible.

Diets that are made up of predominately naked carbs will "train" the digestive tract to prefer simple carbs for energy. Amylase enzymes will be produced in the pancreas and released into the intestines to break down simple carbs at a higher rate than the enzymes for protein and fat digestion (typsin and lipase); this is one contributor to malnutrition. The other contributor is that problem drinkers are not known for their high protein/good fats diets, so that the right nutrients are usually not being supplied in the first place. Even if they are, very little nutrition is actually being digested and utilized.

The sum total of these conditions cause you to gradually become more fueled by energy than by thought. This is quite possibly the genesis of compulsive disorders; at this stage, you are no more evolved than an animal in your lack of rationale. You will begin to compulsively answer to your urges throughout the day, whatever they may be, with very little thinking done to weigh your options or justify your actions.

Your brain does not produce the neurotransmitters required to help you act as a conscious human being who is in control and able to own and direct your energy. You are present physically, but not mentally. You truly are what you eat: if your diet is made up of food or products that predominately produce energy over those that feed the brain with the nutrition required for frontal lobe activity, you will progressively become more energy than thought. Enter the genesis of compulsive behavior.

Pancreatic Inflammation and Injury

Excessive alcohol consumption can cause chronic inflammation of the pancreas and gradually destroy the pancreas' ability to function. Reduced pancreatic function leads to reduced digestive enzymes, which causes malabsorption of nutrients, and leads to malnutrition, weight loss, and poor-quality bowel movements. If insulin-producing islet cells are damaged, diabetes may develop. Chronic inflammation carries with it a heightened risk of pancreatic cancer.

Below is a list of symptoms of pancreatitis. A predominant number of chronic drinkers probably experience these symptoms and attribute it to stomach flu or the onset of an ulcer. Since pancreatitis is so common in problem drinkers, you should definitely consider it as a possibility if these symptoms develop and you have been abusing alcohol for a while. Because the symptoms usually come and go fairly quickly, many people do not initially think to visit the doctor. Even if they did, it is likely that their case would be misdiagnosed because the symptoms are similar to stomach flu. These symptoms should be carefully reviewed; if you are a heavy drinker you should consider the possibility that your pancreas might be in serious trouble. Pancreatic cancer is now the fourth largest cause of cancer deaths in the U.S., in both men and women. Frighteningly, it beats liver cancer by a long shot; liver cancer in men is number eight and in women is not even in the top 12.

Pancreatic cancer is avoidable, since symptoms of chronic pancreatitis usually develop years before the cancer.

Pancreatitis Symptoms

Symptoms of acute pancreatitis include:

- Sudden, intense pains in the middle of the abdomen, often beginning 12 to 24 hours after a large meal or a bout of heavy drinking. The pain may radiate into the back.
- Fever
- Nausea or vomiting
- Clammy skin
- Abdominal distention and tenderness
- Rapid pulse

Symptoms of chronic pancreatitis include:

- Intense, long-lasting abdominal pain that may radiate to the back and chest; the pain may be persistent or intermittent.
- Excessively foul, bulky stools
- Nausea or vomiting
- Weight loss due to malabsorption of food
- Abdominal distention
- Development of diabetes

Adrenal Glands

Alcohol's effect on the adrenals was explored in Chapter 2. This section will highlight the damage done to the adrenals, and the cause of that damage after excessive alcohol ingestion. Healing of the pancreas and the adrenals is given special attention in The 101 Program; they are two organs that are initially hit the hardest by alcohol toxicity, and are always injured to some degree. Special attention is also given because a healthy pancreas and adrenals are primary factors in feeling fit, with the energy and presence of mind to enjoy life.

The adrenal glands are composed of two separate parts: the adrenal cortex and the inner medulla. The adrenal cortex, which accounts for 90% of the adrenals, secretes aldosterone, the hormone that triggers the kidneys to excrete potassium and retain sodium; and cortisol, corticosterone, and cortisone, which together help the body to resist stress, and inhibit the immune response. They promote normal

metabolism of proteins, fats, and carbohydrates, and inhibit inflammation. The adrenal medulla also secretes epinephrine and norepinephrine, which produce the body's fight-or-flight response to stress.

Functions of the Adrenals

- The adrenals release epinephrine, norepinephrine (catecholamines), and cortisol in response to low blood sugar. Epinephrine (adrenaline) stimulates glycogen release from the liver and raises blood sugar during low blood sugar episodes. Cortisol converts glycogen to glucose.
- Due to excessive sugar and alcohol intake, the pancreas is continually over producing insulin to manage high blood sugar. When the resulting low blood sugar conditions occur, the adrenals are taxed by being constantly required to respond to them with cortisol to raise blood sugar. This is a vicious cycle that inevitably results in adrenal fatigue.
- Adrenal fatigue means that the adrenals can no longer meet the demands of the system and produce adequate cortisol and catecholamines required to buffer your biochemical response to stress, which contributes to the desire to drink and many other symptoms.
- When the adrenals are fatigued they take longer to respond to low blood sugar conditions. This further aggravates low blood sugar symptoms known to encourage addictive biochemistry.
- The excess release of cortisol from the adrenals is linked to higher levels of neuropeptide Y, which is directly linked to sugar and alcohol craving.

Hypoglycemic Connection to Alcoholism

Sugar / Alcohol

Similar Processes of Addiction

The biochemical processes by which one becomes addicted to alcohol and/or sugar are identical, as are the symptoms and the withdrawal. These processes and symptoms include:

- Insulin resistance

- Excess carbohydrates and alcohol are naked carbohydrates that produce acetaldehyde. Acetaldehyde is known to be more addictive than alcohol itself and is the key addictive substance in both sugar and alcohol addiction.
- Over stimulation of serotonin, GABA, dopamine, beta-endorphin, and enkephalins during ingestion empties out precursor stores, making them unavailable during non-consumption periods.
- Chronic over stimulation of the above neurotransmitters causes extended periods of low levels of these neurotransmitters which will cause many long term mental and physical symptoms until alcohol/sugar is taken out of the picture and nutritional stores are re-established.
- Low blood sugar, and its ensuing symptoms.
- Simple carb/alcohol craving due to upregulated serotonin and endorphin receptors.
- Reduced HGH
- Over stimulated NPY synthesis in the hypothalamus, creating extreme craving for carbohydrates.
- Diminished synthesis of serotonin, GABA, endorphin, enkephalin, and dopamine due to brain cell damage, malnutrition, and THIQ occupation of receptors (leads to the brain chemistry reducing production of its own opioid neurotransmitters).
- Damages receptor sites on the hypothalamus and pituitary causing their inability to communicate with the neurochemical status of the brain as well as the external environment which diminishes the health of all psychological and physical systems.
- Both sugar and alcohol are used as "medicine" to respond to upregulated serotonin and endorphin brain chemistry symptoms because they both immediately raise these neurotransmitters. This condition is a key marker of addictive biochemistry and the propensity to abuse sugar and/or alcohol.
- Creation of GABA and glutamate imbalances, which produce symptoms of over excitability, nervousness, aggravation, frustration, worry, and anxiety.
- Damage to the adrenals and pancreas in the same manner, promoting and aggravating all known symptoms of addiction and addictive biochemistry.

- Malnutrition caused by damage in the gastrointestinal tract and pancreas.

Hypoglycemia and Dry-Drunk Symptoms

The symptoms listed here are common to both hypoglycemics and problem drinkers; these two conditions cause identical symptoms in the people affected.

- Fatigue
- Anxiety
- Shakiness
- Irritability
- Depression
- Fogginess, lack of focus/concentration
- Aggressiveness
- Excitability/impatience
- Insomnia
- Craving sweets
- Excessive thirst

Withdrawal

Withdrawal is the time period between when alcohol is discontinued and when the brain is able to register the need for, and begin production of, its own feel-good neurotransmitters. This time depends on how long it takes the body to start functioning healthfully again. That functioning relies on all the nutritional cofactors being supplied, properly digested, and utilized in order to supply the neurotransmitter-synthesizing cells with what they need. They must be able to produce, fire, utilize, and metabolize neurotransmitters in an efficient and balanced manner, and in the potency needed for healthy mind and body functions.

The physical withdrawal is in large part due to low levels of GABA and high levels of glutamate. The mental and emotional symptoms are primarily due to low dopamine, beta-endorphin, and serotonin levels, and imbalance. The most dangerous withdrawal condition is the GABA/glutamate imbalance since low levels of GABA, and desensitization of GABA receptors, combined with high levels of excitatory glutamate, is the condition that is responsible for the more

severe and life-threatening symptoms of tremens, delirium, and seizures noted in extreme alcohol withdrawal.

Symptoms of withdrawal include:

- Depression
- Anxiety
- General nervousness
- Extreme carbohydrate cravings
- Physical and mental fatigue
- Outbursts, emotional instability
- Low dopamine, serotonin, beta-endorphin, and enkephalin levels
- Increased levels of glutamate
- Seizures
- Low blood sugar (hypoglycemic) conditions also aggravate the withdrawal phase with a long list of physical and mental symptoms.

Dangers of the Typical Dry-Drunk Diet and Lack of Treatment Addressing the Damage

The all-too-common response to the overwhelming symptoms experienced when one tries to quit drinking is to begin self-medicating with food, cokes, cigarettes, bagels, pastas, and candy to feed the compulsive empty carbohydrate machine that was created by alcohol. The danger of this typical dry-drunk diet that replaces alcohol with other naked carbohydrates is that it continues the addictive state, and keeps you a physical and mental slave to the biochemical factory that produced your addictive biochemistry. Alcohol will be replaced with simple carbs and other sources of sugar for brief periods of relief; eventually a tolerance to that method is achieved, and you will find yourself breaking under the pressure of the symptoms and relapsing back into drinking.

These diets continue the identical cell and bioenergetic damage, nutritional deficiencies, biochemical imbalances, metabolic changes, and symptoms that initially locked in the addiction. They are responsible for the very high failure rate of "treatments" that do not address the root cause of the addiction and its withdrawal symptoms, which are

experienced every day by the former problem drinker who follows this misdirection.

Chapter Nine

Addictive and Addicted Biochemistry

The Cure

In the simplest terms, the root cause of addiction stems
from the fact that a chronic drinker's nutritional status is
severely deficient due to malnutrition, free radical damage,
and toxic overload. In order to reverse the damage that
alcohol toxicity inflicts on the every organ of the system, and
successfully address the cause of the original appeal and
environmental (nutritional, emotional, thought, toxicity, and
EMF) influences that encourage alcoholism, nutritional
deficiencies must be studied, identified, and then addressed.
Once the biochemistry of the individual is well on its way to
being corrected, and the metabolism and damage is healing,
adjunct therapies or treatments to address the other
threatening conditions can be provided and their success
rates made promising. In the ten years I have been
specializing in addictive biochemistry, I have not witnessed
one mind/body energy type healing method produce any
lasting healing results without the biochemical and biorepair
practice of correcting addictive biochemistry being first
established. However, once the biorepair is addressed,
treatments such as EFT, acupuncture, biofeedback etc.
produce very satisfying and healing results; the biorepair
process is accentuated by the energy healing and the energy
healing is accentuated by the biorepair. However, unless the
cells can actually receive and therefore be corrected by the
powerful sublime energy messages that resonate with the
vibrational laws of health, no sustainable measure of healing
will be experienced. In order for these subliminal messages to
get through to the cell bioenergetics and make the vibrational
changes required for a total healing transformation, a clear
biochemical channel must be established and maintained to
facilitate communication. And that channel must facilitate
the progression of the sublime (spiritual) to dense (physical)
vortexes of energy. Your body is a physical representation of

your spirit and when your biochemistry is facilitating that process you will literally shine.

Provision of therapeutic dosages of amino acids, and the vitamin, mineral, and EFA cofactors for building the proteins and neurotransmitters required for emotional, psychological, and physical health is the most important aspect of aggressively addressing the inherent and toxicity induced deficiencies and healing the mind and body. Thus, the first order of business is to detox the body and provide those nutrients. This chapter explores the deficiencies known to those who are addicted to alcohol, as well as those deficiencies caused by inherent and earned addictive biochemistry. It will also go into the scientific validation of the methods and constituents of The 101 Program condictive dietary and nutriceutical protocols.

While the following presentation of amino acids, bodily processes, organ systems, and each system's interdependence on the others for healthy functioning of the whole may be at first an overwhelming labyrinth of molecular information, be assured that The 101 Program is built upon all the well-researched information in this book. The targeted nutritional therapy and dietary practices prescribed in The 101 Program are built upon the validated, evidence-based research and information described herein. All that is really necessary is to follow the program in the appendix with the instructions in Chapters 3 and 6. It is not mandatory that you know the information provided in this chapter; it is provided for those who wish to have the scientific details and proof that what they are doing is not only the right thing, but an absolute must if they want to actually cure their addictive biochemistry. I also provide the scientific picture for those who, like me, find the miraculous functioning of the body interesting and useful. The precision with which our bodies execute millions of processes every second is humbling, and quite frankly gives me a lot of security in knowing that the body really does know it is doing and its natural state is to function toward health. That is why it heals so quickly when you do two simple things; give it the tools it needs to do its job and then get out of its way. This is why my practice is built first on respect for the relationship between the human body and nature, and second; the humility I have learned while becoming acquainted with the superior intelligence our bodies

perform with even in spite of what we do to it. My approach toward health is a simple two-step process: first, I teach you how to get out of your body's way by removing the toxins and denatured substances that are causing the dis-orders and dis-ease you are suffering from, and then I teach you how to assist its natural processes that work toward health. No naturopath, physician or scientist- or even all of them combined now and in all of time, will ever know how the human body does what it does enough to be able to improve upon it- the big picture is simply too big and it changes every second as our cells adapt to the ever changing environment. Each and every cell communicates with the entire universe every second of the day and makes changes in its bioenergetics to respond and report to its environment every second of the day! There is the intelligence of 3 million years of survival; adaptation, repair, and regeneration, built into each cell and we are better served to learn from it and work with it. Our best chance at a healthy life, both in the microcosm and macrocosm, is to take the lesson learned from the cell and strive to cooperate and live in harmony with our environment and the universe, rather than try to improve upon, manipulate, mimic, change, or control it. This attempt has always, and will always get us into trouble. The audacity of man's attempts in this area which saturates the medical, agricultural and biotechnology fields is the number one cause of the health issues that are becoming epidemic today.

When we know better, we do better, and when you understand how your specific body type works, you can better manage it through cooperating with its needs and succeed at any of your health goals. In today's world, people are much more successful when they are educated about how and why something works than they are when they have only a one-dimensional set of instructions, because the knowing why in a Newtonian era that needs scientific facts to support belief provides the validation for the process, and for this reason, I have included this chapter.

Key Nutriceuticals and What They Do

This chapter will provide a complete list of the nutriceuticals that you will be using and how they contribute specifically toward healing the damage caused by long-term alcohol abuse which develops and then imbeds the addiction

into the system. These nutriceuticals are equally important in addressing the root cause of the inherent conditions known to addictive biochemistry that can sometimes be identified as early as childhood.

General Categories

- Vitamins
- Minerals
- EFAs (essential fatty acids)
- Amino Acids

Vitamins

Vitamin A / Beta-Carotene

Vitamin A deficiency occurs during alcohol use because alcohol metabolism promotes excretion of vitamin A from the liver into bile. In a healthy liver, stellate cells store vitamin A; when these cells are activated by cytokines (produced in response to the cell damage inflicted by acetaldehyde), they begin to proliferate and lose their vitamin A stores. These cells then begin to create scar tissue, prohibiting oxygen from entering the cell, and disabling healthy bioenergetics within the cell, which eventually disables the organ and is followed by disease. Vitamin A is also lost when the metabolism of acetaldehyde causes fat to fill the liver cells.

A dose of five times the daily vitamin A requirement has no detectable adverse effects if given alone. However, when this dosage is combined with alcohol intake, there is striking leakage of the mitochondrial enzyme glutamic dehydrogenase into the bloodstream, and therein the possibility of fibrinogenesis. Thus, in heavy drinkers, vitamin A supplementation might accelerate rather than alleviate the development of liver disease. People who are currently or have been heavy drinkers should not take vitamin A supplements. Beta-carotene supplements are a much safer way for former heavy drinkers to satisfy their vitamin A requirements. All beta-carotene requirements are met in the multiple vitamins in The 101 Program protocol.

Vitamin B1/Thiamine

Thiamine is absorbed in the upper and lower sections of the small intestine. It is then carried by the circulatory system to the liver, brain, kidneys, and heart. Vitamin B1 combines with manganese, resulting in an active enzyme that breaks complex carbohydrates down into simple sugars. Thiamine aids in a great many bodily functions in the form of the coenzyme thiamine pyrophosphate (TPP). It has a key metabolic role in the cellular production of energy, mainly in glucose metabolism and in converting glucose into energy; it also converts carbohydrate to fat for storage of potential energy. Thiamine is also needed to metabolize alcohol, helping to convert it to carbon dioxide and water. B1 helps in the initial steps of fatty acid and sterol production. Thiamine is important to the health of the nerves and nervous system. This is possibly because of its role in the synthesis of acetylcholine, an important neurotransmitter in which problem drinkers are deficient. With a lack of vitamin B1, the nerves become more sensitive to inflammation.

Because of its integral relationship to energy and nerve biochemical processes, thiamine is also linked to all mental and emotional biopathways. It is important to the muscle tone of the stomach, intestines, and heart because of the function of acetylcholine at the nerve synaptic junction. Healthy thiamine levels help prevent the accumulation of fatty deposits in the arteries and reduce the progression of atherosclerosis.

Heavy alcohol consumption depletes this vital nutrient and, in cases where the vitamin is limited in the diet, exacerbates health-related issues that stem from deficiency. Heavy alcohol consumption diverts available thiamine away from the brain in favor of alcohol metabolism. After the available thiamine is exhausted, the remaining alcohol is converted to fat. In the interim, however, high levels of the intermediate products of alcohol breakdown (prior to the thiamine-dependent step) are transported through the blood into the brain. In order to dilute the alcohol and its breakdown products, water is drawn out of the tissues (including from the brain) into the blood, causing dehydration.

Those who indulge in refined sugar and flour, processed foods, and junk foods, and who drink alcohol or coffee

regularly, drain their bodies of thiamine. They produce many illnesses related to thiamine deficiency because of the huge demands placed on available supplies to achieve alcohol and sugar metabolism.

Since thiamine is a water-soluble vitamin it is not stored within the body, and any excess is excreted in the urine. Therefore it must be replenished every 5 to 6 hours for optimum thiamine levels during detoxification and healing.

The Role of Thiamine in Hangovers

The biochemical recipe for hangovers involves a thiamine-dependent process. A multienzyme called alpha-ketoglutarate dehydrogenase is the substrate of the energy-producing breakdown of alcohol, at a point where amino acid and carbohydrate metabolism interacts. Alpha-ketoglutarate dehydrogenase is the control for alpha-detoglutarate, which is the substance that is converted into glutamate, which can in turn be converted to GABA, the major inhibitory neurotransmitter in the brain.

At the start of alcohol consumption, inhibition of alpha-ketoglutarate dehydrogenase is likely to lead to a buildup of the alpha-ketoglutarate formed from alcohol, if there are conditions of limited thiamine. This could increase the production of the alternative uninhibited glutamate pathway, and hence lead to an increase in GABA production.

On the other hand, if the excess glutimate is not converted into GABA, toxic amounts will build up and can cause excitatory imbalances in the brain. This produces a broad spectrum of nervous system disorders, from constant low-grade anxiety to seizures.

Benefits of B1/Thiamine in The 101 Program
- Free radical antioxidant; key protector against acetaldehyde free radical damage
- Helps relieve and heal alcohol-induced psychosis
- Helps in blood sugar management
- Addresses the extreme thiamine deficiencies in heavy drinkers and those with liver disease

Symptoms of Thiamine Deficiency
- Encephalopathy
- Anorexia, bulimia
- Fatigue

- Nervousness, nervous system disorders
- Cognitive disorders
- Aggressiveness or hostility
- Anxiety
- Korsakoff's psychosis
- Emotional instability

Vitamin B2 / Riboflavin

Riboflavin is a water-soluble vitamin and is important in promoting the release of energy from carbohydrates, fats, and proteins. It also aids in maintaining the integrity of red blood cells. Riboflavin is an important component of cellular respiration since it takes oxygen from the cells, with the help of other enzymes. Vitamin B2 is crucial in the production of energy via the Krebb's cycle (a biological pathway that converts glucose (sugar) into energy). Riboflavin is involved with the enzyme glutathione reductase, which helps maintain glutathione, a major protector against free radical damage and liver detoxification pathway. This vitamin also has its own antioxidant qualities. It is integral to both the inner breathing of cells, where energy is produced, and the quenching of the toxic exhausts from energy-producing cell respiration.

Riboflavin deficiency occurs in people with long-standing infections, liver disease, and alcoholism. This vitamin is scarce in most foods, so it is best to supplement the diet to insure an adequate intake. Excessive drinking induces mental and physical fatigue because of the fact that many B vitamins are directly related to the Krebbs cycle, and are depleted during their role in alcohol metabolism and the extraordinarily high amounts of simple carbohydrates in the system. They are also used to remove acetaldehyde and detox the body.

Vitamin B2 is now beginning to receive attention for its role in reducing and eliminating beryllium, which is linked to alcoholism. There is a very strong connection regarding the powerful influence that acetaldehyde and THIQ production have toward addiction, and how B2 can reduce that.

Benefits of B2/Riboflavin in the 101 Program

- Protects against cancer

- Protects against anemia
- Helps cell respiration
- Interaction with vitamins A, K, B6, niacin, and folate
- Contributes to the Krebs cycle; required to produce energy
- Metabolism
- Antioxidant

Symptoms of Riboflavin Deficiency

- Contributes to pancreatic injury in alcohol abusers
- Weakness and fatigue
- Burning and itchy eyes
- Lesions of the lips
- Inflammation of the tongue
- Red or bloody mouth
- Dermatitis
- Brain and nerve dysfunction
- Vitamins B6 and niacin deficiency
- Anemia

Vitamin B3/Niacin

The body uses vitamin B3 in the process of releasing energy from carbohydrates, and in forming fat from carbohydrates. Vitamin B3 comes in two basic forms — niacin (also called nicotinic acid) and niacinamide (also called nicotinamide). Niacinamide is the non-flushing form of niacin. A variation on niacin, called inositol hexaniacinate, is also available in supplements. Since it has not been linked with any reports of niacin toxicity in scientific research, some doctors recommend inositol hexaniacinate for people who need large amounts of niacin. Since niacinamide has been researched extensively in regard to alcohol and addiction, and its benefits in treating addictive biochemistry and alcoholism are well documented, I recommend the use of niacinamide over all the other variations of niacin. Niacinamide is extremely important in the reversal of addictive biochemistry for many reasons, especially for its role in helping to maintain healthy blood sugar levels; this is paramount in avoiding the "craving" for alcohol.

B3 and NAD (an enzyme made from B3) activate the enzymes alcohol dehydrogenase and aldehyde dehydrogenase during alcohol metabolism. This lends understanding as to

why heavy drinkers are deficient in B3; it is consumed, like thiamine, in the demands of metabolizing alcohol. When enough B3 is available, niacinamide helps metabolize alcohol and reduce acetaldehyde levels by quickly metabolizing it.

Those with a history of heavy drinking are found to be deficient in B3 and it's easy to understand why. Between the simple carb diets that problem drinkers are known for and the demands of acetaldehyde and alcohol metabolism, B3 supplies are quickly diminished. This poses a problem for a chronic drinker because a deficiency in B3 means that the body is much slower to convert acetaldehyde to acetate; more acetaldehyde is being made available to harm the body, and bind with dopamine, serotonin, and other metabolite complexes to form THIQs. Since THIQs are morphine-like substances, the origin of alcohol addiction in this biochemical pathway is the same as the neuro-biochemical basis of addiction to opiates.

It is also interesting to note that over usage of B3 due to the high demands placed on it by alcohol and sugar metabolism, exhausts leucine, and leaves more isoleucine to over produce insulin – yet another contributor to the hypoglycemic, blood sugar fluctuation and addiction roller coaster.

Since simple/refined carbs are quickly converted to glucose, someone who drinks absolutely no alcohol but is a sugar junkie will produce more alcohol in their system via the fermentation of those simple carbohydrates than a heath conscious person on a whole foods diet. The normal person produces about 1 oz of alcohol per day naturally in their body. A sugar junkie will produce much more than that, which will cause the same euphoric effects of acetaldehyde being converted to THIQs. Since acetaldehyde bonds with serotonin to produce THIQs (preventing that neurotransmitter from supporting healthy states of mind), and B3 (which is depleted during the metabolism of alcohol and its byproducts) is needed for the conversion of tryptophan to serotonin, it will be impossible to supply the brain with healthy concentrations of serotonin. There will be no serotonin to perform the more desirable functions of producing natural optimistic, pleasurable, inspired moods or to aid in your ability to concentrate.

Niacin was the first supplement to gain interest in the orthomolecular treatment of alcoholism due to its enormous contribution toward reducing your desire to drink. It was actually promoted by Bill Wilson, the cofounder of AA. However, even though the benefits of niacin were well researched and its medicinal qualities of relieving depression, low blood sugar symptoms, and the compulsive desire to drink were clinically proven and well documented, the physicians and members of AA refused to endorse Bill's efforts at including it in the AA experience. They rejected further research and the idea of holistically treating alcoholism to the extent that Bill was forced to seek assistance from physicians outside of AA; physicians who in fact further validated niacin's beneficial qualities in treating alcoholism in their own clinical trials. Bill was a maverick, a visionary, and a genius; it is somewhat ironic that his most beneficial contributions, those that he held closest to his heart during his latter years, were rejected by the very group he co-founded. Today, thanks to the work which began with Dr. Abram Hoffer and Bill W. and his original team of physicians, now being continued through people like Mathews-Larson Ph.D., Dr. Kenneth Blum, Dr. Joseph Beasely, Dr. Joseph Tintera, and of course myself and Alternative Approaches to end Alcohol Abuse (AAAA), there is an industry push in the direction of providing treatments that actually cure the biochemical root cause of the addiction, resulting in orthomolecular treatments applied to addictive biochemistry gaining the recognition they deserve. Using orthomolecular science and medicine to cure alcoholism, people are being freed every day from the debilitating symptoms they have struggled with for most of their lives, and which typically resulted in being the genesis of their relapse during previous attempts at quitting using the fatally flawed methods of conventional treatments and support groups. In fact, many conventional treatments and support groups actually *prescribe* what science knows to be the leading causes of relapse.

Symptoms of Niacin Deficiency

Niacin is depleted during consumption of sugar, simple carbs, alcohol, and antibiotics.

- Feeling fearful

- Apprehensiveness
- Worry
- Extreme cravings for simple carbohydrates
- Suspicion
- Depression
- Headaches
- Insomnia
- Agitation
- Inability to concentrate
- Pellagra (dermatitis, diarrhea, dementia)
- Weakness
- Gastrointestinal disturbance

Benefits of Niacinamide/B3 in The 101 Program

- Alcohol withdrawal support
- Required for the synthesis of serotonin from tryptophan
- Known to lower cholesterol and triglyceride levels
- Acts as a coenzyme for utilizing and breaking down proteins, fats, and carbohydrates
- Vitamin B3 is involved in the Krebb's cycle (biological pathway converting glucose into energy), which is a key factor contributing to the mental and physical fatigue experienced by heavy drinkers.
- Co-factor in sex and adrenal hormone synthesis
- Essential component of the GTF (glucose tolerance factor)
- May prevent type I diabetes and help restore beta-cells, or at least slow down their destruction; prolongs non-insulin-requiring remission, lowers insulin resistance, improves metabolic control, and increases beta-cell function. B3 can induce complete resolution in some newly diagnosed type I diabetics.
- Inhibition of nitric oxide production
- Aids antioxidant activity
- Helps reduce anxiety
- In hypoglycemia: improves sugar regulation and is much better tolerated than niacin; high-dose niacin can disrupt glucose control in diabetics.   Through regulating blood sugar, niacinamide prevents abnormal drops in blood sugar, and along with a condictive diet, helps to decrease the craving for alcohol.
- Helps in the recovery from depression, anxiety, frustration, and tension

- Plays an important role in the central nervous system
- Can be synthesized from tryptophan with vitamins B1, B2, and B6 as essential cofactors. Studies show that 60 mg of tryptophan yield 1 mg of niacin.
- Activates the two enzymes responsible for metabolizing alcohol and acetaldehyde (alcohol dehydrogenase and aldehyde dehydrogenase)
- Involved in the production of NAD, a substrate required for redox reactions in glycolysis and in the Krebs cycle during oxidative phosphorylation.
- Required in the synthesis of NADPH, which is needed for the synthesis of both fatty acids and steroids.

Vitamin B5/Pantothenic Acid

Pantothenic Acid is a crucial nutrient for energy metabolism, synthesis of neurotransmitters, and natural body steroid hormones. Hypoglycemia, continued stress, alcohol, and high-simple carb diets deplete vitamin B5 and weaken the adrenal glands, leading to adrenal fatigue and causing psychological and physiological symptoms to develop.

Benefits of B5/Pantothenic Acid in The 101 Program
- Used for conversion of fats, carbohydrates, and proteins into energy
- Key co-factor in the production of neurotransmitters, adrenal hormones, and antibodies; also enhances stamina
- Vital for the production of steroids such as cortisone in the adrenal gland
- Needed to convert phosphatidyl choline to acetylcholine (neurotransmitter involved in memory and learning)
- Key in repairing the damage to the adrenals; absolutely crucial for adrenal health
- Blocks sugar and alcohol cravings by helping produce key neurotransmitters known to help the regulation and release of serotonin, dopamine, and beta-endorphins

Symptoms of B5 Deficiency
- Depletion of B5 indicates fatigued adrenals and makes it impossible for the organ to healthfully respond to stress
- Physical and mental fatigue
- Tingling in hands
- Depression
- Anxiety

- Excitability
- General inability to cope with stress

Vitamin B6/Pyridoxine - PLP, Pyridoxal-5-Phosphate, Pyridoxine

Vitamin B6 (pyridoxine, pyridoxal, and pyridoxamine) is a water-soluble vitamin that is essential in protein metabolism. It facilitates the release of glycogen from the liver and muscle and is involved in the metabolism of fat and nucleic acids. Vitamin B6 and P5P (pyridoxal-5-phosphate, a form of B6) help to construct and break down many amino acids. This plays a critical role in synthesizing, utilizing, and regulating the much-needed serotonin, beta-endorphin, dopamine, and GABA neurotransmitters during this journey toward correcting your addictive biochemistry and maintaining healthy mental processes and mood stability. B6 lowers homocysteine levels; homocysteine is an amino acid responsible for many cardiovascular health issues. In fact, those with low levels of P5P are six times more at risk for heart attack.

Vitamin B6 is essential in minimizing the seizures and over-excitability symptoms of alcohol withdrawal, and in maintaining healthy biochemical composure in relation to nerve function and brain chemistry during the healing process. This is because during withdrawal vitamin B6 is able to synthesize neurotransmitters from raw precursors such as tyrosine, tryptophan, and phenylalanine.

B6 works well for people in combination with folic acid and vitamin B12.

Benefits of B6 in The 101 Program
- Hydrochloric acid production
- Fat and protein utilization
- Red blood cell formation
- Antibody formation
- Maintains sodium/potassium balance (nerves)
- Co-factor in the synthesis of many crucial neurotransmitters
- Promotes healthy skin
- Reduces swelling in tissues
- Helps convert B3 to NAD; since NAD is deactivated by acetaldehyde metabolism, this aids in acquiring and

maintaining good energy because NAD is being made more available for energy-producing contributions.

- Helps produce the inhibitory neurotransmitter GABA, which is helpful during withdrawal due to its calming effects.

- Helps convert Linoleic Acid to arachidonic acid, which is a precursor to Prostaglandin E1 (PGE1). Prostaglandin E1 is essential for healthy functioning of the immune system and nerve cells, and regulates PGE2, a pro inflammatory. Low PGE1 has been indicated in gastrointestinal disorders and some forms of depression. Many problem drinkers experience progressively intensifying allergy symptoms due to vitamin B6 deficiency from alcohol abuse and its resulting prevention of PGE1 synthesis.

Symptoms of B6 Deficiency

- Nervous disorders
- Hair loss
- Irritability
- Increased allergy symptoms
- Anemia
- Dermatitis
- Depression
- Muscle spasms
- Dizziness
- Poor neurotransmitter synthesis

Vitamin B12/Methylcobalamin

Methylcobalamin is the only form of B12 that is used by the nervous system, and provides the type of support and results desired for those detoxing and repairing from alcohol toxicity. Alcohol interferes with B12 absorption so that problem drinkers are extremely deficient in this nutrient.

I recommend methylcobalamin over cobalamin (the standard supplement sold in health food stores) because cobalamin needs to be converted in the liver to methylcobalamin. In a healthy liver only about 1% of cobalamin is converted to methylcobalamin, making it impossible for a healing problem drinker to achieve the required therapeutic amounts.

As a methyl donor, vitamin B12 is involved in homocysteine metabolism, and plays a critical role in proper

energy metabolism, immune function, and nerve function. Vitamin B12 acts with folic acid and vitamin B6 to control homocysteine levels. An excess of homocysteine is associated with an increased risk of heart disease and stroke. Those who abuse alcohol are typically deficient in vitamins B6, B12, and folate, lending deeper understanding as to why they are at increased risk of cardiovascular disease.

Benefits of B12 in The 101 Program
- Needed for normal nerve cell activity, DNA replication, and DNA production
- Co-factor in the synthesis of the mood-affecting, anti-depressant natural compound SAMe (S-adenosyl-L-methionine)
- Co-factor in the synthesis of methylmalonyl CoA to succinyl CoA (lipid metabolism, which removes fats from cells; very helpful for the health of your liver)
- Helps convert homocysteine to methionine and aminoethanol to choline
- Necessary for the proper digestion and absorption of foods and for normal metabolism of carbohydrates and fat
- Lifts mood
- Improves mental clarity
- Increases stamina
- Reduces risk of heart disease

Symptoms of B12 Deficiency
- Chronic fatigue
- Poor appetite
- Walking and speaking difficulties
- General weakness
- Nervousness
- Pernicious anemia

Biotin

Biotin is a B-complex vitamin used in the formation of the enzymes that fuel the human body; it is a key co-factor in metabolizing and utilizing fats and glucose for energy. Biotin is extremely important for the synthesis of EFAs in the body, and could be a key reason why many problem drinkers suffer a list of EFA deficiency symptoms, including everything from brittle nails to depression.

Decreased levels of biotin cause the metabolism to become severely impaired. When enzymes aren't available to break down and build up proteins, the essential building blocks of cellular composition, every biochemical process of the body suffers. For the problem drinker, this further aggravates addictive biochemistry by inhibiting the synthesis of the neurotransmitters that the brain so desperately needs.

Biotin has also been shown to enhance the effectiveness of insulin. A team of Japanese researchers found that deficient biotin levels were associated with type II adult-onset diabetes. In a controlled study, they raised biotin levels by supplementing 18 people with 9,000 mcg of biotin per day. After 30 days, the participants' blood sugar levels fell to nearly half their original levels. In those with type 1 (insulin-dependent) diabetes, they found significant improvements in blood sugar control as well.

Biotin is synthesized from the good bacteria in the intestines, so it is important to supplement the diet with biotin after a round of antibiotics, especially for people who are recovering from long-term alcohol toxicity.

Biotin aids in the utilization of protein, folic acid, pantothenic acid, and vitamin B12. Biotin deficiency will also therefore cause deficiency in these nutrients, which are so important in healthy brain chemistry. Problem drinkers are at great risk for biotin deficiency due to their inherent compromised ability to absorb and utilize those nutrients.

Symptoms of Biotin Deficiency

- Dermatitis
- Depression
- Hair loss
- Anemia
- Nausea
- Muscle cramping
- Impaired neurotransmitter synthesis
- Can lead to compromised adrenal health

Avidin is a protein in raw egg whites that binds to biotin that does not pose a problem in the cooked whites, because heat deactivates it. For this reason, I advise that raw egg whites are not used as a protein source because healthy biotin levels are extremely important for those whom have demonstrated addictive biochemistry.

Lecithin

Lecithin contains Choline and Inositol, which are essential for the breakdown of fats and cholesterol. It is one of the B vitamins, and is considered an excellent source of choline. Once in the body, a key component of lecithin, phosphatidylcholine, breaks down into choline.

Choline

Choline is a B vitamin/fatty acid involved in the:

- Production of neurotransmitters in the brain that regulate mood, appetite, behavior, and memory
- Neurological processes that produce concentration and alertness
- Transmission of nerve impulses
- Processes of all cognitive performances including memory, short-term retention, and learning capability
- Removal of fat from the liver (lipotropic)
- Formation of the neurotransmitter acetylcholine

Choline is most effective in phosphatidyl choline form.

Phosphatidylserine (PS)

Phosphatidylserine is a phospholipid that is extremely important for cell membrane health and is severely depleted during chronic alcohol consumption. This has an overall negative impact on cellular health since phosphatidylserine plays an important role in receptor function, and in transporting cellular waste out and nutrients into the cell. It is an extremely important agent for the treatment of alcohol toxicity damage and to aid in reestablishing healthy HPA axis function. Phosphatidylserine treatment will help sensitize hypothalamic and pituitary cortisol receptors. This is a very important first step in treating a burned out HPA axis since long-term alcohol abuse causes phosphatidylserine deficiency which desensitizes cortisol and all other receptors. This not only diminishes the good effects that cortisol provides for various brain centers, but places a heavy workload on the adrenals due to having to create more cortisol to produce a favorable response for the body from the fewer working receptors. This scenario continues until the problem drinker comes to the adrenal fatigue stage and is unable to produce

healthy levels of cortisol which renders them hyper-reactive to even the slightest amount of stress promoting the psychological and physical desire for alcohol. This is called the negative feedback loop and is the condition, which left untreated, will burn out the body's resources trying to maintain homeostasis and will eventually result in various psychological disorders, stress syndrome, and failing neuroendocrine function.

Folic Acid / Folate

Folic acid is a water-soluble vitamin that functions as a coenzyme and is important for breaking down and utilizing proteins, and for the formation of red blood cells. It is also crucial in creating amino acids; a deficiency will disrupt a broad range of amino acid functions and requirements. Folic acid is a key co-factor in the production of the opioids enkephalin and endorphin in the brain, and a co-factor in the synthesis of methionine from homocysteine. When enough methionine is produced in the body it can, with the presence of other beta-endorphin precursors, enable a sufficient quantity of enkephalins and endorphins to be built. This is extremely important in the former problem drinker's brain chemistry because these key neurotransmitters provide natural relaxation, peace of mind, self esteem, and help to provide a healthy means of coping with stress and relieving some forms of depression.

Cooking, processing, canning, or storing of food can destroy substantial amounts of folate, since the vitamin is sensitive to sunlight, heat, and acids.

Benefits of Folic Acid / Folate in The 101 Program

- Help maintain normal blood sugar levels
- Important for mental and emotional health
- Works closely with vitamins B6 and B12, as well as the nutrients betaine and S-adenosylmethionine (SAMe), to lower homocysteine levels in the blood.
- Promote health of the nervous system, skin, hair, eyes, mouth, and liver
- Aid in the production of DNA and RNA
- Assist in the synthesis of natural opioids; healthy levels of opioids have been shown to substantially reduce the desire and craving to drink alcohol.

Symptoms of Folic Acid Deficiency

- Anemia
- More than usual hair loss
- General weakness
- "Restless leg syndrome"
- Insomnia
- Diarrhea
- Forgetfulness, mental sluggishness
- Depression
- Inflamed, sore tongue
- Numbness or tingling in the hands and feet
- Occurs in the majority of binge-drinkers

Free Radicals and Antioxidants

Free radicals are atoms or groups of atoms with an odd (unpaired) number of electrons. They can be formed when oxygen interacts with certain molecules, and are highly reactive molecules that, once formed, can start a chain reaction like dominoes. Their chief danger comes from the damage they can cause when they react with important cellular components such as DNA or the cell membrane. Cells begin to function poorly or die if this occurs. To prevent this and protect you from free radical damage, the body has a defense system comprised of antioxidants.

Antioxidants are molecules that can safely interact with free radicals to terminate the chain reaction before vital molecules are damaged. Although there are several enzyme systems within the body that scavenge free radicals, the principle micronutrient (vitamin) antioxidants are vitamin E, CoQ10, alpha lipoic acid, beta-carotene, and vitamin C. Selenium, a trace mineral that is required for proper functioning of one of the body's antioxidant enzyme systems, is also sometimes included in this category.

Key Antioxidants

Vitamin C

Vitamin C is a water-soluble antioxidant that is severely exhausted during excess alcohol consumption, due to the high number of free radicals produced by alcohol and acetaldehyde metabolism that must be neutralized. If there is not sufficient Vitamin C available, free radicals will have more

opportunity to inflict damage on all of the organs with which they come in contact, and especially to the liver.

Benefits of Vitamin C in The 101 Program

- Protects the organs from free radical damage, minimizing oxidative stress to organs
- Delays the aging process
- Aids in healing damaged tissues and assists all healing biosystems within the body
- Minimizes oxidative damage to DNA and neutralizes nitrates that are known to cause cancer
- Works as a sedative and has an anti-anxiety affect
- Aids in collagen production, digestion, iodine conservation, shock and infection resistance, and protection against cancer-producing agents (carcinogens)
- Aids in red blood cell formation
- Strengthens the immune system and accelerates healing after surgery
- Helps to prevent common colds
- Key nutrient in blocking sugar and alcohol cravings and helping to reduce all withdrawal symptoms

Symptoms of Vitamin C Deficiency

- Anemia
- Hemorrhages
- Capillary wall ruptures
- Easy bruising
- Dental cavities
- Low infection resistance
- Premature aging
- Poor digestion
- Soft or bleeding gums
- Thyroid insufficiency

Vitamin D

While vitamin D aids in the absorption of both calcium and phosphorous, its most important role is in maintaining blood levels of calcium by increasing the rate of absorption of calcium from food and reducing urinary calcium loss. It plays a role in immunity and blood cell formation, and has been credited for its positive effect on protecting people from diabetes. Vitamin D is needed for the manufacturing of insulin. Its receptors have been found in the pancreas where

insulin is made, and research suggests that vitamin D supplementation may support insulin secretion for people with adult-onset diabetes.

Problem drinkers are excellent candidates for vitamin D deficiencies because two of the major conditions noted in deficient individuals are pancreatic enzyme deficiency and liver disease (including fatty liver).

Symptoms of Vitamin D Deficiency
- Softening of the bones
- Inadequate calcium absorption
- Muscular numbness and spasms
- Tingling

Vitamin E

Vitamin E is an antioxidant that protects cells by deactivating or destroying free radicals. Vitamin E also helps in the formation of red blood cells and facilitates the use of the trace mineral selenium and vitamins A and K. Vitamin E's greatest contribution to those recovering from long-term alcohol toxicity is its ability to clean up cellular waste and protect cells from future free radical damage.

Problem drinkers are likely to be deficient in vitamin E because two of the major conditions that cause deficiency are pancreatitis and a sluggish, possibly diseased liver. Inflammation of the liver can obstruct and reduce bile salts needed for the absorption of vitamin E as well as EFAs; this condition promotes an exhaustive list of potential mind and body illnesses as result of deficiency of these nutrients. Pancreatitis leads to diminished amounts of lipase, the enzyme required to break down fats, and eventually to prevention of vitamin E and EFAs being absorbed by the body.

Symptoms of Vitamin E Deficiency
- Primarily nerve and muscle disorders
- Anemia
- Generalized free radical damage that can be a key or contributing factor in the development of illness

Alpha Lipoic Acid

Alpha Lipoic Acid is an excellent antioxidant, particularly for the liver and brain, due to its ability to clean up free radicals in both fat and water-soluble environments. This is an excellent characteristic, since the brain is approximately 60% fat and those with a history of heavy drinking are likely to have fatty livers. This universally powerful antioxidant has also demonstrated the ability to protect cells in the brain and liver.

Benefits of Alpha Lipoic Acid in The 101 Program
- Recharges C, E, Co Q10, and glutathione
- Both an antioxidant and a B vitamin-like substance
- Reduces lipid peroxidation
- Potent antioxidant in both fat and water-soluble environments
- Abilities extend to both the oxidized and the reduced form
- Improves energy metabolism
- Helps remove fat from the liver
- Protects the liver; helpful in treating liver diseases including alcohol-induced cirrhosis
- Reverses glycosylation (hardening) of cell membranes that is caused by prolonged elevated blood glucose levels; important for heavy and former heavy drinkers
- Can increase insulin sensitivity; important to the former problem drinker in healing insulin resistance

Symptoms of Alpha Lipoic Acid Deficiency
General deficiency of proper amounts of antioxidants can result in everything from cancer and cirrhosis to increased susceptibility to the common cold.

Glutathione

Glutathione is assembled in the body from Glycine, Cysteine, and Glutamine. It is a key free-radical antioxidant and is essential to liver detoxification. It combines with selenium to form glutathione peroxidase, one of the body's own free radical scavengers. Glutathione also helps increase the effectiveness of vitamin C, by converting the oxidized vitamin back to its effective form. Glutathione performs two important functions in liver detoxification: it intercepts toxic

compounds from Phase I liver detox and it combines with Phase II toxic chemicals to form a water-soluble conjugate that can be excreted in the bile and urine. For this reason, it is an excellent nutrient for balancing Phase I and Phase II liver detoxification. However, it is best to take glutathione precursors (detailed above and in the precursor section) because if taken orally, this supplement will be absorbed and broken down mostly in the stomach and small intestine, with very little actually getting to the liver and other organs.

Minerals

Magnesium

Magnesium is a key nutrient for blocking sugar and alcohol cravings, minimizing withdrawal symptoms, and stabilizing blood sugar levels. It has a calming effect and can help tremendously toward reducing delirium and tremors associated with severe and moderate withdrawal. Magnesium also works well with calcium and B vitamins to address many alcohol withdrawal symptoms and related nervous system health issues. It is depleted during heavy alcohol consumption, a deficient state that is a key cause of the hypertension endured by problem drinkers, especially during withdrawal.

Symptoms of Magnesium Deficiency

- Insomnia
- Tremors
- Hyperactivity
- Depression
- Memory impairment
- Delirium tremens
- Confusion
- Cardiovascular health issues
- Cognitive disorders

Manganese

Manganese is an enzyme activator and is required for healthy skin, bone, and cartilage formation, as well as glucose tolerance. It also helps activate the important antioxidant enzyme, superoxide dismutase.

Benefits of Manganese

- Helps body utilize biotin, thiamin, ascorbic acid, and choline
- Key in healthy bone development and health
- Helps maintains normal blood sugar levels
- Promotes optimal function of the thyroid gland; aids in healthy metabolism
- Maintains nerve health
- Antioxidant that protects cells from free-radical damage
- Helps body synthesize fatty acids and cholesterol

Symptoms of Manganese Deficiency

- Impaired insulin metabolism
- Abnormal glucose tolerance
- Impaired lipoprotein (fat) metabolism
- Impaired immune system
- Impaired metabolic function

While manganese is important to many biochemical functions in the body relating to the immune system, bone development, metabolism, and blood sugar management, manganese deficiency is extremely rare in humans. In fact, manganese toxicity is more of a problem in the U.S. than manganese deficiency. This toxicity has been linked to Parkinson disease (many welders have developed Parkinson, probably because of the high manganese content in the welding rods) and many other illnesses found in people who work in or near industrial sites that release it in the air. There are many areas in our industrialized environment that contain toxic levels of manganese and if you think that you might have been over exposed, you should begin researching the sources of manganese toxicity to see if you may be at risk. I do not advise supplementing with high doses of manganese since safe, healthy amounts of this mineral are contained in the condictive biochemistry diet. If you suspect that you may have a slight deficiency, you should get tested and, depending on the results, include the manganese-rich foods listed below in your diet to compensate for this deficiency.

Those with liver disease or diabetes should not supplement with manganese.

- Pineapple
- Ground cloves
- Turmeric

Zinc

Zinc is a predominate factor in good mental health; low levels of it can cause anxiety and nervousness. When zinc is low, copper can rise to toxic levels in the body, creating fearfulness, apprehension, and paranoia. Zinc is also a key co-factor in many neurotransmitter functions. It is excreted out of the kidneys in abnormal amounts as a result of heavy drinking.

Low serum zinc can allow copper to rise and high copper levels are often associated with over-methylation which also indicates low histamine; a very strong contributor to addictive biochemistry. Former problem drinkers who dive into the sugar bowel during recovery tend to continue to demonstrate symptoms of high copper levels due to the fact that sugar and alcohol both cause excessive release of zinc from the body.

A very useful test to ascertain whether under or over methylation and Pyroluria (chronic deficiency of both B6 and zinc) is an issue for you is a whole blood histamine, zinc, copper and Kryptopyrrole metabolic panel. It is reported that 40% to 60% of those addicted to alcohol suffer this condition.

Calcium

Calcium is the most abundant mineral in the body, and is essential to nerve transmission bioenergetics. It affects the contraction and relaxation of muscles.

A balanced supply of calcium and magnesium is extremely helpful toward easing withdrawal. Sufficient calcium will also encourage high-quality sleep.

Symptoms of Calcium Deficiency
- Irritability
- Insomnia
- Nervousness
- Numbness
- Osteoporosis

Selenium

Selenium functions much like vitamin E, protecting the cell membrane from free radicals. Selenium delays the oxidation of polyunsaturated fats, which is one of the

processes that cause the skin to lose elasticity and show signs of aging. This mineral also regulates the supply of oxygen to the heart.

Selenium is essential for the production of prostaglandins, making it extremely important in the treatment of depression due to alcohol abuse, in assisting re-establishment of balanced brain chemistry, and in aiding the recovery of a damaged gastrointestinal tract.

Benefits of Selenium

- Involved in the production of thyroid hormones
- Part of the glutathione peroxidase enzyme that protects the body from free radical damage; this enzyme may also help regenerate the antioxidant vitamin E.
- Component of sulfur amino acid metabolism
- Most highly concentrated in the pancreas, pituitary gland, and liver
- Antagonist to heavy metals including lead, mercury, aluminum, and cadmium

Symptoms of Selenium Deficiency
- Deficiency produces fatty liver infiltration.
- Linked with a variety of degenerative conditions including cardiovascular disease, inflammatory diseases, cancer, premature aging, cataracts, etc.
- Partly responsible for progressive cardiomyopathy, which is common among problem and chronic drinkers
- Contributes to the suppression of the endocrine system, translating to damage and inflammation of the pancreas, liver, and adrenals

Chromium Picolinate

Chromium Picolinate is essential to normal glucose, protein, and fat metabolism. The biologically active chromium molecule involved in the "glucose tolerance factor" (GTF) appears to be a dinicotinato-chromium, glutathione-like complex. This complex facilitates interaction of insulin with its receptor site, thus influencing glucose, protein, and lipid metabolism. This is important for the insulin resistant problem drinker.

Benefits of Chromium Picolinate

- Produces long-term weight loss, increases metabolic rate, controls appetite, reduces serum cholesterol, regulates blood sugar levels, increases energy and/or stamina, and is useful in the treatment of hypoglycemia and diabetes; problems developed by many chronic drinkers
- Acts to regulate sugar and glucose, and to prevent low blood sugar symptoms, thus freeing the former problem drinker from the symptoms associated with low blood sugar; helpful especially during withdrawal and in the first couple weeks of detoxing
- Helps reduce sugar and alcohol cravings
- Assists in carbohydrate metabolism, also transporting carbohydrates out of the system before the excess simple sugars can produce alcohol and lead to the acetaldehyde to THIQ process

Amino Acids

The word protein comes from the Greek word "proteios" meaning "most important". The body breaks down the protein contained in the foods you eat and procures the individual amino acids, which are then reassembled into different types of proteins to meet the specific needs of the various cells of the body. Proteins are the basis of all protoplasm, and therefore all living tissue. They are made of nitrogen in combination with carbon, oxygen, and hydrogen; some also contain sulfur or phosphorus.

Every cell in the body needs and uses amino acids; a healthy, well-balanced supply of amino acids is necessary to produce the various proteins required by the body. There are two types of amino acids: nonessential and essential. The body can manufacture nonessential amino acids, but the essential amino acids must be obtained from the foods you eat. Amino acids have a direct relation with vitamins and minerals; they enable vitamins and minerals to properly perform their specific jobs in the body. Even if the body absorbs vitamins and minerals, they cannot be effective unless the necessary amino acids are present.

Standard amino acids and unique sequential combinations of amino acids are precursors to neurotransmitters, neuromodulators, and hormones, which also have specific

functions in the mind and body. Their synthesis and utilization also relies on complementary vitamin, mineral, EFA, and enzyme availability. Neurotransmitters physically carry information from one nerve cell to another. Neuromodulators are substances secreted from neurons so that their information can be received in various areas of the brain and nervous system. Many molecules act simultaneously as neurotransmitters, neuromodulators, and hormones.

Provision of a healthy, comprehensive amount of amino acids, and their distribution and usage is essential to mind/body/emotional health. Amino acids assist in the exchange of nutrients between the cellular fluids and the tissues, blood, and lymphs. The genetic code contained in each cell's DNA is actually a blue print with directions on how to sustain its life, and repair, and regenerate itself using various combinations of amino acids.

It is for this reason that amino acids become extremely important in the study of addictive biochemistry. When a toxin is introduced into the system, it thwarts the healthy biochemical processes driven by our DNA and other environmental conditions. Due to the extreme nutritional demands placed on the cell's resources to get that toxin metabolized and out of the body, the body's resources, energy and focus is shifted away from repair and replication and is exhausted metabolizing the toxin. Malnutrition ensues and if it is chronic will cause damage to the organs. The impact of the nutrient deficient changes in the composition of healthy cells creates a chaotic environment, causing life-sustaining bioenergetic instructions provided to receptor proteins to be lost, resulting in the cell being essentially excommunicated from its environment. This essentially marks the cell for death, because that is exactly what death is to the cell: excommunication from its environment. These disruptive changes in electrical and chemical information in the cells prevent DNA from functioning in your best interest in the micro world, resulting in biochemical chaos, which prevents you, in turn, from functioning and accomplishing things as you should in your macro world. This leads to destructive, unhealthy changes in thoughts, emotions, and behavior, which then translates into an unhealthy, unmanageable, and

chaotic lifestyle. The macrocosm mirrors the microcosm, and vice versa.

To summarize, amino acids are the "building bocks" of every cell of the body and are intricately involved in all cellular bioenergetics. If they become unavailable or are not usable, as is the case during alcohol toxicity, the result is a deficient and distorted metabolism, compromised physical and mental performance, and a plethora of health issues including life-threatening diseases.

Amino acids are involved in:
- Building all cells and repairing tissue (growth and healing)
- Forming antibodies to combat invading bacteria and viruses
- Healthy blood coagulation
- Regulating the amount of fluids in the tissues and the water balance of the blood
- Maintaining all body flesh, bone, and hair
- Building nucleoproteins (RNA and DNA)
- Formation of all enzymes
- Formation of hormones
- Formation of neurotransmitters and neuromodulators
- Digestion of fats
- Carrying oxygen throughout the body and participating in muscle activity
- Providing a healthy and efficient metabolism

It is important to point out that 'metabolism' means the sum of all the physical and chemical processes whereby protoplasm (all living tissue) is produced and maintained. Therefore, metabolism actually refers to millions of processes within the body; it is not limited to how easily you put on or take off weight.

When protein is broken down by digestion the result is 22 known amino acids. Eight are essential and the rest are non-essential.

Essential Amino Acids

- Leucine
- Isoleucine
- Lysine
- Methionine

- D & L Phenylalanine
- Threonine
- Tryptophan
- Valine

Essential Amino Acids Functions

Isoleucine and Leucine are two of the three major branched chain amino acids (BCAA) (the third being Valine), all of which are intricately involved with muscle strength, endurance, stamina, and the synthesis of the proteins required to build muscle. BCAA levels are significantly decreased by insulin, which explains why people who are heavy drinkers and also go to the gym all week find it very hard to build muscle and get a return on their workouts.

BCAAs also compete (as do other larger-sized amino acid molecules) with tryptophan and tyrosine for transport across the blood-brain barrier.

Functions of the essential amino acids include:

Isoleucine (BCAA)
- Metabolic regulator
- Required for the formation of hemoglobin
- Helps regulate some functions of B3

Leucine (BCAA)
- Metabolic regulator
- Stimulates protein synthesis
- Energy source for muscle tissue
- Primarily metabolized through fat pathways
- Stimulates insulin release
- Excess Leucine decreases the buildup of brain serotonin by inhibiting the transport of tryptophan over the blood-brain barrier.
- Both Leucine and Isoleucine work synergistically with the B vitamins, particularly B6 (Pyridoxine).

Valine (BCAA)

Valine is not processed by the liver before entering the bloodstream and can be used directly by the muscle tissue as an energy source.

- Promotes mental vigor, motivation, muscle coordination and calm emotions
- Involved in the synthesis of vital proteins and peptides

- Functions synergistically with vitamins B6, B2, and B1, biotin, copper, and magnesium
- Excessive drinking, chronic liver diseases and stress create valine deficiency. During deficiency digestion of all other amino acids and proteins will be compromised.

Lysine

- Works with Arginine and Ornithine to stimulate the pituitary
- Helps raise HGH naturally
- Ensures adequate absorption of calcium
- Aids in the production of antibodies, hormones, and enzymes

L-Theanine

L-Theanine is the predominant amino acid in green tea and is a derivative of Glutamic Acid. It is also available in supplement form. It is a non-sedating relaxant that increases the brain's alpha waves, which are those responsible for the state of relaxed alertness; their levels are used as an index of relaxation.

- Raises GABA levels
- Reduces the effects of caffeine; is a caffeine antagonist.
- Clinically proven anti-carcinogen
- Reduces anxiety and promotes relaxation
- Relieves emotional, perceived, and psychological stress
- Promotes learning and retention
- Raises serotonin and/or dopamine in the striatum, hypothalamus, and hippocampus areas of the brain
- Reduces glutamic acid excitotoxicity (excitotoxicity leads to brain cell death)

All of these benefits, combined with the liver healing and rejuvenating catechins also found in green tea, make it an excellent drink for mind and body health if one is not suffering from adrenal fatigue.

L-Threonine

Threonine is an immune system stimulant and a primary nutrient for the thymus. It is required to help maintain the proper protein balance in the body, as well as to assist in the formation of collagen and elastin in the skin. It is a precursor

for glycine and serine and works synergistically with vitamin B6.

Threonine is an important amino acid for the nervous system, due to the high levels contained in the CNS (central nervous system). It has been used as a supplement to help alleviate anxiety and some cases of depression. There is an increased demand for this amino acid during times of stress, especially for the gastrointestinal tract, which relies on it heavily for healthy functioning.

Alcohol, stress, and liver disease deplete threonine. Since threonine is known to be directly beneficial to the thymus, the main gland responsible for building a healthy immune system, depleted levels will translate to compromised immune systems.

During detox, threonine is extremely useful because it is a precursor to glycine, which is an inhibitory neurotransmitter that promotes restful states (reduces anxiety and depression).

- Precursor to glycine
- Helps prevent fatty deposits in the liver
- Aids in detoxification
- Helps build a strong immune system
- Key for healthy GI functioning and should be supplemented during detox to expedite efficient gastrointestinal function.
- Is essential in one of the liver's six major detoxification pathways

Tryptophan

Tryptophan is a precursor to serotonin; it converts into serotonin with the aid of pyridoxal-5-phosphate, a form of vitamin B6. This amino acid is a relaxant for anxiety, eases tension, stimulates growth hormone, and is a well-established anti-depressant for serotonin-depleted type depression, which is the most common amongst problem drinkers and hypoglycemics. It stimulates the immune system and reduces the risk of artery and heart spasms. Along with Lysine it can help reduce cholesterol levels. Tryptophan functions synergistically with Vitamin B6 (in P5P form), B3, magnesium, and some forms of folate.

Tryptophan must compete with five other amino acids to pass through the blood/brain barrier and enter the brain, where it is converted to serotonin. The blood/brain barrier is a

physical barrier between the blood vessels in the central nervous system and the CNS itself; it allows or disallows various substances to pass through, depending on the chemical and nutritious environment at the time. When taking tryptophan, the best possible scenario for maximum effect and absorption is to take it on an empty stomach, with a small glass of freshly squeezed fruit juice such as pineapple (2 oz. juice diluted in 4 oz. of water). The juice will raise the blood sugar a bit, and the resulting rise in insulin will help the tryptophan over the blood/brain barrier. Insulin blocks the larger amino acids and allows the smaller tryptophan molecules through the blood/brain barrier. Another medium that will aid tryptophan in getting over the blood/brain barrier is dried dates.

The biochemical scenario of helping tryptophan across the blood/brain barrier is a large part of the attraction that most hypoglycemics and problem drinkers feel toward sweets. Sugar junkies get a high by using sugar and other simple carbs to move their limited supply of tryptophan over the blood/brain barrier to receive the serotonin/beta-endorphin rush. This rush in turn produces the associated, albeit short-term, feelings of energy, alertness, relaxation, completeness, and the general sense that all is well in the world, while silencing the intense cravings their upregulated systems suffer. This reprieve lasts only about 30 minutes to an hour, until the low blood sugar symptoms kick in once more and send a dark cloud in to block the sunshine. Again, this is a very uneducated, unhealthy, and eventually fatal way to self-medicate. Yes, there is a need in those with addictive biochemistry to enhance serotonin, dopamine, beta-endorphins and catecholamines to feel good and right. However, how they do it determines the quality and length of their lives.

One of the primary reasons behind the serotonin-depleted depression in problem drinkers and hypoglycemics is that the body also produces B3 from tryptophan. When there is high demand for B3 to metabolize sugar and alcohol, B3 becomes depleted, and the available tryptophan will be converted to B3 to continue the job of metabolizing alcohol and sugar. This in turn depletes the tryptophan stores in the body, leaving little to be converted into serotonin. B3 conversion takes precedence over serotonin synthesis if the body is deficient in

B3. When the effects of the alcohol wear off, the depression is felt for a number of neurotransmitter-related reasons; a major one being that much of the available tryptophan has essentially been used (in a roundabout way) to metabolize alcohol and sugar.

In The 101 Program, a B3 supplement is taken with tryptophan to help ensure that the tryptophan will actually be used for serotonin synthesis. This is also a reason why B3 helps to induce sleep; it can make more tryptophan available to be converted into serotonin, which converts to melatonin, which is the body's natural sleep aid.

There is also a huge demand for vitamin B6 in the liver for detoxing excessive alcohol and sugar metabolites so it is often extremely deficient in problem drinkers. B6 is required for the conversion of tryptophan to serotonin, so it too must be taken as a supplement with tryptophan to ensure tryptophan's nutritional contribution to healing addictive biochemistry and the mental disorders that accompany it.

Natural sources of tryptophan are bananas, milk, chicken, turkey, and fish.

DL-Phenylalanine (DLPA)

Phenylalanine comes in two chemical forms: D and L. Although they are chemically identical, they are opposite, mirror images of each other and have similar yet different functions in the brain chemistry. The "left-handed" form is known as L-phenylalanine, or LPA. The "right-handed" form is known as D-phenylalanine, or DPA. A mixture of the two forms is known as DL-phenylalanine, or DLPA.

While tryptophan addresses one side of the spectrum of depression by enhancing serotonin levels and thereby decreasing alcohol and sugar cravings, DL-phenylalanine addresses the other side of the spectrum by increasing levels of beta-endorphin, dopamine, and other catecholamine neurotransmitters. Deficiencies in these neurotransmitters are causes for both depression and alcohol craving. DLPA is used to treat alcohol addiction because of its ability to both enhance and preserve enkephalin, endorphin, and dopamine levels. It has proven to be very successful in treating chronic pain as a result of its natural opiate-type analgesic qualities which are produced by D-phenylalanine inhibiting the

enzyme enkephalinase, the enzyme that breaks down enkephalins.

Phenylalanine supplements should never be taken with MAO (monoamine oxidase) drugs.

L-Phenylalanine (LPA)

L-phenylalanine is a precursor to tyrosine, which is the precursor to the synthesis of the catecholamine neurotransmitters dopamine, norepinephrine, and epinephrine (adrenaline). Catecholamines affect metabolic health, sex drive, ambition, tissue growth and repair, and the immune system. They also influence the quality of many moods and emotions, have anti-depressive qualities, and affect mental acuity, energy levels, memory, learning, and the general sense of confidence.

- LPA can be converted to L-tyrosine, and subsequently to L-dopa, dopamine, norepinephrine, and epinephrine. LPA can also be converted (through a separate pathway) to phenylethylamine (PEA), a substance that occurs naturally in the brain and elevates mood.
- LPA enhances beta-endorphin, enkephalin, and dopamine release. For this reason it is essential for healthy moods, emotions, and nervous system function. Being a precursor to catecholamines and associated with enhancing beta-endorphin and dopamine release, its use is also associated with enhanced memory and learning abilities.
- LPA's effect on the hypothalamus causes a decrease in appetite. The biochemical reasons for this are also beneficial toward reducing alcohol cravings.
- Tyrosine (precursor to catecholamine synthesis) can be synthesized in the body from phenylalanine.
- LPA is depleted by excess alcohol and caffeine.
- LPA enhances clarity of thought, concentration, and memory.
- LPA works synergistically with Vitamins B6, B3, and C, some forms of folate, iron, and copper.
- Natural sources of L-phenylalanine are protein sources such as liver, beef, pumpkin seeds, peanuts, lamb, trout, codfish, chicken, cottage cheese, lima beans, milk, Brazil nuts, and raw, whole chickpeas.

D-Phenylalanine (DPA)

D-phenylalanine is extremely important in achieving healthy brain chemistry in people with addictive biochemistry due to its ability to inhibit the reuptake of endorphins and enkephalins; two natural opioids whose deficiencies are known to be key markers of addictive biochemistry.

D-phenylalanine is the dextrorotary form of phenylalanine and has an entirely different purpose than its molecular mirror form, L-(levorotary) phenylalanine. The L-Forms of amino acids are bio-available and are for protein synthesis and regulatory function. Conversely, D-phenylalanine is not absorbed into the body; it works instead by inhibiting the enzyme "carboxypeptidase A" which is responsible for the breakdown of endorphins and enkephalins. By inhibiting carboxypeptidase A, D-phenylalanine helps to maintain higher levels of endorphins which provide a natural lowered response to pain; reduced nervous system response to physical and psychological/emotional stress; natural euphoric states of mind; aid in maintaining balance between the inhibitory and excitatory neurotransmitters, and a general sense that all is well in the world.

Low endorphin and enkephalin levels heighten sensitivities to physical, psychological, emotional, and perceived stress and have also been shown to increase the production of adrenaline, which aids in over stimulating the sympathetic nervous system. This over stimuli causes its own list of symptoms and intensifies the problem drinker's resident multiple symptoms caused by low blood sugar and over expression of the excitatory neurotransmitters.

Essentially, D-phenylalanine helps to provide the much needed buffer between you and the blunted response to stress syndrome you likely suffer. This natural buffer provides a healing environment for your pituitary that is likely undernourished and overworked. Once the HPA axis has had enough time away from alcohol, and the stress it creates on the body and mind while being properly nourished, it will re-establish normal healthy functioning.

D-phenylalanine is not normally found in the body or in foods. DPA cannot be converted to L-tyrosine, L-dopa, or norepinephrine such as L-phenylalanine. As a result, DPA is converted primarily to phenylethylamine (PEA).

- Enkephalinase (an enzyme that 'ingests' enkephalins) inhibitors such as D-phenylalanine increase enkephalin levels, which decreases craving for alcohol and provides a sense of natural peacefulness and well being.
- Maintaining the brain's endogenous opiate levels is critical in reducing cravings for alcohol. Studies have shown that rats bred to prefer alcohol actually have naturally lower enkephalin levels in the brain. Since L is primarily responsible for enhancing enkephalin/endorphin levels, and D maintains those levels, a key reason for depleted enkephalins/endorphins is the lowered levels of L- and D-phenylalanine.
- DPA is also a strong natural painkiller. It is best used for chronic, long-term type pain due to the fact that there is a "load" time of one to two weeks required, depending on your system and other lifestyle factors.
- DPA is extremely important in achieving healthy brain chemistry in those with addictive biochemistry due to its ability to inhibit the reuptake of enkephalins.

Phenylethylamine (PEA)

Phenylethylamine deserves special mention due to its extremely beneficial effects toward healing and correcting depression, and especially chemically induced depression. It also contributes to many other favorable moods and emotions; one of which is the emotion that some scientists claim to be love, or the physical and emotional symptoms of love.

PEA is a natural chemical (endogenous neuro-amine) similar to amphetamine, and is suspected of causing the `high' experienced by lovers. The theory is that production of phenylethylamine in the brain can be triggered by something as simple as the meeting of eyes or the touching of hands. The heady emotions linked to racing pulses, sweaty palms, and heavy breathing can be clinically explained as the result of an overdose of PEA.[12]

---

[12] The Chemistry of Love
http://www.monash.edu.au/pubs/montage/Montage_96-01/lovedrug.html

- D-phenylalanine (a precursor to PEA), is the preferred form of phenylalanine in producing more phenylethylamine, because synthesis of tyrosine from L-phenylalanine (which can also produce PEA) takes precedence. Little LPA is left for conversion to phenylethylamine, especially in states where tyrosine is deficient.
- In those with high simple carb diets and who drink excessively, DPA supplementation is a must. If the body is severely LPA/tyrosine taxed, healthy levels of PEA, enkephalins, and endorphins cannot be achieved. DPA can help keep the low supplies of these chemicals active longer. This makes it a necessary nutrient to supplement during the initial stages of detox and recovery.
- Urinary levels of PEA metabolites are elevated after exercise along with enhanced levels of beta-endorphin metabolites, giving chemical evidence of the "runner's high" being produced by beta endorphins and PEA.
- Urinary levels of PEA have been found to be low in some forms of depression.
- DPA is not found naturally in foods, leaving most people to rely on what little LPA is available (after supplying the body with adequate tyrosine) for conversion to PEA; many people, especially those with bad/junk food and high simple carb diets, are extremely deficient in PEA, and have upregulated PEA receptor sites.
- PEA is found in chocolate and is attributed as the chemical (along with the sugar/serotonin rush) that produces the sense of completeness, confidence, and feelings of being loved in people who eat it, even if they are detached from others or normally feel unloved.
- PEA levels spike during orgasm and are high during ovulation.
- Over consumption of alcohol depletes the system in such a way that precursors for PEA are not available. This condition leads to the feelings experienced by many long-term heavy drinkers of isolation, insecurity, and of being unloved. These feelings in turn fortify their habit, giving them more (biochemical) need to drink. Drinking will temporarily boost levels of beta-endorphin, serotonin, and dopamine, washing away the undesirable emotions produced by low PEA levels and other symptoms of the addiction.

Methionine

Methionine is an essential sulfur amino acid. It is a part of a process called methylation, by which numerous important compounds in the body are formed. This amino acid is also crucial to the body's detoxification processes. Diets deficient in methionine may result in an unhealthy breakdown and metabolism of protein.

- Critical in regulating the availability of folic acid
- Deficiency has been implicated in depression
- Low levels of methionine will allow histamine to rise and the symptoms from this condition can promote addictive biochemistry.
- Critical for detoxification
- Requires adequate levels of B6, B12, and folic acid
- Combines with cellular fuel ATP to form mood-enhancing S-adenosylmethionine (SAMe)
- Helps produce taurine and lysine
- Main source of methyl groups
- Aids in production of cysteine, an important liver antioxidant
- Lipotropic (fat metabolizer); other lipotropic agents are choline, betain (from beets), folic acid, and B12.
- Essential to remove fat from the liver
- Natural sources of methionine are meat, fish, beans, eggs, garlic, and sunflower seeds.

Non-Essential Amino Acids

Following is an incomplete list of the non-essential amino acids. As noted earlier, this text only highlights those that are known to be most affected and depleted by over consumption of alcohol, thus causing many of the undesirable symptoms and ill health that results from long-term alcohol toxicity.

- Arginine
- Tyrosine
- Glycine
- Serine
- Glutamine
- Taurine

- Cysteine
- Alanine
- Carnitine
- Ornithine

Arginine

Due to its contribution to healing and regenerating the liver, and its role in stimulating and assisting the endocrine system, arginine is very important to those recovering from addictive biochemistry.

- Strengthens the immune system
- Helps prevent tumors
- Stimulates the thymus therefore enhancing the immune system
- Detoxifies ammonia
- Precursor to GABA
- Simulates insulin and glucagon release; it should not be taken unless you are faithful to your condictive biochemistry diet.
- Promotes healing and regeneration of the liver
- Assists in the release of growth hormones
- Crucial for optimal muscle growth and tissue repair

Tyrosine

- Essential precursor for the creation of catecholamines (neurotransmitters that include dopamine, norepinephrine, and epinephrine). Catecholamines critically influence many specific mental behaviors, emotional states, and cognitive ability. Deficiency is directly related to depression, physical and mental stress, and unhealthy reactions to challenging stimuli.
- Works synergistically with vitamin B6 and magnesium for conversion to catecholamines
- Helps overcome depression, improve memory, and increase mental alertness
- Critically important for recovery of healthy brain chemistry
- Promotes the healthy functioning of the thyroid, adrenal, and pituitary glands
- Converts to the thyroid hormone thyroxin, which plays a key role in controlling metabolic rate, and skin and mental health. Many factors of heavy drinking deplete thyroxin release, so short-term tyrosine supplementation in

therapeutic dosages, while stabilizing blood sugar and nutritionally supporting the rest of the endocrine system, can heal thyroid functional deficiencies. Excellent metabolic health can be naturally achieved in this way.

Due to the fact that it must compete with larger amino acid molecules for entry into the brain, tyrosine supplements are best if taken in the morning or early afternoon, an hour before breakfast or lunch, and at least a half hour before the other amino acids in the program. This will help the supplement to have maximum impact.

Tyrosine is naturally found in fish, chicken, almonds, avocados, bananas, dairy products, pumpkin seeds, oats, lima beans, and sesame seeds.

People taking monoamine oxidase (MAO) inhibitors, commonly prescribed for depression, should not take any supplements containing L-tyrosine, as it may lead to a sudden and dangerous rise in blood pressure.

Glycine (Inhibitory neurotransmitter)

This amino acid performs more biochemical functions than any other amino acid. The functions that are most beneficial for a person healing damage from alcohol toxicity and correcting addictive biochemistry are:

- Necessary for Phase II detoxification process
- Precursor to glutathione
- Most important for the neutralization of toxins
- Helps trigger the release of oxygen to the energy-requiring cell-making process
- Involved in glucagon production
- Inhibits sugar cravings
- Plays key role in manufacturing of hormones
- Required for the production of bile salts
- Necessary for a strong immune system
- Contributes to the synthesis of DNA/RNA precursors
- Benzoates found in soft drinks bind with glycine, depleting stores from the body.
- Inadequate supplies result in compromised capability to remove toxins from the body.

Trimethylglycine (TMG)

Trimethylglycine is a substance derived from plant sources such as broccoli, celery, and beets. It is part of the methyl group of substances that turns the potentially dangerous amino acid, homocysteine, into the beneficial amino acid methionine. Health benefits related to TMG include decreased risk of depression and some cancers, adrenal support, and its lipotropic properties, which break down fats in the liver.

- Works with B5, B6, C, and tyrosine to support adrenal function. This is an excellent combination in conjunction with alpha lipoic acid for treating adrenal fatigue.
- Increases insulin sensitivity
- Reduces cholesterol
- Decreases seizure intensity
- Increases levels of hepatic S-adenosylmethionine (SAMe)
- Prevents ethanol-related fatty liver by helping to break down fat in the liver
- Reduces liver triglycerides levels
- Reduces beta-lipoproteins

Serine

- Storage source of glucose for the liver and muscles
- Helps strengthen the immune system by providing antibodies
- Synthesizes fatty acid sheaths around nerve fibers
- Essential for protein synthesis

Glutamine

- Supplemental glutamine stimulates the release of growth hormone.
- Important glycogenic amino acid; essential in maintaining healthy, stable blood sugar levels
- Useful during initial detox for mental fatigue
- Helps the body absorb vitamins
- Blocks sugar and alcohol cravings; helps to keep the intense sugar cravings experienced during the first few days of detox at bay

- Precursor for GABA, a neurotransmitter in which many long-term problem drinkers become deficient. GABA has a calming effect during the initial stages of detox.
- Glutamine is the only alternate source of glucose available to the brain and is very helpful in providing a ready source of brain fuel for hypoglycemics and those experiencing extreme blood sugar drops during withdrawal. This also reduces the brain's reaction of triggering the adrenals for epinephrine, resulting in better blood sugar control and giving the adrenals time to heal.
- Speeds the healing of ulcers, which many problem drinkers develop due to mucosal damage from long-term alcohol use. Also used to aid in the healing of leaky gut syndrome, which many problem drinkers experience.
- Has been proven useful in schizophrenia treatment
- Glutamine, cysteine, and glycine are combined to form glutathione, a powerful liver detoxifier that is essential to liver Phase II conjugation reactions for elimination of toxins in the liver.
- Involved in DNA synthesis
- Works synergistically with B6, C, and manganese

Taurine (inhibitory neurotransmitter)

In healthy individuals, high concentrations of taurine are found in the heart muscle, white blood cells, skeletal muscle, and central nervous system. Taurine is a key amino acid required by the liver for the removal of toxic chemicals and metabolites; it is used to detoxify environmental chemicals such aldehydes (produced from alcohol excess), alcohols, petroleum-based solvents, and ammonia, all of which are present in abundant, harmful levels in the body of a problem drinker. Taurine is an anti-convulsant, and deficiency has been linked to epileptic seizures. Combined with vitamin B6, it has a useful anti-seizure effect in epileptics, and is useful in minimizing alcohol withdrawal tremors and low-grade seizure-type feelings, including anxiety, for this reason.

Taurine is a building block of all the other amino acids as well as a key component of bile, which is needed for the digestion of fats, the absorption of fat-soluble vitamins, and the control of serum cholesterol levels. Taurine can be useful for people with heart disorders, hypertension, or hypoglycemia. It regulates the transport of minerals across, and stabilizes the electrical properties of, cell membranes,

making it vital for the proper utilization of sodium, potassium, calcium, and magnesium.

Taurine has a protective effect on the brain, especially during dehydration. In The 101 Program it is used to treat anxiety, hypertension, poor brain function, and in helping the liver and bile quickly remove toxic waste.

- Enhances effects of GABA
- Helps to stabilize blood sugar levels
- Slows the aging process by neutralizing free radicals
- Used in the liver to conjugate toxins to be removed by the bile
- Required to produce bile
- Combines with bile acids to make gallbladder stones water-soluble
- Helps the liver to excrete excessive cholesterol out of the body through the bile
- Made from two other amino acids (methionine and cysteine)
- Functions synergistically with Vitamins B6, A, zinc, and manganese
- Natural sources of taurine include animal protein such as meat, seafood, eggs, and dairy products, but not vegetable protein.

Cysteine (and Cystine) - NAC (N-acetyl-cysteine)

Cysteine and cystine are inter-convertible. Two molecules of cysteine make cystine, and the body will convert one to the other as needed. Cysteine is one of the three main sulfur-containing amino acids, along with taurine and methionine. It is required during Phase II detox functions in the liver.

Aldehydes (including acetaldehyde), formed from the metabolic breakdown of alcohol, rancid fats, other household chemicals, and environmental pollution are partially neutralized by cysteine.

In one clinical study a group of rats were given a dose of acetaldehyde large enough to kill 90% of them. Rats given a combination of Vitamin C, cysteine, and Vitamin B1 just prior to the same amount of acetaldehyde did not suffer death. The

combination of these antioxidants provided 100% protection against acetaldehyde-induced death.[13]

- Boosts and replenishes glutathione levels. N-acetylcysteine has been shown to be more effective at boosting glutathione levels than supplements of cystine or even of glutathione itself.
- Precursor to taurine
- Most important of all amino acids for detox; especially for detoxing aldehydes such as acetaldehyde, which is the most toxic threat to problem drinkers
- Potent antioxidant and protector against radiation, pollution, and many other free radicals
- Increases immune responses
- Helps regulate liver-detoxifying amino acids sulfate, taurine, and glutathione
- Aids in protein synthesis

Alanine
- Important source of energy for muscle tissue, brain, and the central nervous system
- Strengthens the immune system by producing antibodies, and helps in the metabolism of sugars and organic acids

Carnitine
- Key component in lipid (fat) catabolism and energy production
- Has been shown to help stabilize healthy blood sugar levels in hypoglycemics
- Reduces angina attacks, from which many problem drinkers are known to suffer
- Aids in treatment of diabetes, liver disease, and kidney disease
- Enables muscle cells to use fat for energy
- Improves oxygen utilization
- Helps the liver oxidize the heavy fatty-acid buildup caused by excessive alcohol

---

[13] Pearson, D. and Shaw, S. Life Extension. Warner Books; New York, NY: 1982; 267.

- Can be produced in the body with vitamin C, niacin, iron, and vitamin B6

Ornithine

- Important in the urea cycle
- Precursor to glutamic acid / glutamate
- Enhances liver function
- Stimulates HGH, which enhances endocrine functions

Neurotransmitters- Nutriceutical Precursors

Following is a list of the neurotransmitters most affected by alcohol toxicity, and their individual precursors.

Dopamine

- Niacin, B6, tyrosine, phenylalanine

Norepinephrine

- Tyrosine, phenylalanine, B6, C
- Tyrosine is the precursor of norepinephrine, and L-phenylalanine is the direct precursor of tyrosine.

Epinephrine

- Tyrosine, B6, C, SAMe (methionine)

Serotonin

- Tryptophan B6, C, B3, magnesium, tyrosine
- The proportion of carbohydrates in the diet influences the conversion of tryptophan into serotonin. The synthesis of serotonin, in turn, affects the proportion of carbohydrates an individual subsequently chooses to eat.

GABA

- Glutamine and vitamin B6 (pyridoxine)
- Manganese, taurine and lysine can increase both the synthesis and effects of GABA.

Glutamine

Glutamic acid is a precursor to glutamine; however, glutamine itself can be purchased as an amino acid and taken to address deficiencies during detox. Glutamine and glutimate change into each other during many physiological processes determined by the needs of the body.

Endorphins / Enkephalins

Endorphins are large molecule neurotransmitters that contain smaller, pain-killing pentapeptides called enkephalins.

Addictive biochemistry and alcohol addiction has been linked to low levels of these opioids in the brain and central nervous system. In one experiment, it was found that alcohol-preferring mice had significantly lower whole-brain enkephalin levels than the non-alcohol-preferring mice. The 101 Program addresses this with the inclusion of D-phenylalanine, which inhibits enkephalinase function (enkephalinase is the enzyme that metabolizes enkephalin). The inclusion of D-phenylalanine therefore aids in sustaining brain enkephalin levels, creating brain chemistry that better resembles the non-alcohol-preferring mice.

Volumes of research, including the lab results of AAAA's personal clients, points to insufficient endorphin and enkephalin activity in the brain chemistry of problem drinkers and those known to possess addictive biochemistry. For this reason, The 101 Program places strong emphasis on creating, restoring, and maintaining healthy levels of natural opioids in the brain, and providing the means for the brain chemistry to store, release, and utilize those opioids properly.

Achieving this goal is a two-step process that relies on adherence to the condictive biochemistry diet for success. The first step is the inclusion of endorphin and enkephalin nutrient precursors, which provide the "tools" with which the brain can make these neurotransmitters. The second step is the provision of nutrients known to inhibit the "ingestion" of those neurotransmitters while in the synapse, so that they may be effective for longer periods of time. It is also the goal of these nutritional supplements and The 101 Program Condictive Diet to aid the hypothalamus in properly storing and regulating neurotransmitter release.

Enkephalin precursors are L-phenylalanine, glutamine, tryptophan, B6, B12, folic acid, leucine, glycine, and methionine. D-phenylalanine is an enkephalinase inhibitor. Since the effectiveness of endorphins and enkephalins is interdependent with proper GABA, dopamine, serotonin, and norepinephrine levels, The 101 Program nutritional therapy and condictive diet is designed to meet the requirements for

healthy levels of these neurotransmitters and their proper function.

HGH

HGH precursors are arginine, ornithine, GABA, and lysine. There are two peptide hormones that act in concert to increase or decrease HGH output from the pituitary gland. These are Somatostatin (SS), which decreases HGH release, and Growth-Hormone Releasing Hormone (GHRH), which increases it. In response to elevated insulin levels, the body will produce somatostatin to lower insulin levels. While it is better to have lower insulin levels, it is healthier for this to be achieved by eating properly since somatostatin also suppresses release of many other hormones, including HGH. The general outcome is suppression of the endocrine system as a whole, which leads to health issues like hypothyroidism, accelerated aging, and loss of cognitive resources.

- The amino acid L-Arginine increases HGH by decreasing somatostatin release from the hypothalamus.
- GHRH acts at the pituitary to increase HGH output; it is an HGH release stimulant.
- GABA, L-Glutamine, L- Glycine, L-Lysine, L-Ornithine, and vitamin B3 (niacin) raise HGH by increasing GHRH levels.

Introduction to Fats

So far this text has repeatedly preached the evils of sugar, and its role in the propensity for addictive biochemistry and psychological and physiological disorders. However, it has a strong partner in crime in the standard "modernized" Western denatured diet, which is built for convenience and profit. This 'other half' is the public's uneducated approach to dieting by avoiding all fats.

There are several types of fats, some of which are good for you, and some of which are bad if they are over consumed. The chief fats are triglycerides, cholesterol esters, and phospholipids, which all contain fatty acids.

The three types of fatty acids are:

Saturated

Monounsaturated
Polyunsaturated (PUFA)

Saturated Fats

Saturated fats are usually solid or almost solid at room temperature. All animal fats, such as those in meat, poultry, and dairy products, are saturated. Processed and fast foods are typically prepared with saturated fats for long shelf life and taste. Vegetable oils can also be saturated. Palm, palm kernel, and coconut oils are saturated vegetable oils.

Saturated fats cause the body to produce more cholesterol, so they should be consumed moderately in a well-balanced diet. Saturated fats stimulate the production of LDL cholesterol ("bad" cholesterol), and therefore increase blood cholesterol levels and the risk of heart disease. Saturated fats raise cholesterol levels and LDL-cholesterol levels more than dietary cholesterol itself.

Good, clean, organic meats and dairy products should be consumed in moderation. You should never substitute hydrogenated fats such as margarine for natural animal fats such as butter. Moderation of the right, natural foods is the proper way to approach dietary choices. All other choices, especially if there is a "middle man" involved (any kind of processing- modifying, deleting, adding, etc.), will certainly be deficient in something the body needs and endowed with something it does not.

Monounsaturated Fats

Monounsaturated fats typically remain liquid, even at extremely low temperatures. These fats are also found in vegetable oils such as olive oil, peanut oil, and canola oil. Monounsaturated fat lowers total blood cholesterol by lowering LDL cholesterol without lowering HDL cholesterol (the "good" cholesterol). Monounsaturated fat doesn't have a direct effect on insulin, but it does slow the digestion of carbohydrates, therefore slowing the rate at which they enter the blood stream, which aids in avoiding an insulin "spike" in response to a sharp rise in blood sugar.

Essential Fatty Acids (EFAs)

It is important to first point out that EFAs have more functions than are shared in the context of this book, since this text is focusing specifically on their contributions toward healing addictive biochemistry and the damage done by long-term alcohol toxicity. EFAs are being used to treat everything from schizophrenia to cancer and arthritis. It is wise to research the benefits of EFA supplementation for any health condition, since it is speculated that the root of many diseases, especially those becoming epidemic in the modern world such as degenerative and cardiovascular diseases, can be traced back to EFA imbalances and deficiencies. Their deficiency is implicated in hundreds of modern-day illnesses; the source of this deficiency is irresponsible food distribution systems such as hydrogenation, grain-fed animals used for food, processing, over sugaring foods, removal of fats, and people attempting to eliminate fats from their diets to lose weight.

Essential Fatty Acids must be supplied to the body through the diet and supplementation, and are critically important for those healing from alcohol toxicity and correcting addictive biochemistry. They help repair brain and liver damage, as well as damage in the central nervous system. They improve mental health, are powerful anticonvulsants and anti-depressants, and aid in eliminating cravings for alcohol and sweets. Dietary studies have indicated that EFA supplementation can influence central nervous system serotonin and dopamine synthesis and metabolism, and modify impulsive and compulsive (addictive) behaviors related to deficiencies of these neurotransmitters.

Polyunsaturated Fats (PUFA)

Polyunsaturated fats are usually liquid at room temperature. They can be found in vegetable oils such as corn oil, safflower oil, soybean oil, and sunflower oil. Polyunsaturated fats are also present in fish and fish oils, and help to decrease triglyceride levels. These fats lower LDL cholesterol and total cholesterol, but they also lower HDL cholesterol (remember HDL cholesterol is the good kind).

Therefore, food sources with this fat should be used in moderation.

Within the polyunsaturated category there are two subcategories of essential fatty acids: Omega-3, derived from Alpha Linolenic acid, and Omega-6, derived from Linoleic acid. These are the precursors of the extremely important eicosanoids, which have been made so famous by Barry Sears, Ph.D. (author of <u>The Zone Diet</u>). Eicosanoids are essentially the parental "messengers" that influence the synthesizing and directives of hormones, therefore having an influence in each and every one of the body's biochemical processes, from the cells up.

EFAs...

- Regulate oxygen use, electron transport, and energy production; these are cells' most important moment-to-moment processes.
- Both DHA and EPA (different EFAs) aid in enhancing production of endorphins, serotonin, and dopamine.
- Help form red blood pigment (hemoglobin)
- Keep juice-producing (exocrine) and hormone-producing (endocrine) glands active; extremely important for the recovering problem drinker since EFA status is severely compromised during excessive alcohol use, damaging the endocrine functions.
- Help reduce swelling and provide key nutrients for joint tissues
- Precursors to prostaglandins (PGs); prostaglandin PGE3 is synthesized from EPA, and reduces inflammatory prostaglandins.
- Low levels of Prostaglandin E1 (PGE1) are linked to both alcohol cravings and depression.
- Provide DHA, which is needed by the most active tissues: the brain and adrenal functions. This feature alone is extremely important to the health recovery of the former problem drinker and healing addictive biochemistry.
- Provide EPA, which is required to keep arachidonic acid levels low, thus reducing the amount of bad eicosanoids produced in the body.
- Help the immune system fight infections by enhancing peroxide production.

- Help prevent the development of allergies, and significantly reduce allergic reactions.

The aspect that distinguishes Omega-3 from Omega-6 in regards to someone's health is what kind of eicosanoids they can produce, which is predominately dependent upon your diet. The long-chain Omega-3 EFAs can be synthesized into the good eicosanoids, and the Omega-6 EFAs can be synthesized into the good and also bad eicosanoids.

Good eicosanoids decrease the production of insulin in the body, which is paramount for the recovering long-term alcohol abuser. Excess levels of bad eicosanoids will encourage the pancreas to over produce insulin, giving life to the brain chemistry imbalances which we now know to be key underlying factors to the enhanced response some people have to substances that produce endorphins and serotonin.

Alcohol abuse, through chronic elevated insulin, causes the body to produce more bad eicosanoids than good, at an alarming rate. The body and mind's ability to recover from long-term alcohol toxicity damage is directly linked to re-establishing a balance of good and bad eicosanoids.

Alpha Linolenic Acid (Omega-3 PUFA)

Omega-3 Alpha linolenic acid, via the enzyme Delta-6-Desaturase (D6D) will produce EPA (eicosapentaenoic acid) and DHA (docosahexaenoic acid).

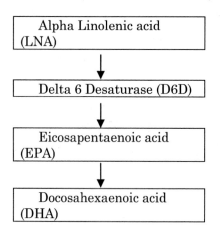

Alpha linolenic acid (LNA) and its derivatives belong to an Omega-3 family of superunsaturates. This family includes

stearidonic acid (SDA), eicosapentaenoic acid (EPA), and docosahexaenoic acid (DHA). If LNA is provided in foods, our cells make SDA, EPA, and DHA. When the conversion of EFAs to their derivatives is inhibited by a lack of the nutrients or over-sugar consumption, it is wise to supplement DHA from black currant seed oil, or EPA and DHA from fish oils (mainly tuna, cod, salmon, and mackerel) or northern ocean algae. Fresh seaweed is one of the rare plant foods that contain EPA and DHA.

Researchers have found that without a sufficient supply of polyunsaturated Omega-3s, the body will use saturated fat to construct cell membranes. The resulting cell membranes, however, are less elastic and denser. This can lead to tissue problems like accelerated signs of aging, and impose a negative effect on the heart because it makes it harder for it to return to a resting state.

Eicosapentaenoic Acid (EPA)

EPA's direct effect on health is its ability to deactivate Delta-5-Desaturase (D5D). D5D is the enzyme that produces bad eicosanoids from Arachidonic acid (AA) from the Omega-6 family. Thus, EPA provides for the overall general health of the body and mind, since it essentially regulates the balance of good and bad eicosanoids.

Below is a list of health issues that can be traced back to unhealthy amounts of AA and D5D in a person's system:

- Addictive biochemistry
- Depression
- Liver disease
- Alzheimer syndrome
- Arthritis and joint pain
- Allergies, extreme food and environmental sensitivities
- Endocrine glandular disorders
- Bad digestion
- Heart disease and strokes
- Cancer
- Multiple Sclerosis

However, in order to have adequate EPA in the system to regulate levels of AA, there must be adequate Delta-6-Desaturase (D6D) to produce EPA from LNA. Because

chronic high levels of insulin deactivate D6D, the root of possibly all alcohol toxicity health issues throughout the body and especially in the brain can be traced back to this broken link in the EFA synthesis chain. When EPA levels are low, AA levels are allowed to rise and wreak havoc on the health of the body. DHA, a critical essential fatty acid for brain health, is significantly decreased because it relies on the conversion of LNA to EPA.

Since alcohol abuse naturally translates to chronically high insulin levels, and in most cases insulin resistance, fish oil is included in The 101 Program nutritional therapy as a direct source of EPA. This is insurance that enough EPA is being provided to the body to accomplish the extremely important jobs of balancing EPA/AA ratios and maintaining a healthy balance of eicosanoids. While The Program calls for an insulin-sparing condictive biochemistry diet, which dramatically reduces and stabilizes insulin levels, it does take a few weeks to get your blood sugar/insulin levels to healthy levels. Once that is done, the body can produce at least the minimal amounts of EPA from LNA on its own. EPA and DHA supplements in the form of fish oil are continued after the initial detox in the Ark phase to provide appropriate amounts of these EFAs and their benefits, since they are severely lacking in today's industrialized diets. EFA supplements have health benefits that reach far beyond healing addictive biochemistry; Dr. Barry Sear's The Omega Rx Zone is a very informative text on this particular subject.

Adequate levels of EPA will help decrease the production of inflammation-inducing cytokines. This is why therapeutic doses of EPA are extremely successful in reducing the pain that results from inflammation such as joint problems, muscle pain, and arthritis. It also helps to actually heal the tissues, while reducing the pain associated with these conditions. EPA increases blood flow, providing more nutrients and oxygen throughout the body. When inflammation is decreased in the brain, blood flow is increased, and nutrients, oxygen, and glucose are able to circulate and efficiently produce, utilize, transmit, and metabolize neurotransmitters. EPA also reduces the formation of the pro-inflammatory hormone PGE2, which in elevated amounts can be an indicator of depression.

Omega-3 Food Sources
Alpha Linolenic Acid

- Flaxseeds (linseeds)
- Mustard seeds
- Wheat Germ
- Pumpkin seeds
- Soy beans (do not eat)
- Walnut oil / walnuts
- Dark green leafy vegetables
- Grains
- Spirulina

Fish oils and fish eggs provide direct sources of EPA and DHA (derived from LNA) and are recommended for their superior benefits and concentrations. Fish oil supplementation is absolutely necessary for the healing former problem drinker due to their long-term high insulin levels, the D6D enzymatic synthesis pathway of LNA to EPA and DHA is severely compromised.

I recommend Cod Liver oil due to the added benefits of vitamin D in this oil. It is speculated today that vitamin D deficiency is epidemic and the number one vitamin deficiency. I also recommend baseball, volleyball etc., over Nintendo to get your natural sources (sunlight) of this seriously depleted vitamin.

Food sources of LNA are predominately grains and green leafy vegetables.

Omega-3 fatty acids are more prominent in meat from wild game, free-range beef, and poultry. Commercial farms feed grains to animals as opposed to grass and use processing methods that makes the meat deficient in necessary Omega-3's and high in Omega 6's.

Good sources are oils made from:
- Cod liver oil (direct source of EPA and DHA)
- Flaxseeds (linseeds)
- Peanuts

Docosahexaenoic Acid (DHA)
DHA is primarily used in the brain to build neural tissue, and is essential for the synapse's transfer of information via neurotransmitters. Research has determined

that this is the only EFA that can stimulate the growth of nerve cells. DHA is also essential in the mitochondria's production of ATP (energy). The tissues that have the highest concentrations of DHA are the mitochondria (where energy is produced), the synapses (which provide a medium in which neurotransmitters provide information between brain cells), and the retina.

DHA is required for:
- Neurotransmitter synthesis
- Signal transmission
- Uptake of serotonin and other neurotransmitters
- Neurotransmitter binding
- Naturally raising serotonin levels in the brain

Nutrients essential for LNA / DHA functions include:
- Magnesium
- Selenium
- Zinc
- Vitamins A (beta-carotene), B3, B6, C, and E

Linoleic Acid (Omega-6, PUFA)

Linoleic Acid (LA) and its derivatives belong to the Omega-6 family of polyunsaturates. This family includes gamma linoleic acid (GLA), dihomogamma-linolenic acid (DGLA), and AA.

Good sources of GLA are evening primrose, borage, and black currant seed. External sources of DGLA are minimal; it can be found in human milk and organ meats in small quantities. AA is found in meats, eggs, and dairy products. It is important when supplementing with GLA to be absolutely faithful to the addictive biochemistry, insulin-sparing diet so that enough EPA is being produced. EPA minimizes the production of bad eicosanoids that can be synthesized from GLA's substrate AA.

Linoleic Acid conversion

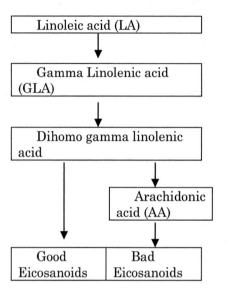

*note: GLA converts to PGE1 (anti-inflammatory)
AA converts to PGE2 (pro-infammatory)

Gamma Linoleic Acid (GLA)

- Alcohol inhibits the enzyme Delta-6-Desaturase, which is essential in converting LA to GLA.
- In the healthy body, GLA is converted to PGE1, which means that it helps to minimize withdrawal and lifts depression.
- GLA also helps to rapidly prevent and repair liver damage.
- Supplementation with GLA has been found to reduce the craving for alcohol.
- If Linoleic Acid is provided by foods and the proper co-factor nutrients are present, cells make GLA, DGLA, and AA. In people with conditions like diabetes and hypothyroidism, the co-factor nutrients should be supplemented.
- Insulin regulates many enzymes in the body, one of them being Delta-5-Desaturase. Just as increased insulin will decrease D6D and prevent healthy amounts of EPA from

being synthesized; it increases D5D enzyme activity, which
will produce more AA from DGLA of the Omega-6 family.

- Bad fats (margarines, shortenings, trans-fatty acids, hard
fats, and cholesterol), lack of minerals (magnesium,
selenium, zinc) and vitamins (B3, B6, C, E), sugar, viruses,
obesity, diabetes, aging, and rare genetic mutations can all
inhibit Omega-6 conversion.

PGE1 – Prostaglandin

- Prostaglandin E1 is a subset of a large family of substances
called eicosanoids, which are localized tissue hormones that
do not travel in the blood like other hormones. Instead they
are created within the cells themselves. They are
regulators and catalysts for hundreds of processes,
including mineral transport in and out of cells (very
important for the brain functions), blood viscosity, dilation
and contraction, swelling and anti-inflammation, and cell
division and growth. Prostaglandins are involved in nerve
cell health, minimizing allergies, maintaining healthy blood
vessels, prevention of blood clots, skin, hair and nail health,
naturally lowering cholesterol, and neurotransmitter
function (many mental conditions such as depression,
mental fatigue, lack of focus and cravings for carbs and
alcohol are attributed to their deficiency). They also help
protect the gastrointestinal tract and aid in the digestive
process. There are three classes of PGs, and two pathways
for PGs to be manufactured. PGE1 and 2 are products of
Omega-6 EFAs and PGE3 is a product of Omega-3 EFAs.
For prostaglandins to be properly manufactured from
EFAs, adequate supplies of biotin, E, protein, zinc, B6, B12
and D6D are required.
- The enzyme that begins the trail of prostaglandins being
produced from EFAs is D6D. This enzyme is diminished
and deactivated by alcohol, sugar, diabetes, malnutrition,
and over eating. However, the most potent deactivator of
this extremely important enzyme is the trans-fatty acids
found in margarines, shortening, and all hydrogenated fats.
It is extremely important for the recovering problem
drinker and anyone with addictive biochemistry to stay
away from hydrogenated fats. Without adequate amounts
of D6D, prostaglandins will not be produced or made
available for the hundreds of mental and physical
biochemical processes that depend on them. Over time, this

can lead to susceptibility to the many illnesses now being attributed to their deficiency.

- Alcohol also inhibits the body's ability to convert Linoleic Acid to the extremely important PGE1 by increasing opioid release in the brain.
- During ingestion, alcohol increases the release of PGE1 in the brain. PGE1 has been shown to elevate mood, and current research shows that a key reason for the craving for alcohol is the drastic fall in PGE1 in the brain after heavy alcohol use. GLA is a precursor of the mood-elevating PGE1, so in the right nutritive environment it contributes positively to reducing alcohol craving. PGE1 also plays a vital role in the prevention of depression, convulsions, and hyper-excitability; common signs of withdrawal and PGE1 depletion. PGE1 slows the release of insulin, which is very important for avoidance of addictive biochemistry.

Omega-6 EFA Food Sources

Linoleic Acid (Omega-6 family)

- Vegetables
- Fruits
- Nuts
- Grains
- Seeds
- Tahini
- Seaweed

Organic eggs (yolks), butter (animal fats), and organ meats are all direct sources of arachidonic acid (the "bad" Omega-6). These should be consumed in moderation.

Oils made from:

- *Canola
- Safflower (avoid)
- Sunflower (avoid)
- Corn (avoid)
- Soy (avoid)
- Pumpkin
- Wheat germ

Supplemental Sources of GLA to be used when D6D is blocked or for preventative health maintenance:

- Evening Primrose oil
- Borage oil
- Black Currant
-

*NOTE: Canola is generally a genetically modified (GMO) oil and therefore I do not recommend it. Principle GMO foods are those that are derived from soybean, maize, canola, and cotton seed oil. Canola is actually rapeseed oil which is high in omega 6 and toxic compounds, and has been processed using methods that cause rancidity and produce trans-fatty acids. As a result of all these factors, canola oil is being linked to many degenerative diseases as well as cancer and brain disorders. I'm afraid that the idea that canola oil was ever a safe or good oil for consumption was due to yet another misleading campaign produced by those that profit from its sale.

Rapeseed used for canola has been selectively bred and genetically engineered in an attempt to reduce the concentration of undesirable and toxic compounds. Rapeseed oil may be good as an emergency insecticide but neither it nor its genetically modified versions should ever be consumed by humans or anything else with parents.

IMPORTANT!

Balancing Omega-3 and -6 food sources

Today's irresponsible food distribution system, predominately saturated in Omega-6, saturated, and hydrogenated fats, does not make shopping easy. You absolutely must take the time to educate yourself according to your palette, and find a way to balance your Omega-3 and -6 EFAs. The goal should be between 1:1 and 4:1 (Omega-6 to Omega-3), 4 being the absolute highest. One way to do this is simply to make the dietary changes that enhance Omega-3 oils while minimizing Omega-6. However, anyone with a degenerative disease, asthma, ADD, allergies, or any condition that is known to be due to Omega-3 deficiency should have their EPA/AA ratios tested. This can be

requested while doing the 101 Comprehensive Services package, or from a personal healthcare provider.

Most sources suggest that human beings evolved on a diet that had an Omega-6 to Omega-3 essential fatty acids ratio of approximately 1:1. Western diets are deficient in Omega-3 fatty acids, and have excessive amounts of Omega-6 fatty acids, compared to the diet on which humans and their genetic patterns were established. Today, Western diets have been calculated at common ratios of 12:1 to 30:1. This dramatic shift toward Omega-6 consumption has been fueled by overuse of processed oils and excessive land animal intake (with the added problem that these animals are grain fed and processed) and is thought to be one of the leading factors in chronic inflammatory illness, cardiovascular disease, cancer, lupus, and a number of other degenerative illnesses.

Also, many of the sources of polyunsaturated fats sold by food distribution systems have been partially or fully hydrogenated to make cholesterol-free substitutes such as margarine, or for deep-frying. Hydrogenating fats also increases profits by extending the shelf life of processed foods. This process oxidizes and alters fatty acids beyond the ability of the human body to recognize and use them.

Westerners are not only taking in far too much Omega-6, they are also deficient in Omega-3. Included are chronic, elevated insulin levels that prohibit Omega-3 EPA synthesis and encourage Omega-6 AA synthesis. The end result is obesity, disease, and many metabolic disorders; one of which is addictive biochemistry.

Balanced Omega-3 and -6 intake, and healthy insulin levels, is paramount in healing addictive biochemistry and reaching your goal of living an illness-free, long life in which that sobriety can be enjoyed. It is important to take the time to research EFAs and learn how to properly incorporate their food sources into your diet. An excellent start is to read The Omega Rx Zone by Dr. Barry Sears (listed in the appendix).

For current or former heavy drinkers, alcohol has inevitably done much to destroy and damage the processes and tissues (especially that of the brain and endocrine system) that rely on EFAs. Anyone with that kind of damage should start healing those tissues and biosystems immediately by incorporating the information in this section into their diet.

Ample amounts of DHA from LNA are required in order for the brain to regenerate healthy brain cells, facilitate transmission, and nourish the cells. It is also important to avoid foods that diminish D6D, such as too many simple carbs and refined sugar (which is entirely off limits during The Krispy Klean Detox, and allowed only *very* occasionally upon graduation to the Ark and Preserve & Protect modules). Essentially, the goal is to provide the proper balance of EFA's in your diet and keep the pathways of their synthesis to good eicosanoids clear.

Omega-9

Omega-9 / Oleic acid is not an EFA because it can be manufactured in the body. Oleic acid is the main constituent of olive oil, and avocados also contain a substantial amount.

Oleic acid is vital to the healing phase in alcohol-damaged organs, especially the brain and liver. It aids in reducing insulin resistance and atherosclerosis, lowering cholesterol, improving blood sugar maintenance, and slowing conversion of sugars into blood glucose.

Hydrogenated Fats (Trans Fats)

Hydrogenated fats are produced by heating liquid vegetable oils in the presence of hydrogen. The more hydrogenation there is, the harder the fat will become (i.e., a stick of margarine has more trans fats than a tub of margarine spread).

Many of the processed foods in today's grocery stores are prepared with hydrogenated fats, which you should avoid. Fast food restaurants and commercially prepared baked goods are also popular sources of these extremely unhealthy trans fats. Fried foods like french fries, onion rings, fish sticks, and breaded items are sources of hydrogenated fats. Trans fats raise cholesterol levels far more than saturated fats because they not only raise LDL (bad) cholesterol, but also lower HDL (good) cholesterol. They also inhibit D6D, which is involved in producing good substrates of Lineolic and Alpha-Lineolic Acids such as GLA, DHA, EPA, and of course their sub groups of good eicosanoids.

Foods that typically contain hydrogenated or partially hydrogenated trans fats include:

- Biscuit, pancake, and cornbread mixes, frostings
- Cakes, cookies, muffins, pies, donuts
- Crackers
- Peanut butter (except fresh-ground)
- Frozen entrees and meals
- Frozen bakery products, toaster pastries, waffles, pancakes
- Most prepared frozen meats and fish (such as fish sticks)
- French fries
- Whipped toppings
- Margarines, shortening
- Instant mashed potatoes
- Taco shells
- Cocoa mix
- Microwave popcorn
- Breakfast cereals
- Corn and potato chips
- Frozen pizza, frozen burritos, most frozen snack foods
- Low-fat ice creams
- Noodle soup cups
- Bread
- Pasta mixes
- Sauce mixes

*This list was excerpted from
http://www.recoverymedicine.com/hydrogenated_oils.htm
Visit the link page at Recovery – Biostructural Medicine, titled "Discover the Truth - Healthcare, Animal Welfare, Environment" at
http://www.recoverymedicine.com/links_biomedica_labs.htm#04. Recovery provides a comprehensive list of resources for those interested in holistic health and healing, the food industry, and how to avoid its inhumane treatment of our food and fellow animals.

The Adrenals and the Pancreas

Particular attention needs to be given to the adrenals and pancreas during the initial stages of recovery and withdrawal, in order to quickly stabilize the body and mind. These two endocrine glands receive the brunt of the daily assault of alcohol abuse. While the liver and brain suffer as well, their

return to health also relies heavily on the proper functioning of these two organs.

Adrenal Health

First and foremost, adrenal health begins with an insulin-sparing diet full of super-nutritious organic foods, aimed at stabilizing blood sugar. The 101 Program provides the nutritional requirements for adrenal health, but anyone participating in The Program must also be mindful to engage in the activities that aid restoration of the adrenals.

Detox: The Krispy Klean Detox provides for the initial detoxification required to begin rejuvenating the adrenals.

Diet: The 101 Program condictive biochemistry diet is an excellent one for healing the adrenals. Elimination of all stimulants and refined sugars, along with targeted nutriceutical support for these glands, is the key to adrenal health.

Key supplements: beta-carotene*, C, E, B5, B6, manganese, glutamine, tyrosine, zinc, and TMG. For badly injured adrenals, natural adrenal glandulars are beneficial because they provide adrenal nucleoproteins and other nutrients that will help accelerate the process of rebuilding the adrenal glands.

*Vitamin A should always be replaced with beta-carotene for former and present heavy drinkers until liver function is known to be healthy and uncompromised by alcohol abuse.

Licorice root extract is an excellent tonic for the exhaustion phase (low cortisol) of adrenal fatigue. The active ingredient in licorice that is beneficial for adrenal fatigue is glycyrrhizic acid (GA). GA inhibits the enzyme that breaks down cortisol, which means cortisol will remain active for longer periods of time, thus prolonging the beneficial effects of this hormone while giving the adrenals a break.

It is important to have an adrenal hormone test (cortisol and DHEA) before deciding to use licorice, because if you are in the adaptation/resistance stage of the general stress syndrome it may promote the harmful effects of too much cortisol if you use licorice. This is the stage at which cortisol is being over produced and typically stays high for long periods of time, wreaking havoc on the immune system and lipid metabolism and causing damage to the hippocampus (brain center responsible for learning and memory). Anyone

who has hypertension should not use licorice extract with glycyrrhizin as it can aggravate that condition and raise blood pressure.

If your adrenals are in very bad shape, organic bovine adrenal extracts in liquid or powdered form may be a strong consideration for recovery.

It is strongly advised not to seek synthetic hormone replacement, such as corticosteroids, for adrenal fatigue. These treatments shut down hormone production from the adrenals and lead to atrophy. Natural hydrocortisone suppresses the adrenals for weeks and sometimes months, even after it is discontinued.

The glandulars I suggest contain the constituents of the adrenal cell, and have only a minuscule amount of hormones in them. Their action is to support, strengthen, and restore normal adrenal function; they assist adrenal function rather than replace it. You never want to replace an organ's function or product with a replacement unless it is for a life saving emergency; you should always seek ways to heal and rebuild it.

For the adrenals this includes:

- Staying away from stimulants.
- Reducing sources of stress.
- Meditating and practicing relaxation techniques such as yoga, deep breathing, etc.
- Exercising
- Maintaining an optimistic attitude
- Adequate sleep is essential to adrenal health and your physical, emotional, and psychological health in general. You must get a good night's sleep! Typically 7 to 8 hours is best for most people. Do not skimp on your sleep!

Pancreatic Health

Long-term alcohol abuse inevitably leads to an injured pancreas. The extent of the damage is primarily determined by diet, activity level, and extent of alcohol abuse. The recovery of this organ, along with the adrenals and liver, is key to being able to enjoy sobriety and prevent relapse, so this organ's health should be a strong focus, especially during the initial stages of recovery.

Insufficient amounts of vitamin A, E, selenium, and carotenoids, over time, are damaging to the pancreas. It will also begin to suffer from a lack of the antioxidants it needs in order to remove the free radicals which alcohol abuse causes.

Chronic and acute pancreatitis is fairly easy to diagnose given the list of noticeable symptoms provided in Chapter 8. To be certain, however, during an attack your doctor can order a blood test to diagnose acute pancreatitis. At the time of an attack, blood contains at least three times more amylase and lipase than usual. If you are not experiencing acute symptoms, consider yourself fortunate and do not dismiss addressing your pancreatic health. A slightly dis-eased pancreas can easily lead to digestive disorders, which will in turn lead to varying states of malnutrition and aggravate addictive biochemistry, so it is a good idea to do the right things to heal and protect an even slightly injured pancreas before it progresses to pancreatitis and/or a diseased pancreas.

Since the pancreas secretes digestive enzymes and hormones that break down carbohydrates, proteins, and fats, the first indication of a compromised pancreas is the inability to properly digest one or all of the above. A simple way to diagnose this is to take pancreatin enzymes that contain amylase, typsin, and lipase. If the aid of these enzymes clears up your indigestion, this could mean that your pancreas is not producing enough of one or all of these enzymes for proper, thorough digestion.

The pancreas also releases bicarbonate, which reduces acid levels in the gastrointestinal tract to aid in proper digestion. Anyone who has an ongoing stomach acid problem could be dealing with a condition that is originating from an injured pancreas.

As with the adrenals, The 101 Program nutritional therapy and diet provide the internal environment for the pancreas to begin healing. However, if your pancreas is in particularly bad shape and requires additional support, I suggest pancreatic glandular extracts with the same synthetic verses natural extract considerations given in the adrenal section of this chapter.

Detox: The Krispy Klean Detox provides for the initial detoxification required to begin rejuvenating the pancreas.

Diet: The 101 Program condictive biochemistry diet is an excellent one for healing this gland. Elimination of all stimulants and refined sugars is key in pancreatic health.

Key Supplements: Beta-Carotene, vitamins C, E, and B12, phosphatidylcholine, methionine, selenium, calcium, zinc, and magnesium.

Much of the damage to both the adrenals and the pancreas results from similar processes to those that damage the liver through acetaldehyde toxicity and free radical oxidative stress. For this reason, much of the protocol for healing the liver in The 101 Program is useful for the pancreas and adrenals. These two organs have been specifically isolated to encourage you to focus on them, consider testing their health, and to pay special attention to their recovery.

Additional Support

- Silymarin (Milk Thistle) - Cleanses the liver. Those who suffer cirrhoses of the liver and are treated with Silymarin have a far higher survival rate, making this an excellent choice for repairing a stressed or damaged liver.
- Super Highway product: Psyllium Husk – Fiber used for bowel cleansing and "massaging" gastrointestinal tract. Please see formula label for additional bowel cleansing support details.
- Acidophilus – Helps to balance bacteria in the stomach, which is very important as many long-term drinkers have bacterial overgrowth, unhealthy digestive flora, and parasite issues to address.
- Pancreatic Enzymes – Used initially in The 101 Program to help thoroughly digest proteins and fats. Long-term drinkers consistently demonstrate insufficient digestive abilities due to the damage inflicted by acetaldehyde on the gastrointestinal tract and pancreas, and long-term high simple carb/junk food diets.
- Protein Shake – Used as a method to assure, from the start of the day, that the body is getting a full-spectrum dose of amino acids to perform healthy biochemical processes, and provide the brain a wealth of precursor amino acids for establishing healthy, balanced brain chemistry throughout the day.

Withdrawal

Decreasing alcohol consumption produces generalized CNS (central nervous system) symptoms of excitability (over expression of excitatory neurotransmitters), due to the chronic adaptive changes in the CNS that result from prolonged excessive alcohol use. Withdrawal is minimized by addressing these changes through the use of aggressive nutritional support, which speeds the process of correcting the brain chemistry, which naturally reduces withdrawal symptoms.

Neurotransmitters that assist this process are:

- GABA
- Beta-endorphins/enkephalins
- Glycine
- Dopamine
- Serotonin

The best way to quickly restore and balance these neurotransmitters is to supplement with their key precursors, while healing the gastrointestinal tract and providing the body with a highly nutritious diet.

Exercise

Regular exercise is one of the three pillars of a healthy lifestyle and is absolutely necessary, especially in today's mentally and physically toxic environment.

Balance physical exercise with mind/body energy healing disciplines

- Bicycling
- Dance
- Weights
- Jogging
- Golf
- Martial Arts
- Recreational Sports

- Yoga
- Tai Chi
- Qi Qong
- HeartMath

Yoga, Tai Chi, Qi Qong (Chi Kung), and HeartMath exercises are just a few of the available mind/body energy healing disciplines that are very helpful for achieving stress reduction, spiritual connectivity, opening the flow of energy throughout the body, healing, and releasing psychological and emotional blocks. Test one or a few out and see what works best for you.

Summary

Alternative Approaches to end Alcohol Abuse (AAAA) continues research in the known biopathways of addictive and addicted biochemistry (listed below). Our professional participation and contributions provide new developments at the cutting edge in orthomolecular medicine and standards of care for healing the body and mind damaged by alcohol, correcting addictive biochemistry, and curing addiction. As a result of our ongoing research in this field, we are producing sophisticated nutritional / biochemical eco-friendly orthomolecular treatments as well as establishing standards of care for best outcomes when integrating the mind/body energy healing practices known universally as vibrational medicine that directly target the biopathways of alcohol addiction. AAAA provides evidence-based treatments validated by both research in all areas of the mind / body / environmental integration and clinical study of the epigenetic influences that can lead to addictive biochemistry such as the effects of malnutrition, distressing emotions, thoughts, environmental toxins, and electromagnetic frequencies. Our studies include:

1) Establishing healthy brain chemistry that produces natural states of psychological and emotional health. This is accomplished by providing a natural, nutrient rich environment that supports the brain in producing healthy levels and function of key neurotransmitters such as beta-endorphins, enkephalins, serotonin, epinephrine, norepinephrine, dopamine, GABA and glutimate.

- Regulation and healthy production of neurotransmitters and hormones to achieve balanced HPA axis function
- Regulation of receptor sites
- Inhibition of premature destruction or ingestion of beta-endorphins, enkephalins, and serotonin
- Prevention of "priming" the brain chemistry for addictive biochemistry
- Correcting impaired "in line" metabolic processes
- Balancing the SNS and PNS to achieve homeostasis and a healthy response to stress

2) Prevention and healing of hypoglycemia, sugar sensitivity, and insulin resistance

3) Aiding in efficient detoxification; healing, regenerating, and rejuvenating the liver and brain

4) Malnutrition and GI-associated disorders - internal bacterial connection to alcohol and carbohydrate metabolism

5) Suppression/damage of the endocrine system and its integral contribution to addictive biochemistry

6) The contribution of EFA and prostaglandin deficiency to the development and continuance of addictive biochemistry, and the most sophisticated usage of these essential nutrients to heal the damage inflicted on all organs by long-term alcohol toxicity.

In Conclusion...

Moderation or Complete Abstinence?

Test Driving a New Biochemistry

First, I would like to make clear that one person drinking themselves to the point of no return, meaning that they cannot completely heal their biochemistry to the point where they would be able to responsibly and safely moderate alcohol consumption does not set the rule for everyone. Many heavy drinkers accept that they have a problem, quit drinking for quite some time, heal, and then are able to drink moderately.

When you transition to the Preserve & Protect maintenance phase of the program, you are healthy and have uprooted addictive biochemistry.

While moderate drinking is absolutely an option for many who have successfully completed this program to this point, it is not the right choice for everyone. If you indulged in alcohol for so long and hard that serious known health issues like hepatitis and cirrhosis, or severely damaged brain function, adrenals, pancreas, or liver scarring are present you should seriously consider complete abstinence.

If this is not the case for you and you decide to allow yourself moderate alcohol use, it is strongly recommended that you remain entirely faithful to the 101 Preserve & Protect lifestyle and are extremely faithful to your condictive diet.

If you decide to drink occasionally, you absolutely must follow the condictive dietary guidelines, especially when it comes to staying away from sugar and other refined carbohydrates. If you begin to once again tax and damage your adrenals, pancreas, and brain chemistry by mainlining processed foods, sugars, and stimulants, you will most likely find yourself drinking more and more, and gradually building back up to your old routine.

Allowing this renewed metabolic damage builds a strong case that you will become dependent on alcohol once again. It is compromised or exhausted endocrine function that caused the trouble with alcohol in the first place; renewing the damage by stressing and depleting the neuroendocrine system again can only open opportunity for the addiction to pay another visit.

 Moderation is different for everyone. A couple of drinks at a cocktail party, a few at a wedding, or an occasional glass of wine with dinner should be safe and actually produces health benefits for most people. A recovering problem drinker should learn from friends who drink moderately and maintain healthy lifestyles, and model his or her behavior after people like this. Everyone is different; the key is to avoid drinking daily or compulsively in unhealthy amounts.

The fundamental value of The 101 Program is that it actually heals you, breaks the addiction, corrects the brain chemistry, and in doing so returns the choice to drink or not to you. When you successfully change your body chemistry, alcohol has a different effect on your body; it is not "medicine" anymore, you don't *need* it to reduce unwanted psychological, emotional or physical symptoms so you will not be

compulsively driven to drink, nor will you view it as a medicine that will help you achieve some state that you can not achieve naturally, such as relaxation, so a dependent relationship with alcohol will not be developed.

After the detox phase and strict adherence to this program for a minimum period of one year (and in more extreme cases up to two years), many former problem drinkers can continue what they have learned in diet management and supplementation, to maintain their corrected metabolism and safely drink in moderation occasionally.

Everyone has a different timeline as to when his or her body chemistry is truly corrected. If you have faithfully done this program for the time period you set for yourself within the guidelines given, and you would like to "test drive" your new body chemistry, do so. If you feel yourself slipping back into an unhealthy habit, take some more time off or consider complete abstinence. Abstinence will have a different meaning for you after doing the program since you will remember feeling wonderful, rather than suffering from hypoglycemia and the other physical and mental symptoms one's body and mind suffers when trying to quit alcohol without addressing the root cause; the reason for the original appeal to alcohol and damage from long-term toxicity.

I've had many clients come to me, initially seeking out the program because they wanted to get healthy and then drink moderately. After doing the program, they felt so good they didn't have any desire to drink. I've also had visits from many men and women from AA who chronically relapse wanting to address their battle with the addiction with The 101 Program. In doing so, they have found a whole new meaning to the concept of "sobriety" because they no longer suffer with the desire, ache, and craving to drink. Nor do they suffer the multitude of "dry-drunk" symptoms with which they were living for years and were causing their relapse. This makes maintaining their chosen complete abstinence much more obtainable and enjoyable. It is the quality of sobriety found through addressing the root cause of the addiction that makes this program the success that it is.

People who have done The 101 Program are predominantly those who have tried numerous conventional methods without success; people who are now living inspired, enthusiastic, happy, and productive lives free of addiction. So don't give up

having only experienced the results of an ineffective, grossly ignorant approach built on years of failure! I invite you to step into the enchanting world 101 Program participants live in daily and enjoy a full life! You can't just give one lifestyle up; you must create a new one. What could be better than creating one that promotes your health and well being through providing for your specific needs?

And please, do not think because I developed and represent a treatment that cures alcohol addiction and respect your choice to healthfully drink or not, that I condone irresponsible drinking or the ill nature of those who drink and become menaces to society, hurtful and sometimes dangerous, if not murderous, when they drink. To the contrary, I am a big fan of people learning to master their lives and the choices in it. The health of the body and mind which is promoted in this book is one enormous step toward that mastery. Since I have personally witnessed people heal and become moderate drinkers, I know that moderation is entirely an option for some.

If alcohol has become a permanent negative issue in your life; if you have killed someone while drinking and driving, have ruined your family, have permanently negatively influenced someone's life etc., then it is a good idea and my recommendation to maintain complete sobriety for a lifetime. In these cases, the impact of the negative relationship with alcohol is permanent and will always have an unhealthy effect on your mind/body health, depleting your life essence and yielding a doorway to addictive biochemistry and addiction- as well as more destruction to the lives of others and yourself.

The 101 Program Formulas

To purchase the standard Krispy Klean Detox supplement formula prepackaged please visit http://the101program.com/KK_detox.html. The prepackaged method saves time, and in most cases money.

Please see the appendix for the complete list of nutritional supplements required for the Krispy Klean Detox.

*The Krispy Klean Detox formula is included in The 101 Program Comprehensive Services package, so anyone planning to enroll in the Comprehensive Services plan should not purchase the supplements separately; AAAA will ship them along with the rest of the 101 Program supplies. For more information on how to enroll in The 101 Program Comprehensive Services package, email info@the101program.com.

Krispy Klean Detox Formula

Vitamins	Dist	Qty bottles	Pot	#c per bottle	# Caps	DT #C	M D	N D	E D
Two Per Day	LE	1	see label	120	120	2	2		
Thiamine (B1)	TL	1	500mg	100	100	2	1	1	
Niacinimide (B3)	SN	1	1.5G	100	100	2	1	1	
Pyridoxine (B6)	SN	1	500mg	100	100	1	1		
Methylcobalamine (B12)	NOW	1	5mg	60	60	1	1		
Ester C	NOW	1	1G	240	240	3	1	1	1
Phosphatidyl Choline Complex	SN	1	420mg	180	180	3	1	1	1
Phosphatidylserine	SN	2	complex	60	120	3	1		2
CoQ10	HO	1	300mg	60	60	1	1		
Minerals									
Cal / Mag	A-B Calm	1lb	Powder / see label	Heaping teaspoon				X	X
EFAs									

The 101 Program Formulas

Cod Liver Oil EPA/DHA w/vit D	CARL	2	see label	liquid	2 Tbl spoon	X			
Protein Shake									
Jarrow Fermented Soy Protein	JW	2	see label	See directions below chart			X	X	
Amino Acids									
5-HTP	Dr. B	2	100mg	60	120	3		1	2
GABA	NOW	1		170G	170 G	2G		1 G	1 G
DL-phenylalanine	SN	1	750mg	60	60	750 mg		1	
Alpha Lipoic Acid	CL	1	300mg	60	60	1	1		
NAC	NOW	1	600mg	250	250	3	1	1	1
Liquid Amino Fuel	TL	1	liquid	Dosage is 2Tbls			X		
Super Highway									
Tri-Cleanse (psyllium husks plus)	PH	1	See label for instructions				1		1
Additional Support									
Pancreatic Enzymes	SN	1	500mg	100	100	3	1	1	1
Thistle Cleanse	Z	2	Herbal extract			1	1		
Melatonin	LE	1	3mg	100	100	1 – 3 as needed for sleep			
Acidophilus	NL		Purchased by participant			See program breakout			

*Use only pharmaceutical grade Tryptophan.

*Standard Process products are prescription only organic nutriceuticals and must be ordered through a licensed practitioner or through The 101 Program (AAAA) for the purposes of this detox protocol.

Chart Legend
Potency = Potency of each cap
DT #C = Daily total caps taken
DT P = Daily total potency taken
MD = Morning dose
ND = Noon dose
ED = Evening dose

Distributors Legend

A-B Calm
NN = Nordic Naturals
CL = Country Life
DrB = Dr.'s Best
GOL = Garden of Life
HO = Healthy Origins
IT = Iron Tek
LE = Life Extension
NOW = NOW
NL = Nature's Life
PH = Planetary Herbals
SN = Source Naturals
SP = Standard Process
TL = TwinLab
Z = Zand

*GABA may cause a "tingling" effect in some individuals very similar to that of the niacin "flushing" side effect. This response subsides after a few days, as the neuroendocrine system balances and can better accommodate GABA. For best results, empty the capsule into a small glass of water and sip it for about an hour. GABA is a very important ingredient in the protocol, as it is the primary inhibitory neurotransmitter (induces a calming effect), and stimulates Growth Hormone from the pituitary, which favorably affects the entire neuroendocrine system.

Acidophilus is not provided because I recommend the liquid (live) Nature's Way product that can't be shipped but can be bought in any health food store for around $10.00.

For ease of digestion and to minimize caps taken throughout the day, we suggest opening the amino acid capsules for the recommended dosage and pouring the powder of each cap in one container. When it is time to take this supplement, mix the powder with water and drink. Do not mix powder with juice, since it will make blood sugar rise, and prevent the amino acids from doing much of what they're intended to do.

Resources and Links

Food, Herbs, Health Education

Alternative Approaches to End Alcohol Abuse
http://the101program.com

Healthy Food Resources:
http://101programsnacks.wholefoodfarmacy.com
http://www.rawfood.com
http://www.thebestdayever.com
http://davidwolfe.com
http://www.thevegetariansite.com/index.htm
http://www.rawgourmet.com
http://www.living-foods.com
http://vegweb.com/recipes/raw/
http://teaforhealth.com
http://www.eatwild.com
http://www.greenteahaus.com
http://www.glycemicindex.com

For excellent pasture raised meats
http://eatwild.com
http://eatingfresh.com

For an excellent introduction to the Paleolithic diet I
recommend after the Krispy Klean Detox explore these links:
http://paleodiet.com
http://healing.about.com/od/paleolithic_diet
http://www.paleofood.com

An excellent, ethical fish distributor that delivers to your
door can be found at http://vitalchoice.com. Please read about
how important it is to know where your fish comes from and
who is doing what to it, at
http://www.vitalchoice.com/purity.cfm.

For a complete list of safe and unsafe fish to eat visit
http://www.thegreenguide.com/gg/pdf/fishchartissue97.pdf

For a study on essential EFAs, how to balance Omega-3 and -6 intake, and the importance of including them in your diet, see http://www.westonaprice.org/know_your_fats /know_your_fats.html

An excellent broad-based quick link reference for the true health purist, as well as those that seek to live in harmony with this planet, is Discover the Truth - Healthcare, Animal Welfare, Environment at:
http://www.recoverymedicine.com/links_biomedica_labs.ht m#04

For help locating an accredited Naturopath in your area http://www.naturopathic.org

For a good education about the pharmaceutical/psychiatric trade, and a wealth of information about the criminal rampant prescribing of anti-depressants, see
http://www.prozactruth.com/index.html

For reliable information regarding nutrition and health and the politics of both:
Mike Adam's www.newstarget.com (highly recommended)
http://www.hsph.harvard.edu/nutritionsource/index.html

To get involved politically to ensure people's continued rights to natural supplements, visit the International Association for Health Freedom (IAHF), at
http://iahf.com/index1.html

Health World Online
http://www.healthy.net

Suggested Reading

7 Weeks to Sobriety, Joan Mathews-Larson Ph.D.
Integral Psychology, Ken Wilber
The Integral Vision, Ken Wilber
Syndrome X, Jack Challem, Burton Berkson, M.D., and Melissa Diane Smith
The Zone, Barry Sears, Ph.D.
The Omega RX Zone, Barry Sears, Ph.D.
Potatoes Not Prozac, Kathleen DesMaisons

Get Skinny on Fabulous Food, Suzanne Somers
Eat Great, Lose Weight, Suzanne Somers
Naked Chocolate, David Wolfe and Shazzie
How to Defeat Alcoholism: Nutritional Guidelines for
Getting Sober, Dr. Joseph D. Beasley, MD (any of Dr.
Beasley's many books are an excellent addition to anyone's
library and education)
Sugar Blues, William Dufty
Life Extension, Pearson D and Shaw S

For a broader/spiritual conceptualization of addiction and
the process of healing:

Coyote Medicine, Lewis Mehl-Madrona
Molecules of Emotion, Candace B. Pert
Seat of the Soul, Gary Zukav

Mind / Body Energy Healing

Holosync http://www.centerpointe.com/holosync
HeartMath - Sheva Carr, Licensed HeartMath coach and
Acupuncturist. http://www.fyera.com
EFT, Emotional Freedom Technique, www.emofree.com

Integral Institute

http://www.integralinstitute.org
Integral Institute is a 501 (c)(3) non-profit organization
dedicated to bringing the **Integral Approach** to bear on
personal and global issues.
What's "Integral"? It simply means more balanced,
comprehensive, interconnected, and whole. By using an
Integral approach—whether it's in business, personal
development, art, education, or spirituality (or any of dozens
of other fields)—we can include more aspects of reality, and
more of our humanity, in order to become more fully awake
and effective in anything we do.

Integral Healing

Integral Health, The Path to Human Flourishing, Elliott
S. Dacher, M.D.

Dedication

Never underestimate the powerful influence you have on others in the most every day mundane, unexpected moments. It is in these moments, I believe, that we are influenced the most profoundly. It is in the quiet, subtle, unsuspecting moments, comfortably shared with loved ones, that we receive the most powerful and meaningful messages that stick with us for a lifetime. One of those moments, experienced when I was a teenager, would eventually produce this book. One uneventful day my grandmother, Gladys Petralli, who was nutrition-minded years before it was popular to be so, told me a story about her dentist; 20 years previously he had told her that she would need dentures soon. She immediately began studying and practicing truly optimal nutrition straight from God's kitchen (the earth); removing all adulterated/processed foods from her family's diet. Some 40 years after that dentist's statement, my grandmother passed away with a full set of beautiful pearly whites – all hers. A portrait was taken just before she passed on, which I have hanging above the desk where I work with my clients and write this book. Every time I look at that picture of her smiling with her bright, vibrant, glowing essence, and that beautiful smile with all those perfectly healthy teeth, I feel supremely vindicated in my work (through my client's and those that have done The 101 Program successes). I also remember that 5-minute conversation that changed my life forever; she had provided me the living proof of the importance of nutrition and its role in healing.

So yes, I was raised with an education that promoted the importance of nutritious foods, avoiding the for-profit, not health, junk that food companies were calling food, and being conscious of what I ate. I was given protein shakes and multi vitamins with breakfast before school, and urged to learn how to properly prepare foods for optimal nutritional benefit. And now, my daughter is being raised in the same fashion and Grandma continues to live through her, as she does through me. Every time I prepare a "colorful" salad (which is what my daughter calls the multi-veggie salads I've prepared for her since before she was 2), a protein shake, or give my daughter her vitamins with breakfast, Grandma is there. Aside from the spiritual grounding my grandmother also provided, I can

Alcoholism: The Cause & The Cure The Proven Orthomolecular Treatment

and

The 101 Program

Bringing the Most Advanced Holistic Detox Center to You

Genita Petralli, H.H.P., N.C., M.H.
Foreword by Dr. Abram Hoffer M.D., Ph.D.

**Edited by Carrie White, Open Window Consulting
Proof Reading and contextual contributions by
Heather Noel Culin
Cover design by The Creative Collaboratory**